DUO-PIANISM

A Dissertation

by

HANS MOLDENHAUER

PREFACE

This study was first stimulated by a strong interest in duo-pianism. The writer and his wife, Rosaleen Moldenhauer, have been playing together on two pianos for a period of ten years. While their activities in this field have led them to frequent public performances and to a weekly half-hour radio broadcast, now in its seventh consecutive year, their two-piano association was undertaken and still is regarded by them as a sideline to their profession as music teachers. Duo-pianism, for their purposes, constitutes primarily a satisfying form of musical ensemble; its daily application is found in the home, and its chief function is that of providing constant enjoyment and edification.

Out of the hobby grew a specialized study. The decision to collect all pertinent information into a full treatise was prompted by Chicago Musical College, Dr. Rudolph Ganz, president, when the research project "Duo-Pianism" was accepted for a doctoral dissertation in musicology. Dr. Hans Rosenwald, director of the Graduate School at the Chicago Musical College, acted as counsel in the shaping of the material into a comprehensive study; the writer is gratefully indebted to him for his advice and encouragement.

In preparation of the treatise, a representative group of duo-pianists, composers, and pedagogues was consulted in personal interviews and by way of extensive questionnaires. Many original thoughts were contributed and subsequently incorporated into the text. Appreciation is expressed especially to the following for their most gracious response to the request for opinions and data:

> Appleton and Field
> Bartlett and Robertson
> Abram Chasins
> Dougherty and Ruzicka
> Gold and Fizdale
> Morton Gould
> Rosina Lhevinne
> Luboshutz and Nemenoff
> Philip Manuel (Manuel and Williamson)
> Darius Milhaud
> Morley and Gearhart
> Beryl Rubinstein
> E. Robert Schmitz[1]
> Dorothy R. Sinnitt
> Vronsky and Babin
> Whittemore and Lowe

---

1. Deceased.

Grateful acknowledgment is extended to the publishers of copyright books and magazines, and to the authors of such source material, who have kindly granted permission to quote from their various publications, as indicated in the text.

Music publishers and recording companies also have lent much helpful cooperation by supplying data pertaining to the indices of "Original Two-Piano Music" and "Recorded Two-Piano Music".

During the compilation of reference material, the following libraries were of special assistance, and the appreciation of the author is due to them and their workers:

Chicago Musical College Library; Eloise Corley, Librarian

Newberry Library, Chicago; Bernard Helfrich, Music Librarian

Public Library, Spokane; Elizabeth Gilbert and Mary Johnson, Reference Librarians.

Radio Station KGA Spokane, Harvey Wixson, General Manager, for the last seven years has sustained a weekly half-hour broadcast of two-piano music, thereby providing invaluable workshop facilities. The availability of this laboratory for practical experimentation has been instrumental in the evolution of this study.

Thanks are due, first and last, to the wife of the writer, his companion on two pianos, for her long-year partnership in duo-pianism, for the tireless help given in all detail work, and for her constant inspiration.

Spokane, Washington, April 1950   H.M.

CONTENTS

TABLE OF ILLUSTRATIONS

---

1. Fitzwilliam Virginal Book.
2. Oeuvres Complètes de François Couperin, Second Livre de Pièces de Clavecin, Neuvième Ordre
3. Bach-Gesellschaft Edition

CHAPTER I

INTRODUCTION

Duo-Pianism: *Ars Novissima Artis Novae*

Of the young art of music, duo-pianism is one of the most recent branches. But like the highest twig of a tree, the art has shown a rapid growth during the last half century. It is now recognized and reckoned with as a field of music making all of its own distinction, as an artistic vehicle of the highest order, and as an ensemble discipline without peer.

The sudden rise of duo-pianism presents a phenomenon. Where the history of vocal and instrumental arts underwent a slow and often cumbersome evolution, two-piano playing in its present form sprang into being almost overnight, notwithstanding the germinal beginnings scattered over some three hundred years. As late as in December 1933, Josef and Rosina Lhevinne, then at the height of their career as duo-pianists, began an essay on two-piano art with this somewhat resigned statement:[1]

"Two-piano playing is practically virgin territory and this, perhaps, is its chief interest."

The short span of fifteen years later, the same Rosina Lhevinne feels compelled to modify her earlier viewpoint when making the following opening remarks to another essay on duo-pianism:[2]

"Two-piano playing is taking a very prominent part in the musical world of today. In fact, the interest for these concerts has almost become a vogue."

A comparison between the two quotations, emanating from the same source, is striking, and the sudden mutation is surprising. However, this complete change of opinion as professed by one of the most influential

1. *Four Hands That Play as Two,* "The Etude," December 1933, p. 809.
2. *The Spirit of Ensemble,* Pan Pipes, February 1949, p. 162.

forces in the art of duo-pianism is confirmed by the following casual remark coming from a professional concert reviewer. This quotation is only one of the many similar statements throughout the press:[3]

> "Duo-piano programs are now in vogue with some noted artists devoting themselves to this branch of musical art. It is in fact giving solo piano recitals a contest for popularity."

It seems a long way, both chronologically and historically, from the music written for two virginals in the late sixteenth century to the inclusion of a two-piano team into the illustrious array of artists celebrating the Goethe Bicentennial Convocation and Music Festival at Aspen, Colorado, in the summer of 1949. More than three hundred and fifty years have passed between the first evidence of keyboard ensemble music and the final recognition of this art form as an autonomous and self-sufficient expedient of music making.

Final recognition there needed to come, for duo-pianism until recent times was regarded alternately, and according to one's prejudice in the matter, an exhibitive act of musical vaudeville and even an artistic atrocity, or a model of intimate chamber music with its subtlety and restraint, and at the same time an instrument for brilliant concert display with the means of scaling orchestral heights. In the presence of such diversified conceptions, and their many variations within the extremes, the medium always had to be controversial.

Time has given its verdict. Two-piano teams now appear on every concert series, season after season, in every city or town. Duo-pianists rank as favorites with their audiences. Radio programs regularly feature two-piano teams or their recordings. Special duo-piano clubs are being organized. Conservatories offer piano ensemble classes in their curricula. The public acclaim indicates that two-piano programs are refreshingly adventuresome and that the field is wide open at a time when piano solo programs have fallen into much of a cliché.

Composers of the first rank are prolific in their creations of original scores for two pianos. The objection of long standing that there exist too few original compositions and too many arrangements, has constantly given way under the flood of new original works and the revival of older scores which were unearthed by research-minded duo-pianists. The popular fancy is captivated by the medium, and countless amateur teams are attracted by the fascination of piano ensemble, in which they discover new approaches and problems and at the same time experience new attitudes unheard of in solo performance.

---

3. *Opera and Concert,* April 1949.

Considering the sudden growth in popularity which has brought duo-pianism to the fore, the amount of available literature on the subject, and of vital statistics pertaining to it, is surprisingly small. What little information there exists to which duo-pianists and lovers of the art can turn, needs to be gathered from many sources: An essay here, a dictionary reference there; some magazine articles in the manner of informal interviews with leading teams, often prompted by the motives of publicity rather than by scholarly inquisitiveness; a slim number of professional papers, mostly unpublished and widely scattered in the libraries of colleges and universities; a few more or less substantial annotations to concert programs or record albums.

During the preparation of this volume, some of the leading libraries of the country have been consulted for reference material, yielding only scanty results as far as the specific research project of duo-pianism is concerned. Not a single exhaustive treatise of the complex matter could be found, indeed an amazing fact in view of the existing public interest. A tentative explanation may be that duo-pianism, although it is one of the most highly appreciated arts in the field of music today, grew into prominence almost overnight. In the words of Wier, "its rise to popularity has been comparatively sudden, therefore information regarding its past history, present status, special technique, literature and probable future has not been available."[4]

The comparatively largest reference to the subject is made in an essay on "The Art of Two-Piano Playing", written by Vera Brodsky. Even this article, however, constitutes merely a contributing section within the standard work *The Piano* by Albert E. Wier; it appears in almost identical form in *The Macmillan Encyclopedia of Music and Musicians*. All other references regarding duo-pianism are very limited in scope. They either are contained in encyclopedias of music or they come from articles in magazines and newspapers and consequently must fall short of comprehensive information. Most of these essays stress merely the aspects of performance, pointing out the commanding place which the two-piano ensemble has taken on the concert platform. They all mention the sudden rise to popularity, and many are attributing this phenomenon largely to the peculiar opportunities afforded by the combined instruments for achieving a semblance of orchestral effects.

A number of suggestions on some details of practice and performance are made by the various authors, most of whom belong to noted concert

4. Statement by Albert E. Wier, in an introductory note to the essay on *Two-Piano Playing* by Vera Brodsky in the *MacMillan Encyclopedia of Music and Musicians*, 1938, p. 1898.

teams in the field. While generally agreeing on the characteristics of antiphonal and polyphonic effects produced on two pianofortes, the opinions on technical execution are diversified. The available repertoire usually is mentioned only as far as the nucleus of standard compositions is concerned. References to the working methods of composers in the field, both of original two-piano scores and of arrangements for this medium, also are very limited. Likewise, historical data are sketchy, and collective biographical information concerning famous duo-pianists is non-existent.

It can be considered common knowledge that a vast literature exists for the pianoforte as a *solo* instrument. Aside from the hundreds of thousands of compositions written for it, there are voluminous treatises of the history, mechanics, and aesthetics of the pianoforte. There are innumerable books on pedagogy, technic, and interpretation. Countless articles have been written by artists, scholars, and teachers. The sum total of this material is within easy reach of the piano student, the amateur, the artist or the scientist whenever he may desire or need some special information.

For the novice in the field of duo-pianism, professional and amateur alike, the great scarcity of adequate reference material is conspicuous. No approximately complete list of the repertoire is available at the present time, and the catalogs of the individual music publishers must be depended upon for exclusive information in this direction. The same situation prevails in regard to a special list of recordings of all two-piano music, which would provide access to a source of invaluable help for all aspirants in the field. Here again, reference to individual commercial catalogs needs to be made, precluding a comprehensive survey which must encompass the older releases as well as the more recent recordings.

The reasons why there has been so little scholarly research in the field of duo-pianism are difficult to ascertain. Evidently, there has been sufficient interest to stimulate, warrant and render highly practical an encyclopaedic investigation of the complex matter. The theory may perhaps be advanced that the medium for intrinsic reasons is not likely to produce many scholars. Any specialized study demands as its fundamental requirement the active participation and resultant definite experience in the object of research. Of the permanent two-piano teams which could answer this requisite, the professional group of concert artists rarely brings to the task the detached, objective, "disinterested" attitude which a scientific investigation postulates as its prime condition. The rank and file of duo-pianists, on the other hand, seldom continue their association long enough to accumulate the knowledge and furnish the experience which need to be the storehouse of the investigator; then, with the separation of the partners, their interest in the medium usually wanes.

The essence of the proceeding paragraphs brings into sharp relief a peculiar discrepancy: In plain evidence is, on the one hand, the tremendous popularity of an art which has suddenly risen to universal recognition and wide-spread utilization in the field of music. On the other side, there exists a startling lack of available information on the subject; very little effort has been made to evaluate the past and present manifestations of the art with treatises and statistics, and thereby to prepare and further the future development of a decidedly original branch of musical experience and accomplishment.

Duo-pianism has come of age. The pioneers among the performing artists have completed their task, setting out courageously into the world of music, standing up against prejudice and belittlement, breaking the ground and planting the seeds. Now the bloom of the movement and the harvest of public acceptance has begun. With it, interest in the medium has been stimulated, and an intellectual curiosity is aroused. The desire for information confronts the practitioner of the art, and in increasing measure the necessity evidences itself to satisfy such demand.

As a consequence, the following treatise constitutes an attempt to organize the material as it presents itself today. The study is intended and undertaken as an inquiry into the history, nature, applications, and problems, as well as the literature of duo-pianism. With the phenomenon still passing through a state of evolution, there cannot be the full perspective as to its historical aspects, nor can there be an answer to all existing problems. There will crystallize, however, some statistical facts, and there will emerge some tentative explanations. There is to be a dissertation in the full meaning of the word, a formal discourse, a dissecting of pertinent factors and an examination of ingredients. Motivation and propulsion for the entire procedure are provided by that primary and perpetual curiosity which alone is capable of revealing the innermost truth of existing facts or situations, lest one allows himself to succumb to the psychosis of a phenomenon.

Full attention will be given to the accepted standards of a dissertation which require that the branches of history, aesthetics and pedagogy be duly represented and allied. The inherent factors of the research project will be subjected to the methodical laws of generalization, comparison, causation, and evaluation. It must be emphasized, however, that no single thesis can represent the final statement on a given problem, or the absolute coverage of a particular subject matter. Rather, even a dissertation, actual and complete as it may appear at the moment, serves only as a link in the chain of constant transformation, as an incentive and indeed a challenge to further investigation. Where the poet feels moved to speak for mankind:

"It is given us
Nowhere to rest . . . "
(Hyperion's Song of Fate)

where science advances as an ever discovering and never static force, so is the search for artistic truth a perpetual motivation in the life of those who are destined to seek. Final satisfaction and happiness will be found in the *pursuit* of truth as an absolute objective, for

"The way *is* the goal."

Duo-pianism still offers an open road. The art appears today as one of the last frontiers in the domain of music, with challenge and opportunity for the pioneer. A province still unexplored, it may justly be called

Ars Novissima Artis Novae.

BOOK I

THE HISTORY

For Two Virginals.

GILES FARNABY

GILES FARNABIE

CHAPTER II

THE PIONEERS

To begin with the history of duo-pianism, it is necessary to retrace the development of the pianoforte as far as into the sixteenth century. During that time, the virginal was very much in vogue with English musicians. The collective name *virginal* designated a small form of harpsichord or spinet which looked very much like a clavichord as far as its rectangular shape was concerned, and which had no legs. The strings, being plucked rather than struck by hammers, produced a delicate tone which was fascinating in its manifold sonorities. The name of these instruments, "The Virginals," originated as a compliment to Elizabeth, the Virgin Queen, who was an excellent player.

There were numerous leading English composers who wrote for the virginal, and a large repertoire for this instrument has been handed down to the present through the many generations since. Much of the literature consists of dances, with such movements as the galliards and pavanes apparently very fashionable at the time. Then there were preludes, variations, fantasias and liturgical pieces. The virginalists must be credited primarily with the all-important contribution of developing a keyboard style suiting the harpsichord idiom. After more than three hundred and fifty years, there remains much cause to marvel at their ingenuity in matters of tasteful figuration and brilliant passage work; of undiminished delight are the robust virility as well as the graceful charm of that pianistic era past.

From this early period of keyboard music stem the first three extant duets of which knowledge is possessed. Two of these duets are for four hands on one keyboard, and one is written for four hands on two keyboards. Nicholas Carleton (early 16th century) entitles his duet *A verse for*

9

two to play on one Virginall or Organe, and Thomas Tomkins (1573-1656)[1] calls his ensemble piece *A fancy for two to play.* The title of the composition for four hands on two keyboards is simply *For two Virginals.*[2]

This quaint and delightful little tune was created, and its two-keyboard setting invented, by Giles Farnaby (c. 1560-c. 1600) whose eminence as a prolific composer of the Elizabethan era was rivaled only by that of William Byrd (1538-1623). The small work is found among more than fifty others from Farnaby's pen in that monumental collection of keyboard music of the sixteenth and seventeenth centuries, the Fitzwilliam Virginal Book which comprises nearly three hundred pieces. In Farnaby's tune for two virginals, there are only two sections, each containing four measures; each part is marked for repetition. The spontaneous freshness of the piece has not been impaired by the centuries, and the workmanship displayed in the combination of the two instruments remains most interesting. The tune has a folk-like quality. Miller writes on this little work:[3]

"The last two measures suggest a possible figuration of the original melody. The part marked "Virg. I" carries this tune in the upper voice with simple accompaniment. The second virginal part, considerably more difficult, is virtually a figuration of the first virginal part. There is much duplication between the two, as for example, in the right-hand parts in the fourth measure. . . . If the two parts are performed consecutively, the second makes an effective variation of the first. Although there is no signature, the composition is in G major, with F-sharp used almost consistently. The style, on the whole, is typical of the virginal school, except that it perhaps calls for less virtuosity than usual."

It may be worth mentioning that in the original manuscript the part for the first virginal is written fully by itself, apart from that for the second instrument. This procedure differs from the now customary method of scoring the two parts immediately above each other.[4]

A theory concerning the question when people first were interested in two-piano playing, is advanced by Dougherty and Ruzicka, duo-pianists, as follows:

"In the 17th Century, barber shops were equipped with virginals (one of the earliest precursors of the pianoforte). And in the interim while waiting for their elaborate hair-dos, patrons diverted themselves in vying with one another in their keyboard ability and consequently playing in ensemble."

Actually, there are no historical records of the first time that the fore-runners of the pianoforte were paired for private entertainment or public

---

1. The life span of composers has been given throughout this chapter, to allow for a proper perspective during this early period. Life data are omitted beginning with J. S. Bach.
2. See Illustration No. 1.
3. Hugh M. Miller *The Earliest Keyboard Duets,* The Musical Quarterly, October 1943
4. Fitzwilliam Virginal Book, Vol. I, Introduction p. XXIV.

performance. The origin of the art is shrouded in the mists of antiquity. However, it appears very likely that two clavichords or harpsichords were combined as soon as composers discovered that the same harmonization and contrapuntal devices which were carried out by human voices could also be assigned to a number of instruments.

From the time of Giles Farnaby, far more than one hundred years were to elapse until Johann Sebastian Bach wrote his great compositions for two claviers. Only scanty material has been preserved from the intervening period, but what little evidence there exists is both illuminating and significant. The French school of clavecinists, with François Couperin (1668-1733) recognized as the supreme master, exerted its style of keyboard treatment far beyond the French borders; indeed, it was Couperin "The Great" who profoundly influenced the harpsichord writing of Bach.

It is in a set of suites by Couperin called "Ordres" that can be found the *Allemande à deux Clavecins,*[5] at the beginning of the Neuvième Ordre.[6] The piece is brilliant and masterly, taxing with its technical difficulties, and, unlike Giles Farnaby's *For two Virginals,* equally demanding on each of the performers. Moreover, it is in every respect representative of Couperin and his clavecin style.[7]

Several members of the Couperin family were held in high repute as eminent performers on keyboard instruments. Assuredly, there must have existed a strong incentive for these distinguished musicians to combine several harpsichords for ensemble purposes. Thus it becomes clear why Couperin gave to a number of his works the provision allowing for their performance on two harpsichords, besides the additional employment of viols, flutes, or any other instruments "which might be at hand." In an autographed *avis,* the composer himself suggests that two harpsichords should play antiphonally, or in unison, with the orchestra. His directions for execution, while leaving the widest liberty for the application of instrumental combinations, beyond doubt authorizes the use of two harpsichords in a concertante style.

Some works by François Couperin which belong into this category and may be performed authentically on two harpsichords, are the following:

> *Six short Pieces*
> *Le Parnasse (L'Apotheose de Corelli)*
> *L'Apotheose de Lulli*
> *Suite No. 3: L'Imperiale*

---

5. See Illustration No. 2.
6. *Oeuvres Complètes de François Couperin,* Second Livre de Pièces de Clavecin, publié par Maurice Cauchie.
7. For further comment on this work, see Book III *The Literature,* Chapter XXIII, *The Standard Repertoire.*

Allemande à deux Clavecins.

François Couperin

Philip Manuel of the Manuel and Williamson harpsichord ensemble, Chicago, has made a special study of the music of this period and considers it as fully legitimate to adopt for performance for two harpsichords not only the aforementioned compositions, but also Couperin's two bagpipe tunes *Musette de Taverni* and *Musette de Choisi*.[8] Manuel, for like reasons, also includes into the two-harpsichord repertoire Couperin's so-called portraits *La Jeuillet* and *Madame Letiville,* charming bits of characterization and Gallic finesse of wit.

To the same type of early program music, with all its allusions to the dance, belong Jean Philippe Rameau's (1683-1764) *Mme. Cupis* and *Mme. Marais.* The name "portraits" given to these tone pictures appears to be very fitting. The two pieces are taken from Rameau's *Concerto No. V.* Like with the works by Couperin just mentioned, the instrumentation of this concerto is fairly in the abstract, allowing most any combination for optional usage. The treble part mostly was played by a violin or flute or oboe against the part of the viola da gamba. Very effective, however, and so authorized in the composer's special *avis,* is the combination of two harpsichords.

Compositions of the same period which provide suitable settings for two harpsichords include also Raison's (fl. 1685) *Hail, the King!* and Le Begue's (1630-1702) *The Bells,* both pieces to be performed by either organ or harpsichords.[9]

Before leaving the French school of harpsichord writing, a late representative of the clavecinists may be anticipated at this time. He is Armand Louis Couperin (1721-1789), who, in the tradition of the *Allemande à deux clavecins* by his illustrious namesake and uncle, François, has written several works for two harpsichords. Armand Louis does not fail to explicitly prescribe this instrumental combination as the definite medium for performance. One of two major compositions is entitled *Symphonie à deux Clavecins,* the title evidently being in keeping with the practice of the time which applied the term *symphonie* to any polyphonic composition.[10] The work is in the key of D major and has three movements which are marked *Moderato et marqué, Andante,* and *Presto.* The very same tempo indications are used for the movements of a second keyboard ensemble composition of Armand Louis Couperin which is called *Deuxième Quatuor à deux Clavecins* and which is in the tonality of E flat. The

8. Philip Manuel writes on these musettes: "The musette from Taverny was perhaps first heard in the small commune by that name in the north of France. Couperin suggested that these voices for drones and chanters be played on all sorts of instruments. Members of the spinet family in unison he deemed an especially fine medium."
9. Information by Philip Manuel.
10. The three-part Inventions of J. S. Bach also were named *Symphonies* by their author.

original scores of these two works are kept in the archives of the Conservatoire in Paris.[11]

It now becomes necessary to return to the first years of the eighteenth century and to encounter another change of locality. Across the Alps, in Italy, a leader in the early development of keyboard music was experimenting on his own account with the combination of two instruments. He was Bernardo Pasquini (1637-1710), an important musician of the time, whose compositions are both vigorous and graceful. Pasquini's influence upon his German colleagues was considerable; he and Handel, for instance, had much in common.

Even a hundred years before Pasquini, Giovanni Gabrieli (1557-1612), the respected teacher of Schuetz and Praetorius, had already experimented with the antiphonal effects possible to obtain on two separate instruments. His composition *Pian e Forte*[12] indicates Gabrieli's objectives. His intended medium most likely were the two organs of St. Mark's at Venice where Gabrieli was the organist.

Pasquini, however, specifically wrote for the harpsichord. The British Museum in London possesses three volumes of chamber music by the great Italian. The first volume contains 14 pieces for two harpsichords, preceded by a partita. The latter is dated May 6, 1703, as the time of its composition; the day given at the end of the collection is December 3, 1704. The original notation of the 14 sonatas "a due cimbali" is in the form of figured basses. A separate bass line or part is designated for each instrument, and explicit indications are given as to which harmonic and melodic improvisations can be executed by the performers. The first two pieces do not have the superscription "Sonata," but since they are in all respects similar to those pieces which follow afterward and bear that title, they can justly be classified under the same term. Over the first piece are written the mere words "A due Cimbali," with only the year 1704 given as the date of origin; the designation of the second piece is simply "2a." Interspersed among the sonatas for two cembali are also pieces for one instrument; these compositions bear the heading "basso continuo."

Several settings for two pianofortes have been effected from some of Pasquini's early two-keyboard sonatas.[13] F. Boghen edited the sonatas in G minor and F major, and the Sonata in D minor, now frequently per-

---

11. According to an information received by Philip Manuel; the latter secured the copies in his possession from the *Bibliothèque* of the French institution.
12. Written "abstractly," for any combination of voices or instruments.
13. For the publishers of the various editions, see Book III, *The Literature*, Chapter **XXIV**, *Original Two-Piano Music*.

formed, was arranged by W. Danckert as well as by J. S. Shedlock.[14]

Arnaldo Bonaventura who is the author of a monograph on the music of Bernardo Pasquini,[15] brings his interesting comments in connection with these sonatas for two cembali to the culminating statement that

> ". . . nell' idea di scrivere Sonata per due clavicembali il Pasquini ha precorso i grandi tedeschi, quali l'Handel e il Bach che pur si compiacquero di somigliante genere di composizioni."[16]

As far as the reference of the Italian writer to Handel's great liking for harpsichord ensemble music is concerned, small evidence of such preference has remained. Only one composition for two harpsichords is definitely known to have been written by the great master of the oratorio, George Frederick Handel (1685-1759). It is a *Suite à deux clavecins* which Handel wrote during his youth. However, only one of the two parts has been discovered and was incorporated into Volume 48 of the monumental edition by Dr. Friedrich Chrysander. Shedlock assumes that the existing part is the principal one.[17] From it, Manuel and Williamson have reconstructed a supplementary part. They used original material given out by Harpsichord I, and "other Handelian figures[18] when the canonic or antiphonal style of the music seems to give way to ideas other than those announced by Harpsichord I."[19]

In this restored version, Manuel and Williamson program the work as *Suite in C minor* for their duo-harpsichord performances, offering two movements (Prelude and Courante) of the original four. The *Suite in C minor* is one of two works known to have been written by Handel for two keyboard instruments. The other comparable composition is scored for two organs, but unfortunately this work also exists only as a fragment.

A contemporary of Handel and Bach, Wilhelm Hieronymus Pachelbel (c. 1685-1764) is said to have composed a toccata for two claviers. This work is mentioned explicitly by both Spitta and Schweitzer in their exhaustive biographies of J. S. Bach. However, both references are quite

---

14. J. S. Shedlock, the editor of *Selection of Pieces Composed for the Harpsichord by Bernardo Pasquini*, writes on p. V of his preface: "The third Sonata will be found at p. 42; an attempt has been made to evolve the music from the figured basses. If this attempt to imitate Pasquini's style be not acceptable, the basses are given as the composer wrote them, and anyone who cares, can work out upper parts according to his judgment." The entire Sonata, in Shedlock's edition, is found on pages 42-48. It contains three movements: *Allegro-Adagio-Vivace*.

15. Arnaldo Bonaventura, *Bernardo Pasquini, Monografia*, Roma, Casa Editrice "Musica," 1923

16. ". . . In the idea of writing Sonatas for two harpsichords, Pasquini has preceded the great Germans, Handel and Bach, who liked so much the same genre of composition."

17. See p. IV of Shedlock's preface to *Selection of Pieces Composed for the Harpsichord by Bernardo Pasquini*.

18. The extraneous material includes a *Courante* by Handel, published by Schott & Sons.

19. Information from program annotations by Manuel and Williamson.

short, and no source of further information is made available. Prosniz lists the piece on p. 58 of his *Handbuch der Klavier-Literatur* 1450-1830, *Historisch-Kritische Uebersicht*. Eitner mentions the composition as "Toccata auf 2 Clav. ex Eb" and traces the location of the original manuscript to the *Kircheninstitut* in Berlin. However, Manuel believes that Pachelbel's toccata was written for the two *manuals* of one harpsichord rather than for two separate instruments. It is to be recalled that the term *clavier,* signifying "keyboard," used to be the generic name for any keyboard instrument, including the harpsichord family, the clavichord, and the organ. In consequence, the deduction whether a work written for two claviers was to be performed on one or two instruments depends on the number of staves in the score.

Only an examination of Pachelbel's original manuscript, not accessible at this time, can reveal the actual intentions of the composer and thereby provide the answer concerning the correct execution of the music in question. Some printed works of W. H. Pachelbel are incorporated in the volume of clavier compositions by his father, Johann Pachelbel (1653-1706).[20] These three pieces are entitled *Musikalisches Vergnuegen,* suggested to be played "sowohl auf die Orgel als auch das Clavier," (on the organ as well as on the clavier). The indication as to execution, combined with the fact that W. H. Pachelbel was an organist to whom two claviers in all likelihood meant two manuals, makes Manuel's theory appear as supported by probability. Nevertheless, the final classification of the "Toccata auf 2 Clav." will need to be established by the evidence found in the manuscript itself.

This concludes the brief examination of relics from the epoch of the early pioneers in the keyboard ensemble field. From the mists which shroud the early dawn of the art, there emerges the morning clearness of duo-pianistic history. Over it rises the sun-like genius of Johann Sebastian Bach.

---

20. Denkmäler Deutscher Tonkunst *Klavierwerke von Johann Pachelbel, nebst beigefuegten Stuecken von W. H. Pachelbel,* edited by Max Seiffert.

CHAPTER III

BACH

There can be little doubt that a family of keyboard virtuosos as eminent as the Scarlattis at frequent occasions placed two harpsichords together, be it for the instruction accorded by Alessandro, the father, to Domenico, the son, be it for a friendly contest of skills, for improvisation or formal composition. It is in the realm of possibility, although it does not appear probable, that Domenico was a pupil of Bernardo Pasquini and thus came to know the latter's sonatas for two cembali. There is also room for conjecture regarding a contest on harpsichords between Domenico Scarlatti and Handel when the two men had become acquainted in Venice in 1708. Together they went to Rome where Cardinal Ottoboni arranged for the competition, an event probably similar to the famous contest between Mozart and Clementi, and apparently a favorite pastime with the elect patrons of the art at that age. Scarlatti and Handel may and may not have competed on two harpsichords at the time; however, Domenico Scarlatti's contribution to modern technical execution is so great, and his influence even to Mendelssohn and Liszt so evident, that he needs to be given prime mention in any discussion relative to pianism.

Whereas the Scarlattis left no tangible account of their duo-keyboard activities, it is the work of Johann Sebastian Bach which stands, like in so many other fields of musical art, as a towering cornerstone in the early period of duo-pianism. It was quite common practice in those days to arrange several cembali together. Bach considered the playing on two, and sometimes more, harpsichords as a special edification and he indulged in various combinations of keyboard ensemble at home with the many qualified members of his family as well as in company of his musical friends.

20

A distinct incentive was provided when, in the year 1729, Bach was made the director of the Collegium Musicum at Leipzig. The society had been founded by Telemann in 1705 and could be called an academy of music. The college studies were held during the winter in Richter's Coffee rooms where several harpsichords were at the disposal of the musicians. A number of good harpsichordists could be found among the students gathering around the great master; his two eldest sons were particularly accomplished players. Due to Bach's position as director of the group, it was expected from him to produce new music of his own at these meetings. It is only natural that Bach was moved to write for various combinations of the keyboard instruments at hand; the outgrowth of this incentive is a wealth of compositions for two and more harpsichords.

Of all the brilliant music ever written for clavier ensemble, the multiple cembali concerti by Bach can be counted among the most sparkling. They are filled with the effects of running dances, alternated by sections of stolid dignity; whirling figures rival with passages of shimmering delicacy. Vera Brodsky writes about these concerti as follows:[1]

"With his contrapuntal bent, Bach must have revelled in the opportunities afforded by the employment of twenty or thirty fingers for rhythmic and other effects, complex figurations and fullness of tone. . . . But never were those compositions mere vehicles for the display of empty agility, as exploited by Corelli and Vivaldi. Bach integrated his solo instruments with the orchestra, and foreshadowed the type of concerto which served as the model for all his great successors."

Possibly Bach may have received the first suggestion of writing a multiple concerto for harpsichords from his revered idol, Dietrich Buxtehude. This Swedish master became famous in Germany for his activities in Luebeck. His reputation was so great that he made that city a goal of pilgrimage for many a musician anxious to advance in his art, including the young Johann Sebastian Bach. Manuel holds that Buxtehude wrote a concerto for three harpsichords of which, however, Prosniz makes no mention. In any event, the various chamber groups as they performed in Buxtehude's "Evening Music Makings" at Luebeck, permanently kept Bach's fancy stimulated. Whatever amount of inspiration he then received for the medium of keyboard ensemble, the outgrowth of his vision in this particular field of *Kammermusik* eventually brought on no less than three concerti for two claviers, two concerti for three claviers, and one concerto for four claviers. As will be seen, Bach in addition arranged two fugues from his monumental contrapuntal treatise *Die Kunst der Fuge*

1. *"Two Piano Playing,"* an essay in *The Macmillan Encyclopedia of Music and Musicians,* p. 1898.

for two claviers, an act of significance for the function of duo-pianism then and now.[2]

Before embarking on a discussion of Bach's concertos for multiple claviers, a remark on the status of the concerto form during his time seems appropriate. The original idea of the concerto did not entail the extreme prominence of the solo instrument; rather, each instrument was treated on an equal basis, *paris inter pares*. The modern tendency at Bach's time, however, was toward the featured display of solo parts. In the fifth Brandenburg concerto, more than an indication of this trend is to be noticed in the soloistic treatment of the clavier; the instrument is allowed to occupy the field by itself for considerable length of time.

The tendency towards featured display eventually and logically developed into the direction which Parry describes as follows:[3]

> ". . . when later Bach wrote concertos for clavier and for two and more claviers with orchestral accompaniment, it was inevitable that the individuality of the solo instruments should be more and more emphasized, because Bach's impulse, begotten of ample experience, necessarily impelled him to get the utmost effect out of the passages which the performers had to play alone, and this could not be effected without giving them a conspicuous share in the proceedings. The tendency in the modern direction was more noticeable in concertos for claviers than in concertos for violins or wind instruments, because the clavier was so much better adapted to play solo passages without the orchestra."

Spitta analyzes the same development in a penetrating essay contained in his biography on Johann Sebastian Bach. Pertinent passages from this treatise will be quoted in connection with the discussion of the Concerto in C Major for two claviers which follows later.

Of the three concertos for two harpsichords,[4] only two such works had been known for some time. They were the *Concerto No. 1* in C Minor and the *Concerto No. 2* in C Major. Now there is still a third concerto which, like the first, is in the key of C minor. The Concerti Nos. 1 and 3 are known to be harpsichord arrangements of concertos which at first were written for two violins.[*] Therefore, only the Concerto No. 2 in C Major can strictly be considered an original composition for the medium of two claviers.[5]

---

2. Bach was also credited for a long time with a *Duetto* which, however, later research ascribed to his son, Wilhelm Friedemann Bach.

3. Parry, *Bach*, p. 132-133.

4. The exact title in Volume 21 of the Bach Gesellschaft edition reads: "Drei Concerte für 2 Claviere mit Orchesterbegleitung."

5. Vera Brodsky writes—in *The Piano* by Wier, p. 350—that there are "three original concertos for two claviers," a statement which may be misleading.

* Arnold Schering holds that the *Concerto No. 1* was originally a concerto for violin and oboe and was written in D minor. According to Dr. Schering, "the original violin and oboe voices can, with very little difficulty, still be traced out of the right hand parts of both pianos" (Preface to *Concertos for Two Pianos by Johann Sebastian Bach*, Edition Eulenburg, Nos. 730-731).

As to the arranged Concertos Nos. 1 and 3, the quality of these transcriptions for two claviers is controversial. The keyboard version sometimes is unfavorably compared with the effect of the original concertos for two violins. Albert Schweitzer speaks of the "quite incredible haste and carelessness" with which Bach would transcribe violin concertos for the musical evenings at home and for the concerts of the Telemann society. He writes:

> "Violin effects to which he could easily have given a pianistic turn are not remodelled at all. Later on he improves them here and there in the score, but leaves them as they are in the clavier part. The reason for this was that he himself played the clavier part and did as he pleased with the notes before him, making a new part out of them."

A possible explanation for such "haste and carelessness" could be construed from the pressure which was made upon Bach for piano concertos at the weekly meetings of the Collegium Musicum. The constant need for new music found him with either little time or lacking inclination to regularly provide original scores. Schweitzer goes even farther when he condemns the arrangement of the *Concerto No. 3* with the following words:[6]

> "How Bach could venture to transfer the two cantabile violin parts in the largo of this work (the original D minor concerto for two violins) to the cembalo, with its abrupt tone, must be left to himself to answer. Had he not done it himself, we should be protesting in his name today against so un-Bach-like a transcription. This is not the only case in which he makes it hard for his prophets to go forth in his name against the evil transcribers."

David Ewen, on the other hand, holds that in transforming the concertos from the idiom of the violin to that of the piano, Bach was much more than a mere arranger. Ewen states:[7]

> ". . . he rewrote the works to fit them to the new medium, often changed the key, enlarged the harmonic construction, and revised the melodic line to make it more suitable for the keyboard. He can rightly be called the father of the piano concerto."

An interesting comparison of the respective aptitudes of the violin and of the pianoforte as instruments, and an estimation of their realization in the concertos of Bach, is undertaken by Parry. He writes:[8]

> "The aptitude of the violin for expressive melody induced the composition of many movements of extraordinary beauty like those in the concertos. The qualities of the clavier moved Bach in a different manner. He was very urgent about executing melodious phrases in a cantabile manner on that instrument, and not infrequently essayed movements of a song-like character for it; but for the most part the influence of the keyed instrument was more in an abstract direction, suggesting purely artistic developments. It would be hard to find more suggestive contrasts than such as are presented between the slow movements of the violin concertos and those in the fine concertos for two claviers in C and C minor. The latter were probably written later in life and present the tokens of much more spacious development and more

6. Schweitzer *Johann Sebastian Bach*, Vol. I, page 413
7. David Ewen, *Music for Millions*, page 14.
8. Parry, *Johann Sebastian Bach*, pp. 135-136.

maturity of style, especially in the quick movements; and in these cases the order of merit is reversed, for the slow movements are of less appealing quality than the quick movements. Bach in these cases laid hold of the rhythmic capacity of the keyed instrument and the opportunity which the activity of so large a number of human fingers afforded for producing rich effects and giving the impression of great fulness of tone. The differences may be summarized in the sense that the violin is superbly suggestive for melody and the clavier specially adapted for part-writing; so when Bach writes slow movements for the clavier he makes them serve as phases of contrast to the quick movements, in which some rather abstract melody is discussed with a certain aloofness of manner, or treated with elaborate ornamentation, such as was more suited to the instrument than passages of sustained melody pure and simple."

Probably the most realistic judgment which has been accorded to the two transcribed Concertos Nos. 1 and 3 is given by Wilhelm Rust in his preface to Vol. 21 of the Bach Gesellschaft edition. Rust maintains that the extraordinary beauty of the compositions will offer a rich amount of compensation for such disadvantages which the instrument as well as the performer always will incur when they attempt to reproduce musical thoughts which can attain their full effect only through the noble mouthpiece of the queen of the orchestra, the violin.

Entirely aside from the degree of edification which can be derived from their performance, the preservation of the Concertos Nos. 1 and 3 constitutes an important factor in the history of musical literature. The original manuscript of the first concerto for two violins no longer exists, and a complete loss of this work would have been suffered were it not for the survival of the arrangement for two claviers. As to the *Concerto No. 3* in C minor, this is in reality a transcription of the well known Concerto in D Minor for Two Violins and Orchestra. In this case, Bach's subsequent arrangement for two claviers was destined to serve the restoration of the double violin concerto in that the original score of the latter disappeared. The parts for the two solo violins and an unfigured bass in Bach's own hand survived, however; these particular manuscripts are preserved in the State Library in Berlin. The Concerto was restored by Bach authorities in an authentic edition; at this occasion, the score of the Concerto for Two Claviers in C minor was of decisive importance through its comparison with the solo parts and the unfigured bass.[9] The two-clavier arrangement thus again was instrumental in preserving the original music.

The *Concerto No. 1* in C minor, of which the version for two violins has been lost altogether, possesses musical contents of great interest and beauty. As the work opens, the two soloists and the string orchestra give a concerted announcement of their subject. The two clavier parts are interlaced with each other, and the striving appears to be for balance

9. Paul Affelder, program notes to *Double Concerto for Two Violins in D Minor*, Columbia set MX 90.

rather than contrast. The middle movement, *adagio,* is in E flat major. It is distinguished by a beautiful melody, unfolded at first by the second piano. The first piano repeats it in the dominant with a fugal suggestion which, however, proves deceptive. The burden of the dialogue is given to the two claviers, and the orchestra is kept subordinate. In the finale, marked *allegro,* the two solo instruments and the orchestra commence again in lively fashion and complete agreement. During the development there appears a counter subject in the bass, and numerous episodes vary with each other. An inversion of the principal subject is introduced before the close of the work.

Important as the Concerti Nos. 1 and 3 necessarily are to this discussion, chief attention is commanded by the *Concerto No. 2* in C major. With this work, Bach not only erected a milestone for the two-piano idiom as a creative medium, but he also established a new prototype within the entire realm of musical composition, more specifically in regard to the evolution of the concerto form. Wilhelm Rust, in the afore-mentioned preface to Volume 21 of the Bach-Gesellschaft edition, traces the beginnings of the idea to treat both claviers in an obligato style or in concertizing manner. He arrives at the conclusion that the *"accompagnement"* which remains an important factor of the solo clavier concerto and of the concerto for other combinations, must be silent in the concerti for two and three claviers. "Here it indeed would be a musical Pleonasmus of the most disturbing kind." The thought to abolish the orchestra in the *tutti* sense, and as the chief protagonist of the soloist, was originated by Bach and put into practice in this concerto; the logic of the procedure has continued to exert compelling influence, as was recently evidenced by the methods which Stravinsky has employed in the creation of his own concerto for two solo pianos.

Various authors have elaborated on the significance of the C major concerto which came into being, through the vision of Bach's genius, to represent a concise form of the concertante style. Applied to a combination as resourceful as two harpsichords, the style was pre-eminently qualified to continue its influence throughout the following generations of new musicians and new instruments. There are indications that Bach from the beginning had in mind to treat the two claviers *a capella,* without orchestral accompaniment. As a matter of fact, the second movement of the concerto is marked *"Quartetto tacet"* (string orchestra silent). This direction by the composer is another bold step toward the exploitation of the orchestral qualities inherent in the harpsichord of which the pianoforte later was to become the successor and heir.

To throw further light upon the motivations underlying Bach's tenden-

cies to treat the harpsichord in a solo and at the same time orchestral
style, it is helpful to quote what Ernest Newman, critic of the *London
Times,* is stating on the harpsichord and its music:

> "The harpsichord can produce so many varieties and mixtures of tone-color that
> sometimes the effect is quasi-orchestral. At a hundred points, as we listen, we see
> how true it is that this music was born out of the very being of the harpsichord:
> for the harpsichord shows us the music, as a whole and in every point of detail,
> as the composer conceived it."

To these summary remarks, Manuel and Williamson, duo-harpsichordists, add in greater detail some pertinent information on the ancient instrument:

"The 'Regal Cembalo' reached the peak of its development about the
middle of the Eighteenth Century. It was considered the solo keyboard
instrument par excellence; it was the chief support for singers; it was the
orchestra conductor's indispensable ally; and it was frequently used in
the churches.

"Following are but a few harpsichord truths concerning which com-
mentators have given false impressions: within each register, nuance is
possible; cantabile of lyric lines can often find their tenderest expression
at the clavecin; dynamic accent is not only possible at the harpsichord, but
it is constantly employed by the player; the life of tone is remarkably
long—indeed, with certain combinations, one gets a distinct impression
of organ peal (the ornamentation of the music of the period, when rightly
treated as melodic invention, represents a style, and has nothing to do
with durability of tone—music of the time written for violin, organ, or
voice was equally replete with 'graces').

"After one has listened to a harpsichord for a given time, his ear
deposits the strumming, rustling, chiming quality into its rightful place
of characteristic tonal background, and one gathers the great number of
varieties of timbre which sing from the different types of strings. Flutes,
flageolets, oboes, clarinets, stringed instruments, even drum beat when
desired, emerge from the general swirl of sound."[10]

In full realization of this resourcefulness and independence of the
instrument, Bach set out to create the prototype of the "Concerto without
an Orchestra." In his *Italian Concerto,* he frankly attempted to attain
with a single solo instrument the effect of an entire body of instruments
such as were usually employed in the traditional concerto grosso. Proving
successful with his theory, how much more, then, must Bach have felt
moved to dispense with the accompaniment of an orchestra when he
utilized the resources of a combination of harpsichords.

10. Special reference to the present significance of the harpsichord and its music will
be made in Chapter XI, Section *The Trend.*

As it is, the concerto can readily be performed without the assistance and background of the string orchestra. It thus proves the self-sufficiency of the two solo instruments. Indeed there are indications that the orchestral scores were added to the solo parts at a later time.

Rust believes that the work in its final form was created over intermittent periods of time because of certain rather obvious mistakes contained in the several manuscripts which have been preserved. Rust also feels that this gradual development in which the wonderful concerto grew to the final form in which it now presents itself, is accountable for "that highest stage of maturity which characterizes a perfect work of art."

In his evaluation of the composition, Rust makes the following comments:[11]

"As a clavier composition, the C major concerto No. 2 at any rate is the most effective. It combines the most perfect skill of composition with the highest flight of musical thought. Vital and exuberant Bach—particularly the last movement flows along and leads the listener by the most beautiful pictures of youthful fantasy. Not less perfect is the tonal language through which those thoughts are brought to expression."

David Hall[12] considers as outstanding "the brooding slow movement of this otherwise spirited work," and Alfred Einstein[13] enthusiastically writes of the concluding movement:

"Rarely does a concerto have so grand a conclusion as the glorious fugue in Johann Sebastian Bach's C major Concerto for two claviers . . ."

Extensive comments on the C major concerto are also available from the biographies by Schweitzer and Spitta. Pertinent excerpts from these essays will be quoted in the following paragraphs; they serve to underscore the epoch-making importance of this work.

Schweitzer, who was seen to doubt the quality of the Concertos Nos. 1 and 3, arranged for two claviers, voices the greatest admiration for the C major concerto. He writes:[14]

"The one original concerto, however—No. 2, in C major—compensates us for all our disappointed expectations in the two others,—if we can speak of disappointment in connection with Bach. The fact that it was originally conceived for two claviers is shown at once not only by the rich writing for the two solo parts, (in the third section of the splendid fugue they are in three parts throughout,) but also by the subordinate position given to the orchestra. It is not an orchestral concerto with two soli cembali, but a concerto for two claviers with orchestral accompaniment. Perhaps, indeed, the first movement existed at one time without instrumental accompaniment. Certain indications go to show that this was added later,

11. Wilhelm Rust, in his preface to Vol. 21 of the Bach-Gesellschaft edition, section *General Remarks*
12. *The Record Book*, p. 216.
13. *Mozart*, p. 289.
14. Schweitzer, *J. S. Bach*, Vol. I, pp. 414-415

and that Bach wrote it out at first not in score but in parts. Otherwise we cannot explain how it happens that in two places of this first allegro,—bars 83 and 108— the orchestra enters with the major third, while the clavier parts maintain the minor third,—which grows logically out of what has gone before,—and do not make it major until the following crochet. Bach would certainly have noticed this error had he had the clavier and orchestral parts before him in the score. The curious thing is that the mistake was not noticed, in performance, and at once corrected in the clavier parts. (Footnote: The observation is Rust's; see his preface to B.G. XXI, p. 8. The error is of course corrected in the B. G. edition. Rust's hypothesis that Bach resorted to this concerto form from the desire to omit the third (accompanying) clavier from the other concertos for two claviers,—in which, however, it is a necessity—cannot be regarded as proved).

"An accompanying piano is not necessary here, the two solo claviers themselves supplying the most essential harmonies. The *cembalo accompagnato* is here really the orchestra, consisting of a simple string quartet, which in reality only plays a figured bass that has a good deal of rhythmical interest. In a performance in a small room it can be quite well replaced by a third piano. An ordinarily good player could easily play the part direct from the orchestral score. We could even arrange for the two pianos all that is really indispensable in the orchestral accompaniment."

A penetrating analysis of the C major concerto is given by Philipp Spitta in his biography of Bach. The following quotations are taken from this essay:[15]

". . . it is easily conceivable that the mere use of a second harpsichord for the figured bass would suggest to the composer that it might be raised from its dependent position to a more prominent one. For it must be regarded as an indubitable fact that in the C major concerto no instrument is meant to play the figured bass part; and even in the older C minor concerto—to judge from the parts which date from Bach's time—it was not regarded as indispensable. Finally, it must not be forgotten that a composition for two claviers was nothing new. Bach may not have had the form suggested to him by Hieronymus Pachelbel's Toccata for two claviers, if indeed he knew of it; Couperin had written an Allemande for two claviers which Bach, his great admirer, must certainly have known.

"Be that as it may, the C major concerto leaves not a moment's doubt as to Bach's conception of this form. There is no longer any idea of strife or opposition between the solo instruments and the tutti; the tutti has nothing to do but supply an accompaniment to the harmony, or to support the passages played on the claviers. In the Adagio it is silent, and in the other movements it could quite well be dispensed with without detriment to the construction of the work. Its use is to give fulness and colour. The few short episodes and polyphonic phrases which it has to itself are apparently accounted for by the fact that Bach could not endure the tedium of writing parts which were not *obbligato*. The working-out falls entirely to the share of the claviers, but with this exception it exactly follows the method prescribed by the concerto form. A tutti phrase (bars 1-12) and a solo-phrase (bars 12-28) come into prominence in the first movement, which is developed out of their different combinations and contrasts in different keys. Within the limits of these two chief groups, however, the solo instruments have concerted passages of a very animated kind among themselves. This movement can thus be called a concerto in a two-fold sense, both because it preserves the form of Vivaldi's concerto style, which proceeds from the contrast between the solo and the tutti, and also because it actually contains a strife or competition between two instruments, although these are of different kinds. The last movement of the

15. Spitta, *Johann Sebastian Bach*, Vol. III, pp. 144.146.

concerto generally has a dance character and some kind of three-time, and, as compared with the more pathetic first movement, it must always be gay, light, and brilliant. This requirement is fulfilled by Bach in the C major concerto; but the employment of the fugal form is remarkable. The fugue belongs to the sonata form, or to that of the concerto in the sonata style; it has nothing in common with the strict concerto form, since that originates not in polyphony, but in homophony, and its working-out is not thematic but episodic. Bach often employs a fugue for the last movement, especially where the clavier appears as a solo instrument; this is the case, for instance, in the fifth Brandenburg concerto, in the concerto in A minor for clavier, violin, and flute, and also in the fourth Brandenburg concerto, the violin part of which was re-arranged by Bach for the clavier. There, and in the C major concerto, he succeeded in a most masterly way in suiting the form to the character of the movement, by the style of invention and treatment, especially by means of longer episodes, or even interludes, quite in the free style; and he was led to introduce them by the style of the harpsichord and the organ, which always influenced his imagination. Although the fugal style would appear to afford but little temptation for anything of the kind, Bach contrives in this movement to employ the two claviers in such a manner as to make them appear as two factors of equal importance. By this means, the working-out of the fugues, even putting aside the interludes, is characteristic and especially interesting. The two allegro movements, and, in no less a degree, the delicately woven and melancholy quatour which serves as an Adagio, reveal a fresh though controlled inventiveness, a feeling of strict moderation, which, when united to the highest perfection of form—for the work corresponds absolutely to the ideal of the concerto —make the work a classic model."

As to the slow movement, marked *Adagio overro Largo* and in 6-8 time, it reveals in its minor key a mood of beautiful melancholy, governed by sublime poise, a combination of emotion and control of which this great genius was the unexcelled master.[16]

The concerti for three and four claviers at this time do not enter into the discussion. Their nature and significance will be referred to at a later time.[17] As a matter of record only, it is pointed out that the two concerti for three claviers and orchestra are in the keys of D minor and C major respectively; they can be found in Vol. 31 of the Bach-Gesellschaft edition. Tradition has it that these concerti were composed by Bach for the special purpose of performance with his two eldest sons who assisted him in the circle of the Collegium Musicum. The concerto for four claviers, contained in Vol. 43 of the Bach-Gesellschaft edition, is a transcription of the concerto for four violins, two alti, violoncello, violone and cembalo by Antonio Vivaldi.

Significantly, all of Bach's compositions for two or more claviers and orchestra were classified as *"Kammermusik."* As has been pointed out, this explicit designation of the chamber music genre, while rooted in the tradition of Buxtehude, is not throughout in compliance with the evolution

16. For further comment on this work, see also Book III, *The Literature*, Chapter XXIII, *The Standard Repertoire*.
17. See Book II, *Nature, Applications, and Problems*, Chapter XII, *Definitions*.

of the concerto form. The distinct featuring of individual instruments to more recent concepts has become the essence of the *concerto* form whereas chamber music in the present terminology represents the intimate fusing of instruments rather than their solo display. This definition, however, will be examined more closely in later chapters when the problem of "Duo-pianism: Concert or Chamber Music?" is subjected to a special discussion.[18]

Of paramount interest in this survey are the two fugues for two claviers which were written by Bach in connection with, and as a supplement to, his last and crowning work, *The Art of Fugue.* It is generally known that the scoring of this gigantic work provides no indication as to the employment of certain prescribed or recommended instruments for performance of the music. Therefore, Bach's dissertation on the possibilities of fugue writing stands as a largely theoretical work. Arguments pro and contra the various media of rendition have been as old as the repeated attempts to give the work a hearing.[19] This fundamental problem probably cannot be solved to everyone's complete satisfaction, and all reconstructions of the most likely instrumentation remain matters of conjecture, not of authenticity.

One of several theories advanced is that of Willi Apel, expressed in his *Harvard Dictionary of Music.*[20] Apel holds out the opinion that the work was intended for keyboard performance; his reasoning is worded as follows:

> "Another problem of the Art of Fugue is that of medium and performance—the question as to whether it is keyboard, orchestral, or chamber music. The lack of any instrumental specifications in either the autograph or the first edition, together with the use of the scholarly name 'Contrapunctus' as a designation for the various pieces, characterizes the Art of Fugue as a work which is not dependent upon specified medium or sound, a work which is rooted in the contrapuntal tradition of the Flemish School rather than in the ideas of the Baroque period. Therefore any kind of performance must be considered justifiable which is in conformity with the austere spirit of the composition. On the other hand, the fact should not be overlooked that all the pieces, with the exception of the mirror-fugues (Nos. XII and XIII of the Peters ed.) are within the reach of the hands of a keyboard player. Evidently, in composing the work, Bach was thinking constantly of keyboard performance, if only for instructive purposes."

The last remark may be amplified by adding Parry's statement that "Bach delighted in combining the beautiful with the educationally helpful."[21]

18. Book II, *"Nature, Applications, and Problems,"* Chapters XVI and XX.
19. The first public performance, promoted by W. Graeser, took place at Leipzig in 1927, followed by a sensational revival of the work which encompassed the entire musical world.
20. See section, *Art of Fugue*, p. 59.
21. Parry, *Johann Sebastian Bach*, p. 501.

Within this important argument, the appendical arrangement for two claviers by Bach himself is of great significance. The arrangement includes those two marvelous three-part fugues of which the second is the inversion and mirror of the first in all parts. To begin with, it is to be realized that there is the very practical aspect of extreme difficulty, and indeed that of partial impossibility, to play certain portions of these three-part fugues on one keyboard instrument. The parts often are so far distant from each other that two notes which are to sound simultaneously cannot be reached except by a jump; such a leap, however, would gravely mar the texture and impair the continuity. Bach arranged the fugues in a manner[22] whereby two of the three voices are assigned to one clavier while the other harpsichord takes the third and an additional fourth part; the latter was composed by Bach especially for this arrangement. There are also some free additions at the outset of each fugue, so that one can really speak of enlargements rather than arrangements.

Of the Bach biographers, Spitta comments on these arrangements for two claviers as follows:[23]

> "In order to make this 'eye music' appreciable by the ear, Bach arranged the fugues in such a manner that one clavier plays two parts, while the other takes the third and a free part added in besides. A few free additions are also made at the beginning of each fugue. The newly added parts give fresh evidence of Bach's enormous talent in contrivances of this kind. The result, however, has but a doubtful value as a work of art, and was never intended for insertion in the complete work, since it is a distortion of the idea of writing a fugue in only real parts, all capable of inversion; while the introduction of a second clavier radically alters its style and character."

Notwithstanding Spitta's reservations, the two fugues in Bach's own setting for two claviers have been given frequent concert performances and for a time even enjoyed something of a vogue.[24]. Their revival and continuing popularity appear deserved because of the workmanship of these compositions which is indeed stupendous. In the fashion of an orderly complication all ideas of the first fugue are turned upside down in the second fugue, inner voices of the first are made outer voices of the second, and what was given out by the first clavier is tossed to the second instrument which plays the notes as though they were now seen in a mirror. The fugues are perhaps the most sensational examples of Bach's incredible command of the contrapuntal idiom. A sovereignty so absolute that "while every note is calculated with mathematical exactitude, the music at every point sounds spontaneous and inspired. Bach is here the master of that contradiction in creation toward which every composer

---

22. See Illustration No. III.
23. Spitta, *Johann Sebastian Bach*, Vol. III, p. 198.
24. The fugues form part of the repertoire of Manuel and Williamson, duo-harpsi-chordists.

Beilage 2   "DIE KUNST DER FUGE"

Fuga a 2. Clav.*)   Joh.Seb.Bach

*) Im Berliner Autograph als Beilage 2.   B.W. XXV. (1)

B.W. XXV. (1)

Beilage 2   "DIE KUNST DER FUGE"

Alio modo. Fuga a 2. Clav.*)

Joh. Seb. Bach

*) Im Berliner Autograph als Beilage 2.

B.W. XXV.(1)

Duo-Pianism

must aspire; the power of unlimited freedom of expression within the severest of self-imposed limitations."[25]

The wonder excited by these fugues is expressed by Albert Schweitzer in an enthusiastic commentary which also includes a reference to their arrangement for two claviers. Schweitzer writes in his biography on the master:[26]

> "All the possible fugue types, including those of which Bach himself had never made use, are represented in the Art of Fugue. We do not know which to wonder at most—that all these combinations could be devised by one mind, or that, in spite of the ingenuity of it all, the parts always flow along as naturally and freely as if the way were not prescribed for them by this or that purely technical necessity.
>
> "His purpose in this work being a purely theoretical one, Bach writes the fugues out in score, and calls them 'counterpoints.'
>
> "The last four fugues are grouped in pairs, each of a pair being note for note an exact inversion of the other, as if we were reading it in a mirror. They are in three parts; the negative stands immediately under the positive. Here again Bach soars playfully above every technical difficulty. The pieces are bright and animated from beginning to end, as if it were a pure accident that one of them happened to be the reflection of the other.
>
> "Bach himself must have felt the purest pride in them. He arranged the last pair for two claviers, adding a fourth obbligato part so that both instruments should be fully occupied. In this form the last two pieces of the *Art of Fugue* were given as a supplement, and when the work was republished in the nineteenth century this part of it was fastened on by the pianists and soon became the most popular of all."

With a dearth of original two-clavier compositions from the early classic period, and especially in view of the highly significant position which this instrumental excerpt from the *Art of Fugue* occupies, even more frequent performances of this complex and brilliant work are to be encouraged. No better examples than these two fugues for two claviers can conceivably be found to demonstrate Bach's amazing contrapuntal mathematics which miraculously always produce great music. They also leave the student with the conviction that Bach exhausted the possibilities of the fugue; what he did not do with the mechanics of this form, what he did not accomplish in this manner of composition, most likely cannot be done.

It may be of some interest that the fugues precede the torso of a great fugue on three subjects, including one on Bach's own name, which breaks off abruptly and remains unfinished because death prevented the composer from completion. In the strictest sense, therefore, the two fugues for two claviers can be assumed to constitute the master's last work completed by his own hand.[27]

25. A. Veinus, in the program notes to Victor Album *The Art of Fugue*.
26. Schweitzer, *Johann Sebastian Bach*, Vol. I, p. 427.
27. The Chorale-Prelude "Wenn wir in hoechsten Noethen sein" is known to have been dictated from the death-bed to his son-in-law, Altnikol; Bach then was totally blind.

The manuscript of these two fugues consists of only one sheet of four pages, the size being that of a *"Bogen in Hochformat."* The inscription, while narrow, is very clean. The sheet is marked *"Beilage No. 2"* and represents one of the three existing appendices to *The Art of Fugue.* The autograph is in possession of the former Royal Library in Berlin.[28]

It remains to give some attention to the *Duetto* for two claviers which for a long time was considered a work of Johann Sebastian Bach but now is ascribed to his son, Wilhelm Friedemann. The composition is actually contained in Vol. 43 of the Bach-Gesellschaft edition and is also mentioned specifically by Shedlock in a footnote on page IV of his preface to *Selection of Pieces composed for the harpsichord by Bernardo Pasquini.* Shedlock calls the work an interesting composition and he attributes it, judging from the character of the music, to a mature period of Bach's creative life.

The score of this *duetto* is reproduced on pages 47 to 68 of the aforementioned volume of the Bach-Gesellschaft edition. While the headline immediately above the music consists only of the word *"Duetto,"* the preceding engraved title page reads:

Sonate fuer zwei Claviere,
F dur

In the preface of Vol. 43 the work is traced to, and its publication based upon, a copy which was made from the original manuscript by Ambrosius Kuehnel; the preface further contains a statement to the effect that the composition for the first time is published in print. It is in the final report ("Bericht") of Vol. 46, page 223, that the revision of authorship is effected. A small footnote to the thematic index makes the following terse announcement: "This is a composition of Wilhelm Friedemann Bach."

Grove's Dictionary of Music and Musicians[29] also makes reference to this *Duetto* which was first published as an original work of Johann Sebastian Bach, but proved to be one by Wilhelm Friedemann.

The Sonata is in three movements with the tempo markings *Allegro Moderato, Andante,* and *Presto.* Entirely disregarding the question of authorship, the composition stands as an important contribution to the literature of music for two unaccompanied claviers; in fact, it is one of the earliest works of this genre possessing similar dimensions. The historic and musical status of the *Duetto* both render the composition

---

28. For additional comment, refer to p. 115 of Vol. XXV of the Bach-Gesellschaft edition. The fugues are also contained in Part XI of the Peters edition.
29. Section *Duet,* Vol. II, p. 103.

deserving of much greater attention by duo-pianists than it has received
in the past.

From the temporarily doubtful position held by the *Duetto in F major*
in regard to its origin, and the subsequent attribution of authorship to
Wilhelm Friedemann, the discussion now leads to the sons of Bach and
more specifically to those who have left compositions for two claviers.
Indubitably, the example set by their illustrious father in writing so many
works for multiple harpsichords served to stimulate an interest in Bach's
sons to also compose in this medium. In addition, the frequent ensemble
performances at home and in the Collegium Musicum could not fail to
be conducive to the necessary initiative.

Karl Phillipp Emanuel must be mentioned first. He wrote two concertos
for two claviers and orchestra, one in the key of E flat, the other one
in F major. In addition, Prosniz lists *4 Kleine Duetten fuer 2 Klaviers*
as having come from his pen.[30] These particular duets are given as unprinted; however, the location of the original manuscripts is not indicated.

Wilhelm Friedemann Bach, the recognized author of the *Sonata (Duetto)
in F major*[31] has also written a concerto in E flat major for two harpsichords
and orchestra. His two sonatas for two claviers in the keys of D and F
are sometimes called "Concerti for Two Solo Claviers" *(Konzerte fuer
zwei Klaviere allein)*. The one in F major, in three movements *(Allegro
e moderato—Andante—Presto)* is especially beautiful and bears out the
very great talent of Bach's most gifted, but unfortunate son. When performed on two harpsichords,[32] the poignancy of style and feeling conjures
up reflections on the purity of musical conception and expression during
the age of *Empfindsamkeit* of which this sonata is a typical exhibit.

Johann Christian Bach, the "London Bach," has left a charming sonata
for two claviers in G major which Altmann lists as *opus 15, No. 6.*[33] The
work is thoroughly characteristic of Johann Christian's style which was
facile and graceful rather than profound. Through his contribution to
the medium, Bach's youngest surviving son becomes the third of the
brothers to give vivid proof of having carried on the cherished tradition
of harpsichord ensemble playing, a tradition with which their father had
so richly invested them.

There is evidence that, for quite practical reasons, playing on two
claviers was an older form of keyboard ensemble than that of duet playing

---

30. *Handbuch der Klavier-Literatur 1450-1830*, p. 73.
31. Published in Vol. 43 of the Bach-Gesellschaft edition.
32. Manuel and Williamson gave the work a hearing on July 25, 1949 at Northwestern
    University.
33. Altman, *Verzeichnis von Werken fuer Klavier vier—und sechshaendig, sowie fuer
    zwei und mehr Klaviere.*

on one instrument. Dr. Burney writes enthusiastically on his acquaintance with Karl Philipp Emanuel Bach, mentioning specifically the latter's skill in duet playing with another local musician at Hamburg. So impressed was the Englishman that, upon his return, he felt inspired to himself write *Four Sonatas or Duets for the Harpsichord*. They were published in the year 1777, when harpsichords rarely exceeded the range of five octaves. It is obvious that so short a compass of the keyboard was little suitable for the association of two performers before the same instrument, especially if the circumstance is taken into consideration of "the ladies at that time wearing hoops which kept them at too great a distance from each other."[34] In order to remedy the inconvenience, Dr. Burney proceeded to have a special harpsichord built by Merlin; it had six octaves and was expressly intended for the playing of duets. If there is no printed duet music to be found before 1777, the cause for this surprising fact lies in the practical considerations just mentioned. That very condition of too narrow a keyboard for duets was, on the other hand, conducive to the performance on, and to the composing for, two instruments, so that this early period is seen to have actually produced a larger literature of music for four hands on two claviers than for four hands on one keyboard.

In the widest perspective, it must be observed that the older composers did not employ the combination of keyboard instruments as much as it was to become the usage in later periods; this seeming neglect, however, was mainly based on the nature of the instrument itself. The harpsichordist, with the help of two manuals and their coupling facilities, and sometimes even a pedal keyboard, was capable of drawing from the instrument its capacity of tonal range and sonorities. The compact mechanical properties of the harpsichord were very different from those of the fully developed pianoforte with its greatly widened compass and otherwise enlarged possibilities. In short, the harpsichordist could more fully exploit the resources of his instrument than a pianist can. Consequently, there was no real need felt by harpsichord players and composers to add an additional performer. A similar example of self-sufficiency in instrumental music is offered by the development of the organ, its literature, and its players. The organist, throughout the long history of his instrument, was always considered, and has remained, the sole executive in control of all mechanical resources.

In closing this discussion, it appears appropriate to make short reference to the compositions which Johann Sebastian Bach has written for the harpsichord with two manuals and pedal keyboard. Such instruments were frequently used by organists of Bach's day and age and served

34. Dr. Burney, in his essay on music in Abraham Rees's *The New Cyclopedia*, 1849.

the purpose of allowing "organ" practice at home. It is known that Bach owned three harpsichords of this type. Important works such as the *Passacaglia and Fugue in C Minor,* later arranged for the organ, and Bach's six so-called *Organ Sonatas* were written primarily for execution on these instruments. Schweitzer makes the following comments in this connection:[35]

"In the strict sense of the term, it is wrong to speak of Bach's 'organ sonatas.' The two manuscripts in which they have come down to us—one from Friedemann's possession, the other from Emmanuel's—prove that they are really works for the clavicembalo with two manuals and pedal. This instrument was at that time in common use. It was excellently adapted for playing in three real parts, which accounts for the sonatas being in strict trio-form. This does not imply that Bach never played them on the organ also."

The parts or voices of the aforementioned harpsichord compositions are scored on three staves, of which two are designated for the manuals and one for the pedal keyboard. It appears quite justifiable that works of this type, if not played on the organ (for which they practically have been claimed), should be performed on two pianofortes. In our day, this combination will most closely approximate the original character of the music. No notes need to be changed in a distribution of the scoring over two pianos, and the occasional doubling of certain voices will do no violence to the texture. In the opinion of Manuel and Williamson, it is very likely that "Bach gave . . . . similar performances, possibly collaborating with a pupil or one of his sons."[36]

Two-piano arrangements and transcriptions of the works by Johann Sebastian Bach have been devised in uncounted numbers by noted composers of every generation which has followed the great German master. Favorite objects of transcription are the chorale preludes, of which several present-day English composers have made notable arrangements. There exists an impressive two-piano version of the monumental *Passacaglia in C minor* by the American Abram Chasins. Louis Victor Saar has arranged the same work, in addition to the lofty *Chaconne,* and the *Prelude in E major,* both originally composed for the violin. Guy Maier's transcription of the famous *Air* from the Suite in D Major ("Air on the G String") has the declared objective of making the contours of Bach's exquisite piece emerge with as much loveliness in the two-piano version as in the original scoring. The large multitude of available arrangements and transcriptions prevents a further enumeration at this time.

The existing controversy over the legitimacy of transcriptions, or the

35. Schweitzer, *Johann Sebastian Bach,* Vol. I, p. 278.
36. Manuel and Williamson here refer to the *Passacaglia in C minor* which they themselves perform in their concerts on two harpsichords.

degree of their justifiableness, does not enter this survey until a later discussion of the particular problems.[37] It may be recalled, however, that Johann Sebastian Bach himself ranks foremost among the transcribers of all times and could well be termed the chief and fountainhead of the "ancient and honorable history"[38] of transcriptions. He repeatedly used the works of his contemporaries and of earlier composers as vehicles for excursions into musical realms of his own, and often the original form is all but abolished. The concerto for four claviers, transcribed by Bach from Vivaldi's concerto for four violins, proves a good case in point.

To a man like Bach, the contradistinction between original composition and transcription probably mattered little. It certainly never became for him an issue of consequence, let alone one of bitter controversy. The important thing was the Music, and it remained immaterial whether this music was created through his own inspiration, or merely filtered through his craftsmanship and thereby re-created. For Music was his constant need; it was the daily bread of his soul and the expression of his spirit. Whatever substance or form he chose, the music to come forth was a transfiguration of the spirit.

37. See Book II, *Nature, Applications, and Problems,* Chapters XVI, XIX, XX, XXI, XXII.
38. Brodsky.

CHAPTER IV

MOZART

A complete change of style and taste took place in the few years between the death of Johann Sebastian Bach and the musical advent of Wolfgang Amadeus Mozart. It became evident that a transition had occurred from the grave, serious, and elaborate style of writing which was the outgrowth and essence of the Baroque era; the metamorphosis was to lead into the period of the Rococo, with its lightness and elegance.

This transformation was effected only gradually. As early as in the harpsichord compositions of F. Couperin, and in some of the optional dance movements in the suites by J. S. Bach, the so-called "Galanterien", this trend toward the *gallant style* can already be noticed. Wilhelm Friedemann and Karl Philipp Emanuel Bach imbued the tendency with a new kind of expressiveness *(Empfindsamkeit)* which was strongly foreshadowing romantic feeling. It was Johann Christian Bach who endowed Mozart with the Italian gallant style, its facility and gracefulness. From the weighty grandeur of the Baroque era, the emphasis now shifted to pleasantness and elegance, prettiness and sometimes even frivolity. From emotional austerity, from complexity and severity of the formal design, from profundity of thought, the tastes were turning into almost opposite directions with their respective connotations and manifestations.

Apel writes concerning the *gallant style*:[1]

> "The appearance of this new style indicated the change from the church to the 'salon' as the cultural center, from fugal treatment to accompanied melody, from architectural greatness to playful pettiness, from cantatas and masses to amorous songs."

1. *Harvard Dictionary of Music* by Willi Apel; section on *Gallant Style*, p. 289.

These changes in matters of artistic taste generally were caused and propelled by outside influences, primarily the revolution in social attitude. However, the new type of "professional musician," exemplified by such men as Handel, Karl Philipp Emanuel Bach, Haydn and Mozart, no doubt furthered and accelerated the development within the realm of musical culture, and at the same time helped this revolution to stay within solid channels.

Much emphasis has been placed on the influence which the "London" Bach, Johann Christian, as well as the "Hamburg" Bach, Karl Philipp Emanuel, have exerted upon Wolfgang Amadeus Mozart. It is true that Mozart considered Karl Philipp Emanuel the "father of keyboard art," and that his association in London with Johann Christian Bach provided him with a great incentive for clavier composition, besides fundamentally influencing his style. However, at the very beginning of this discussion of Mozart's active interest in the two-piano medium, mention must also be made of Georg Christoph Wagenseil, a South German, the highly respected teacher of the Habsburg Archduchesses. The name of Wagenseil, which at his own time identified an important musical figure, now has become all but obscure. Yet, an early and definite impression was exerted by Wagenseil upon the young Mozart. For it was not so much Karl Philipp Emanuel Bach who gave Mozart the first conception of the clavier concerto in which he should become so eminent; rather it was the style of Wagenseil whose clavier works were shown to Mozart in London as early as in 1764. They must have instilled the youthful composer with Wagenseil's idea of the piano concerto, a concept of a much simpler nature than that of Karl Philipp Emanuel Bach.

Of particular importance to this investigation is the fact that Wagenseil was the composer of a concerto for two claviers.[2] The score of this concerto is expressly mentioned by Mozart's father, Leopold (in November 1767) as being in the family's possession[3] and no doubt it was shown to the children. The manuscript of this concerto for two claviers is now kept in the archives of the Gesellschaft der Musikfreunde in Vienna. Besides the double concerto, there exists also a divertimento for two claviers, opus 5, from the pen of Georg Christoph Wagenseil, and it can well be assumed that this composition likewise came to Mozart's attention.

Possibly Mozart's interest in the two-piano idiom was further stimulated by Johann Ladislaus Dussek's compositions in this medium. Dussek, a distinguished Bohemian pianist, made a powerful impression wherever

---

2. Listed by both Prosniz and Eitner.
3. Einstein, *Mozart,* p. 290.

he went and ranked among the finest of the artists whom the mechanical advance of the pianoforte called into action. He wrote a concerto for two pianos and orchestra in B flat, a sonata for two pianos in E flat, and two duos. As a pupil of Karl Philipp Emanuel Bach, Dussek most likely had the medium suggested to him by the latter; in any event, his legacy to the then scanty literature gives evidence of his considerable interest in the idiom.

Much has been written about the ensemble playing of young Wolfgang Amadeus, the "wonder child," and his sister, Maria Anna, who was four years older than he. They toured Europe three times together during their youth, scoring success after success in the capitals and at the courts. Their proficiency must indeed have been astounding, and they excited wonder and admiration particularly by their playing "*à quatre mains.*" However, how many of their ensemble performances actually were on two keyboards can only be conjectured. The authentic pictures and available accounts of their concert activities describe the pair seated at *one* piano. Nevertheless, their ensemble activities no doubt entailed some work on two keyboards. Mozart's subsequent fondness for the combination evidences his practical experience in the medium. The predilection for the idiom eventually became sufficiently strong to stimulate a number of compositions for two pianofortes, although the historically recorded performances of these works actually were given by Mozart with partners other than his sister, "Nannerl." Such keyboard partners included Josephine v. Aurnhammer, Barbara Ployer, and Constance v. Weber; the latter was to become his wife.

As far as the first famous instance of public two-clavier playing is concerned, it is fortunate that reference can be made to several sources of information. Various historical documents pertaining to the event have been preserved. It seems that Emperor Joseph II instigated a friendly contest of skill between Mozart and Clementi at the court of Vienna, for Mozart was commanded there on December 14, 1781. In a letter dated December 22, 1781, Mozart writes:

> ". . . the day before yesterday, the 14th, I played at court. Another pianist has arrived here, an Italian, whose name is Clementi, and he was also engaged to play. I received fifty ducats yesterday for this, which I at present stand greatly in need of."

Clementi had come to Vienna with the reputation of being a clavier-player of unheard-of excellence. He relates his first meeting with Mozart to his pupil L. Berger in the following words:

> "I had only been a few days in Vienna when I received an invitation to play before the Emperor on the pianoforte. On entering the musicroom I beheld an individual whose elegant attire led me to mistake him for an imperial valet-de-

chambre. But we had no sooner entered into conversation than it turned on musical topics, and we soon recognized in each other with sincere pleasure brother artists—Mozart and Clementi."

Mozart himself gives a vivid description of the musical encounter which followed. In his letter of January 12, 1782, the atmosphere of the competitive musicale is brought close to the reader by the following account:

"After we had paid each other all manner of compliments, the Emperor gave the signal that Clementi should begin. 'La santa chiesa cattolica!' (The Holy Catholic Church first!) said the Emperor—Clementi being a native of Rome. He preluded, and played a sonata.

"The Emperor then said to me: '*Allons, d'rauf los!*' ('Now then, fire away!'). I preluded, and played some variations. Then the Grand Duchess produced some sonatas by Paisiello (in his own miserable manuscript), of which I was to play the allegro and Clementi the andante and rondo. Then we selected a theme from them and carried it out on two pianofortes. By the way, I had borrowed the Countess Thun's pianoforte for myself, but only played upon it when I played alone. The Emperor wished it to be so. The other instrument was out of tune, and three of its keys stuck fast. 'Never mind,' said the Emperor. I look upon it that the Emperor knows my musical skill and knowledge, and wished to do me justice in the eyes of the foreigner. I know upon very good authority that he was thoroughly satisfied with me. He was very gracious, spoke to me a great deal privately, and even alluded to my marriage."

In the same letter, Mozart expresses his opinion regarding the musicianship of his Italian rival. The verdict is not entirely flattering:

"As to Clementi, he is a good player, and when this is said, all is said. He has great facility with his right hand; his principal passages are thirds; but in other respects he has not an atom of taste or feeling—all is mere mechanism."

An explanation of Mozart's harsh judgment of his competitor's musicianship is attempted by Frank Kidson (F.K.) in his essay on Clementi in *Grove's Dictionary of Music and Musicians*. At the same time, some further interesting details of the historical event are revealed. Kidson gives this account:[4]

"In 1781 Clementi started on his travels, beginning with a series of concerts at Paris; from thence he passed . . . to Vienna . . . where, at the instigation of the Emperor Joseph II, he engaged in a sort of musical combat at the pianoforte with Mozart. Clementi, after a short prelude, played his sonata in B flat—the opening of the first movement of which was long afterwards made use of by Mozart in the subject of the '*Zauberflöte*' overture—and followed it up with a toccata, in which great stress was laid upon the rapid execution of diatonic thirds and other double notes for the right hand, esteemed very difficult at that time. Mozart then began to preludise, and played some variations; then both alternately read at sight some MS. sonatas of Paisiello's, Mozart playing the *allegros* and Clementi the *andantes* and *rondos;* and finally they were asked by the Emperor to take a theme from Paisiello's sonatas and accompany one another in their improvisations upon it on two pianofortes. The victory, it appears, was left undecided. Clementi ever afterwards spoke with great admiration of Mozart's 'singing' touch and exquisite taste, and

4. *Grove's* Vol. I, pp. 667-668.

dated from this meeting a considerable change in his method of playing: striving to put more music and less mechanical show into his productions. Mozart's harsh verdict in his letters (Jan. 12, 1782; June 7, 1783) was probably just for the moment, but cannot fairly be applied to the bulk of Clementi's work. He disliked Italians; the popular prejudice was in their favour, and they were continually in his way. He depicts Clementi as a 'mere mechanician, strong in runs of thirds, but without a pennyworth of feeling or taste.' But L. Berger, one of Clementi's best pupils, gives the following explanation of Mozart's hard sentence:

" 'I asked Clementi whether in 1781 he had begun to treat the instrument in his present (1806) style. He answered *no,* and added that in those early days he had cultivated a more brilliant execution, especially in double notes, hardly known then, and in extemporized cadenzas, and that he had subsequently achieved a more melodic and noble style of performance after listening attentively to famous singers, and also by means of the perfected mechanism of English pianos, the construction of which formerly stood in the way of a cantabile and legato style of playing.' "

The contest between Mozart and Clementi attracted wide attention. Their alternate improvisation on a given melody, with each virtuoso in turn playing the leading part and the other supplying an obbligato on the second instrument, is the first recorded instance of a practice which was to reach its full flowering under the hands of Moscheles, Mendelssohn, and their contemporaries. Now obsolete as an artistic manifestation, the custom was fitting at a time when every ranking musician was virtually expected to be also a composer; as such, he had to be capable of the extemporaneous handling of musical materials.

The public competition between two leading virtuosos of their age, entirely aside from its duo-pianistic interest, is but one symptom among other signals of the changing times. A new avenue of subsistence for the composer was opening up, that of giving public concerts. Formerly depending on the employ by either court or church, musicians now began to try their fortunes in free lancing. The instrumental virtuoso found out that he could be self-dependent and independent to a much larger degree than heretofore. This change of economic outlook worked its way even deeply into the textural core and structural fiber of the music produced by the composer. The new attitude of the instrumentalist became a co-determining cause for the revolutionary change from polyphony to homophony, in that the instrumental virtuoso "either needed no support at all in presenting himself or he stood out so far above his assistants that they seemed merely to provide an accompaniment. Thus the so-called *homophonic* forms came to be developed, forms born of the nature of harmonic music, in which a single voice took the lead while the rest merely filled in."[5]

It appears almost certain that the improvisation by Mozart and Clementi on two pianos was carried out mainly in the manner of homophonic

5. Paul Bekker, *The Story of Music,* p. 135.

music, with one player taking the melodic lead, and the other supplying the harmonies of the accompaniment. Whatever the artistic worth of this contest may have been, it stands as a historic event in the annals of duo-pianism, recording the first "Grand Duo" in its characteristic combination of flamboyancy and rivalry.

In a strictly chronological sense, there are on record earlier performances on multiple claviers. Mozart played his *Concerto for Two Claviers in E flat major, K. 365,* together with Josephine v. Aurnhammer on November 24, 1781, in a concert at Vienna; this event occurred three weeks before the contest with Clementi. As early as October 22, 1777, Mozart personally took part in the premiere of his *Concerto for Three Claviers, K. 242,* at Augsburg. Therefore, the contest with Clementi on December 14, 1781—spectacular and sensational at it otherwise is—has no claim to be pointed out as the first piano ensemble performance on record as which it is sometimes represented.

When embarking on a survey of the compositions which Wolfgang Amadeus Mozart wrote for the combination of two pianofortes, it is suitable for various reasons to begin with the *Concerto in F Major, K. 242.* This work, known as the "Lodron" concerto, originally was composed for three claviers and orchestra; afterwards, however, Mozart himself arranged it for two pianofortes. In the latter form, the concerto has enriched the duo-pianistic literature and consequently is included in this investigation.

The concerto, Mozart's seventh in his series of concertos for the pianoforte, is one of a number of works which were created for specific pupils. It was composed for and dedicated to the Countess Antonia Lodron and her two daughters, Luise and Josefa. The dedication, probably written by Mozart's father, is in the flowery style of the eighteenth century. It reads:

"Dedicate al incomparabile merito di S. Exc. la Sgra. Cont. Londron, nata Cont. d'Arco et delle sue figlie le Sgre. Cont. Aloisia et Guiseppa."

This carefully written title page may be translated as follows:

"Dedicated to the incomparable merit of her Excellency the Signora Countess Lodron and her two daughters, Countesses Luise and Josefa, by their most devoted servant, Wolfgang Mozart."

The concerto was composed in February 1776 in Salzburg, only a short while after Mozart's twentieth birthday. In this year, and during those preceding and following it, Mozart was furiously active, producing in abundance what *Grove's Dictionary* refers to as "typical examples of Mozart's 'gallant' style in its extreme development."

The autograph of the concerto is preserved in the Prussian State Library at Berlin. Special interest here centers on the arrangement for two claviers which is added to the autograph and which bears this heading, written in Mozart's hand:

"I Soli del Concerto a tre Cembali, accomodati a due."

Mozart makes reference to the arrangement for two claviers when he asks his father, on June 27, 1781, for copies of *"2 Concerte auf 2 Clavier."* This request can be interpreted only as applying to the concerto for two claviers in E flat major, K. 365, and to the arrangement for two claviers of the concerto, K. 242.

A comparison between Mozart's concerto for three claviers and orchestra and the works which Johann Sebastian Bach wrote for the same combination, inevitably suggests itself. It is to be wondered how Mozart reconciled his homophonic style of composition with so great a number of pianofortes. Furthermore, the question needs to be raised what reasons may have prompted Mozart to arrange the concerto for only two instruments subsequent to its original form.

Some comments concerning these problems are provided by Jahn who writes:[6]

"We must not look for the same contrapuntal independence of the three instruments which we find in Bach's concertos, but there is no mistaking the cleverness and delicate sense of effect which are displayed in the varied combinations of the instruments—the doubling of parts, the strengthening of the melody or of the bass, the position of the accompaniment, and the alternation of the instruments. The main object of the first movement is to give equal and yet individual effect to each of the three claviers, although the third is hardly on a level with the other two; in the two last movements the third instrument is still more in the background, being chiefly confined to accompaniment, so that in the finale it does not even take part in the cadenzas. This made it easier for Mozart to arrange the concerto for two instruments; the solo parts, so altered, are preserved in his handwriting."

As to form and content of the work, it is in the customary three movements which are marked, respectively, *Allegro, Adagio, Rondeau—Tempo di Menuetto*. The key is that of F Major. The concerto is comparatively short, consisting of only 565 measures (First Movement: 280 bars, Second Movement: 73 bars, Third Movement: 212 bars.). The character of the composition can best be defined by the term charming. "The tone of the concerto is lively and cheerful; the whole is treated in an easy and happy vein of humour, which entertains the players quite as much as the audience." (Jahn). There is a distinct increase in Mozart's power to project the solo instruments. The orchestra is treated with a certain

---

6. Jahn, *Life of Mozart*, Vol. I, p. 326.

measure of independence in this concerto, and the distinction between *tutti* and accompaniment is not a very marked one. Rather, the soloists and the orchestra mutually assist and promote each other, and "their union results in a perfect work of art." (Jahn)

No record exists of a public performance by the three ladies to whom the concerto was dedicated. The premiere, as was mentioned previously, took place in Augsburg, on October 22, 1777. An organist of that city, J. M. Demmler, then played the first piano part, Mozart himself the second, and the piano manufacturer Stein the third. Mozart seems to have especially enjoyed this concerto, and it gave him satisfaction that it was repeatedly and successfully brought to performance. He informs his father of the Augsburg premiere and subsequently notifies him of a performance in Mannheim on March 12, 1778. The concerto then was heard at Cannabich's and Mozart writes in a letter, dated March 24, 1778, about the event as follows:

"Madelle Rosl Cannabich spiellte das Erste, Madelle Weber das zweyte, und Madelle Pierron (serarius unser haus-Nymphe) das dritte. wir haben 3 Proben gemacht, und es ist recht gut gegangen."

Alfred Einstein who considers Mozart's piano concertos as "the peak of all his instrumental achievements, at least in the orchestral domain" and who finds in them the realization of the composer's ideal for musical expression does not think quite as highly of this concerto. Einstein states:[7]

". . . among the twenty-three concertos for piano and orchestra, there is only one that is below the highest level—the concerto for three pianos (K. 242) written to be played not by Mozart himself or any capable soloist, but by three lady amateurs."

Mozart's evident fondness of the work, the repeated performances under his direction, and his supplemental arrangement for two pianos (the latter indicative of his lasting concern with this music), all are factors which hardly support Einstein's verdict. Nor does Mozart's chief biographer, Jahn, agree with Einstein's statement, for he calls the concerto "a perfect work of art." In its two-piano version, the composition has, of course, found general acceptance and employment within the duo-pianistic repertoire. Josef and Rosina Lhevinne introduced the work to the United States during the season of 1939-40 when they played it with the New York Philharmonic Orchestra under the direction of John Barbirolli.[8] Pierre Luboshutz ranks the F major concerto as a standard work in the repertoire of all two-piano teams, and Manuel and Williamson perform it on two harpsichords with the accompaniment of strings, oboes

7. Einstein, *Mozart,* p. 287.
8. Rosina Lhevinne, in collaboration with Vronsky and Babin, since has recorded the concerto in its original scoring for three pianos; Thomas K. Sherman conducts The Little Orchestra Society in the orchestral portion.

and horns. The concerto has also been arranged for two solo pianos, without orchestral accompaniment, in an edition by Josef Wagner.[9]

The *Concerto for Two Pianofortes in E flat Major, K. 365,* was written in 1780. It may have been composed by Mozart with the intention of rendering it a performance together with his sister, Maria Anna. There is no record, however, that they ever played it in public. Instead, Mozart performed the work twice in concert with his pupil, Josephine von Aurnhammer. The latter seems to have been instrumental also in the creation of the *Sonata in D Major, K. 448,* and probably was a motivating force for the inception of another sonata for two pianofortes which, however, remained a fragment *(Anh. 42).*

Mozart's association with the young lady is both an interesting reflection of his character and an amusing incident. It seems that Josephine's family would have been glad to receive him as more than her teacher, and as more than a temporary lodger after he had actually taken up residence in their house. The von Aurnhammers from the first pressed the association by often inviting the young composer. Mozart writes to his father, on June 27, 1781:

> "I dine almost daily with Herr Aurnhammer; the young lady is a horror—but she plays divinely. . . ."

The "fat lady-daughter" was known as a brilliant pianist; in fact, she was one of the leading clavier players of the day. Mozart considered this fact very well, but he firmly resisted the advances of the girl and of her family; he maintained his reserved attitude although his father was on friendly terms with Herr von Aurnhammer and appears to have favored a closer connection. The immediate neighborhood into which young Mozart entered with the Aurnhammer family by taking up lodgings there, did not last long. As he wrote to his father, the quarters offered to him were

> ". . . only fit for rats and mice, but not for human beings. The stairs need a lantern to light them at noon-day. The room might be called a cell, and to get to it, I had to pass through the kitchen, and above the door there was a small window. They indeed promised to put up a curtain, at the same time requesting me to draw it aside again as soon as I was dressed, otherwise they could not see at all, either in the kitchen or the adjoining rooms. The wife herself called the house a rat's nest—in fact it was really dreadful."

Mozart apparently had good reasons to be dissatisfied with the quarters which had been offered to him. In addition, there were other strong motives which caused him to discontinue the close association with the family. Mozart does not hesitate to state these reasons to his father. As

9. *Schirmer Library, No. 1578.*

became quickly evident, Fräulein von Aurnhammer was in love with the handsome, gifted, already famous musician who was only 24 years old at the time. Mozart's drastic description of Josephine leaves no doubt as to his and her feelings. If he expressed plain disgust in regard to his living quarters, he is even more provoked when he speaks of Josephine:

"If a painter wanted to depict the devil according to nature, he could not do better than have recourse to her countenance. She is as fat as a peasant girl, and also sweats, that one might spit. She is revolting to look at, dirty and untidy, and she goes about so unclad that one can actually read: 'I pray you, gaze here.' "

Nevertheless, Mozart was patient with her, for Josephine confessed to him that she realized her situation. He writes home:

"Then she told me: 'I know that I am not pretty, on the contrary I am plain. I have no wish to marry . . . some clerk who earns a bare living . . . so I have no other choice but to earn my living by my talents.' "

Good-naturedly, Mozart aided Josephine in her musical advancement. However, when she demanded too much of his time with practice hours, and when Mozart found out that she was seriously in love with him, he began to shorten the lessons. Finally, when he learned that Josephine encouraged gossip of their forthcoming marriage and joint concert tours, he left the house altogether. The following is Mozart's own description of the developments which must have caused him considerable embarrassment:

"I wrote to you how she plays the clavier, and why she begged me to assist her. She is not content that I should pass two hours every day with her, she would like me to spend the whole day there, and then she makes herself agreeable; or rather, worse than that, she is seriously in love with me. I thought it was a joke, but I know it for certain now. When I first observed it (for she took liberties, reproaching me for coming later than usual, or not staying long enough, and other such things) I felt constrained to tell her the truth politely, for fear she should make a fool of herself. But it was of no use, she became more deeply in love. Then I tried being very polite until she began her nonsense, when I turned cross. Then she took me by the hand and said, 'Dear Mozart, do not be so angry, and you may say what you like, I am so fond of you.' It was the talk of the whole town that we were going to be married, and people wondered at my choice. She told me that when anything of the kind was said to her, she laughed at it; but I know from a certain person that she acknowledged it, with the addition that we should set out on our travels together as soon as we were married. That made me really angry. I gave her my true opinion on the subject, and reproached her with abusing my kindness. I have left off going there every day, and only go every other day, so as to break it off by degrees. She is an infatuated fool. . . ."

In spite of all his personal distaste for Fräulein von Aurnhammer, Mozart admitted that she played "divinely, enchantingly." Realizing that she was one of the best pianists in Vienna during that time, he continued to assist the young lady in his usual amiable manner. He performed with her the *concerto a due* (K. 365) at a private concert at the Aurnhammer's on November 24, 1781, when they also played together a sonata which had been composed especially for this occasion and which "went remarkably well." The applause for the concerto is reported to have been enthusiastic. At one of his own concerts, on May 25, 1782, Mozart gave the concerto a repeat performance, collaborating again with Josephine von Aurnhammer. His musical partnership with the girl seems to have been sufficiently strong to even cause him to postpone a journey to Salzburg later in the year because he had promised to play at one of her concerts (October 26, 1782).

As has been pointed out before, there is great likelihood that the concerto for two claviers came into existence due to Mozart's wish to play it with his sister. Koechel gives "early in 1779" as the date of composition, while André asserts that the work was written in 1780. At any rate, the origin of this concerto for two pianofortes is placed into the period immediately following Mozart's return from the great journey. The work was composed at Salzburg and may stand in connection with the fragmentary double concerto for piano and violin with orchestra (Anh. 56).[10] A certain indication that the concerto was composed for the purpose to be performed by Mozart himself together with Maria Anna, derives from the fact that the manuscript remained in Salzburg in the safe keeping of the father and the sister. Afterwards, on June 27, 1781, Mozart requests that the "2 Concerte auf 2 Clavier" be sent to him. Later, in the fall, he again asks for the concerto when he writes "The Frl. von Aurnhammer torments me terribly because of the double concerto" (September 12); he issues a similar reminder on September 26. After the manuscripts had been sent to Vienna, he enlarged the original orchestration by adding to the accompaniment the parts of two clarinets on a flyleaf. Two trumpets and tympani also were added to the scoring of the corner movements.[11]

The concerto is in three movements with the indications *Allegro, Andante,* and *Rondeaux,* the latter marked *Allegro.* The autograph of the work is preserved in the Prussian State Library at Berlin. The title of the original manuscript reads *Concerto a Due Cembali,* and no doubt was meant to apply to the employment of either harpsichords or pianofortes, the newer instruments being preferred by Mozart himself.

The following is a quotation of Jahn's comments on this concerto for two claviers:[12]

---

10. Regarding the latter fragment, Einstein holds that one of the greatest losses of the art was suffered by Mozart's failure to complete this work.
11. For the full scoring and further details, refer to Book III, *The Literature,* Chapter XXIII, *The Standard Repertoire.*
12. Jahn, *Life of Mozart,* Vol. II, pp. 91-92.

"In design and treatment it is essentially similar to the earlier triple concerto. There is no intention apparent of making the two instruments independent; the players emulate each other in the delivery of the melodies and passages, sometimes together, sometimes in succession, often breaking off in rapid changes and interruptions; the melodies are sometimes simply repeated, sometimes with variations so divided between the two instruments that neither can be said to have the advantage over the other. There are somewhat greater difficulties of execution than have been usual hitherto, a few passages, for instance, in octaves and thirds, but very modest ones; the passages generally have more variety and elegance. The orchestra is simply and judiciously, but very delicately treated, the wind instruments in sustained chords, as a foundation for the clavier passages; the effect of the crescendo and a greater attention to light and shade show the influence of Mannheim. Altogether the concerto is a well-arranged composition, clear and melodious, as well as accurately constructed, with a free, cheerful expression, which is most strikingly shown in the fresh gaiety of the last movement."

Another interesting commentary on the work is given by Alfred Einstein. It reads as follows:[13]

"It is a companion piece both to the *Sinfonia Concertante* in the same key (K. 364), which it cannot quite equal, and to the Vienna Sonata for Two Pianos, in D major (K. 448, written in 1781), which is likewise not to be matched. But the Concerto contains a brilliant contest between the two players, and the orchestra, with its majestic beginning, enters significantly into this eager dialogue. . . . But there is not only a brilliant contest. Side by side with places of what one might call 'mechanical' gaiety . . . there is a strange darkening of the mood in the recapitulation. The pastoral *Andante*, too, quivers with a mood of longing, and has passages of extraordinary luxuriance. And even in the *Rondo*, which is frankly merry, the middle portion, in C minor, moves into what seem dangerous and mysterious regions—regions, too, of contrapuntal seriousness. But the seriousness is not quite so deep as might appear, as is shown by the fact that Mozart later borrowed one of the C minor passages and put it into the mouth of Papageno, just at the point where the latter's comic anxiety reaches its peak. In general, the Concerto is a work of happiness, gaiety, overflowing richness of invention, and joy in itself, and thus is evidence of how little the secret of creative activity has to do with personal experience, for it was written just after the bitterest disappointments of Mozart's life. In the early years in Vienna he performed it several times with Fräulein Aurnhammer, and for these occasions he enriched the instrumentation of the opening and closing movements by the addition of clarinets, trumpets and timpani."

Leopold Godowsky is the composer of two cadenzas to be used in connection with this concerto. It can be stated, in closing, that the work is a perennial favorite in the standard repertoire of all duo-pianists.

After the discussion of the two concerti for multiple pianos with orchestral accompaniment, the inquiry now proceeds to those compositions which Mozart wrote for two solo pianofortes. The major works in this idiom which were completed by the composer, are the *Fugue in C minor (K. 426)* and the *Sonata in D major (K. 448)*. At the very outset of the survey which is to center upon these works, Einstein's regret must be

---

13. Einstein, *Mozart*, pp. 295-296.

shared that[14] "Mozart . . . yielded to the desire to write for two pianos . . . only twice, for in both cases he produced incomparable masterpieces."

As to the *Fugue in C minor, K. 426,* this work has become known in two versions: the one for two claviers, and another for string quartet. The primary scoring is for two claviers and was completed on December 29, 1783. The arrangement for string quartet, enlarged by a short adagio serving as an introduction (K. 546), was written in June, 1788.

When the concerto for three claviers, K. 242, was under discussion, a comparison between Bach's and Mozart's textural styles and treatment of musical forms first suggested itself. There is no doubt that Mozart realized Bach's supreme greatness which finds its foremost manifestation in the playful mastery of his complicated means of expression, in the synthesis of the deepest human emotion with the highest degree of intellectual penetration and projection. At times, Mozart must have been affected by the awareness that a prophet had gone before him, as the young Brahms in a later era was to suffer deeply from his realization that he walked in the shadow of another titan, Beethoven. What was Mozart's reaction when he saw himself confronted with the musical language of polyphony which was forceful and perfect, but antiquated and unpopular as far as the tastes of his own day were concerned? What was his solution to this problem which was certain to involve his artistic conscience?

Alfred Einstein takes up these questions in his biography on Mozart when he writes:[15]

"We need not trace here in detail Mozart's difficulties in connection with Bach or with polyphony. It need only be emphasized that they were real difficulties, a true crisis of creative activity. Mozart was too great and fine a musician not to feel deeply and painfully the conflict produced when his habit of thinking in terms of *galant* and 'learned' music was shaken by the encounter with a living polyphonic style. Bach did not live to experience the musical dualism of the second half of the eighteenth century. The smallest gavotte, the shortest *passepied* from one of his clavier suites, though it may appear *galant,* is in reality as polyphonic in feeling as one of the organ chorales or the *Kunst der Fuge.* Can it be believed that Mozart was not deeply aware of the super-human grandeur of this music, as an overpowering quality that was not to be found in the work of any of his contemporaries? Where in contemporary music were there compositions with the free logic of voiceleading, the scope and consistency of structure of Bach's organ trios? Mozart was never completely finished with this experience, but it enriched his imagination and resulted in more and more perfect works."

One of those "more and more perfect works" was the *Fugue in C minor.* The composition was intended for performance on two pianofortes or two harpsichords, for the title inscription reads *Fuga a Due Cembali. di*

14. Einstein, *Mozart,* p. 273.
15. Einstein, *Mozart,* p. 153.

Wolfgango Amadeo Mozart mp. Vienna li 29 di decembre 1782. Until 1934, the autograph was known to be in the possession of the estate of Edward Speyer at Ridgehurst near London.

There are some explicit directions available as to the manner in which Mozart wishes this great fugue, and other fugues, to be performed. The particular information is gained from a letter to his sister, dated April 20, which accompanied the manuscript then sent to her. Mozart writes in this letter:

"I have taken care to write *'andante maestoso'* on it, that it may not be played too fast; for, if a fugue is not played slowly, the recurring subject is not distinctly and clearly heard, and so loses its effect."

This expression of concern regarding the proper tempo is only one indication of the fact that Mozart saw himself preeminently occupied with the work. He at one time began a prelude for it, but it remained a fragment *(K. Anh. 44)*. The composer's desire to preface the grandeur of the fugue with a fitting introduction, finally was realized when he arranged the work for string quartet, or for string orchestra, on June 26, 1788. The arrangement probably was prompted by the then close association between Mozart and Gottfried, Baron Van Swieten; the latter was a somewhat autocratic musical amateur and patron who became the founder of the "Musikalische Gesellschaft," a forerunner of the "Gesellschaft der Musikfreunde." To the arrangement, Mozart added "a short *adagio a 2 violini, viola e basso,* for a fugue, which I wrote long ago for two pianos." Einstein believes that this introduction "corresponds in significance and weight to the fugue itself." The form and substance of the music amply support this statement.

Some interesting comments on this magnificent work are given by Jahn and Einstein, two of the authorities who have made exhaustive studies of the creative work of Mozart. Jahn expresses his views in the following words:[16]

"The effect of the C minor fugue (426 K) . . . rests neither on the sound effects of the pianoforte nor on those of the stringed instruments. It is so broadly conceived, so earnestly and with such ruthless severity carried out, that the external means of expression fall into the background before the energetic enunciation of the laws of form, obeyed consciously, but without servility."

The comment by Alfred Einstein culminates in the statement[17] that Mozart in the Fugue in C minor

". . . sums up the fruit of his contrapuntal studies and of everything he had learned from Johann Sebastian Bach. It is a strict, four-voiced fugue, with a deeply serious, 'dualistic' theme—half imperious and half complaining; and it contains all

16. Jahn, *Life of Mozart,* Vol. II, p. 392.
17. Einstein, *Mozart,* p. 273.

the devices of inversion and stretto. Only at the end does it assume a more pianistic bearing, but its relation to the 'objective,' contrapuntal portions of the pieces for mechanical organ is unmistakable."

It may be the very austerity of thought and design which has prevented the work from attaining a popularity similar to that of the compositions listed under Koechel Nos. 365 or 448, the latter complying with the more familiar conception of what is considered "Mozartean" in musical expression. It lies beyond the confines of this discussion to investigate such causations; instead, it must suffice to close with a quotation by Ernest Hutcheson, who speaks for the connoisseur when he voices his belief that "the fine Fugue in C minor deserves more attention than it has received."[18]

The other important work for two solo pianofortes is the *Grand Sonata in D Major, K. 448.* There exists a considerable discrepancy among authorities regarding the period during which this work originated. Jahn establishes the particular time as soon following the composition of the Fugue in C minor; he believes that the sonata was written at the beginning of the year 1784. However, the Koechel Verzeichnis, in the revised edition by Einstein, gives November of the year 1781 as the date of composition, Vienna being the place where the work was written. As evidence, Mozart's letter to his father, dated November 24, 1781, is quoted in which he reports on a private concert at Aurnhammer's as follows:

"wir (i.e. Mozart and Miss Aurnhammer) haben das Concert à Due gespiellt, und eine Sonate in zweyen, die ich express dazu componiert habe, und die allen succès gehabt hat . . ."

Additional evidence can be construed from Mozart's letter of January 9, 1782, in which he writes:

". . . bey der Sonate auf 2 Clavier hat die frl: v. Auernhammer die Erste Parthie gespiellt. . . ."

Jahn bases his own theory probably on a reference to the two-piano sonata which is made by Mozart in a letter dated June 9, 1784, and addressed to his sister:

"Tomorrow Herr Ployer has a concert in the country, at Doebling, where Madle. Babette is to play her own concerto in G (K. 453), and I the quintet (K. 452, with wind instruments), and then we are both to play the grand sonata for two pianos."

The particular letter was mailed from Vienna only on June 12, but the concert at Agent Ployer's in Doebling probably took place on June 10, 1784. At that occasion, Mozart played the sonata with Barbara Ployer as his partner in the presence of Giovanni Paisiello, the eminent composer of the Italian school whose well-known jealousy and addiction to intrigue no doubt contributed to Mozart's pronounced dislike for Italians.

---

18. Ernest Hutcheson *The Literature of the Piano*, p. 76.

The original manuscript of the work was last known to be preserved in the Veste Koburg, a possession of Duke Ernst. Of the three movements of the sonata, the middle section is in the key of G major, while the corner movements are in the tonality of D major. The tempo markings read, respectively: *Allegro con spirito—Andante—Allegro molto.*

Jahn states that "the piece at the time definitely required a virtuoso performance and up to the day is effective in its brilliancy." An additional commentary by Jahn[19] terms the sonata

"a capital bravura piece for the time at which it was written, effective even now, and interesting from the interweaving of the two parts. The first movement is the best, the working-out forcible and effective, though not elaborate; the andante is somewhat tedious, owing to the repetition of the entire first part."

Alfred Einstein accords the work a very high place among all of Mozart's creations. His remarks on the sonata read as follows:[20]

"Quite different in character (from the Fugue in C minor, K. 426), but of no less value, is the Sonata in D major (K. 448), written in November 1781 for performance by Fräulein von Aurnhammer and himself. This work is galant from beginning to end; it has the form and the thematic material of an ideal sinfonia for an opera buffa; no cloud obscures its gaiety. But the art with which the two parts are made completely equal, the play of the dialogue, the delicacy and refinement of the figuration, the feeling for sonority in the combination and exploitation of the different registers of the two instruments—all these things exhibit such mastery that this apparently 'superficial' and entertaining work is at the same time one of the most profound and most mature of all Mozart's compositions."

Einstein concludes that Mozart himself must have felt the suitability of the two-piano medium as an ideal vehicle for his creative expression. A number of extant fragments are providing the affirmation necessary to justify such an assumption. There exist no less than four manuscripts from Mozart's own hand, all of which constitute fragmentary compositions for two pianofortes. These autographs will be discussed in detail shortly. However, it should be stated first that the nature of Mozart's fragments encompasses a two-fold function, and that their significance varies according to the original intent and purpose. The incomplete compositions either were undertaken with the objective to result in finished works later on, in which event the sketches really are to be termed "fragments"; or they merely served as incipits or "springboards" for the composer's inspiration. Regarding the latter function, Einstein offers the following explanation:[21]

"He needed only the beginning: his imagination and unerring taste provided the appropriate continuation, the *filo* of ideas, the choice of the character of additional movements."

19. Jahn, *Life of Mozart*, Vol. II, p. 460.
20. Einstein, *Mozart*, p. 273.
21. Einstein, *Mozart*, p. 136.

Over one hundred such fragments have been preserved. Some of them indubitably had been intended for subsequent completion, like the great *Mass in C minor,* or the *Sinfonia Concertante* for violin, viola, violoncello, and orchestra (Koechel, Anhang 104). Likewise, the four fragments belonging to the two-piano category do not have the features of mere trial runs. Rather, each of them appears to possess such qualities as to bespeak Mozart's intention to complete each new work then undertaken. The indications leading to this assumption will presently be investigated.

The manuscripts of the four fragmentary two-piano compositions are listed in the Koechel Verzeichnis as *Anhang Nos. 42, 43, 44* and *45.* They will be discussed in this order although, from a chronological point of view, they may not have originated in the same sequence.

The fragment marked as *Anhang 42* represents the beginning of a sonata for two claviers. The key is that of B flat major. 52 measures have been preserved, eight measures of an *Adagio (Grave)* and 44 measures of a *Presto* movement. The autograph is kept in Paris; it is contained in the collection of Ch. Malherbe which forms part of the Bibliothèque du Conservatoire. The title is inscribed *Sonata à 2 Cembali.* The composition was begun in spring 1782. Like the sonata, K. 448, this work probably was intended for a performance with Josephine von Aurnhammer. The character of the music is highly dramatic. It foreshadows the species of the "Sonata Pathétique" of which Beethoven was to create a prototype not many years later. However, as Einstein states, "the period of the pathetic concerto had not yet arrived, and Mozart doubtless felt that he could hardly set any other piece against the D major work." Thus the sonata was abandoned and had to remain a fragment because of its insufficiently gallant ("gesellschaftlichen") character.

The fragment of another sonata for two pianofortes can be viewed in autograph at Salzburg, where it is kept in the Mozarteum. Listed in the Koechel Verzeichnis as *Anh. 43,* this sonata also has the tonality of B flat major. In 2-4 time, it breaks off after only 16 measures. The dedication from Mozart's hand reads *"per la Signa Constanza Weber—Ah—."* The dedicatory remark reveals an interesting clue regarding the motivation which prompted this work. While the association with Josephine von Aurnhammer for purely musical reasons had been conducive to the production of a number of works, in this case the incentive sprang from motivations based on the composer's romantic attachment. The fragment falls into the time of Mozart's courtship which was to result in his marriage to Constance within the year. M. Blaschitz places the date of the composition to the end of the year 1782, but it probably was written somewhat earlier, considering the period when Mozart's romance with Constance v. Weber reached its full flowering. The music possibly represents a theme for variations and is of a calm and cheerful character.

The fragmentary *Allegro for Two Pianofortes, Koechel Anh. 44,* is controversial as far as the date of its composition is concerned. Blaschitz ascribes the fragment to the year 1785, but Einstein considers it in connection with the C minor Fugue, K. 426, in that it is also in the key of C minor. Because of the sameness of tonality, Einstein deducts the great probability that the Allegro was intended as an introduction to the fugue. If this assumption is correct, the fragment could have been composed at Vienna in December of the year 1782, the fugue having been completed there on December 29, 1782. The autograph is among the manuscripts in the Mozarteum at Salzburg. The fragment is marked *Alla breve.* Its only 22 measures have prompted Jahn to the following statement:

"It is remarkable how these few bars confirm the observation that the choice of a minor key was with Mozart an invariable sign of a special effort of his productive powers."

The fourth and last of the fragments, marked as *Anh. 45,* also belongs to the manuscript collection preserved in the Mozarteum. This composition is the beginning of another fugue for two claviers. However, the extant 23 measures, written in 3-4 time and in the key of G major, reveal a basic character altogether different from that of the great Fugue in C minor, K. 426. The autograph bears the title *Fuga à due Cembali.* Its composition is placed by M. Blaschitz into the year 1782, and Einstein traces it to spring of that year. There is a good deal of likelihood that the fugue was undertaken by Mozart with the intention to play it himself with Constance v. Weber as his partner. Constance, with whom he was in love at the time, had taken a pleasure in fugues, and Mozart's sketch, like the one listed as *Anhang 43,* probably was motivated by his desire to further the musical interests of his future wife.

The spirit of the music, totally different from the nature of the C minor fugue, is clearly projected by the opening measures which are reproduced on page 64 of this volume.

In the foregoing survey, it has been shown how Mozart, besides the number of his finished compositions for two claviers, made several additional creative efforts in this medium. It became evident how all of these attempts aimed at distinct forms. One of the commencements was meant to become a sonata, another possibly a theme with variations if not a sonata also. Still another fragment suggests the possibility of an intended introduction for the Fugue in C minor, K. 426, and the last of the manuscript sketches constitutes a definite beginning of another fugue. All com-

Koechel Anhang 45

mencements bespeak a clearly defined purpose; all are so "grand and forcible" (Jahn) that the fragmentary state of these compositions must be forever regretted. Nevertheless, the existence of the sketches provides an important part in the ample evidence of Mozart's strong interest in the two-piano medium. The fact that he left altogether eight manuscripts of works for two pianofortes—four completed (Koechel Nos. 242, 365, 426, and 448) and four in fragmentary condition (Anh. 42, 43, 44, 45)—is sufficient proof and testimony regarding his fondness for this instrumental combination. Moreover, Mozart also wrote a number of compositions for four hands on one keyboard, and it can be construed that some of these duets may indeed have been intended for performance on two claviers. The history of the four-hand *Sonata in C major, K. 521,* which can be traced from the autographs, reveals the illuminating fact that Mozart submitted the composition to the recipients in two separate parts, inscribed *"Cembalo Imo"* and *"Cembalo II do,"* respectively. In view of the apparent impracticability to place two parts alongside each other on the same note rack, the conclusion presents itself that the work was meant to be played on two instruments; assuredly, this procedure was followed in the music room of the persons to whom it was dedicated. The recipients of this sonata were the sisters Natorp, Nanette and Babette. It is to be pointed out that the two cembalo parts are treated as of equal importance, with no partiality in the assignment of the musical material being shown to either the cembalo primo or the cembalo secondo. Rather, the two parts engage in a friendly rivalry, providing a most brilliant effect, especially in the opening and closing movements. It is, of course, to be considered of great significance that Mozart marks the original manuscripts as if the work was definitely to be performed on two claviers. Einstein, among other authorities, therefore concludes that the work was fully intended to be thus rendered, and that the composition can only gain by being played on two instruments. The two parts of the autograph of this vigorous work which is "stirring, imaginative, and rich in melodic beauty" (Berkowitz) can be inspected in the Fitzwilliam Museum at Cambridge.

Another work which originally seems to have been intended for execution on two claviers rather than for duet performance on one keyboard, is the *Andante with Five Variations, K. 501.* The theory that a definite two-piano tendency exists in this composition, again is advanced by Einstein; it appears supported by the evidence from the autograph which is in the possession of Rudolf Nydahl at Stockholm. Before the *accolade* (the brace employed to connect two or more staves), the manuscript shows the inscriptions *"Cembalo Imo"* and *"Cembalo II do."* These specific indications for two separate claviers have been scratched out, however, and replaced by the direction to use *"mano dritta"* and *"mano sinistra."* The similarity of primary concept and intention between the Andante and Variations, K. 501, and the Sonata for the Natorp sisters, K. 521, is apparent, and little doubt therefore exists that Mozart originally here had in mind another work for two pianofortes. Presumably, the duet version was decided upon because Mozart's publisher and friend, Hoffmeister, expressed a distinct preference for this particular ensemble form. The latter, however, was *not* "the more usual combination" at that time as Einstein suggests; rather, compositions for two pianofortes were more popular for causes which will presently be demonstrated. The variations themselves are most engaging, and their charm frequently inspires two-piano teams to include them into their recital programs.[22]

Both Thompson *(International Cyclopedia of Music and Musicians)* and Silvio Scionti *(The Fascination of Two-Piano Playing)* list among Mozart's works for two pianofortes a Sonata in F major. There exists, however, only a *Sonata in F major, K. 497,* for four-hand duet on one keyboard; this work naturally could be played on two instruments like all other four-hand duets. Sir Donald Tovey has termed this particular sonata one of Mozart's greatest instrumental works; it is this superior

---

22. Duo-pianists Appleton and Field have recorded the work in 1949.

rank of the composition which may have induced an occasional performance on two-piano programs, thereby causing its subsequent attribution
to the duo-pianistic literature.

At any rate, the duet is "a superb piece of chamber-music in no way
inferior to that of the great quartets and quintets of its period in Mozart's
career." The work, composed at the height of Mozart's creative life,
beyond doubt is one of the finest specimens of the entire chamber-music
literature. It remains "a veritable model for all other four-hand music
and is pervaded by that atmosphere of sublimity which is felt in Mozart's
greatest products" (Berkowitz). As has been suggested, it is the very
caliber of this and other duet works which offers an inducement to include
them from time to time on two-piano programs. Further encouragement
to such procedure, together with a certain amount of authenticity, is provided by the theory that Mozart himself had in mind the employment
of *two* claviers for the performance of his four-hand works. This assumption is based on the likelihood that Mozart, while preferring the pianoforte
to the harpsichord, still saw himself largely confronted with the presence
of the older instrument which was to be only gradually replaced. In the
preceding chapter, reference has already been made to the narrowness of
the harpsichord keyboard and the difficulties attending the playing of
duets on that instrument. Besides the physical disadvantage, the problem
of freedom enters into ensemble performance on only one harpsichord,
in that it definitely limits the keyboard sovereignty of each participant.
It is precisely this element which has always stood in the way of duet
playing on one keyboard. On this particular point, Jahn elaborates as
follows:[23]

> "Pianoforte music for two performers was then far from having attained the
> popularity which it now possesses, especially among amateurs. Those who wished
> to play for the sake of playing, and to give full effect to their performance, would
> not readily shackle themselves with a fellow-performer, and lose their absolute
> sway over the instrument. Duets were considered an exceptional kind of amusement,
> not without its peculiar charm. This charm consisted in the richer elaboration of
> material which they allowed, and in such a division and alternation of the parts as
> should set the two players in competition. Mozart, who excelled in this kind of
> treatment, often employed it, and even transfers entire cantilene with their accom-
> paniments to the bass part, not always, as Marx rightly observes (*Lehre von der
> Musikalischen Composition*, III, p. 601), with a good sound effect . . .
>
> "Compositions for two pianofortes were more popular, as affording more scope for
> display to the performer, but the inconvenience attending their performance has
> prevented the cultivation of this branch of composition. It appears at one time to
> have been a favourite one with Mozart, owing, no doubt, to some special circum-
> stances."

The circumstances last mentioned by Jahn have been amply discussed in

23. Jahn: *Life of Mozart*, Vol. II, pp. 459-460.

the preceding paragraphs. To conclude the consideration of the duets for one keyboard, with respect to their performance on two claviers, it is maintained that for the sake of strictness in classification, Mozart's works listed under Koechel Nos. 497, 501, or 521 should not be placed into the category of *original* music for two claviers. This decision is made notwithstanding the theory that Mozart may have intended to use two instruments for the performance of his duets.

With greater justification, a work like the *Fantasy for a Barrel Organ (K. 608)* could be included into the duo-pianistic repertoire. This beautiful Fantasy in F minor, composed on March 3, 1791 at Vienna, was conceived as *Ein Orgel—Stück für eine Uhr* (Mechanical Clock). The curious instrument, based on the simple principle of the pin-and-barrel, has been in existence for some 500 years; it seems that all inventors who for so many centuries have attempted to provide mechanical means for the easy dissemination of music, inevitably were drawn to experimentation with some type of a mechanical clock or barrel organ. In the eighteenth century, much encouragement was lent this activity by such famous musicians as Handel, Quantz, the sons of Bach, Haydn, Graun and Kirnberger. Mozart's own works for instruments of this kind are scored sometimes on three and sometimes on four staves. The autograph of the Fantasy, K. 608, cannot be located and must be assumed lost; the only existing copy, which is preserved in the Prussian State Library in Berlin, was not written by Mozart. In view of the fact that the score is laid out in four parts, and under due consideration that the barrel organ now is obsolete, it appears thoroughly justified to adapt this work for performance on two pianos. The medium quite logically presents itself for suitable projection of this four-voiced music. One such edition for two pianofortes has been arranged by F. Busoni;[24] it is a setting completely in accordance with the rich musical content of the beautiful work. Manuel and Williamson also include the piece into their repertoire because they feel that "the use of two harpsichords permits a reading of the barrel organ tune perhaps closer to the composer's first conception of the Fantasia with its frequent and involved superimpositions of parts." Regardless of the medium, more frequent performances of the Fantasy in F minor are to be encouraged, because it is one of the most profound works created by Mozart. In Einstein's words,[25] ". . . the crown of his labors with the fugue is found in the Fantasy in F minor for an organ-mechanism in a clock, dating from the last year of his life. . . . Here his mastery achieved full freedom in the conquest of the 'strict style' . . . "

24. Breitkopf & Haertel, Leipzig.
25. Einstein: *Mozart*, p. 153.

So much for Mozart's final triumph in the realm of the severest intellect. However, the field in which his fancy truly had found free play for the combination of the concertante and contrapuntal styles of treatment, for the fusing of the galant with the "learned" manner of composition, was the idiom of four-hand clavier music. More specifically, it was the medium of two claviers through which his intention of giving equal importance to each of the partners could be carried to realization most readily and most completely. Here Mozart succeeded in the synthesis of the old and the new, of intellectual profundity with that happy playfulness which so often, and somewhat superficially, is assumed to be the most typical manifestation of Mozart's musical genius.

There is reason to believe that Mozart himself derived a great deal of satisfaction from his creative work in the two-piano idiom. Whatever the degree of his predilection, it is to him that the art owes "the purest examples of the concertante style" (Einstein), a legacy sufficient to make duo-pianism a domain in the system of instrumental combinations.

CHAPTER V

THE GRAND DUO

Josef Haydn does not appear to have been attracted to writing for two pianofortes. The reasons for this lack of interest in the medium are more or less subject to speculation; the most likely explanation would probably be found in his preoccupation with other instrumental combinations. As it is, Haydn has left only one single four-hand work, to be played on one keyboard and entitled *Il Maestro e lo scolare, variazioni a quadri mani per un clavicembalo.*[1] Ruthardt, in his otherwise so reliable *Wegweiser durch die Klavier-Literatur*[2] attributes to Haydn a Sonata in D major and a Fugue in C minor, both for two pianos. The error is self-explanatory: these two works obviously belong into the Mozart catalogue.

If Mozart is said to have brought music from the church to the salon, Beethoven transplanted it further to the concert hall. More yet, he took it "from the castle to the cottage and made it the most democratic thing in the aesthetic world."[3] There are many reasons for this new development which are amply exposed in any standard book of music history. Interest and concern within this discussion are centering only upon Beethoven's apparent failure to write for the combination of two pianofortes. One chief reason why he did not feel drawn to the medium may have been a physical factor. The perfection of the piano mechanism, still a recent invention, now was fully under way. Performers partook as leaders in the exploration of new sonorities as well as in the devising and developing of a commensurate technic. A great flowering of solo virtuosity set in. This type of virtuosic display included technical mastery and prowess

1. Prosniz *Handbuch der Klavier-Literatur 1450-1830*, p. 76.
2. Chapter XII, Music for Two Pianofortes, Four-Hands.
3. Schauffler, *Beethoven, The Man Who Freed Music.*

as much as the ability to convey, through this new and seemingly omni-
potent musical instrument, the all-embracing spirit of revolution, unrest
and change; it projected the message of liberty and demonstrated how one's
entire emotional life could be poured into and expressed through one
single medium.

Superseding the narrow compass of the harpsichord, the much extended
range of the pianoforte offered a supreme challenge to the soloist to set
himself up as master of the added resources. With so much opportunity
for discovery and conquest, a pronounced individualist like Beethoven
hardly could think of sharing the platform of newly-won musical freedom
with another pianist. As far as he was concerned, the thirty-two piano
sonatas which he composed over a period of twenty-six years, constituted
his pianistic credo. He reached in them so complete a measure of self-
fulfillment that after composing the last of the sonatas, opus 111, he
lived on for five years without writing any other. Although he still was
to erect the crowning monument of his works for the pianoforte, the
Variations on a Theme of Diabelli, opus 120, Beethoven himself declared
that he now found the piano "an unsatisfactory instrument." He indeed
had fully exhausted the possibilities of the sonata form and the sonorities of the instrument as he envisioned them and "having nothing more to
say he preferred to remain silent." (Ewen).

Thus, by not writing for the combination of two pianofortes, Beethoven
not so much showed a lack of interest in the idiom, but he actually could
not visualize the medium itself at that time. There is no room for speculation whether he would have discovered duo-pianism for himself had
he lived on longer. As a piano virtuoso, his was a pronounced soloistic
temperament; the reasons for his attitude towards the pianoforte were
based on the fact that the solo instrument brought out his romantic-revo-
lutionary individuality most strongly and effectively.

Finally, Beethoven's musical age was that of homophonic forms of texture. This is to say that he mainly created music in which a single voice
was reigning supreme over the rest of the tonal material; the latter served
largely the function of filling in. It seems likely that the combination of
two pianofortes, calling for a contrapuntal treatment and a concertante
style as its dominant features, not only offered no advantages to Beethoven's principal structure of piano composition, but actually proved anti-
climactic to the means of expression which he and the Romanticists had
just begun to discover for themselves.

It is merely left to mention the few compositions which Beethoven did
write for four hands on one piano, the only evidence of a slight interest
in piano ensemble during his youth. These works include a *Sonata in D,*

opus 6, which was published in 1797 and *Three Marches, opus 45,* published in 1804. The *Variations in C, on a theme of Count Waldstein,* were brought out by Simrock as early as 1794.[4] Finally, there exist four-hand variations on a theme inspired by words of Goethe, "I Think of You." These variations, in the key of D major, were composed in 1800 for the Countesses Josefine Deym and Therese Brunswick.

The foregoing data give evidence that all four-hand works by Beethoven were written in his early years, and mainly for the benefit of his patrons. Once his independence, economically and artistically, had been established, he ignored the idea of the piano-ensemble and preferred to make his chosen instrument the lone voice of his lonely soul.

Although Franz Schubert, like Beethoven, left no original work for two pianofortes, his was unquestionably the first great genius for four-hand music. He himself was very fond of duet playing. As a composer, he possessed a fine feeling for the registers of the instrument. In his piano duets, he demonstrated his awareness of sonorities which remained unexploited in solo playing, and while he materialized this cognizance by writing for four hands on one piano only, he nevertheless pointed thereby to duo-pianism as the logical future development.

Schubert's advance in this direction is documented by the wealth of four-hand music with which he has endowed the literature. Much of this duet music is habitually played on two pianos and, when thus rendered, actually is enhanced in its effect because it then appears freed from the limitations of the original medium. Schubert's *Grand Duo (Sonata in C major), opus 140,* as an example, is known to have been played on two pianos by Clara Schumann and Johannes Brahms. This "Grand Duo," believed by some musicologists to be Schubert's own arrangement of the disputed "Gastein'" Symphony, is "more orchestral in conception than any of Schubert's other four-hand music. It is a spacious work of symphonic proportions, and on every page one finds some extraordinary touch of the inspired Schubert." (Berkowitz) Another duet work by Schubert which is frequently performed on two pianos rather than on only one keyboard, is his intensely dramatic *Fantaisie in F minor, opus 103.* The scoring of the work is rich and sonorous, and the melodist Schubert here invents some of his most beautiful and haunting themes. Small wonder that many duo-pianists have incorporated this and other of Schubert's four-hand piano compositions into their repertoire.[5] The practice has persisted even to the extent of making some of these duets mistakenly appear as

4. Victor Babin has made a two-piano transcription of this work.
5. To cite one typical instance, Dougherty and Ruzicka included the *Fantasy, opus 103,* in their recital of chamber music for two pianos which was given at the Library of Congress on October 29, 1944, during the Tenth Festival of Chamber Music.

original two-piano works. Yet, the sublime beauty and profundity of Schubert's compositions, and their felicitous scoring for the full range of pianoforte sonorities, disarm all objections which may be felt regarding their rendition on two keyboards.

The name of Muzio Clementi first entered into this survey when in 1781 he engaged in a contest of skill with Mozart at the court of Vienna. Mozart's contemporary and sometime rival was to remain overshadowed by the former's supreme genius. Nevertheless, Clementi's indisputable merits for the development of the pianoforte as a mechanism, and of pianoforte playing as a scientific skill, place him into the first rank of historical personalities in this field. The branch of duo-pianism, in particular, is indebted to Clementi for his two charming sonatas for two pianofortes, *opus 12* and *opus 46*. Both are in the key of B flat major and especially the smaller one which consists of only two movements, is a gem.[6]

Clementi's interest in the duo-piano field is further ascertained by the frequent ensemble performances which he gave in partnership with John Field, the eminent Irish pianist and composer. Field was a pupil of Clementi who later used him to exhibit his pianos. It was Clementi who in 1804 introduced the "Inventor of the Nocturne" to Russia where Field was to become so eminently successful. The concertizing and piano demonstrating activities of teacher and pupil included frequent duo-work, so that the pair of sonatas for two pianos offers relatively small evidence of the actual degree of duo-pianistic interest which Clementi displayed during his long career.

J. L. Dussek has already been mentioned as one of the notable composers who were interested in the two-piano medium during this period. Credit must also be given to Johann Nepomuk Hummel, a pupil of Mozart, who left an opus posthumous for two pianofortes entitled *Introduction and Rondo*.[7] To the same generation belongs Daniel Steibelt. He was a colorful figure in the world of music who at one time attracted attention by entering into a contest of pianistic skill with Beethoven. Within this survey, it is of interest that Steibelt numbers a set of duos for two pianos among his compositions. Further to be mentioned here is Ferdinand Ries, the pupil of Beethoven, who composed a *Sonata for two pianos,*

---

6. Manuel and Williamson extend their programs of two-harpsichord music to these sonatas by Clementi, with somewhat doubtful justification if style history becomes the criterion. It is known that Clementi, as an artist, pioneered the modern pianoforte; in addition, he was engaged in the business of piano manufacturing, and naturally sought to propagandize his product.

For further comment on Clementi's sonatas, see Book III *The Literature*, Chapter XXIII *The Standard Repertoire*.

7. This work was revived by duo-pianists Levin in a recent Carnegie Hall concert.

opus 32, and a *Duo, opus 142*; he also wrote a trio for two pianos and harp. The sonata was written in 1816. It is not known whether Ries showed it to Beethoven; however, probability implies that he submitted the work to his teacher for inspection.

The great outburst of Romantic individualism, coupled with the flowering of pianistic virtuosity which followed in the wake of Beethoven's career, produced exponents of the instrument such as Moscheles, Cramer, Czerny, Hummel, Kalkbrenner, Weber, Mendelssohn, Herz and Thalberg. All these men were thoroughly representative of the pianoforte technic founded by their master, Beethoven, and they might justly be called the group of technicians. In addition, each of them embodied the new life of the virtuoso, that glamorous career of frequent public concerts in which a pianist was expected to render a formal program as well as to be qualified to appear as an improviser. The technic of the virtuosos kept pace with the mechanical evolution of the instrument which was steadily being improved by the manufacturers. The sum total and culmination of their achievements was reached in the appearance of Franz Liszt.

A definite advancement of two-piano art during this period is due especially to the close friendship and collaboration between Moscheles and Mendelssohn. Ignaz Moscheles, a power in his day and still a name denoting lustre and commanding respect, first felt moved to write a piece for two pianofortes when in 1822 he went to England and participated in a concert which had been planned by his friend Cramer. The occasion is typical for the now beginning vogue of the *Grand Duo,* when virtuosi discovered that playing on two keyboards afforded the chance for much sensational display such as was not possible on a single instrument.

Moscheles himself provides a description of the circumstances furnishing him with the incentive for the composition which later became one of the most famous in the duo-pianistic repertoire. He writes as follows:[8]

"I found J. B. Cramer on the point of giving his yearly concert. He showed me two movements of a Sonata which he wished to play with me, and expressed a desire that I should compose a third movement as a finale; only I was not to put any of my octave passages into his part, which he pretended he could not play. I can refuse him nothing. I shall therefore be obliged to strive and write something analogous for him, the disciple of Mozart and Handel."

The finale which Moscheles hastily wrote to complement Cramer's Sonata is the same *Allegro* movement which now is well-known and frequently played under the title *Hommage à Handel.* Moscheles afterwards added an introduction to it, converted the movement into an independent piece and in this form published it for two pianos. The novelty was first

8. *Recent Music and Musicians as Described in the Diaries and Correspondence of Ignaz Moscheles,* pp. 43-44.

performed at Cramer's concert on May 9, 1822, and is reported to have created a furore. A contemporary account of, the event gives this glowing description:[9]

> "To hear Moscheles, of whom the newspapers said 'that his execution is most wonderful, and more wonderful because he always makes the right use of his genius,' playing together with 'glorious John,' and in addition to that, in a composition on which both had worked, was 'an unrivaled treat, an unprecedented attraction.' "

This work was not the only contribution which the composer Moscheles made to the two-piano literature. Together with Mendelssohn, he contrived a *Duo Concertante,* consisting of variations on the march theme from Weber's *Preciosa;* this duo is listed in Moscheles' catalogue as *opus 87b.* A later work is the *Symphonic Heroic March on German Folk Songs, opus 130,* and there exists also a *Grand Duo Concertant in A.* Moscheles, in addition, was one of the first who conceived of writing an added second piano part for simultaneous performance with an original piano solo. He decided on a selection of ten Preludes from The Well-tempered Clavier by Johann Sebastian Bach and composed for the added concertizing piano his *Melodic-Contrapuntal Studies, opus 137.*

Of all these two-piano works, however, Moscheles' *Hommage à Handel,* given the opus number 92, was to become a favorite showpiece of his time and of subsequent generations. The work is still often played and much enjoyed, even though it may have acquired the reputation of being a somewhat dusty conservatory war-horse. Authentic records speak of several performances which were given to the composition by Moscheles in partnership with his devoted pupil and life-time friend, Felix Mendelssohn-Bartholdy. Ever since the two met for the first time in 1824, when Mendelssohn was a handsome boy of fifteen while Moscheles already was carried by the full tide of artistic success, the latter was to exercise a great influence upon the young genius.

On October 21, 1840, Moscheles writes as follows from Prague about a concert in the famous Gewandhaus at Leipzig during which he played the *Hommage à Handel* together with Mendelssohn:[10]

> ". . . At the Fête in the Gewandhaus, given me by Mendelssohn, there were about three hundred connoisseurs invited, who surrounded the three Härtel pianos. The room was brilliantly lighted, there was a full orchestra and chorus, a hundred and forty strong. It was so pretty to watch Mendelssohn and his lovely wife, before the music began, doing the honors for the various guests, and taking care that every one had refreshments offered them. Here is the programme:—

---

9. *Recent Music and Musicians as Described in the Diaries and Correspondence of Ignaz Moscheles,* p. 44.
10. *Ditto,* p. 275.

FIRST PART

"The two *Leonora Overtures*, gloriously performed. Mendelssohn's *42nd Psalm*. A noble work. The solos excellently given by Madame Frege.

"*Hommage à Handel*. Played with fraternal enthusiasm by Felix and myself.

SECOND PART

"*Overture to the Hebrides*. My *G minor Concerto*.

"The Orchestra, conducted by Felix, played splendidly; there was not a slip. I played 'con amore.' Chorley declares, better than ever I did before. Applause deafening. J. S. Bach's 'Triple Concerto' with Madame Schumann, Felix, and me—judge how it went. To wind up I played some 'Studies.' "

There is also a record of an earlier performance of *Hommage à Handel* by Moscheles and Mendelssohn when they played the duo at the former's concert in Leipzig on October 9, 1835,[11] and eleven years later, in 1846, both again performed the work at the Birmingham Festival. Mendelssohn's *Midsummer Night's Dream* music was conducted by the composer on the same evening. [12] Another performance, also by Mendelssohn in collaboration with Moscheles, is reported to have taken place on September 25, 1844. The particular concert was arranged in impromptu fashion when Moscheles visited Mendelssohn at the latter's summer vacation spot, the resort town of Soden, near Frankfort. The recital was given before a crowded audience, following the initiative of Felix who insisted on the concert "though there is a regular congress of pianists here."[13]

Felix Mendelssohn himself had taken an early interest in two-piano work. In fact, when he appeared in public for the second time, as a boy of 13, he took part in a duo for two pianos by Dussek. The occasion was the concert given by Aloys Schmitt on March 31, 1822. Schmitt was well known as a successful teacher and seems to have been occupied to some extent with activities in the two-piano medium. His own *Konzertstueck Op. 23* attests to this interest.

During the long and intimate friendship and musical association between Mendelssohn and Moscheles, both appeared jointly at frequent occassions in two-piano performances. One of these duo-concerts occurred in London on June 1, 1832, when they shared honors in the program presented by Moscheles. They played Mozart's Concerto for Two Pianos into which Felix inserted two long cadenzas, one for each performer. The concert reviewer of *Harmonicon* said of these display passages:[14]

". . . each introduced his own cadenza, in which musical skill and powers of execution were exhibited that certainly none in the present day could surpass and very few would dream of rivalling."

---

11. Stratton *Mendelssohn*, p. 77.
12. *Recent Music and Musicians as Described in the Diaries and Correspondence of Ignaz Moscheles*, p. 325; also Stratton, *Mendelssohn*, p. 122.
13. Stratton, *Mendelssohn*, pp. 111-112.
14. *Harmonicon*, Vol. X, p. 154.

At another of the annual concerts of Moscheles, the two friends played a composition based on the *Gypsy March* from Weber's *Preciosa*. The work, as has been mentioned previously, was composed by Mendelssohn and Moscheles in partnership with each other. It is in the variation form, and it can be found in the official opus lists of both composers under the name of *Duo Concertante*. The scoring, which originally was for two pianofortes with orchestra, later was reduced to two solo pianos. The first performance took place on May 1, 1833, in London. The premiere of the work is said to have been practically in the manner of an improvisation, in that the piece at that time was only roughly sketched out. Nevertheless, the notice in the *Harmonicon* gave the composition much praise. Laudatory comment was bestowed especially upon the cadenzas which the reviewer considered to be of the most masterly kind. That first performance, according to available sources of information, excited the admiration of a crowded room. Eleven years later, a hearing was given to the work on July 9, 1844, when Mendelssohn and Moscheles played it again in London, on the occasion of a farewell soiree at the house of Klingemann.

In addition to the ample documentary proof of their many joint appearances in public, there also exist several reports of the extemporaneous two-piano playing in which Mendelssohn and Moscheles seem to have indulged at frequent occasions. Their particular procedure remains of questionable artistic merit. However, the two great musicians must have derived much personal pleasure from these improvisations. To quote the words of Moscheles, they allowed themselves "all manner of musical extravagances" when they extemporized jointly or alternately on the two instruments while Abraham Mendelssohn, who by that time was quite blind, sat mystified and amused. It seems that this sort of musical fun became an almost habitual practice with the two, for as late as in 1846 Moscheles reports from Leipzig, where he had gone after his appointment to the faculty of the Conservatory:[15]

"We spent the evening at the Mendelssohns' in a social quiet way. . . . After supper we amused ourselves on two pianos, and at last had a grand improvisation together, in which Felix was so inspired that in my enthusiasm I almost forgot my own part in listening to him."

In the following excerpt from a letter written by Moscheles' son, the approximate procedure of a "grand improvisation" under the hands of Mendelssohn and Moscheles is described in greater detail:

"A subject once started, it was caught up as if it were a shuttlecock; now one of the players would seem to toss it up on high, or to keep it balanced in mid-octaves with delicate touch. Then the other would take it in hand, start it on classi-

15. *Recent Music and Musicians as Described in the Diaries and Correspondence of Ignaz Moscheles*, pp. 328-329.

cal lines, and develop it with profound erudition, until perhaps the two, joining together in new and brilliant forms, would triumphantly carry it off to other spheres of sound. Four hands there might be, but only one soul, so it seemed as they would catch with lightning speed at each other's ideas, each trying to introduce subjects from the works of the other. It was exciting to watch how the amicable contest would wax hot, culminating occasionally in an outburst of merriment when some conflicting harmonies met in terrible collision. But soon they would seem to be again fraternizing in perfect harmonies, gradually leading up to the brilliant finale that sounded as if it had been so written, revised and corrected and were now being interpreted from the score by two masters."

During the entire period of Mendelssohn's residence in Leipzig, a veritable round table of musicians, and particularly pianists, gave constant incentive to ensemble playing on multiple keyboards. Bach's concerti for three claviers were frequently performed by Mendelssohn in collaboration with such illustrious colleagues as Clara Wieck, Thalberg and Moscheles. Typical of the close collaboration then prevailing among virtuosos of the first rank was a concert in London, given on June 1, 1844. This event is mentioned here because of its reflection on some characteristic practices of the "Grand Duo," particularly that of improvisation. Horsley gives a vivid account of the concert which also reminds of the then still prevailing custom to extemporaneously produce a cadenza during concert performance, a practice which was almost obligatory for every self-respecting virtuoso of that period:

"Bach's triple Concerto in D minor was performed by Moscheles, Thalberg and Mendelssohn. Thalberg not being given to extempore playing, it was agreed that no cadenzas were to be introduced. When the first pause was reached in the finale, Moscheles, perhaps from the force of habit, started off with a brilliant cadenza. At the second pause it was Thalberg's turn, and though taken by surprise, he got through very well. Lastly came Mendelssohn's effort."[16]

The following is Horsley's description of the cadenza which Mendelssohn then improvised:[17]

"It began very quietly, and the themes of the concerto, most scientifically varied, gradually crept up in their new garments. A crescendo then began, the themes, ever newly presented, rose higher and higher; and at last a storm, nay a perfect hurricane of octaves, which must have lasted for five minutes brought to a conclusion an exhibition of mechanical skill, and the most perfect inspiration, which neither before nor since that memorable Thursday afternoon has ever been approached. The effect on the audience was electrical . . . at the end rounds of cheers were given for the great artist, which sounded like salvos of artillery."

The general statement can be made that Mendelssohn's contribution to the history of duo-pianism largely was that of the performing artist. It was he who shared with Clara Schumann in the premiere of Robert Schumann's *Andante and Variations, op. 46,* at a memorable concert in the

16. Stratton, *Mendelssohn*, p. 173.
17. Horsley, *Choir*, Vol. XV, p. 81.

Leipzig Gewandhaus on August 19, 1843.[18] While it seems to be common knowledge that Mendelssohn throughout his life showed an active interest in two-piano performance, the important fact that he also composed two concertos for two pianofortes is very little observed. These works have remained unpublished to this day, although the awareness of their existence gives enough cause for fascination to duo-pianists. The original scores are contained in the forty-four volume collection of manuscripts in the former Royal Library at Berlin. [19] It is hoped that conditions will soon permit to uncover these autograph scores from their oblivion and to subject them to the curiosity of all those interested in the duo-pianistic medium.

The friendship between Moscheles and Mendelssohn with all its enthusiasm and exuberance is but one characteristic example for the general artistic spirit and the flambuoyance of the age. Remote and alien as this attitude of heroic grandeur and glorified virtuosity may appear to a different era, it was productive of great musicians and of a type of music which, in spite of its frank emphasis on display, was cradled in the great tradition of the Viennese school. Thus it came to be substantial in essence and, moreover, it was heated in the flaming fire of romantic spirit with its manifold connotations. While the pianoforte underwent a continual improvement of its mechanical properties through the efforts of inventors and manufacturers, the development of playing technic kept pace with this evolution. Virtuosi like Cramer, Czerny, Kalkbrenner, Pixis, Herz, and Thalberg constantly met in friendly contest and frequently shared the platform in sensational two-piano exhibitions.

Such showy display did not remain limited to the combination of only two pianofortes. The English periodical *Quarterly Musical Magazine and Review* reports as early as in September 1825 on the unusual activities of German pianists in the French capital during the spring of that year. A concert, given by Moscheles at the Académie Royale de Musique, included a remarkable performance of an arrangement for three pianos and twelve hands. The composition heard was the overture to Weber's *Der Freischuetz;* it had thus been arranged by Moscheles. The executants formed an array of illustrious pianists: Moscheles himself, Henri Herz, Schunke, Pixis, Felix Mendelssohn, and Camille Pleyel.

Another typical example for the exhibition of great fraternity among virtuosos during the period of the Grand Duo was the concert which the French pianist Henri Herz gave on the occasion of a visit to London in 1831. Henri Herz, born in Vienna and later becoming a naturalized

---

18. This event wil be given further attention during Chapter VI, *Salon, Chamber Music, Symphonic Workshop.*
19. Stratton, *Mendelssohn,* p. 207, Appendix B, Catalog of Works.

Frenchman, was unusually popular during his lifetime. He met every-where with an enthusiasm which in this day of calm and dignity is hardly imaginable. Herz was one of the greatest technicians of his generation and at the same time one of the most prolific composers for the pianoforte. His works are now forgotten, except the well-known piano exercises under the title *Hanon*. At the concert referred to, Herz was joined by Cramer and Moscheles in duet performances which were designed to be sensational attractions in view of the popularity enjoyed by each of these outstanding virtuosos.

The collaboration often transcended the purely pianistic partnership and extended to the venture of joint composition; a case in point is the *Duo Concertante* by Moscheles and Mendelssohn which has been referred to before. Again it needs to be remembered that the classic tradition was still strong enough to impel, if not postulate, the ability of a concert pianist to improvise freely and to provide samples of his skill and talent as a composer. It is therefore not too surprising that, alongside the records of frequent duo-piano performances, a sizable number of two-piano com-positions has come forth from this epoch of the "Grand Duo." It is the latter term which indeed is used as title or subtitle for very many of these compositions, and no better name could be found to typify the entire period. The nomenclature *Grand Duo* aptly describes both the association of illustrious virtuosos joining in performance, and the appro-priate kind of music written by or for such two-piano combinations.

There are far too many compositions of this genre to enumerate. A goodly number of them has been forgotten by posterity, and their essential superficiality explains why their appeal had to be ephemeral. Among the more representative works, deserving of mention are two "Grand Duos" by Joh. Bapt. Cramer, *opus 24* and *opus 37*. The earlier work also exists in a version for harp and piano, an ensemble form which was a favorite combination of the period. Both Kalkbrenner and Czerny collaborated with famous harpists of their day in duo-compositions for their respective instruments (Kalkbrenner with Dizi, and Czerny with Parish-Alvars.) The scoring of these duos renders them suitable for ready execution on two pianos, and in this combination they were given frequent performances. Friedrich Kalkbrenner also composed a *Concerto for Two Pianos and Orchestra, opus 125*, a *Marche in G* and a *Grand Duo in D, opus 128*.

Karl Czerny, the disciple of Beethoven, and beyond doubt one of the most prolific composers of all times, endowed the two-piano literature with an abundance of material. A *Grande Polonaise brillante, opus 18*, was followed by *Three brilliant Fantasies on favorite Motives from the works of Schubert, opus 339*, and by the *Duo brillant, opus 358*. In *opus*

797, Czerny presents an entire two-piano cycle of *Ten brilliant Fantasies*. *Six Potpourris, opus 212*, include one composition with the unusual combination of two pianos, six hands. The *Variations on Montecchi* are scored for two pianos with the accompaniment of a quartet. In his employment of the two-piano medium, Czerny did not confine himself to purely virtuosic display as the frequent use of the adjective "brilliant" in his titles might imply. His concept of duo-pianism envisioned a higher function: As one of the very first composers, he seems to have realized the practical advantages of the idiom for the faithful reproduction of orchestral music. A reference by Saint-Saens, contained in his *Musical Memories*, [20] allows an interesting glimpse into the state of musical affairs in the city of Paris during the early 1850's; because of this record, it becomes possible to give due credit to Czerny whose influence and authority far exceeded that of an expert piano technician. Saint-Saens remarks that concerts then were provided by a society formed at the Conservatoire and restricted to its members. "There was no other symphony concert worthy of the name in Paris at the time." The symphonic repertoire was limited. "Not only did the Conservatoire audiences know little music, but the larger public knew none at all. The symphonies of the three great classic masters were known to amateurs for the most part only through Czerny's arrangement for two pianos."

The labor of love which produced the two-piano settings of these symphonic works, deserves to be here recalled, especially since these arrangements for some time apparently were instrumental in the promotion of great music. The industrious Czerny's efforts represent the first large-scale instance of the role which duo-pianism was to assume in the hands of Liszt, Brahms, and other symphonists; it becomes the function of two pianos to provide the closest semblance to the orchestral idiom, and consequently to serve as its nearest substitute.

Karl Czerny was a part of the same proud circle of musical friends to which also belonged men like Johann Peter Pixis, Henri Herz and Sigismund Thalberg, the distinguished pupil of Moscheles. Each one of these famous virtuosos is known to have composed in the fashion of the Grand Duo. A favorite form was that of the variations, based either on original themes, or on melodies from popular operas of the day, like *The Huguenots* or *Norma*. Grand Opera and Grand Duo entered into a somewhat bombastic alliance. At one time, six celebrities of the pianistic stage convened and jointly composed a set of variations known as the *Hexameron*. Even Chopin and Liszt collaborated in this project which also enlisted the efforts of Czerny, Herz, Pixis, and Thalberg. The theme for

20. pp. 192-193.

their Grand Concert Variations was chosen from *The Puritans,* and the separate contributions to the unusual composition may have been intended as a memorial for Bellini who died, at the age of only thirty-three, soon after the first performance of his last opera. The original edition of the variations was for solo piano. In 1835, the set appeared in print under the title of *Hexameron,* alluding to the six co-authors of this unique work. Liszt, who had written the introduction and the finale, subsequently arranged the piece for two pianos; at that time, the variations by Chopin, Czerny, and Pixis were omitted.

Serving as a typical specimen, the work is reminiscent of all the grandeur and flamboyancy so characteristic of the entire period. It is a perfect exemplification of the musical thought and style during an epoch which is as remote to this day as the Victorian era itself.[21] The Grand Duo then enjoyed a veritable vogue. Acclaimed and tremendously popular, the practice ran its course, sometimes the dangerous course of the all-too-grandiose, the superficial and bombastic. Yet, this phenomenon was eminently in keeping with the taste and style of a period which considered grandiloquence its birthright. The character and substance of the music often portray themselves in the titles among which *marches du couronnement* and *hymnes triomphales* abound. Jean Henri Ravina composes a *Grand Duo sur l'Opéra Euryanthe de C.M. v. Weber, op. 9,* and later adds his *Souvenirs de Russie, Grand Duo, op. 64 bis.* Ferdinand von Hiller writes a *Duett ueber Luetzows Wilde Jagd von C.M. v. Weber op. 108* and another *Grosses Duett op. 135.* Otto Goldschmidt, a pupil of Chopin and Mendelssohn and the accompanist and husband of Jenny Lind, like Hiller injects the patriotic element in his *Grosses Duett mit Zugrundelegung des Liedes 'Die Wacht am Rhein' op. 21;* his next composition, entitled *Fruehlingserwachen, op. 22,* again is dedicated to the literature of original works for two pianos.

The picturesque array of titles in the Grand Duo genre of composition could be extended readily. Instead, it is preferred to close this sparkling chapter of duo-pianistic history with one more illustration taken from the concert stage. No other figure would be more suitable to provide a faithful image of the pianistic ideal during the epoch of the Grand Duo than the person of Louis Moreau Gottschalk, the American pianist and composer. With his qualifications as a virtuoso, Gottschalk succeeded in gaining the respects of Chopin and Berlioz. His popularity was synonymous with idolatry. Considering the impressionability of his audiences, Gott-

---

21. Appleton and Field discovered a copy of the yellowed score while browsing through a dusty pile of uncatalogued music at a New York clearing house for European publishers. The duo-pianists gave the first presentation of the work in the United States, at their Town Hall concert in 1944.

with an inquiry concerning their contribution to duo-pianistic advancement. At once, the salient fact emerges that each of the three has left a major work for two pianos. In essence and manner of projection, these compositions constitute a complete antithesis to the flamboyant practices of the Grand Duo. They represent the turning-point and salvation from the decadent course which two-piano music had taken for a time; they also accomplish the restoration of a legitimate development of the art. These three works are to be termed legitimate because they follow the inner laws of musical creation, rather than the temptations and corruptions caused by vanity and superficiality. They are to be called legitimate also because they possess the artistic qualities to make them enduring, fully alive today as then, and pro-creative of perpetual inspiration with generations of artists old and new.

The three compositions referred to are the *Rondo, opus 73,* by Chopin; *Andante and Variations, opus 46,* by Schumann; and *Concerto Pathétique,* by Liszt.

A virtuoso by profession himself, Frédéric François Chopin towered far above his colleagues by virtue of his genius which was both strongly nationalistic and peculiarly personal. His hyper-sensitive individuality, his fastidious and even exclusive style of composition, his temperamental disposition combined in producing the prime character of ever-fluctuating nuance in his musical conception. This chief quality was little conducive to two-piano discipline, for reasons which can be considered self-evident.

Actually, very little is known of Chopin's activities in the duo-pianistic realm. Carl Mikuli, his pupil, relates the fact that a second piano was regularly used by Chopin for demonstration during his lessons, but this application falls into the pedagogic category and therefore will be discussed in a later chapter.[3] Chopin and Liszt are known to have paired on at least one occasion at a meeting in one of the salons of Paris. It is probable that their performance, patterned after the impromptu style of the Grand Duo, was more in the nature of a social gesture than considered as serious art. The age of glittering virtuosity was not disposed towards that mutual adjustment and integration of powers which must be the Alpha and Omega of duo-pianism. Instead, each virtuoso carried his own standard of keyboard execution to greater and greater heights, exploring new solo effects of sonorities and dynamics. Private and public two-piano playing in the "Grand Duo" tradition was continuing to be a popular attraction, but the underlying attitude of the virtuoso regarding his sporadic duo-performances was not in keeping with a sincere approach

3. See Book II, *Nature, Applications, and Problems,* Part C, *The Educational Medium,* Chapter XXI, *Pedagogic Applications.*

to, and with the maxims of a true ensemble in which the collective purpose needs to supersede the individual tendency.

The prevailing outlook can perhaps best be illustrated by the following characteristic incident: Liszt and Thalberg had announced separate recitals for one and the same evening. Liszt is said to have paid a call to his rival, suggesting a joint concert on two pianos. Thalberg's reply was: "I do not like to be accompanied."

Little as there is known about Chopin's two-piano activities, his *Rondo in C major, op. 73,* nevertheless reveals a certain amount of interest in the medium. This rondo for two pianos which Chopin gave to the literature, was published posthumously. Despite the late opus number, it is really an early work, dating from the year 1828. Opinions on the musical merits of the composition are divided. Hall, for instance, writes that "this early Chopin piece is light fluff, easy to listen to but hardly of great consequence."[4] However, Brodsky calls the piece "glittering and beautiful . . . one of the most delightful pieces in two-piano literature."[5] Hutcheson, on the other hand, speaks of the Rondo as of "an unimportant composition of the master and pupil type, with an easy part for the second pianist."[6] The weakness pointed out by Hutcheson probably has been felt by many duo-pianists, and it is for this reason that Lee Pattison made an arrangement of the Rondo with a more equal distribution of pianistic material between the two players.

The Rondo, by all means, is a fine exhibition piece. It is well worth study and, moreover, holds a good deal of historical as well as aesthetic interest; the latter derives from Chopin's stature which is generally upheld as a prototype of individualism in piano music. The problem for the Polish composer was, in short, to reconcile two Chopins who were to concertize with each other. Thus formulated, his attitude towards, and his difficulty with, the two-piano medium become self-evident. Entirely aside from all other considerations, however, Chopin's Rondo remains a fine example of the early *salon* type of composition in the duo-pianistic idiom. This genre combines charm and sentiment with outward glitter; it has remained in popular favor throughout the century which since elapsed.*

In the midst of an era which harbored the refined elegance and sometimes blasé attitude of the salon as well as the flamboyant and exuberant manifestations of the Grand Duo, there awakened, rose and flourished the

4. David Hall, *The Record Book,* p. 824.
5. Albert E. Wier, *The Piano,* p. 350.
6. Hutcheson, *The Literature of the Piano,* p. 222.
* For further comment on this work, refer to Book III, *The Literature,* Chapter XXIII, *The Standard Repertoire.*

genius of Robert Schumann. Earnest and introspective, yet enthusiastic and passionate, Schumann was a true son of German Romanticism and a champion of his artistic ideals. His all-encompassing temperament and deeply poetic disposition were dominant traits of a new language in music which later also provided articulation to the great voice of Johannes Brahms.

Like Chopin whom he admired, Robert Schumann wrote only one work for two pianofortes, but this piece can well be called the essence of all his creative efforts. It may equally well be considered as an all-inclusive manifestation of German Romanticism. For the development of duo-pianism, the composition is the first striking example of the two-piano medium in the field of chamber music. Moreover, the work arrived at a time when it was to fulfill a most urgent mission of artistic salvation. This historic function is worded by Schauffler in his work on Schumann as follows:[7]

> "At a time when the Variation form of classical days had been degraded, by such luminaries as Herz and Huenten, down to the level of a mere vehicle of fireworks, Schumann . . . in the Andante and Variations filled it again with pure poetry."

The composition numbers as Robert Schumann's opus 46. The composer set to work on it early in 1843, shortly after he had gone through a crisis of mental exhaustion brought on by the tremendous strain of the preceding three years during which he had created an enormous output. As a consequence, Schumann had been compelled to give up composition temporarily. When he began writing again after this enforced rest, his first inspiration conceived of the *Andante and Variations*. The work was originally scored for two pianos, two violoncellos and horn. In this setting, unconventional as it is, it evidences Schumann's departure into the field of chamber music, after he first had concentrated on the piano solo, then on the art song (particularly during the year of his marriage), and next on the orchestra.

The unusual combination of the original version probably was prompted by Schumann's predilection for deep and rich sonorities. The score was tried out during March of 1843 in the warehouse of the well-known Leipzig publishers Breitkopf and Haertel. In a letter addressed to Dr. Haertel, Schumann announces the work as follows:

> "I have written a Variation Cycle for two pianos, two violoncellos and horn which I would be glad to hear once. Mendelssohn will be so good as to take a part. Our room space is too limited for this, so would it be possible to use your warehouse for it in the next few days?"

At the trial performance, Schumann was not satisfied. The composition met with certain problems of balance in the original instrumentation which

---

7. Schauffler, *Florestan*, p. 495.

caused it not to sound very well. Since Schumann also realized the difficulty in assembling such an unusual combination of instrumentalists and the resulting danger of oblivion to which the work would be exposed, he proceeded to rescore the composition for two pianofortes alone, without accompaniment. The first performance in this definite version took place at a Gewandhaus concert in Leipzig under the hands of Felix Mendelssohn and Clara Schumann, on August 19, 1843.

The particular concert was given by Pauline Viardot-Garcia and was also shared in by the violinist Joseph Joachim, then a boy of twelve. Clara Schumann and Mendelssohn played Schumann's opus 46 from manuscript. During the debut performance of the work, a fire alarm was sounded, and the disturbing incident then prevented the composition from having the same success which it later attained. According to general agreement, Schumann's *Andante and Variations* have since ranked with the best original works written for the combination, and the composition holds a firm place in the first line of the repertoire with all two-piano teams.

Intimacy and affection are breathing throughout the music. These qualities are almost pre-determined by the character of the theme itself; they are carried through in the treatment of the voices which are gentle in their dialogue, but strong when they unite in common aspiration. No performer nor listener can misunderstand the specific nature and message of this music. It is fully illustrative of those peculiarities which are commonly ascribed to the genre of chamber music. While the two-piano combination for the first time is made the vehicle of a musical branch honored by tradition and aristocratic substantiality, the medium at once becomes fully representative and even typical of that entire artistic genre. Therefore, the *Andante and Variations* will first come to mind whenever duo-pianism, with its widely ranging gamut of aspects and applications, is called upon to present its finest facet. With the introspective glow of chamber music, it counteracts and balances the features of symphonic dimension which are no less inherent in the idiom.

"Ausserordentlich fein und stimmungsvoll" ("Extraordinarily fine and poetically impressive") is the comment of Ruthardt on Schumann's op. 46. Although the composer when he wrote the piece had not quite recovered from the exhaustion of the years 1840 to 1842, the work is undoubtedly one of his finest. 1843 is to be recalled as the year during which Mendelssohn and Schumann collaborated in establishing the Leipzig Conservatory. The work was written during Schumann's best period, at the time when he was abandoning the habit of composing exclusively at the piano keyboard and when he realized himself at the height of his powers.[8]

---

8. For further comment on this work, see Book III, *The Literature,* Chapter XXIII, *The Standard Repertoire.*

On a concert tour to Vienna, late in 1846, Clara Schumann played her husband's opus 46 with Anton Rubinstein who then was sixteen years of age. It is reported that receipts at this concert barely balanced expenses. Another record of a public performance of the *Andante and Variations* dates from the year 1850; the work then was jubilantly received in Hamburg where Robert and Clara had gone on a highly successful concert trip. The composition was also frequently played by Clara Schumann and Johannes Brahms. The beautiful *andante* melody, the passages of the variations which have been described as "the interweaving of garlands of flowers," and the lovely and serene conclusion, all could not fail to have their particular meaningful message for the two. But to this episode of duo-pianistic evolution, attention will be turning only at a somewhat later time.[9]

During the current survey, Franz Liszt was first met with in the two-piano field when the *Hexameron* was mentioned, something of a curiosity in which he had a major share. Originally co-authored by six composers, the score was subsequently arranged by Liszt into a piece called *Grand Concert Variations* on the March in *I Puritani* for two pianos. In returning again to Liszt, his record in the field of duo-pianism will now be more closely observed. Attention needs first to be given to the major contribution to the original literature for two pianos which the art owes to him.

This work is the *Concerto Pathétique* in E minor. The concerto was composed in 1850 originally as a "Grosses Konzert-Solo" for Adolphe Henselt, one of the most celebrated pianists of the nineteenth century. A reference, found in one of Liszt's letters to Carl Reinecke (dated March 19, 1851), makes mention of the composition under the title "Concerto without orchestra." The work underwent a first metamorphosis in 1865 when Liszt rewrote it for two pianos; at this time, he also extended the score of the new version which he now called *Concerto Pathétique*. The music of this concerto and the form into which it was cast occupied the composer's mind for a period extending over altogether 27 years. As late as in 1877, apparently not yet satisfied with the edition of 1865, Liszt effected still another alteration. In the same year, he played this final version of the *Concerto Pathétique* with Ingeborg von Bronsart, one of his pupils, at a concert of the Tonkuenstler-Versammlung, at Hamburg.

The work is in one movement and therefore represents a formal analogy to the structure of a symphonic poem. Several tempo changes occur and the sub-division into various sections or movements is thereby implied. The principle of thematic development is the same as in the symphonic

9. See Chapter VII, *Brahms.*

poems. A forerunner and possibly a model of Liszt's *Concerto Pathétique* was a work of the same title and general outline composed by Ignaz Moscheles.

The mere fact that this composition occupied Liszt's creative thoughts for so long a period of time, can be held indicative of a particular purposefulness with which the composer seems to have dedicated himself to the work. Could it be supposed that Liszt in this music suffered through the various stages of romantic ardor, as conquering hero at first and compassionate martyr afterwards? There is room for assumption that the gradual transformation leading to the final setting for two pianos had its motivation in philosophical roots such as Paul Bekker points them out with the words:[10]

> "When individuality has been exploited to the limit of its possibilities, the desire for a common unity grows up once more. This great, unrealizable spiritual longing is innate in all romanticists, leads them always further in their individual ways, and thus determines the deeply pessimistic character of all romantic art."

Does it seem possible that the "desire for a common unity" befell Liszt, that most self-righteous of all soloists, when he arranged the *Concerto Pathétique* for two pianos? Could it be true that in this work, labored over by him for so many years, he tried to gain artistic salvation through a transfiguration of all passion into the higher sphere of compassion? Did he seek to find delivery from the proud but lonely peak of his virtuosity and to arrive at a more comforting province of the art in which companionship is the essence of satisfaction? In the projection of *two* voices to proclaim mankind's rhapsodic yearning, love, and suffering, did he aspire to a sublimation for himself, denouncing artistic egotism and accepting the social principle?

If these in truth may have been salient motives for its creation, then the *Concerto Pathétique* possesses a prophetic meaning for much later trends. Liszt who indeed had lead pianism to its zenith, with this work was searching himself for new horizons, for new direction of the art in order to avoid its decline.

From the realm of philosophical speculation, the discussion now returns to more factual considerations. Stimulated and encouraged by the composer's repeated experimentations with the work, several additional arrangements were created following Liszt's own final version for two solo pianos. Of these revised editions, the one by Eduard Reuss, written in 1880, first commands attention in that it was executed under the supervision and with the full sanction of Liszt himself. The Reuss arrangement, which was for one pianoforte and orchestra, twenty-six years later received a

10. Bekker, *The Story of Music*, pp. 247-248.

parallel when Richard Burmeister devised a similar setting. The latter
version draws the following comment by James Huneker who writes about
it in his book on Liszt:[11]

"Richard Burmeister made an arrangement of Liszt's *Concerto Pathétique* in E
minor by changing its original form for two pianos into a concerto for piano solo
with orchestral accompaniment. Until now the original has remained almost an
unknown composition; partly for the reason that it needed for a performance two
first rank piano virtuosi to master the extreme technical difficulties and partly that
Liszt had chosen for it such a rhapsodical and whimsical form as to make it an
absolutely ineffective concert piece. Even Hans von Bülow tried in a new edition
to improve some passages by making them more consistent, but without success.

"However, as the concerto contains pathetic musical ideas, among the best Liszt
conceived and is of too much value to be lost, Mr. Burmeister ventured to give it
a form by which he hopes to make it as popular as the famous E-flat major concerto by the same composer. The task was a rather risky one, as some radical
changes had to be made and the character of the composition preserved.

"To employ a comparison, Mr. Burmeister cut the concerto like a beautiful but
badly tuned bell into pieces and melted and moulded it again into a new form.
Some passages had to change places, some others to be omitted, others again repeated
and enlarged. Mr. Burmeister went even so far as to add some of his own passages—
for instance, a cadence at the beginning of the piano part, the end of the slow
movement and a short fugato introducing the finale. As to the new form, the result
now comes very near to a restoration of the old classical form: *Allegro—Andante—
Allegro*."

In this survey of duo-pianism, the versions for solo piano and orchestra
evidently are of much less interest than the further revision which was
edited by Lee Pattison in 1921. Pattison arranged the *Concerto Pathétique*
for two pianos and orchestra and thus performed it in partnership with
his teammate Guy Maier. The premiere of Pattison's version took place
in Chicago on November 25, 1941, at a concert with the Chicago Symphony
Orchestra.

In each stage of the extensive experimentation which the *Concerto
Pathétique* has undergone, the work successfully emerges with its emphasis
on musical substance rather than on mere technical showiness. In spite
of the controversial aspects regarding its form, the volume and essence
of its purely musical ideas make the composition rate high among all of
Liszt's creations. The concerto also marks a definite advancement in the
realization of the orchestral color potentialities which are inherent in
the two-piano medium. These latent propensities, as will soon be pointed
out, may have meant to Liszt a suitable approach to the fixation of his
tonal ideal, in that his own notion of sound perfection strove for symphonic richness. Since his imagination revolved around the pianoforte,
he was unable to find an utterly satisfying combination in the resources
of the orchestra, and even a full orchestral body sounded to his mind only
like a glorified piano instrumentation. This is why for Liszt the combi-

11. Huneker, *Franz Liszt*, pp. 177-178.

nation of two pianos was the logical avenue toward the attainment of even greater richness than the solo piano would afford; it was the road toward the materialization of his individual symphonic ideal which even the orchestra could not yield to him.

The *Concerto Pathétique,* in the comments from its critics, has received both praise and derogation; the adjectives attributed to the work range from "sublime" to "banal." Hans Rosenwald, the friend of the late Hungarian composer Béla Bartók, relates the interesting fact that this modernist, although being dedicated himself to sparing and lucid means of expression, yet professed a special fondness for the concerto which he frequently performed together with his wife. This was but one manifestation of Bartók's general appreciation of Liszt, "whose contributions to the further evolution of music have been more significant than those of either Wagner or Richard Strauss."[12]

In addition to the *Concerto Pathétique* and the *Grand Concert Variations* on the March in *I Puritani,* Liszt also made a masterly arrangement for two pianos of his own *Don Juan* Fantaisie. This work was originally written for solo piano. It is a most effective composition, breath-taking in its brilliancy and splendor, and the impression obtained is even more powerful in the transcription for two pianos. But the chief reason why Franz Liszt is to be recognized as one of the great pathfinders in the art of duo-pianism, rests with still another of his numerous creative efforts. That particular distinction is based on the monumental arrangements of his twelve symphonic poems for two pianofortes. The following enumeration of titles which identify these works, will serve to make the reader familiar with the enormous extent of Liszt's compositions for two pianos.

The twelve symphonic poems include:

1. *Ce qu'on entend sur la montagne*
2. *Tasso*
3. *Les Préludes*
4. *Orpheus*
5. *Prometheus*
6. *Mazeppa*
7. *Festklänge*
8. *Héroide funèbre (Heldenklage)*
9. *Hungaria*
10. *Hamlet*
11. *Hunnenschlacht*
12. *The Ideals*

Some of the foregoing works are well known in their orchestral forms, but the fact that all of them are available in Liszt's authentic two-piano

12. Margit Varro in *Contributions to Béla Bartók's Biography.*

versions is little observed. Yet, these arrangements must be considered as of paramount importance because they bring into clear relief the twofold significance which duo-pianism was destined to assume in symphonic music. First, the effect of the medium is orchestral even when the original intention aims for a specific two-piano sound. On the other hand, the idiom serves as the closest substitute to orchestral effects and therefore lends itself as the most suitable medium for the arrangement and rendition of orchestral scores. Regardless of the point of departure which lies within the attitude of the composer himself, the natural tendencies of duo-pianism render it a *symphonic* medium. This trend of thought was materialized in the many experimentations by both Liszt and Brahms. The idea to employ the two-piano medium as a symphonic workshop occupied the champion of "program" music as much as the staunch apostle of the "absolute," for it was Brahms who at the same time used duo-pianism as a convenient form for his own musical essays. Both great composers realized that the combination of two pianofortes can provide the closest semblance to the orchestral idiom, both in sonorities and in the organic discipline of ensemble performance. What was to become a highly perfected artistic skill in the two-piano scores of such orchestral masters as Debussy, Ravel, Reger, Milhaud, or Stravinsky, is due to the vision and ground work of Liszt and Brahms and thus remains their historic merit.

Any explanation of Liszt's symphonic thought needs to be sought in his thoroughly pianistic ideology. He was both the supreme virtuoso and poet of the pianoforte and as such could hardly hear or think other than in terms of his chosen instrument. This is why Anton Rubinstein, in his *Conversation on Music,*[13] comments on the symphonic poems by Liszt in the following words:

> "His orchestral instrumentation exhibits the same mastery as that of Berlioz and Wagner, even bears their stamp; with that, however, it is to be remembered that his pianoforte is the *Orchestra-Pianoforte* and his orchestra the *Pianoforte-Orchestra,* for the orchestral composition sounds like an instrumented pianoforte composition."

The distinction between the "orchestra-pianoforte" and the "pianoforte-orchestra" is necessarily the prerogative of the individual composer; it is based on the tonal image in his own mind and the attitude resulting therefrom. As far as the duo-pianistic medium is concerned, however, the symphonic character of the idiom is absolute. Whether this symphonic quality of the two-piano sound will stimulate an expansion into full orchestral instrumentation, or whether the latter is synthesized into the two-piano medium, is of no consequence in considering and accepting the essentially independent nature of the medium itself. It remains the prerogative of duo-pianism to be symphonic both in cause and result.

13. Reprinted in *Franz Liszt* by James Huneker, pp. 157-158.

CHAPTER VII

BRAHMS

It is only one step from the twelve symphonic poems by Franz Liszt with their dual existence as orchestral works and as two-piano condensations, into the duo-pianistic laboratory of another great composer. In the mind of Johannes Brahms, the two-piano medium assumes a new meaning, and under his hands it receives a new practical application. In the course of this review of the evolution of duo-pianism, a number of important historic phases have been examined up to now. The Farnabies and Couperins, the Pasquinis and Bachs were observed entertaining themselves with the combination of two keyboards; homage was paid to Mozart for raising the medium to the concert stage. Notice was next taken of the "Grand Duo" driving the young art into the dead-end of empty showiness; and then Schumann was seen coming forth to bring about its glorious resurrection. But it was Johannes Brahms who was destined to achieve the greatest heights of duo-pianistic composition and to secure a place of magnificence and unequalled originality for the idiom in the history of musical art.

Brahms' attention to, and his extensive employment of the two-piano combination was based on reasons which at the same time were very personal and very practical. The former are found in his relationship to the Schumanns, Robert and Clara, which deeply influenced both his private and his creative life. Well-known are the help and friendship, the advice and encouragement which Robert Schumann bestowed upon the younger composer. Not less familiar is the affectionate loyalty which Brahms so richly returned. It is not deemed necessary to here dwell on a speculation regarding the specific nature of relations which existed between Clara

93

Schumann and Johannes Brahms. This controversial issue has been ex-
haustively debated by various biographers, and the argument has reached
the point of agreement that the exact degree of their relationship eludes
fixation. No amount of uncertainty exists, however, concerning the fact
that the young composer for a period of at least two years, 1854-1855,
was deeply in love with Clara who, from her end, exerted a marked power
and influence over Johannes throughout his life. Not only was Clara the
first authority consulted by Brahms whenever a new composition was born,
but she also provided the first stimulus and continual inspiration for the
creation of a sizable number of works. Especially important to the current topic of duo-pianism is the fact that Clara became the living incentive
for the practical interest which Brahms took in the two-piano medium,
beginning at an early stage of his creative productiveness and lasting into
the most mature period of his work, culminating in the *Fourth Symphony*.

The motives for this interest are not difficult to analyze: Johannes
and Clara had entered into a communion of their souls, theirs had become
a true *Seelenverwandtschaft*. They longed for frequent communication,
for the contact and interchange of their strong personalities. Both were
pianists *par excellence*. Musically, therefore, the logical way to achieve
this amalgamation of ideas and emotions, to effect the longed-for companionship and the intercourse of the unsaid and the unspeakable, was
in joint performances on two pianos. In this form of ensemble each was
able to assert the strong artistic individuality which he had acquired by
birth and training. He could command the entire width of the keyboard
and draw from the full depth of its sonorities; he could project his
assertiveness and ruling strength. At the same time, their attentions now
focused upon one another, their minds united in common aspiration and
converged on that destiny which was to bless them with greater joys than
are ever given to the stark loneliness of the solo performer. In the concentration of their personalities, they won the experience of a perfect
partnership in duo-pianism, when the two musicians were indeed becoming *one*.

From this "Seelenverwandtschaft" as the spiritual association between
Clara and Johannes may best be termed, duo-pianism as an art form was
to benefit immeasurably. For Brahms not only saw himself inspired by
her friendship to write some early sketches for the two-piano medium,
but even much afterwards, when the romantic attachment to Clara Schumann had cooled, and when many miles separated the two, he repeatedly
invited her advice and criticism by resorting to this form of scoring
which provided a simple and convenient insight into an otherwise complicated composition.

The expediency last mentioned leads the discussion to the more practical reasons for the frequent employment of the duo-pianistic idiom by Brahms. Actually, it was the two-piano laboratory which furnished him with a tool for symphonic experimentation more readily accessible than any other, and one which at the same time proved to be most suitable in its closeness to orchestral conception. To the mind of Brahms, the tonal ideal was to be sought in the full employment of the symphony orchestra. Throughout his artistic development he aspired toward that final triumph and satisfaction to see himself the master of the orchestral body, commanding its challenging complexities and elusive subtleties. Like Franz Liszt, Brahms began his career as a pianist, a concert virtuoso to be sure. But unlike Liszt, he always thought of his chosen instrument as of the *pianoforte-orchestra,* an instrument which could be made to serve as a "surrogate" orchestra in its allusions of colors and sonorities. The two-piano medium permitted him a convenient mode of experimentation with vast symphonic projects. It encouraged the manipulation of majestic architectural plans. It stimulated the endless invention of polyphonic designs, the unhampered employment of rhythmic ideas. The combination of two pianos, moreover, satisfied his ever-present desire for emotional and structural discipline, in that each part could be made to act upon the other as an instrument of control and restraint as well as of propulsion. Different as his outlook and resulting attitude were from Liszt's conception of the medium, Brahms, much more than Liszt, made duo-pianism a form of symphonic workshop. With him it was the vehicle for ideas, the medium for sketches, drafts, or blue-prints. When more and more such two-piano scores were left along his long road to mature symphonic sovereignty, so large an arsenal of original material had come forth from the workshop that duo-pianism could rightfully claim it as its own domain. The testing ground had become a monument.

These two chief motivations for the frequent and long-lasting employment of the two-piano medium by Brahms, the personal and the practical, are often overlapping. At times, they are so closely integrated that a distinction becomes impossible. For that matter, any analysis of primary motives carries only subordinate significance when the ultimate result defies its evaluation in terms other than those of the absolute. Therefore, the following discussion of all such compositions by Johannes Brahms in which duo-pianism forms an integral part of the evolutionary process, will be restricted to purely factual comments.

Duet playing was a natural form of music-making in the Schumann home, a home of pianists. Ensemble performance occurred frequently; it was cultivated for its own sake through the rendition of original duet works, or it served the convenient condensation and reproduction of larger scores. To these traditional applications the function of the workshop was added. The piano duet became an experimental station in the process of creation. Brahms, having taken up residence in the Schumann home at Duesseldorf, living near the woman whom he admired and adored, found an ideal musical companion in Clara. She willingly offered her cooperation although their partnership was not at all times on an entirely equal basis. John N. Burk, who is the author of a book on Clara Schumann, describes the character of their musical relationship as follows:[1]

> "Clara was a little in awe of Brahms. When he was touchy about a new score of his own—its justification or its interpretation—she respected the rights of the composer, and said not a word. Sometimes he was so erratic and arbitrary in his tempi that it was impossible to keep with him. If a new work was in process of birth, he resented prying questions, and Clara allowed him his privacy, merely wondering in her diary what might be coming forth."

Of the many compositions which periodically were to come forth, those works will now be examined in which the two-piano medium was either the tool or the objective. Interest first centers upon a sonata for two pianos which Brahms produced in the spring of 1854. Initial mention of this work is made by Grimm who, on April 9, wrote to Joachim:

> "Kreisler (Brahms) is a most amazing man. He hardly delighted us by his *Trio* (the early version of the B major trio), when he already has finished again three movements of a *Sonata* for two pianos, which to me appear still more heaven-storming."

It is comparatively little known that the *First Piano Concerto in D minor, opus 15,* evolved from this sonata which, in its turn, came into being only in lieu of a symphony. The project of the symphony is mentioned by Brahms in a letter to Schumann, written in January 1854. The first movement then had already been orchestrated, and the second and third movements had been drafted. However, Brahms soon stated: "A good deal is wrong in the composition," and he subsequently postponed the project; actually, it was to take him another twenty years to produce his first symphony.

Two events took place during the early months of the year 1854 which exerted tremendous power over Brahms' thoughts and no doubt influenced his decision to abandon the symphony. These events, at the same time, shaped the very character of the sonata for two pianos into which the symphonic project then was converted. One of the two incidents was the fateful attempted suicide by Robert Schumann on February 27 when he threw himself into the Rhine, only to be committed to an insane asylum

---

1. Burk, *Clara Schumann,* p. 306.

and slow death after his rescue. Little later, in March, Brahms was submitted to another soul-shaking experience when he for the first time heard Beethoven's *Ninth Symphony* performed. To him, the first movement of this work appeared like "a musical correlation of the Schumann catastrophy" (Kalbeck). The impression of Beethoven's last symphony was nothing short of discouraging as far as his own aspirations to large orchestral forms were concerned. Ewen goes as far as describing Brahm's state of mind as "possibly terrified at the thought of venturing into Beethoven's world."[2]

As has been mentioned before, Brahms was not to recover from this depression and rally to compose his own *First Symphony* for a period of some twenty years; only then he had fully developed and evolved his own strong individuality, had acquired the self-reassurance of maturity and knew himself in command of the orchestral technique. Even in the early Seventies (the *First Symphony* was not completed until 1876), Brahms told his then intimate friend, Herman Levi, in Karlsruhe: "I shall never compose a symphony. You have no idea how one feels if you always hear such a giant (Beethoven) marching before yourself."[3] So overcome was he by the hearing of the *Ninth Symphony* in March 1854, so marked was his feeling of uncertainty, his sense of inferiority in dealing with the orchestral idiom, that he helped himself by revamping the sketches of his first symphonic ideas, recasting them into a sonata for two pianos. The pianoforte was the instrument which by then he had mastered in all its resources. In his want of an articulate orchestral language, in his insecurity with the technic of symphonic instrumentation, it was particularly the combination of two pianos which afforded him with an outlet for his orchestral thoughts. "In his dilemma, Brahms helped himself by binding to the piano what would not yet take hold in the yearned-for orchestra." (Kalbeck)

What there had been of an intended symphony, was soon converted into the *Sonata in D minor* for two pianos. The composition was completed in the spring of 1854, and it was played for the first time by the young composer and Clara Schumann at Klems. John N. Burk gives the following description of the occasion:[4]

> "On May 24, he suddenly produced the manuscript for a *Sonata in D minor* for two pianos (the first two movements were eventually to be used in the *First Piano Concerto*). They tried it through several times, and she was excited by this first full unfolding of the violent, demonic, darkly impassioned artist. As Brahms thundered through it, he seemed to tear at the piano, as if he must have a more dynamic and far-flung medium. The concept was plainly orchestral—Brahms was in deep self-search for the symphonic unfolding which Schumann had set as his goal."

2. David Ewen, *Music for Millions*, p. 107.
3. Kalbeck, *Johannes Brahms*, Erster Halbband, p. 165.
4. Burk, *Clara Schumann*, p. 306.

Clara Schumann's own diary entry on this event reads as follows: "I tried over the three movements of his sonata. They struck me as quite powerful, quite original, conceived with great breadth and more clarity than any of his earlier works. We played them twice, and on Sunday I shall play them with Dietrich."

Clara's first impression of the sonata grew with each further performance. Dietrich, himself an important composer, made the acquaintance of the work after his return from Leipzig to Düsseldorf. He then saw the sonata in a very careful manuscript, and some parts of the thematic material remained so unforgettable to him that he had no difficulty to recognize the music again when it reappeared in its various transformations later on.

Brahms was not satisfied as yet. There still was some element which the composer felt to be a fundamental inadequacy in this work. The material, conceived orchestrally at first, now seemed too rich for the two unaccompanied pianofortes. Grimm who, after Brahms and Dietrich, played the sonata with Clara Schumann, suggested the concerto form for it. The composer, best realizing himself that the music was essentially orchestral, agreed to a compromise between the two projects—symphony and piano sonata—and subsequently proceeded to combine the two versions. From the further revision eventually emerged the *Concerto in D minor for Piano and Orchestra, opus 15*. It is in the Maestoso and Adagio movements of this concerto that two movements of the sonata for two pianos are found again, now somewhat "simplified and lightened," as Brahms wrote to Joachim in April 1856. But the music of the opening movement unmistakably still was as rugged and militant as it had been when it was first conceived under the dire impression of Schumann's attempted suicide and subsequent confinement to an asylum. A slow scherzo in Sarabande tempo was omitted from the concerto. Temporarily discarded, it eventually underwent a transformation of its own and was given a rebirth when it appeared later in the second section of the *German Requiem*. There it was made to form the theme of a funeral march in the chorus "Behold All Flesh."

The gradual metamorphosis of one complex musical idea, from the germinal symphonic sketches to the final casts as piano concerto, and chorus respectively, is the interesting first example of the duo-pianistic laboratory of which Brahms was to avail himself so frequently later on. The two-piano sonata served in the important function of constituting the hub, chronologically and materially, in this long process of evolution. Indeed, the very form and character which the *Concerto, opus 15,* finally assumed are due to the intermediary position which is held by the two-piano sonata. From the latter, the concerto derived the addition of the pianoforte instrument, and thereby the essential piano idiom; from the first symphonic drafts came the orchestral garb and general conception of power and expansiveness. It is always to be remembered that it was the "uncertainty and helplessness of the young composer" (Kalbeck) which first caused him to veil his compelling orchestral thoughts in a two-piano sonata. Only after toiling for years with this titanic project, he arrived at the final form in which symphony and pianoforte found their synthesis. Thanks to the transformative position which the sonata for two pianos occupied, and the generating force which it exerted, Brahms could turn the D minor Concerto into his first symphonic achievement. Moreover, he created with it the first work of an entirely new genre which became known as that of the symphony with piano obligato. The proportions and the chief tenants are symphonic, the heroic attitude is general rather than soloistic, and even the key of D minor is reminiscent of Beethoven's Ninth which threw its shadow over the very origins of the work.

The sonata for two pianos in D minor, in Kalbeck's words[5] remained the "main work of 1854 which, originally intended as a symphony, then had been reduced to a sonata for two pianos, because the composer felt himself too weak to command the orchestra for a finale which would have been equal to his powerful intentions and commensurate to the first three movements." It has been seen how Brahms approached and temporarily solved the problem of this early orchestral weakness by resorting to the combination of two pianofortes. Evans, in his specialized discussion of the piano works by Johannes Brahms,[6] affirms this conclusion when he describes the first period of Brahms' writing for the instrument as "symphonic," because of its orchestral character. Brahms seemed to take his parts directly from the orchestra and convert them into the language of the pianoforte which then was more familiar to him. In contrast to Liszt who thought in a pianistic vein even when he wrote for the orchestra, Brahms inwardly felt compelled by the sonorities of the orchestral idiom even while he composed for the piano. His was the "piano orchestra," with all the implications of the latter, and it is easy to conclude that the

5. Kalbeck, *Johannes Brahms,* Vol. I, Chapter 7, p. 291.
6. Evans, *Handbook to the Pianoforte Works of Johannes Brahms,* Chapter V. This chapter, entitled "The Symphonic," falls short of an elaboration on the two-piano aspects. The work also lacks a discussion of the *Sonata for Two Pianos, opus 34 b,* and of the *Variations on a Theme of Haydn, opus 56 b.* In Index I, Section C (p. 305) entitled "For Two Pianos," the two-piano setting of the *Third Symphony* is omitted although this version, like that of the *Fourth Symphony,* was arranged by Brahms himself. On the other hand, the section lists among the two-piano arrangements one of the *Concerto in B flat Major for Piano and Orchestra, opus 83;* the latter work, however, was given by Brahms only an arrangement for one piano, four hands.

combination of *two* pianofortes gave him an even closer semblance of the full symphony orchestra.

The same anguish and struggle which accompanied the evolution eventually resolving in the D minor Concerto, was to attend the creative process culminating in the *F minor Quintet*. Even the sequence of stages in the course of the metamorphosis was similar, a sonata for two pianos forming the pivotal center between the primary version as string quintet and the final cast as quintet for piano and strings. The work was first created in 1862.[7] Originally it was scored as a string quintet with two violoncellos. Kalbeck mentions a few unsatisfactory attempts which were made to play this work in rehearsals. Brahms probably felt some fundamental inadequacy; possibly the strings alone proved incapable of expressing his capacious ideas, or else he had not yet acquired sufficient mastery in suitably writing for them. Realizing the shortcomings of the score, Brahms actually burned the manuscript of the original string quintet later on. Before committing the work to the fire, however, he proceeded to transcribe it into a sonata for two pianos. This version of the music, later published (in 1872) as *Sonata for Two Pianofortes, opus 34 b,* was completed during the winter of 1863-1864. On April 17, 1864, Brahms played the work together with the Liszt disciple, Karl Tausig, as his partner at a concert of the "Singakademie." The event was a special "Brahms-Evening," entirely devoted to the composer's own works. The collaboration between Brahms and Tausig at this time produced one of the most notable combinations in duo-pianistic history. Tausig was achieving a career which was nothing short of phenomenal despite his youth, and Brahms then had reached the height of his own pianistic mastery.

Again the two-piano version of this great chamber music work in F minor was to function as an intermediary objective only and as a stepping stone to further development. Clara Schumann's critical advice was instrumental in causing Brahms to search for still another medium through which to project this music. This definite form was ultimately arrived at when, in the summer of 1864, the composer arranged the material in its final version by scoring it as a quintet for piano and strings. The work, now commonly called the *F minor Quintet, opus 34a,* "shows souvenir-vestiges of its arduous evolution,"[8] but it nevertheless became one of the most popular among the chamber music compositions by Johannes Brahms when it was published in 1865.

As to the Sonata for two pianos which here demands the greater interest, it appears in Vol. XI of the Breitkopf and Haertel edition of

---

7. According to the Revisionsbericht to Vol. 8 of the *Johannes Brahms: Saemtliche Werke;* some sources place the origin a little earlier, circa 1861-1862.
8. Schauffler, *The Unknown Brahms,* p. 56.

the "Johannes Brahms, Saemtliche Werke." The sub-title of the headline: *After the Quintet, Op. 34 bis,* is an ambiguous one. According to the evidence submitted in the preceding investigation, the two-piano sonata not only was completed, but had even been publicly performed, before the scoring as piano quintet was undertaken. Only the opus numbers of the two versions have been reversed by the composer, contrary to their genesis. Afterwards, an identical procedure was applied by Brahms to the opus numbers for his Haydn Variations. They were classified as opus 56a and 56b respectively, regardless of the reverse sequence appertaining to their chronological order of composition and performance. Besides the misleading subtitle of the work ("After the Quintet, opus 34 bis"), a reference by Alfred Einstein gives additional cause to assume an erroneous succession of the two versions in date of composition and, more important, in their order of conception and development. Einstein writes:[9]

> "Schubertian also is the Quintet in F minor, op. 34; but the dramatic dialogue between the two bodies of sound is so marked that the work can be refashioned without essential change into the Sonata for Two Pianos, op. 34 bis."

The use of the word "refashioned" tends to give a wrong impression, both in material fact and in regard to the essentially theoretical position which two-piano writing occupied in the creative processes of Johannes Brahms. Also based on error is the opus number "34a" given to the Sonata by Vera Brodsky who calls the work "a unique achievement of duo-piano composition."[10]

At any rate, the musical substance is essentially the same in both opus 34a and 34b, although the quintet version has succeeded in achieving greater popular acclaim. Concerning the music itself, Schauffler maintains that[11]

> ". . . the Master never invented lovelier melodies, or wrote with a more exuberantly creative fecundity, and nowhere else worked out his material with the passionate verve of youth so perfectly balanced by the profound mastery and inner creativeness of a recently attained maturity."

Some comments by Ewen on the work contain the statement that[12]

> "Its elusive and subtle beauties are not easily grasped, and it was some time before its greatness was fully appreciated. It is profuse with thematic material, developed with consummate mastery, and it abounds in subtleties of expression which require intimacy for full appreciation."

Niemann, whose frequent comparisons between the music of Beethoven and Brahms are well known, discovers many elements of analogy in the

9. *Music in the Romantic Era,* p. 224.
10. A. E. Wier, *The Piano,* p. 351.
11. Schauffler, *The Unknown Brahms,* p. 403.
12. Ewen, *Music for Millions,* p. 119.

latter's opus 34. He writes of the work that it is

". . . full of pathos, grand and monumental, rebellious, harsh, and audacious to the verge of asperity, defiant in its strength and powerful in its sonority. . . . But it has generally escaped attention that the Brahmsian spirit of gentleness and resignation is striving against this defiant and passionate spirit. This appears in the first movement, often in a quite surprising manner, in a variety of mournful, touching passages, which are worked into the organic structure; among these are the second-theme group in F minor, with its thoroughly elegiac feeling, and the mysteriously subdued third-theme group in C-sharp minor. But it is quite patent in the slow movement, with its luxuriant profusion of tender, dreamy, Schubertian melodies. . . . And finally it is illustrated in the last movement with its Beethovenesque unrestrained humor, now jovial and boisterous, now full of ironically mocking laughter."

As far as the last movement is concerned, a brief comment by Hutcheson is noteworthy. Hutcheson points out[13] "that the martial third movement acquired greater force in the two-piano arrangement, since neither pianist need exercise restraint in mercy to the strings."

An analogy is frequently drawn, and indeed is suggesting itself, between the opus numbers 34b and 56b by Johannes Brahms. Like the F-minor Sonata (Quintet), the *Variations on a Theme by Haydn* also were published in alternate form. The two versions are for orchestra (opus 56a) and for two pianos (opus 56b), respectively. At once, it should be anticipated that critics find it impossible to attribute superiority to either of the captions and that "each version, in its own right, embodies a contribution of the first importance to its respective field." (Veinus) This unqualified acclaim of the variations in their two-piano setting is in marked contrast to the prevailing opinion regarding the two versions of opus 34 of which the quintet form is generally held to outrank the two-piano sonata.

There is another reason which counteracts a close analogy between the two compositions. The earlier work was definitely intended and designed as a specimen of chamber music, while the variations from all apparent signs are dominated and pervaded by their orchestral conception. This fundamental difference is formulated by Fuller-Maitland in the following statement:[14]

"Though the quintet, opus 34, appeared as a duet for two pianos, and the "Haydn" Variations similarly disposed count as a separate opus number, not as a transcription of an orchestral piece, yet it will be best to consider the former among the *chamber* compositions and the latter among the *orchestral*, seeing that the ultimate disposition of both is fixed by general consent and the master's own decision."

After these initial comments, the survey now proceeds to a discussion proper of the Haydn Variations, opus 56, by Brahms. There has always existed some uncertainty in regard to the evolution of this work. The

13. Hutcheson: *The Literature of the Piano*, p. 237.
14. Fuller-Maitland, *Brahms*, p. 94.

orchestral variations which, incidentally, constitute Brahms' first ambitious work exclusively for symphony orchestra and which therefore represent a direct preparation for the *First Symphony, Opus 68,* seem to possess chronological precedence, because of the opus number *56a* given to them by the composer; the two-piano version, bearing the opus number *56b,* superficially would appear to be second in line. However, as in the case of the F minor quintet, closer investigation reveals factually a reversal of priorities.

Several important details bear out the correctness of the assumption that the two-piano version preceded the orchestration of the work. The autograph of the duo-piano score, formerly in Spitta's possession, is given at the end the inscription: *Tutzing, July 1873.* Tutzing is a small town on Lake Starnberg in Upper Bavaria where Brahms had gone in May for his summer vacation. The composer then had a copyist make an easily readable duplicate of the manuscript score, to take it to Bonn for the Schumann Festival which began August 17. During the latter event, Brahms and Clara Schumann played the Variations on two pianos at a friendly gathering. The first printed edition of the two-piano version appeared in November of 1873.

Early in the same month, on November 2, the orchestral variations were premiered at a concert of the Vienna Philharmonic Society. This version was published only two months after the two-piano edition; it appeared in printed form early in 1874. However, the principal argument for conclusion that the orchestral variations were completed later than the two-piano score, derives from a letter which Brahms wrote from Tutzing on September 1. At that time he had returned from Bonn, and the two-piano variations had already found their first performance. The letter was addressed to his friend Levi in Munich; in this communication, Brahms asked Levi for music paper with 16 staves *"Quer-Format."* It is on the very same type of paper that the orchestral score of the Variations 6, 7 and 8, as well as of the Finale, was written, while two different kinds of paper were used for the earlier parts of the work. The original manuscripts here discussed are in the possession of Simrock.

Even without this evidence, it could well be assumed, according to the earlier discussion of the composer's working method, that the two-piano variations took precedence and reached an earlier completion even while Brahms from the beginning may have had in mind an orchestral dimension of the work. Kalbeck confirms this conclusion when he writes:[15]

"Which version is the original, cannot be decided with absolute assurance; the probability speaks, as far as the conception is concerned, for the priority of the

15. *Johannes Brahms,* Vol. II, Chapter X, p. 463.

orchestra variations, while in regard to the *time* of execution the precedence ("Vorrang") remains assured to the *piano* variations."

As to the work itself, it is "unquestionably one of the most vital creations in the entire two-piano repertoire" (Veinus). The theme was first drawn to Brahms' notice by Karl Ferdinand Pohl in the autumn of 1870. It was among some unpublished music supposed to have been written by Haydn. Brahms copied the second movement of a Divertimento in B flat for wind instruments. This movement was entitled *Chorale Sancti Antoni* and contained the theme which is now believed to have been originally a popular German chorale of Haydn's day. Subsequently, the melody was appropriated by Brahms; the chorale now became the point of departure for eight variations and a finale.

The theme is notable by itself; "its charmingly irregular rhythmical plan, beginning with two five-measure periods, continuing with four fours, and ending with a three, might have been conceived by such a master of exotic rhythms as Brahms himself."[16]

Unusual as it is, the theme provides a wonderful, hymn-like foundation for the excursions which Brahms undertakes from it and around it. It has great nobility and it furnishes a maximum of inspiration to the composer who presents every facet of romantic emotion ending in a passionate outburst of utmost grandeur. Even so, Niemann has termed the work an "intellectual tour de force," probably because Brahms, formalistically the most classic of all romantic composers, has "followed here his customary procedure of building a solid, even severely cerebral scaffolding beneath the surface expanse of warm, vibrant romantic music." (Veinus)

Of the many critical commentaries which exist on the work, only those by Schauffler, Tovey, and Veinus are here referred to. An interesting theory is advanced by Schauffler who at the same time deals with the programmatic interpretation of Kalbeck. Schauffler writes as follows:[17]

"For all its wide variety and wealth of contrast, the majority of its movements have one feature in common besides their often thoroughly hidden theme. Variations II and III are in the mood of those Allegrettos—like that of the C minor symphony—which Brahms developed as substitutes for the traditional light and rapid middle movements of his larger works; while Nos. V, VI, and VIII are true scherzos. We know that the Master liked to indulge in subtle and purely musical greetings to the shades of his mighty predecessors. Did he give the Variations their marked scherzoso character as a tribute to Haydn for his pioneer deed in first popularizing the term scherzo?

"Next to the finale, No. VII, a delicate idyll for the innocent flute, in Siciliano rhythm, is the most effective variation. It is marked grazioso. Kalbeck, whose weakest point was his desire to embellish absolute music with far-fetched literary programs, seriously contended that this work represents the temptations of St. Anthony the

16. Schauffler, *The Unknown Brahms*, p. 460.
17. *Ditto*, p. 417.

Great in the Egyptian desert; and that, of these temptations, 'the most terrible because the sweetest,' 'a Leda awaiting her swan,' a super-houri who embodies 'the quintessence of human voluptousness,' is none other than—the blameless Siciliano! Programmatists have seldom fallen to lower depths of absurdity than this."

Tovey's comments contain a piece of advice on how to listen to the Variations; it seems quite feasible that his remarks in connection with this work could be generalized and elevated into a procedure of how best to enjoy *any* set of variations. Tovey states:

"The listener need not try to recognize Haydn's melody throughout Brahms' Variations; he will have no difficulty in doing so wherever Brahms wishes; and an elaborate analysis would show something like a nervous system of melodic connexions. But the best way to enjoy these is to become familiar with the whole work. To begin with the finishing touches is not the best way to enjoy the whole. In music, as in all art that moves in time, the listener should fix his attention on some element that pervades the whole, not upon some guess as to the course of events. In a set of classical variations the all-pervading element is the shape of the whole theme. How its external details may be treated is a matter of decoration and wit."

Complementing Tovey's analysis, Veinus makes the following lucid remarks:[18]

"The melodics of each of the variations have a substantial beauty of their own and are quite independent of the St. Anthony Chorale. Brahms finds no need to keep continually before us the original melodic surface. Coherence between variations is to be sought in the position of each in the work as a whole, rather than in the physiological resemblance of each to the chorale prototype."

Further reference material in connection with this work can be found in a later chapter.[19] In closing the present discussion, it may be said that the parts of both instruments are treated masterfully, and that Brahms seems to have surpassed all previous achievements in the field of two-piano composition with this monumental work. The composer himself delighted in playing the variations frequently in partnership with Clara Schumann and with Elizabeth von Herzogenberg. His own approval may be considered as reliable a measure stick of estimation as would be applied only by the most severe judgment.

The composition of the Haydn Variations in their orchestral form convinced Brahms that he was now ready to undertake his first symphony. The latter was completed in 1876; three others followed within a period of nine years. After it has been observed how the two-piano medium entered as a crucial element into the genesis of the opus numbers 15, 34, and 56, further interest is aroused concerning the degree to which the duo-pianistic laboratory may have been employed also in the preparation of the major symphonic assignments. Inquiry into this phase yields only a

18. Program Notes to Brahms *Variations on a Theme by Haydn*, Victor Musical Masterpiece Series, M-799.
19. See Book III *The Literature*, Chapter XXIII, *The Standard Repertoire*.

few scanty records, for Brahms was generally reserved in his communications about his own works, and he became even more reluctant to mention them when they still were in a state of incompletion. The probability presents itself that Brahms now did not feel the need of a preliminary or intermediary two-piano version any more. He had matured into the clairvoyance of his orchestral conceptions and he now possessed the technical facility to express himself freely in the complex idiom of symphonic textures and structures. Thus knowing himself finally as master of the orchestra, he yet continued to regard the two-piano combination as an adequate medium for the conveyance of symphonic thought, line, form and colorit.

This distinctive function of duo-pianism Brahms upheld to the last. His own arrangements for two pianos of the *Third* and *Fourth Symphonies, opus 90* and *opus 98* respectively, evidence anew his belief in the expediency of the duo-pianistic idiom. Both arrangements were published by Simrock, but there is proof that the two-piano editions were not merely written upon commission, to satisfy the request of the publishers. Rather they came into being simultaneously with the orchestral scores, possibly as sketches for the latter, or more likely as the means of an immediate performance with the "surrogate orchestra" of two pianos. The purpose of the two-piano drafts therefore was one of rendering instantly audible that which was being created in the composer's mind. Preliminary hearings of the music made possible the most exacting tests regarding doubtful aspects in detail and proportion, and subsequent changes of the primary scoring may often have been the result of these preparatory examinations.

When Brahms first informed his close friends in Wiesbaden, Ehlert and Beckerath, of the existence of the F major Symphony, he wrote to them: "I have played the symphony often on two pianos with Bruell for the friends (in Vienna) . . . "[20] It can therefore be assumed that the two-piano medium fufilled a certain function in the creation of this symphony, Brahms' opus 90, and that again it formed a part of the workshop routine which the composer apparently had developed and for which such outstanding examples have been found in the histories of the D minor Piano Concerto, the F minor Quintet, and the Haydn Variations.

The two-piano arrangement of the *Third Symphony,* later published by Simrock, is also mentioned by Clara Schumann. In her diary she writes:[21]

20. Kalbeck, *Johannes Brahms,* Vol. III, Chapter VII, pp. 383-384.
21. Burk, *Clara Schumann,* p. 400.

"I have been able at last to play over the Third Symphony (arranged for two pianos) with Elise. When I had heard it the other day, I missed too much to have a real idea of its beauty. How I long to hear it again, now that I know every bar! It was cruel of Brahms to send me no more than half the arrangement. If I had been able to study the symphony beforehand, what a difference it would have made!"

There exist also records of similar two-piano drafts for the *Fourth Symphony*. One such sketch was played by the composer with Dr. Julius Roentgen. The draft showed an opening which was different from the beginning eventually adopted for the symphony; apparently, the original opening bars of that particular sketch were abandoned.[22] Additional and definite evidence is available of an arrangement for two pianos which was being prepared simultaneously with, if not prior to the instrumentation of the orchestral score. This knowledge derives from a communication sent by Brahms to his publisher Simrock. The letter, incidentally, is characteristic for the composer's reluctance to commit himself concerning any of his works as long as they still were in the process of preparation. It seems that Simrock had been eager, for what he termed "practical reasons," to receive a piano edition of the symphony, intending to print it together with or soon after the orchestral score. Brahms' answer, while it opposes the publisher's impatience with aloofness, reveals beyond doubt that such a piano arrangement already existed at that very time. The following is a quotation from the letter by Brahms to Simrock:[23]

"What practical reasons are there that I should soon edit a four-hand condensation (of the symphony)? First of all, I have not the slightest idea as yet whether I shall have printed the thing at all! On the other hand, however: if something most human should happen to me (so that I could not have any voice in the matter any more), then the symphony is to belong to you automatically, i.e. it is to be a gift to you as it lies here with me, in orchestral score and piano arrangement. Otherwise, however, I still want to think about it!"

The piano arrangement explicitly mentioned in the letter, indubitably was the two-piano version of the *Fourth Symphony* which was published by Simrock later on. Elizabeth von Herzogenberg and Clara Schumann who had been the first to be intimated into the existence of this symphony, received from Brahms a two-piano condensation of the entire work[24] which is probably identical with the arrangement just mentioned. The symphony was completed in 1885, and it happened to be played when Brahms attended his last concert on March 7, 1897, less than a month before his death. Pervaded by the melancholy of autumn, and carried by a "disciplined emotion of heroic character" (Ewen), this music brought to a culminating conclusion the composer's noblest symphonic aspirations. It

22. Schauffler, *The Unknown Brahms*, p. 168.
23. Kalbeck, *Johannes Brahms*, Vol. III, Chapter 8, p. 455.
24. Burk, *Clara Schumann*, p. 403.

is the proud merit of duo-pianism to have served as pivot and tool in this creative upsurge from beginning to end.

It remains to make brief reference to the works for piano duet, four hands on one keyboard, which have come from the pen of Johannes Brahms. They seem to have been inspired by much the same personal and practical motivations which caused their counterparts on two instruments to come into being. The chief difference between the duos for one and for two pianos seems to lie in the choice of subject matter; whenever the musical material is of a lighter and symphonically less complex nature, the more condensed scoring for one piano appears appropriate and sufficient. This theory applies equally well to the *Waltzes, opus 39,* the four volumes of *Hungarian Dances,* and the two sets of *Liebeslieder Walzer, opus 52* and *65.* The earlier *Variations on a Theme of Schumann, opus 23,* are more profound, poetic and more spacious in their masterful construction.

Vera Brodsky makes mention of Brahms' own two-piano adaptations of his Hungarian Dances,[25] but with these arrangements may be meant the excellent transcriptions by Robert Keller. As a matter of course, every duet score will lend itself automatically to performance on two rather than on one keyboard, with results which insure the greater freedom of the performers, and in addition offer the interchangeability of parts as a definite practical advantage. In consequence, duo-pianists frequently resort to this mode of performance,[26] and the justifiableness of the procedure has already been discussed in connection with the duet works of Schubert. However, the confines of classification restrict this survey to the works specifically designated by the composer for execution on two pianos.

As a matter of fact, Brahms has left one more work for incorporation into the strictly duo-pianistic category. This further addition to the original two-piano repertoire are his arrangements of five waltzes from *opus 39.* The original set of sixteen waltzes, composed for four hands on one keyboard, was transcribed by Brahms also for piano solo. These waltzes contain some of the master's most delicious melodies. They possess in abundance the captivating qualities of sweetness, leisure, and delight. In Einstein's words,[27] they are "something like an act of reverence to Vienna and to Schubert." Corresponding in essence with the *Liebeslieder* waltzes, "the character of the individual dances sometimes approximates

25. In Wier, *The Piano,* p. 351, and in *The MacMillan Encyclopedia of Music and Musicians,* p. 1899.
26. A recent recording of the *Liebeslieder Walzer* employs the two-piano team of Luboshutz and Nemenoff for the duet part of the work.
27. Einstein, *Music in the Romantic Era,* p. 225.

to the lilting Viennese waltz, but oftener to the easy-swaying *Laendler*" (Hanslick).

The five waltzes selected by Brahms from his opus 39 for arrangement in two-piano form are those numbered in the original cycle as Nos. 1, 2, 11, 14, and 15; the last is the well-known little gem in A flat major. The arrangements were dedicated to Frau Seraphine Tausig, the wife of his good friend, the celebrated pianist Karl Tausig. While the two-piano version gives marked predominance to the first piano part and relegates the second instrument to an accompanying role almost throughout, the total effect achieved is a most felicitous blending and constitutes a full exploitation of duo-pianistic sonorities.

The character of these little pieces is truly intimate, and if examples ever come to be cited for the classification of certain two-piano works into the genre of *chamber* music, these miniatures most ideally embody the term. "In no work of Brahms has his pensive side, his quiet, deep delight in simple, domestic joys, been so frankly and simply revealed as in these waltzes. Through them one comes quickly into personal and affectionate touch with him."[28] A further characterization is hardly needed to describe the intimate nature of the chamber-music genre as a whole.

It is with his ingratiating contribution to the literature of chamber music, the two-piano settings of *Five Waltzes from opus 39*, that leave is now taken from the Master Brahms. If duo-pianism can claim to have provided him with a medium for the articulate expression of his early symphonic conceptions, and with a perfect working tool thereafter, it is from his strength, in return, that two-piano art derived the power and glory of its First Golden Era.

---

28. From the program notes of a Whittemore and Lowe recital.

CHAPTER VIII

THE FIRST GOLDEN ERA

Up to this time, the duo-pianistic evolution has been surveyed collectively in its two most important aspects which are those of composition *for* and of performance *in* the medium. The fact that composer and performer in many cases were identical, encouraged this procedure as the most logical course to follow. From about the middle of the nineteenth century on, however, an intensive cultivation of two-piano playing as a specialized ensemble art became noticeable. It soon developed into a full-grown concert activity, causing its specific applications and problems, and evoking an appeal and reaction all of its own. For reasons of this specialization, it seems advisable to now follow individually the separate branches of this fast growing musical system.

Attention will first be devoted to the development of artistic performance. Subsequently, a survey is proposed with regard to those composers who have contributed to the literature and who indeed are forming an array of distinguished names. Next, the discussion will proceed to an investigation of the extent to which duo-pianism has spread in its manifold utilizations. In conclusion, a prognostic estimation is to be attempted through an analysis of the trend which two-piano art has taken and through an outlook into the expected future.

To begin with, the spotlight will be focused upon the group of professional musicians who, through their performances, have promoted and perfected the concert form of duo-pianism during the later part of the nineteenth century. Within this group, two principal types of performers will be incurred who devoted themselves to duo-pianistic endeavors. There are first those who occasionally combined for sporadic performances. While they were helpful in propagandizing the still much neglected field, they do not occupy the same high rank in the history of the art as those who formed the earliest permanent teams which frankly specialized in this ensemble type.

During the following discussion, the first group of occasional two-piano combinations is anticipated although their activities in many instances overlapped far into the period when permanent teams already existed, and when the reputation of the art had begun to be grounded on the accomplishments of such specialized duo-pianists.

It was in the wake of the meteoric career of Franz Liszt that a virtuosic *Goetterdaemmerung,* a "Twilight of the Gods" of the keyboard, was throwing its shadows on the musical stage. Men like von Buelow, de Pachmann, d'Albert, and Busoni continued the great tradition of their master, with aplomb and splendor, but they were unable to further raise the standards of his accomplishments. Each of these virtuosos achieved a most distinguished career, to be sure, and they all carried to its glorious conclusion the brilliant and romantic musical era of the nineteenth century. None, however, had the genius to equal, let alone to surpass the pianistic record height which had been achieved by Liszt.

Still encountered with many of these virtuosos is a practice which had been observed in the period of the Grand Duo, during the time of Moscheles and Herz: The occasional collaboration between two such keyboard titans, each of whom was primarily famous as an exponent of solo virtuosity, continued to constitute a favorite attraction with performers and audiences alike. Superficially seen, this practice would appear merely as a continuation of the Grand Duo, but an important difference lies in the fact that now the idea of presenting a full-length two-piano recital is first encountered. Both artists begin to take equal shares in the proceedings, while previously the concert-giving solo virtuoso used to invite his colleague only for a special two-piano number or a grand finale.

The concept of the two-piano recital as an individual type of concert therefore seems to have been born at this time. It may have originated as a symptomatic gesture coming from those who seriously professed their own quest for new horizons in a time of pianistic *fin de siècle.* Several such concerts are known which were given by idolized exponents of the keyboard whose reputation, now as then, rests on their gigantic individual accomplishments. The members of such sporadic two-piano combinations are deserving of credit for having been among the first pioneers of an art form which they themselves may have regarded only as an ephemeral "novelty." Nevertheless, by their promotion of the duo-pianistic idea as such, they were instrumental in stimulating the formation of the first specialized and permanent two-piano teams.

Such artists who joined in occasional ensemble appearances, although their primary and usual aspirations were devoted to the field of solo virtuosity, included Rafael Joseffy and Moritz Rosenthal, Vladimir de Pachmann and Maggie Oakey, and Eugen d'Albert and Teresa Carreño. The mere assembly of these distinguished names already would be apt to conjure up the faded glory of a proud and brilliant era.

Typical examples for the new type of two-piano concerts were provided by Joseffy and Rosenthal who have made duo-pianistic history by giving what has been termed "a magnificent pair of concerts" in New York and Brooklyn in the years 1888 and 1890. Considering the reputation of supreme proficiency which each of the two virtuosos held in that day, the artistic level of their joint performances indeed must have been extraordinary. Their brace of concerts was nothing short of epoch-making and provided a tremendous stimulus for further efforts in the two-piano field.

Moritz Rosenthal, one of the truly great among pianists, also has to his record a performance of Chopin's *Rondo in C major* which he played together with his teacher, Carl Mikuli. The latter, himself a pupil of Chopin, at the time was director of the conservatory in Lemberg. Their public performance of the only composition which Chopin wrote for the two-piano medium, took place in 1872.

Not less sensational than the concerts by Joseffy and Rosenthal were the joint appearances of Eugen d'Albert and his wife Teresa Carreño, both phenomenal virtuosi of the late nineteenth century. They are recorded to have given a few memorable two-piano recitals in Europe which, taking into consideration the marked personalities of these artists, must indeed have been unusual. Silvio Scionti feels inclined to comment on their duo-pianistic adventures with the following words:[1]

> "What a singular experience such a recital must have been to an audience, with a kind of musical contest between a Walküre and a Wotan, two giants of pianism at two keyboards. From accounts of their almost incessant domestic battles, this could not have been two-piano playing at its highest perfection as, first of all, this art demands transcendant understanding, sympathy, and psychic cooperation between the participants."

Another famous virtuoso of the same period was Vladimir de Pachmann, whose accomplishments in certain special phases of piano art still are un-rivalled. Following one of his concerts in England, de Pachmann made the acquaintance of a young lady pianist whose name was Maggie Oakey. She soon became one of his pupils and, in the year 1884, his wife. They subsequently joined forces in a two-piano combination. In 1890, the de Pachmanns gave a number of concerts in Europe and America; they visited the United States for the first time in 1892. Everywhere they were

1. *The Fascination of Two-Piano Playing*, "The Etude," September 1939, p. 567.

received with the greatest acclaim, and they will always need to be remembered among the important husband and wife teams of duo-pianistic history.

Other occasional two-piano concerts by keyboard masters of superior stature are recorded to have been presented by such pairs as von Bülow and d'Albert, Rachmaninoff and Siloti, Myra Hess and Irene Scharer. Stirring beyond measure in their audience appeal as these sporadic performances of prominent piano virtuosos no doubt proved to be, they lacked the frequency and regularity to serve as an effective promotion for the art. Moreover, they could hardly be expected to possess the finesse in ensemble playing which is frequently achieved by players of less brilliant individual equipment who set their aim of artistic satisfaction upon the perfection of the team work as such.

The reasons why the teaming of solo pianists with superlative individual equipment will not automatically produce the best results, contrary to superficial expectation, are formulated by Silvio Scionti in the following statement:[2]

"Two virtuosi of the pianoforte have been heard together in an occasional two-piano recital, but rarely with marked success. Their limited number of rehearsals and their unavoidable concern over the loss of solo personality would naturally impair the possibility of that resourceful tonal adjustment and color and subtle rhythmical freedom (the life of music) which distinguishes two-piano art from two-piano playing."

It must always be remembered that none of the great virtuosos who have been mentioned in the foregoing paragraphs, in any sense specialized in the two-piano field such as it already had become the established practice and accepted condition for the regular and permanent two-piano teams of truly professional standings to which attention will be turning shortly. Important as these occasional two-piano concerts had been in their function of conditioning the public to a full-length recital program entirely devoted to the duo-pianistic idiom, such events still were considered more of a sensational entertainment than really regarded as part of the regular fare in the musical calendar. The concert going public, accustomed to associate the name of either Joseffy or Rosenthal with a soloist of the highest caliber and as a drawing power in his own right, could not but see in the collaboration of two so brilliant stars something of a "double feature" attraction. While audiences enjoyed the unusual collective offering, they yet persisted in individual evaluation. The personal reputation of the soloists in a sense became the very detriment of their duo-pianistic aspirations. As long as each of them was mainly known for his consuming artistic personality in solo performance, the purpose in coupling their

2. *The Fascination of Two-Piano Playing,* "The Etude," September 1939, p. 567.

individualities had to remain incomprehensible to the average music lover.

It must also be pointed out that sometimes even the artists themselves lacked the vision of a clear artistic objective in the combination of two pianofortes. They laid themselves open to the suspicion of performing a stunt when, at times, they chose to play original solo compositions on the two instruments in unison with each other. This trick plainly was intended for audience effect, but artistically it had to remain worthless because of the stifling precision necessary in such duplication of identical parts. Little wonder then that the public looked upon two-piano playing largely as an exhibitive feat, depending in its interest and appeal on purely mechanical matters, such as how it was possible for the two artists to start together without any outside signals and how they managed to maintain perfect timing throughout the composition. The severe reproach of lacking artistic freedom in the two-piano medium literally was invited by this unfortunate practice, and it had a stifling effect on the recognition of the art for many years to come.

The growing realization that a two-piano team needs to be an organic unit rather than a duplication of soloists, was one of the chief motivations for the formation of the first combinations which frankly specialized in this new musical idiom and with all their energies aspired to raise it to the level of an accepted concert medium. It may also have been the reaction against the powerful influence of the individual champion of the piano, his glorification, and his autocratic and monopolistic reign, which created the desire to counteract the dazzling effects of solo virtuosity by the more subtle nuances of an ensemble art. The latter tendency may have been further generated by the growing awareness that, after the seemingly unsurpassable standards set by Liszt, a *non plus ultra* in solo performance had been reached. Confronted with an apparent dead-end, the imagination was stirred into the exploration of new possibilities, and thereby the ground was being prepared for an altogether new orientation of which duo-pianism became a manifestation. While the many went on to spend their efforts as epigones of the great solo pianists, a few resolved to form the first two-piano teams of more than casual association, and, as a consequence, of true and lasting significance.

This then was the time when the spearhead of permanent ensembles appeared on the musical scene, duo-pianists who acquired their reputation entirely through the excellency of their two-piano work rather than by individualistic accomplishments. Forerunners were the Hungarian brothers, Louis and Willi Thern, who made Vienna their home. They fully deserve the title "pioneers of two-piano art," in that they were the very first musicians to form an ensemble with the specific intent of specializing in two-piano recitals, and with the declared purpose of perfecting this medium to a full-fledged concert activity.

The Thern brothers were the sons of Karl Thern (1817-1886) who in 1841 became a conductor at the Budapest opera and from 1853 to 1864 was a professor at the Conservatory in the Hungarian capital. Both boys received their training mainly from their father. Louis Thern (1848-1920) in addition was a pupil of Moscheles and Reinecke at the Leipzig Conservatory; he eventually became a professor at the Conservatory in Vienna. Willi Thern (1847-1911) likewise studied with Moscheles and Reinecke, and there is little doubt that the great interest which both their teachers took in two-piano art provided an important and possibly decisive stimulus to the brothers to entirely devote themselves to this medium.

The extended concert tours of Louis and Willi Thern took place in the years from 1864 to 1868. These journeys led them through Germany, France and Belgium, the Netherlands and England, and brought about a serious interest in two-piano playing as a self-dependent form of musical culture. Although undertaken as an initial venture in practically virgin territory, the duo-piano artistry of the brothers attained considerable fame at their own time, and their ensemble became "the delight and astonishment of all Europe" (McKinney). The public recognition must have been gratifying to them. Their father and mentor, who travelled with them, wrote a number of original two-piano compositions especially for them, having in his own right acquired status as a composer of three operas and much other music. The older Thern is also remembered for a number of two-piano arrangements which are still effective, as for instance that of the *Turkish March* by Beethoven.

While the Thern brothers must be credited with having established the historic precedence of forming the first specialized concert two-piano team, and while theirs was also the first career of extended touring, another combination was not less acclaimed at the end of the nineteenth century. The names of these duo-pianists were Louis and Suzanne Rée. The male member of this team, Louis Rée, was of Scotch ancestry; he was born in Edinburgh in 1861. After first studying at the Stuttgart Conservatory, he became a pupil of Leschetizky. Rée eventually settled in Vienna, the home town of his pupil, wife and two-piano partner, Suzanne Pilz. Following their marriage, they gave many successful two-piano recitals and established themselves in the annals of duo-pianism as one of the earliest permanent teams with outstanding merits. Moreover, they rank in history as the first famous husband and wife combination.

Louis Rée, in addition to his activities as concert pianist and teacher, also distinguished himself as a composer. His works include a piano concerto, numerous piano pieces, waltzes for four hands, and several compositions for two pianos, notably the *Suite Champêtre* and a set of *Variations*.

The first duo-pianists for whom this designation specifically was coined and to whom it actually was first applied, were the American sisters, Rose and Ottilie Sutro. It was their two-piano association which inspired the originator of the name "duo-pianists" to create this poignant term for the executants of two-piano music. Now in common usage, the term also supplied a derivation for the art itself: *Duo-pianism*.

Both Sutro sisters were born in Baltimore, Rose in 1870 and Ottilie in 1872. They began studying the pianoforte with their mother when each was eight years of age; eventually, they became pupils of Karl Barth at the Berlin Hochschule. They were appearing in two-piano recitals from 1894 on. Their debut took place in Steinway Hall at London, England, and their American debut followed in Brooklyn, New York, during the same year. Their concerts, distinguished by a unique character, covered most of Europe during extended tours until the outbreak of the First World War in 1914. The artists were distinguished by many honors, among which was that of a private performance for Queen Victoria.

The eminence of the Sutro sisters is borne out by the fact that they enjoyed the friendship and respect of Brahms, Saint-Saens and Richard Strauss. Among the notable composers who wrote for them were Max Bruch *(Double Concerto, opus 88)*, Schuett, Hollaender, Floersheim and Rudolph.

From 1914 on, when the war interrupted their concerts in Europe, the activities of the Sutros were carried on in America. Their career attracted wide attention and helped to break the ground for the new art form. They have edited a large number of two-piano arrangements, which still are widely used; with these added to the influence exerted by the pair through the media of concert and radio, their work in behalf of two-piano art represents a lasting promotion.

As a matter of record, it is mentioned that the Sutro sisters probably were the first musicians of American nationality to make two-piano playing their professional specialty. The success of their activities, achieved in the centers of both continents and therefore embracing the entire sphere of Western civilization, did much to promote the young musical culture of their own home country.

It remains the historic merit of the three pioneer teams just discussed—Louis and Willi Thern, Louis and Suzanne Rée, and Rose and Ottilie Sutro—that duo-pianism became a recognized form of musical ensemble art in the late nineteenth century. Thanks to their highly specialized performances, and the public acclaim attending them, a legacy of success and artistic acceptance was quickly established for this youngest branch of instrumental combinations. The fertile soil thus provided, a great flowering of music in the two-piano medium began with the turn of the century. A veritable array of new teams launched the upsurge. Whereas Romanticism as a period and pianistic solo virtuosity as one of its manifestations still held full sway, an increasing number of keyboard artists began to seek their fortunes in the new and challenging enterprise of joining forces in a pianistic companionship. Solo virtuosity with its pronouncedly individualistic, egocentric, and sometimes erratic utterances was deliberately opposed by a new type of mutual compatibility, long known and cultivated in other branches of chamber music, but never before tried out among pianists themselves. Together with the growing realization that the "twilight of gods of the keyboard" had arrived, there appeared the dawn of a new promise for all piano art.

So much success and distinction was being achieved for the young movement that, in retrospect, it appears justifiable to classify the entire period, from the Therns to the Lhevinnes, as the *First Golden Era* of duo-pianism. During the first decade of the twentieth century, the Sutro sisters continued their successes in Europe, but their triumphs were soon paralleled by newcomers to the field who considerably deepened the ranks of professional teams and achieved even greater heights of accomplishment in the perpetual quest for perfection. The duo-pianists who will here be singled out from the gross of their colleagues, are those who beyond doubt command a rank of historic importance. They are the teams of Bauer and Gabrilowitsch, Hutcheson and Randolph, Maier and Pattison, and Josef and Rosina Lhevinne. The careers of all these artists have been so outstanding, and their fame remains so radiant even several decades after their retirement, that their permanent position in two-piano history stands beyond question.

The success of the duo-pianistic association between Bauer and Gabrilowitsch presents something of a paradox. Notwithstanding the supremacy as a solo virtuoso which each of the partners could claim for himself, irrespective of the occasional character and fluctuating frequency of their two-piano recitals, these pianists seem to have established with comparatively few concerts a standard of perfection which up to this day has remained a measure of accomplishment to many. Vincenz Ruzicka, a member of the contemporary two-piano team of Dougherty and Ruzicka, is only one of those who hold the explicit opinion that Bauer and Gabrilowitsch still are unsurpassed as the finest team of all times, past and present.

Harold Bauer (1873-) and Ossip Gabrilowitsch (1878-1936) both are primarily noted as outstanding solo piano virtuosos. Bauer, of German-English parentage, was born in New Malden, near London. Until the age of 19, he studied to become a violinist, but from 1893 on he quickly established his reputation as a pianist in France, Russia, and throughout Europe. His debut in the United States took place in 1900.

Bauer is a pupil of Paderewski whose acquaintance he made, curiously enough, in a role approximating that of duo-pianist. When Bauer first went to Paris as a violinist, expecting the musical world to bow before him, he had very little money. He soon found out that engagements in the field of his first choice were not easy to obtain, but that piano accompanying was apt to be more marketable.

> "Bauer decided to use his knowledge of the instrument and, after a few weeks practice, succeeded in securing several engagements. His first chance came very soon. He was asked to substitute for another man who was to accompany Paderewski on a second piano. 'At that time,' says Bauer, 'I knew about enough to be able to play the essential notes in a difficult passage—those that could not be spared!' Paderewski was evidently impressed, for he gave him helpful hints from time to time, and got him a job."

Thus writes Gdal Saleski in his book *Famous Musicians of a Wandering Race.*[3] Harold Bauer's rapid rise to fame as a pianist, and his ensuing triumphant career, still are commonly remembered and therefore need no elaboration at this time.

The late Ossip Gabrilowitsch was an eminent Russian pianist and conductor, trained at the Petrograd Conservatory. His teachers included Rubinstein and Leschetitzky. In 1918 he became the conductor of the Detroit Symphony Orchestra, a position which he held with great distinction.

Bauer and Gabrilowitsch, in addition to their individual attainments as solo performers and scholars of the first rank, reached the highest level of ensemble accomplishments. The artists thereby demonstrated that the simultaneous pursuit of solo and group activities in music is not inconsistent with the possibility to attain the greatest success in either. They have earned for themselves lasting merit by making invaluable contributions towards the establishment of duo-pianism as an independent art form, both in popular acclaim and critical approval. Their position in the history of performing exponents is indeed exceptional in that they succeeded to elude the general norm by achieving the pinnacle of the art without devoting their entire career to two-piano playing. They understood to reconcile their unquestioned status as individual virtuosi with the achievement to reach the foremost rank among the accomplished two-piano ensembles of all times. With their great individual reputation and

3. P. 291.

popularity, and notwithstanding their manifold separate activities, they succeeded in making a historic contribution to duo-pianistic advancement with their noble annual two-piano recitals. Their supreme accomplishments have continued to exert a lasting influence upon the development of the art. It is the fact that their activities were of an incidental and irregular character which makes their position in the field nothing short of phenomenal. Whatever casual contributions they made to the art, they have remained of a significance sufficiently great to place Bauer and Gabrilowitsch into the front line of the truly outstanding duo-pianists now as then.

Of an essentially different type was the renowned team of Hutcheson and Randolph. Their association, which has proved a strong promoting force in the history of duo-pianism, came about through the sympathetic collaboration of two highly trained pianists and pedagogues, each of whom attained to prominent positions in the world of music education. Ernest Hutcheson (1871-) is of Australian-American extraction. He studied with Vogrich, Reinecke and Stravenhagen, first acquiring reputation as a child prodigy. His career led him from the directorship of the piano department at the Peabody Conservatory in Baltimore to that of the Institute of Musical Art and subsequently, in 1940, to the presidency of the Juilliard School of Music in New York. Hutcheson is the author of a book on piano literature (1949) and also gained repute as a composer; his concerto for two pianos and other works for the duo-piano medium were the direct outgrowth of his intimate familiarity with the art.

Harold Randolph (1861-1927) made his debut in 1885 at Baltimore. Among his teachers were Carl Faelton and Asgar Hamerik; it was the latter whom he afterwards succeeded as director of the Peabody Conservatory.

In their two-piano association, Hutcheson and Randolph attained a high level of accomplishment. Their status in the field was based on a scholarly approach and intellectual penetration of the medium. Consequently, it is appropriate to speak of these duo-pianists as of the "academic" team. Reserve and control, critical self-observation and scientific search for aesthetic truth were the apparent tenants of their artistic combination.

In marked contrast to the qualities just mentioned, the characteristics which distinguish the team of Maier and Pattison are those of enthusiasm, spontaneity and exuberance. The artists seemed to possess an ever-present flair for the improvisational, and throughout their long career, the quality of eternal youth was a salient impression radiated by their work.

Maier and Pattison constitute one of the most celebrated two-piano teams on record. Attaining to international fame, they represented, following the Sutro sisters, one of the earliest all-American combinations. Guy Maier was born in Buffalo in 1892. He studied at the New England Conservatory of Music in Boston and was a pupil of Proctor, Juon, and later of Schnabel in Berlin. Lee Pattison, born in Grand Rapids, Wisconsin, in 1890, had his training with Baermann and also with Schnabel. The friends made their debut as duo-pianists in Jordan Hall in Boston in 1916 and shortly thereafter proceeded to New York's Aeolian Hall for their first appearance in the metropolis. Both recitals were extraordinarily successful.

In 1918, during the First World War, Maier and Pattison performed in Paris. When they discovered how popular the two-piano combination could be, they gave impromptu performances behind the front lines in France. After the war, Maier and Pattison became the pacemakers of duo-pianism in the concert field. They played with many of the leading orchestras on both continents and gave uncounted recitals. The European centers in which they appeared included, among others, London, Paris, Berlin, Amsterdam and The Hague. They also visited Australia and Honolulu. Extensive tours of the United States took the team into many remote communities which previously had never witnessed a two-piano performance. Thus bringing their art to every section of the country, Maier and Pattison indeed became the "barnstorming" pair of duo-pianists.

Foremost composers felt inspired to write concertos and other special two-piano music for this famous team. Notable among those who contributed works in the larger forms are composers like Ernest Hutcheson, Leo Sowerby, Arthur Bliss, and Edward Burlingame Hill. Others who saw themselves stimulated by the art of Maier and Pattison to write in the two-piano idiom included Leopold Godowsky, Albert Elkus, Marion Bauer, Daniel Gregory Mason, and Ernst Bacon. Many now well-known compositions were introduced to American concert audiences by the celebrated team, such as *En Blanc et Noir* by Debussy, *Jeux de Plein Air* by Germaine Tailleferre, *Puppazetti* by Alfredo Casella, and *Moy Mell* by Arnold Bax.

The unbroken two-piano association between Maier and Pattison extended from 1916 to 1931. It terminated after both partners married and moved to different sections of the country. Their official farewell tour took place in the season of 1929-1930. Since that time, they have appeared together only occasionally. Guy Maier formed a new two-piano partnership with his wife, Lois, and this ensemble also achieved some success. A great deal of distinction was further attained by Maier in his capacity as an arranger of numerous two-piano scores and as a tireless editor and writer on musical subjects. Both he and Pattison, who gained much attention as a composer of piano pieces and songs, eventually devoted themselves entirely to pedagogy. In the field of music education, they have continued their fruitful influence upon the evolution of two-piano art to which they have so eminently contributed.

Maier and Pattison are still regarded so highly among audiences and authorities alike that Silvio Scionti, himself a leader in the duo-pianistic movement, aptly describes their significance with the following words:[4]

> "The present wide-spread revival of interest (in two-piano art) . . . must be credited to the magnificent initiative of the famous duo-pianists, Guy Maier and Lee Pattison."

No better tribute to the historic status of this team could be paid, and a future gallery of famous duo-pianists will prominently display the busts of this triumphant pair.

Apparently intending to bestow the highest praise upon the team, a critic once said regarding a certain pair of pianists which has been discussed in the foregoing paragraphs: "Widely differing and unusually complemental in temperament, (they) . . . for years played so skillfully against each other as to make their ensemble seem the result of one instrument and one intellect."[5] This particular commendation can readily be extended to many of the leading combinations; it indeed seems to represent the highest tribute and final recognition which possibly could be achieved. However, the Lhevinnes replaced the trait of "playing *against* each other" with the no less characteristic quality of all-pervading sympathy and unanimity which transcended all other aspects of their teamwork. Their art was marked by a perfect fusion of two personalities and closely approached the ideal of perfection. If Bauer and Gabrilowitsch are held by many to have been the most brilliant and accomplished two-piano team of past history, they certainly are finding close rivals for the highest rank in the combination of Josef and Rosina Lhevinne. For several reasons, it would appear that the crown of the Golden Age of Duo-Pianism eventually must fall to the Lhevinnes. Such final causes include the permanent nature of their association, the frequency of their sterling performances, and the unparalleled influence which they have exerted throughout a long period of time over a vast audience.

These matchless artists actually seem to have dominated the entire duo-pianistic period which in the title of this chapter has been called "The First Golden Era." The beginnings of their association, as appears natural in this and similar cases of the husband and wife ensemble, lay in the mutual attraction of the partners. Added to their personal attach-

---

4. *The Fascination of Two-Piano Playing*, "The Etude," September 1939, p. 567.
5. Howard D. McKinney in *Advocating Freer Use of Two Pianos*, Fischer News Edition, October-December 1933.

ment, the congeniality of musical interests led, wih the inevitableness of
a basic law, into the merging of their lives and talents. For the musical
world, this partnership in marriage and profession produced a team of
the greatest importance in the history of duo-pianism.

An account of their meeting is given by Gdal Saleski who writes as
follows:[6]

> "When Josef was nineteen years old, he met a young lady, Rosina, a little younger
> than himself, at one of the numerous house parties of the neighborhood in Moscow,
> where he lived. Both played the piano and became close friends. Rosina went to
> Safonoff at the Conservatory and, like Josef, finished the course by winning the
> gold medal, being the first girl to achieve that honor. She wanted to continue her
> studies and the director advised her to coach with Lhevinne. This led to a romance,
> but the formalities required in Russia at that time had to be complied with, so they
> could not marry until after his service in the army. After this another tour of a
> year, made necessary by a contract, was fulfilled. Finally the marriage took place,
> and the couple took up residence in Tiflis, where Josef had been engaged as pro-
> fessor in the Conservatory. Here they spent three years, during which period the
> plans for their joint recitals and his world tour were launched and perfected."

Rosina Lhevinne herself describes the birth and growth of the famous
piano ensemble with her husband in the factual manner which distinguishes her personality and her art:[7]

> "My entrance into the field of two-piano playing was quite by chance. In 1898,
> when Mr. Lhevinne and I were married, eight days after my graduation from the
> Imperial Moscow Conservatory, I firmly decided not to attempt a career of my own.
> Cesar Cui, the composer-general who knew my work, did not approve of this
> decision, and one day paid us a visit. He appeared in his glorious uniform gray
> coat lined with scarlet, white gloves and a sword. The purpose of his visit was to
> ask us to take part in a charity concert of which he was the chairman. He requested
> we play a new suite by Anton Arensky, our harmony teacher.
>
> "The next day after the concert, the newspaper gave as much space to the
> composition and the phenomenon of having two grand pianos on the stage, as
> to our playing. The success of this concert impelled us to decide on a certain
> professional career for me as well. However, we never gave recitals devoted only
> to two pianos. Our programs always consisted of two groups played by Mr. Lhevinne
> alone and two groups played by us together. In some way I think this arrangement
> made our programs more interesting, for the original literature for two pianos is
> very limited and the solo literature is certainly vast and beautiful. It also gave the
> opportunity to the public to hear an artist of Mr. Lhevinne's stature play alone,
> as well as in two-piano ensemble. We played many solo recitals and with the
> major orchestras of Europe and America, but I held to my original idea not to
> attempt an independent career.
>
> "However, in 1938 at our fortieth anniversary concert in Carnegie Hall with
> Orchestra, Mr. Lhevinne insisted on my playing a concerto by myself. The program
> consisted of the Chopin E minor Concerto which I played, the Tchaikowsky Con-
> certo played by Mr. Lhevinne, and finally the Mozart E Flat Concerto for two
> pianos. Of all the many concerts we played together, it is this and the one we
> played in 1940 in the Hollywood Bowl that I recall most vividly. During these

6. Saleski, *Famous Musicians of a Wandering Race*, p. 345.
7. Rosina Lhevinne, *The Spirit of Ensemble*, Pan Pipes, February 1949.

many years, we made a very gratifying observation of the public's increased appreciation of two-piano ensemble work."

Josef Lhevinne (1874-1944) was to pass away only a few years after that memorable concert in Hollywood Bowl. He will, however, always live in the annals of piano art as one of the greatest virtuosos of all times. That he and his wife, Rosina Lhevinne (1880-), who had retired from solo activity after their marriage, succeeded in a compromise which did justice to Mr. Lhevinne's outstanding solo virtuosity and yet permitted them to support their two piano ideals with unfailing devotion, is ample evidence of their supremely harmonious personalities. The same deep human understanding and love permeated their life and their music, welding the two experiences into one great reality. If ideals mostly lead a phantom existence, Josef and Rosina Lhevinne made theirs come true. They therefore may rank in duo-pianistic history as the "ideal" team.

After her husband's death in 1944, Rosina Lhevinne has continued her work as one of the world's outstanding teachers. Victor Babin does not hesitate to term her "the one single authority who knows most about piano playing." Mme. Lhevinne is a member of the faculty at Juilliard in New York; she also spends some time in Los Angeles, teaching at the local Conservatory. She has written a number of articles on duo-pianism, and her lucid remarks on this topic will be frequently incurred in later chapters.[8] Nor has her interest in the art of piano ensemble resigned itself to memoirs and theories alone. Quite recently, in 1949, Rosina Lhevinne joined duo-pianists Vronsky and Babin in a recording of Mozart's *Concerto for Three Pianofortes (Koechel No. 242),* and it is in this youthful work that she herself exhibits the spirit of enduring youth.

A closing word: It is indeed good fortune that so many of the Great of duo-pianism who have been recorded in this chapter, are still among the living. Most respectfully, the hope is expressed that they will bear no misgivings for having been relegated to a Golden Era which assuredly is one of past history. May it be that they will accept the laurel which is offered to them by the humble disciples of their art. Because they still are active in musical affairs, because their guiding hand still can be reached, and their influence continues to be exerted over a new generation, it would indeed be irreverent to attempt a further evaluation of their historic stature at this fleeting moment. Yet, whatever amount of perspective time has already permitted for a final appreciation, in essence consolidates the firm belief that duo-pianistic art will always place them in the foremost rank of its ministers.

---

8. Her comments are quoted throughout Book II, *Nature, Applications, and Problems.*

CHAPTER IX

THE PRESENT HEIGHT

It was just stated that Rosina Lhevinne recently collaborated with duo-pianists Vronsky and Babin in a recording of Mozart's *Lodron Concerto*. Through Mozart's ever-young and sparkling voice, the representative of the Golden Era joins hands with the standard bearers of today. All retrospect is banished, and thoughts are turned into the presence. For never yet came into being a new era, later classified as such, without the watchword: *En avant!*

The task of giving an outline of history's great two-piano teams, at this time enters into a most difficult stage. Any survey demands distance, and historic appraisal requires as prime condition that perspective and detachment which only time can give. Time indeed becomes the essence, the chief factor in the process of evaluation. But since this survey now has arrived at the two-piano teams of yesterday and today, it is of necessity found to be quite impossible to establish a norm which would permit their advance classification according to historic merits. The full extent of their assets and exploits will be judged by time, and time alone. Instead of evaluation, this chapter will therefore be confined to giving a statistical report. The program of this assignment is only to present an enumeration of such artists who have successfully held the concert stage for some length of time and who over the years have found acclaim with audiences and critics alike. Their reputation assures that they all have in common that absolute cohesion which nowadays is synonymous with duo-pianistic teamwork. They all are possessed and carried by the conviction that theirs is a unique art form with a singular expressive power. They all are poten-

124

tially "great" teams, and while the ultimate selective process regarding their eminence remains history's chief privilege, and sometimes caprice, it is the purpose of this record to present them here with a short listing of biographical data.

The field of practitioners is indeed a large one in this day. From the comparatively few veteran teams, a long line of outstanding ensembles has come to the fore to satisfy the ever-growing public demand. The present flowering of the art, which had been prepared and cultivated by the now classic tradition of the first two-piano teams from the Therns to the Lhevinnes, has catapulted into prominence many fine combinations. By 1930, the field was alive with rivalling teams. Their competition quickly led to critical comparison. Discriminating observation in turn suggested and established definite standards which allowed for ready classification. The novelty appeal of the medium soon was superseded by the deeper satisfaction which the connoisseur enjoys. Duo-pianists no longer went out as pioneers; they now had to uphold a tradition and were expected to add to that endowment their own share towards further perfection.

Three principal groupings appear convenient in the presentation of teams which have, with the sum total of their efforts, achieved the present height of duo-pianism. The first class, *Teams of Yesterday,* will include such two-piano combinations which were active primarily in the thirties and since have dropped out from regular concert work. The second group, *Veteran Teams of Today,* presents those duo-pianists who, having been already prominent in the nineteen-thirties, are still continuing with their careers and more than ever are holding the spotlight on the musical scene. As third and last division, *The Young Generation* is given its right, with a listing of teams which came to the fore during the last decade.

Within each group, an alphabetical sequence is adhered to. Comments are confined to biographical data; additional remarks may be found appropriate when a team definitely has been dissolved and therefore invites its final appreciation. The length of a sketch does not represent any reflection and consequently allows for no conclusion as to the importance of the team under consideration. Omission from the list likewise is no criterion and may be due to the absence of proper information. Lack of perspective is the chief impediment in the nature of any contemporary survey; because of this hindrance, definite boundaries cannot be drawn. However, the procedure as suggested in the foregoing paragraph will provide a practical platform for encyclopaedic information on the leading teams of duo-pianists to this date (1950).

1. TEAMS OF YESTERDAY

BRODSKY AND TRIGGS

Vera Brodsky (1909-) and Harold Triggs (1900-) both are American born. As Juilliard fellowship winners, they studied with Josef and Rosina Lhevinne, and formed their two-piano ensemble in 1932. Their activities as duo-pianists included many concerts and radio broadcasts. In the course of their career, Brodsky and Triggs appeared with the major symphony orchestras. Since 1937, they gave courses in two-piano ensemble at the Curtis Institute of Music in Philadelphia and the Juilliard School of Music in New York.

Vera Brodsky is the author of an important chapter on duo-pianism in the standard work *The Piano* by Wier, and of a similar essay in *The MacMillan Encyclopedia of Music and Musicians*. Harold Triggs, who in 1937 became the head of the Arthur Jordan School of Music, Indianapolis, has written compositions for two pianos as well as for orchestra, string quartet, voice and piano.

FRAY AND BRAGGIOTTI

Jacques Fray and Mario Braggiotti became a two-piano unit in 1928 and since that time were popular both in Europe and America. Fray comes from a French banking family and Braggiotti from the well-known Italian family bearing that name. The duo-pianists first won public recognition in Paris at the Salle Pleyel for their unique two-piano arrangement of Maurice Ravel's *Bolero*. An auspicious career ensued, leading them to many continents. They became well-known through the media of concerts, phonograph recordings, and, since 1931, radio broadcasts.

The team-work of Fray and Braggiotti was distinguished by great imaginative powers and possessed by an exceptional flair for the ensemble art. Their heterogeneous appeal has been exceptional, and their style of playing and repertoire was satisfying to the varied tastes of international audiences.

After dissolving their team in the early 1940s, both Fray and Braggiotti from time to time have formed new partnerships, continuing to champion their preferred medium of musical expression. Each is reputed as an expert pianist in his own right.

HALL AND GRUEN

The woman member of this American team of duo-pianists, Frances Hall, was born in Erie, Pennsylvania, in 1899 and studied at the Juilliard Graduate School. She has concertized on two continents. Her partner, Rudolph Gruen, was born in St. Louis, Missouri, in 1900. He is a pupil of Harold Bauer and has toured America, Germany and New Zealand.

Gruen is also noted as a composer. His contributions to the literature of original two-piano compositions include a *Humoresque* and a *Scherzo;* in addition, he has been active as an arranger of two-piano scores.

KELBERINE AND BEHREND

Alexander Kelberine (1904-1940) was a notable Russian pianist and teacher. His training was received under Siloti and Busoni. He toured Europe and America as a soloist. With his wife, Jeanne Behrend, he gave numerous two-piano recitals. His reputation as an arranger and creator of distinctive transcriptions for two pianos is widespread.

Jeanne Behrend is one of the most successful of native American pianists. Josef Hofmann and Rosario Scalero were her teachers in piano and composition respectively, and she became the first pianist to be graduated by the Curtis Institute of Music in Philadelphia. Miss Behrend is especially noted for her courageous pioneer work in the field of native American music.

RUBINSTEIN AND LOESSER

Although Beryl Rubinstein and Arthur Loesser have carried out their duo-pianistic activities as a sideline, they nevertheless have attained to the highest proficiency in the medium. Their collaboration as colleagues on the faculty of the Cleveland Institute of Music of which Rubinstein is director, no doubt has been conducive to their two-piano work.

Both are American born. Beryl Rubinstein (1898-) studied with José da Motta and Ferruccio Busoni. He toured the country as a child prodigy. Besides being an accomplished pianist, he rose to considerable stature as a composer. His *Suite for Two Pianos* is discussed in a later chapter.[1]

Dr. Rubinstein has contributed to this investigation a most interesting exposition of his views concerning duo-pianism. His letter is reproduced elsewhere in this volume.[2]

Arthur Loesser (1894-) is a pupil of Stojowski. He became known as accompanist for Mme. Schumann-Heink with whom he went on tour. Loesser also achieved note and success in the field of composition.

HEINZ AND ROBERT SCHOLZ

This Austrian team has been active concertizing in Europe since the early twenties. The Scholz brothers made their first American tour during the season of 1937-38. A major feature of their recitals, and a service to great music generally, has been their performance of Bach's *The Art of Fugue* on two pianos.

---

1. See Book III, *The Literature,* Chapter XXIII, *The Standard Repertoire.*
2. See Book II, *Nature, Applications and Problems,* Part B, *The Creative Medium,* Chapter XVIII, *The Challenge,* Section 2, "Acceptance and Reservations."

The birthplace of the brothers is Steyr, Upper Austria; Heinz was born in 1897 and Robert in 1902. They studied under Petyrek and toured widely throughout Europe. Annual participants in the Salzburg Festivals, where both also teach at the Mozarteum, they specialize in the works of Mozart whose piano compositions they have edited.[3]

Both brothers have attained high status as composers. Heinz Scholz is noted for études and contrapuntal studies as well as for transcriptions of the old masters. Robert Scholz is the composer of a *Concerto* for two pianos, a *Passacaglia* for two pianos and orchestra, a *Preludio, Fughetto and Toccata,* and an *Oriental Suite* for orchestra or two pianos.

SILVIO AND ISABEL SCIONTI

Silvio Scionti (1882-   ) is Italian born. A native of Sicily, he was trained in Palermo and Naples, becoming a pupil of Cesi. He is well-known as a pianist and teacher, conductor and editor. His residence now is in Texas.

Scionti first engaged in a two-piano ensemble with his pupil Stell Andersen (1897-   ) who afterwards gained repute as a solo recitalist. They toured Europe and America together and scored considerable success. Scionti then formed a new and equally successful team with his wife, Isabel, a native of Texas, who was a master of music degree student under him at the Chicago Musical College. Their Carnegie Hall debut took place in 1938, and they subsequently gave an all-Bach two-piano program at Town Hall (1941). Their concert tours led them to Europe, Mexico and Hawaii.

Silvio Scionti is the author of a number of two-piano transcriptions, notably of works by Bach.

MISCELLANEOUS

There are other teams which attained a considerable reputation during that period, as for instance Ida Deck and Andrew Haigh; the Canadians, Scott Malcolm and Reginald Godden; Dorothy and Carl Parrish; Muriel Packard and Harold Bristol. Mention is also made of the occasional two-piano performances of the noted Artur Schnabel (1882-), Austrian pianist and Leschetizky pupil, with his son, Karl Ulrich Schnabel (1909-   ). The latter has also joined forces with the young American pianist, Leonard Shure (1910-   ), a pupil and later assistant of Artur Schnabel.

3. Published by the Universal Edition, Vienna.

2. VETERAN TEAMS OF TODAY

BARTLETT AND ROBERTSON

A British husband and wife combination which for many years has concertized extensively in Europe, South Africa, the United States and Canada, and Latin American countries.

Ethel Bartlett (1901-) was born in the County of Essex, on the edge of Epping Forest. At the age of ten, she was brought to London and educated there. Her teachers included Tobias Matthay and Artur Schnabel. It was during her period of study at the Royal Academy of Music in London that she met Rae Robertson, also a pupil of Matthay.

Robertson was born in 1898 in Inverness, a small highland village in the north of Scotland. He attended Edinburgh University where he received a master of arts degree, and also studied at the Leipzig Conservatory.

After their marriage, each continued with his own artistic course, only to realize after some time that "as rising young pianists, they found individual careers, no matter how successful, incompatible with mutual happiness." In 1927, they solved their personal and professional problem by merging into a duo-piano ensemble, becoming the first English artists to specialize in this field. Their debut in the United States occurred in 1929.

Bartlett and Robertson are distinguished by an untiring research concentrated on unpublished manuscripts of music for two virginals, harpsichords, or clavichords. Miss Bartlett, herself an accomplished harpsichord player, in 1944 made a transcription of pieces taken primarily from the Fitzwilliam Virginal Book and arranged them for two pianos in a cycle entitled *Elizabethan Suite*.

Aside from their concert work as duo-pianists, Bartlett and Robertson have become well-known as editors and annotators of classical and modern piano music.

GABY AND ROBERT CASADESUS

French team, composed of husband and wife. Robert Casadesus (1899-) is well-known as piano virtuoso, pedagogue, and composer. He was a pupil of Diémer and Leroux at the Paris Conservatoire, and won the Conservatoire's first prize in 1913. His American debut took place in 1935. He heads the piano department of the American Conservatory at Fontainebleau.

Mme. Casadesus, the former Gaby L'Hote, likewise is on the faculty of the institution at Fontainebleau. As duo-pianists, Gaby and Robert Casadesus have carried out their activities on an international scale.

The compositions of Robert Casadesus include several original works for two pianofortes, notably a concerto. He also wrote a symphony, a violin concerto, chamber music, and piano pieces.

JOSE AND AMPARO ITURBI

This two-piano team consists of brother and sister. They are of Spanish descent. José Iturbi was born in Valencia, in 1895. He studied at the Conservatory in his native city and won the piano prize at the age of thirteen. Subsequently he went to Barcelona, becoming a pupil of Joaquin Malats, and afterwards to Paris. He graduated from the Conservatory in the French capital at the age of seventeen. In 1919, the Conservatory of Geneva offered Iturbi the chairmanship of the piano department, a position which he held for four years. The artist has also gained recognition as conductor of leading orchestras.

Amparo Iturbi, José's younger sister, first appeared publicly in 1925. She received her entire musical instruction from her brother. Following their debut recital as duo-pianists in the Salle Gaveau at Paris and after repeated concert tours throughout Europe, the pair gave their first performance in New York with the Philharmonic Symphony under the direction of Alexander Smallens, at the Stadium concert of July 7, 1937.

José and Amparo Iturbi are active in many fields, including that of the motion pictures. It is through their repeated screen appearances that the exciting character of their two-piano performances has become popularly known.

NEMENOFF AND LUBOSCHUTZ

The male partner of this husband and wife combination, Pierre Luboshutz, is Russian born, (1894-   ). He studied with Risler and Blumenfeld and is a graduate of the Conservatory of Moscow. His debut as a prodigy was made in 1902, and his first appearance with an orchestra occurred under the baton of Serge Koussevitzky, in a performance of the Concerto in D minor by Brahms.

Genia Nemenoff was born in Paris of Russian parentage. Her studies were with Isidor Philipp. The artists first met in Paris in 1929 when Miss Nemenoff enrolled in a master class conducted by Mr. Luboshutz at the Paris Conservatory.

They were married in 1931 when Luboshutz was on his second tour of the United States and Nemenoff on her first. Each of them pursued an individual career for a time, and their duo-pianistic partnership began in extempore fashion. They played on two pianos informally for the sheer pleasure it gave them, and for the entertainment of their friends. When a concert manager heard them perform on one of these occasions, a professional alliance of their talents was suggested.

Nemenoff and Luboshutz entered into the duo-pianistic concert field in 1936. During their first three years before the public, they gave 198 recitals.

Their concerts have included frequent performances with the leading symphony orchestras, like the New York Philharmonic Society. They have repeatedly played under the batons of Toscanini (NBC Symphony Orchestra), Koussevitzky (Boston Symphony Orchestra), and Ormandy (Philadelphia Symphony Orchestra; nine re-engagements within one season).

Pierre Luboshutz is recognized as one of the outstanding arrangers in the two-piano field.

VRONSKY AND BABIN

Both Vitya Vronsky and Victor Babin are natives of Russia. They are husband and wife in private life. The woman partner of the team was born in the Crimea and is a daughter of Mikhail Vronsky, maestro of singing and former *regisseur* (stage director) of La Scala, Milan. She studied piano at the State Conservatory in Kieff. Her graduation, which she achieved at the age of 15, was followed by a concert tour of European Russia during which she gave more than one hundred recitals. In 1926, Miss Vronsky arrived in Western Europe to combine the beginnings of her international career with additional studies. Her teachers were Cortot, in Paris, and Egon Petri and Artur Schnabel, in Berlin. In the following years she gave solo recitals and appeared with many orchestras in all principal cities of the European continent and England.

Victor Babin was born in Moscow in 1908. At the age of 13 he entered the State Conservatory in Riga, majoring in piano and composition. After his graduation in 1927, Babin went to Berlin to continue his studies. His teachers then were Artur Schnabel in piano and Franz Schreker in composition. He graduated *cum laude* from the Hochschule fuer Musik, performing at this occasion a piano concerto of his own composition. Recitals and orchestral appearances followed which took him to England and through both Western and Eastern Europe. Always dividing his time between concert activities and creative work, Victor Babin has to his credit, apart from many two-piano arrangements, published works for violin, cello, voice, chamber music, piano solo, and two pianos; he also composed a concerto for two pianos and orchestra, as well as one for violin.

Vronsky and Babin met in Berlin in 1929 while both were pupils of Artur Schnabel. They were married in London in the year 1933. The impetus to play together on two pianos was received when, at a private house in London, they heard Artur Schnabel and Myra Hess informally perform duets by Schubert. Their debut as a two-piano team occurred in London in 1935. Thereafter they appeared in recitals, with symphony orchestras, and on radio broadcasts. Their activities extended over England and the European continent, including the Scandinavian countries.

The American debut performance of Vronsky and Babin took place on February 13, 1937 in Town Hall, New York. Since that year, their annual concert tours have taken them across the continent and have extended to Canada, Hawaii, Cuba, and Mexico.

After the outbreak of the Second World War, Babin joined the United States Army Air Force. During his period of service, Miss Vronsky taught piano to mental patients at St. Elizabeth Hospital in Washington, D.C., experimenting with the therapeutic influences of music study. Following the termination of hostilities, Vronsky and Babin resumed their concert activities in America as well as in Europe. They have partaken in the production of an educational musical movie "short" in Hollywood and were chosen to perform at the Goethe Bicentennial Convocation and Music Festival at Aspen, Colorado, in the summer of 1949.

MISCELLANEOUS

Of European combinations, the following belong to the group of veteran teams of today: Castagnetta and Kaye; Wiener and Doucet; Paul Schoop and Lothar Perl. The last named duo-pianists started their concert work in Switzerland and now reside in this country.

If a prediction as to the future historic significance of any of the afore-mentioned teams can be attempted at all, and if the consistent acceptance by audiences and critics will be considered a valid criterion, it would appear that there are three veteran teams on the concert stage today which are likely to secure a permanent place in the annals of the art. "Newsweek" magazine wrote on December 27, 1943:

> "As a concert attraction, the duo-piano team has flowered only within the past twenty years, and in those years four teams have almost overcome the axiom that while one piano might be art, two were near-vaudeville entertainment."

Of the four teams referred to, the Maier-Pattison combination at that time had already been dissolved.[4] The other three teams singled out were those of Bartlett and Robertson, Luboshutz and Nemenoff, and Vronsky and Babin.

3. THE YOUNG GENERATION

APPLETON AND FIELD

Vera Appleton and Michael Field both are American born. Miss Appleton comes from Tulsa, Oklahoma, while Michael Field is a native of New York. Both are graduates of the Juilliard School of Music where they were fellowship students under Carl Friedberg, himself a pupil of Schumann.

Out of their joint recitals and broadcasts of student days arose their

---

4. Maier and Pattison were discussed in the preceding chapter, *The First Golden Era.*

professional two-piano work which was carried on after Vera Appleton's marriage to Alexander Bressler, and the birth of a son.

The duo-pianists place emphasis on this statement: "Unlike other two-piano teams whose performances together in public are an expedient of their marriage, the Appleton and Field combine came about as a perfect musical mating of two major talents especially synthesized for and wholly dedicated to this specialized ensemble art."

On their extended annual tours, they champion the new in music, but they are also conducting an unceasing research for undiscovered or forgotten two-piano material. In the fall of 1949, they presented a series of three Town Hall programs, giving a cross-section of the literature under the title "Two Pianos through Four Centuries."

For several years, Appleton and Field have taught piano ensemble classes during the summer sessions at their alma mater, the Juilliard School of Music in New York.

DOUGHERTY AND RUZICKA

Celius Dougherty and Vincenz Ruzicka made their debut as duo-pianists in 1939. Before that time, each was already an established pianist; however, the success of their first two-piano appearance induced them to abandon their individual careers and to devote themselves entirely to ensemble playing as their profession.

Celius Dougherty was born in Glenwood, Minnesota, and holds a bachelor of arts degree from the University of Minnesota. His later studies were with Josef Lhevinne, and in composition with Rubin Goldmark. Dougherty has gained much recognition as a composer; his works include, in addition to those for two pianos, compositions in the fields of the string quartet, violin and piano sonatas, songs and opera.

Vincenz Ruzicka was born in Chicago, Illinois, of Czech-Viennese parentage. He started his career as a child prodigy. At the age of only twenty-one, he was appointed chairman of the music department at the University of Texas. He had appearances as piano soloist with several major orchestras on this continent as well as abroad.

Dougherty and Ruzicka met for the first time while they were students at the Juilliard School of Music in New York. During that period, they engaged in two-piano playing at many informal social gatherings. Afterwards, while following widely separated careers, the memory of those impromptu performances was like a magnet which inevitably drew the artists together. Their debut as a duo-pianistic unit took place in Town Hall, New York, in the year 1939. They have distinguished themselves with the first performances of many important contemporary works. Their own arrangements include an uncut version of Schumann's *Andante and Variations, opus 46,* transcribed from the original scoring for two pianofortes, two violoncellos, and horn.

GOLD AND FIZDALE

Gold and Fizdale constitute one of the youngest teams on the concert stage. Their appearance in the field was comparatively recent. The debut performance in New York (1946) was hailed by Virgil Thomson with the words "Duo-pianism reached heights hitherto unknown to the art!"

Arthur Gold (1919-   ) was born in Toronto, Canada, of Russian parentage. He arrived in the United States at the age of 15, to become a pupil of Rosina and Josef Lhevinne with whom he worked for six years before allying his talents with those of Robert Fizdale.

Fizdale's home town is Chicago. He also stems from Russian parents. Like Gold, he was a child prodigy. His teachers included Ethel Lyons, Howard Hanks, Louis Rabyn and Ernest Hutcheson. The two-piano proficiency of Gold and Fizdale was attained under the tutelage of Lhevinne and Hutcheson. Their professional debut occurred at the Arts Club in Chicago in 1944, and their first Town Hall recital followed in 1946.

When Gold and Fizdale gave a concert in Paris in 1949, three foremost contemporary composers—Paul Bowles, John Cage, and Alexi Haieff—traveled from three different countries to the French capital to hear them play their works which had been written especially for these duo-pianists. The team has consistently placed emphasis on *original* two-piano compositions and is exerting a constant stimulation upon the creation of new scores.[5]

MORLEY AND GEARHART

The American duo-pianists, Virginia Morley and Livingston Gearhart, both spent their student days at the Fontainebleau Conservatory of Music where they were artist pupils of Robert Casadesus. Their debut as a two-piano team took place in Paris and was followed by seven recitals in the French capital and a number of other engagements in France and Switzerland. After this European tour, they returned to their own country.

Mr. and Mrs. Gearhart in private life, the duo-pianists were born and educated in the United States. Virginia Morley is a native of California and studied piano and composition at Mills College. Livingston Gearhart was born in Buffalo, New York, and had his first studies with his mother who was a pupil of Leschetizky. He subsequently became a scholarship

5. Refer also to the closing paragraphs of Chapter X, *The Composers.*

pupil at the Curtis Institute in Philadelphia, and afterwards continued his studies in Europe, having Nadia Boulanger as his teacher in composition.

Livingston Gearhart has attained note as a composer and arranger and also as an educator, being the co-author of a book for violin students and having developed a system of teaching sight reading.

Morley and Gearhart have become widely and popularly known through their frequent radio appearances on the Fred Waring program.

WHITTEMORE AND LOWE

Of this native American two-piano team, Arthur Whittemore was born in Vermillion, South Dakota, and educated at the University there. He received a master's degree in composition from the Eastman School of Music at Rochester, New York. For some time he was director of music at the College for Men, University of Rochester.

Jack Lowe was born in Denver and began his musical career as a violinist. He subsequently became a scholarship student in composition at the Eastman School of Music where he attained to his master's degree.

Whittemore and Lowe met at Eastman. When they went together on a vacation trip to San Juan, Puerto Rico, a two-piano concert by accident had been arranged for them even though they had never before combined their talents on two instruments. It was then that they embarked on their career as a duo-piano team. Their American debut occurred in 1940; it took place in New York's Town Hall.

During the Second World War, as members of the United States Navy and stars of an all-Navy musical, Whittemore and Lowe played close to 750 performances before nearly a million service men and women. They returned to the professional concert field after four years in the service.

Among many other first performances of important works for two pianofortes, Whittemore and Lowe have premiered Ralph Vaughn Williams' *Concerto for Two Pianos and Orchestra* in the United States. (Cincinnati, November 1949) Notable among the large number of their arrangements for the two-piano medium is that of Max Reger's *Variations and Double-fugue on a theme of Bach, opus 81.*

In 1950, Arthur Whittemore and Jack Lowe received citations as among the thirteen outstanding alumni during the first hundred years of the University of Rochester.

MISCELLANEOUS

The gross of contemporary duo-pianists comprises a professional group far too large and too quickly changing to allow even an approximate coverage. However, a few present-day teams of significance may be singled out: Loretta and Murray Dranoff, pupils of Clarence Adler; Constance Keene and Abram Chasins, a husband and wife combination of which the male partner has achieved great distinction as a composer and arranger; the Levins; Rawicz and Landauer, very popular in England; Shrago and Leviton; Alfred and Herbert Teltschik.

Of a somewhat unique status in the entire two-piano field are the Franciscan Nuns Jeanne Madeleine and Francis Terese. They are twin sisters who were blind at birth. Although American born, they began their early braille training at the age of six at the Nazareth Institute in Montreal, Canada, and learned to use the braille method in all their work. A series of surgical operations has resulted in their ability to now distinguish light from darkness and to move about unassisted among familiar surroundings. However, they still type and transcribe their notes exclusively by way of the braille system. As duo-pianists, Sisters Jeanne Madeleine and Francis Terese have acquired a large repertoire. They are recitalists and recording artists of standard concert music and also feature several compositions of their own.

The foregoing brief listings must suffice to indicate the present height of duo-pianism. The survey may have appeared unduly concise to those whose enthusiasm over some particular team or teams is running high. Yet, a sober and reserved attitude towards one's own epoch, its representatives and accomplishments, seems only proper and fitting; it assuredly avoids the risk of overstatement. If glamour be desired, this quality is abundantly provided by the brilliant careers of these highly successful teams, and by the harvest of public recognition which they are reaping with their activities. The actual reputation of the artists must speak for itself, lest the danger of premature glorification is incurred in the absence of a true perspective.

So much, however, can be said without prejudice or partiality: If the two-piano concert today is held in high estate among critics and laymen alike, it is the performing artists who are chiefly responsible for this success, because of their choice of programs and the elevated plane of their renditions. Therefore, salutations are due to the teams of today. They carry forward the tradition of the art, confident that their level of duo-pianistic achievement will favorably compare with that of past history and will measure up to the standards of future generations.

CHAPTER X

THE COMPOSERS

For posterity, musical compositions constitute historic evidence as much as documents or other relics. They testify in behalf of the epoch in which they were created. Like the monuments of architecture, painting, or literature they present the following generations with a living memorial after the decay of the rest. From an extant work of music, not only the innermost thoughts of the composer himself can be derived and reconstructed, but also the preoccupations of the people among whom he lived and gained his inspiration.

In previous chapters, it was found advisable, if not compelling, to devote considerable attention to the earlier masters of two-piano composition. The purpose of such detailed investigation was to properly trace the amount of their interest in this mode of creative expression. For it is a composer's contribution to any given medium which reflects the general interest in that idiom among musicians and audiences of his time. Whatever amount of acclaim performers may achieve, whatever degree of enthusiasm is aroused in the listeners, they are always ephemeral manifestations, having but little import on the next generation. The written composition, however, carries a living tradition into the future and functions as the most important document in the kaleidoscope of musical history.

Farnaby and Couperin, Pasquini and Handel, Bach, Mozart, Schumann, Liszt and Brahms formed the lifeline along which the birth and growth of duo-pianism was traced. Now the survey turns to a more encyclopaedic coverage of the many other ranking composers who have been active in the two-piano medium during the last one hundred years. Indeed, there is a veritable array of illustrous names among the composers who lived before and throughout the Golden Age of duo-pianism. The galaxy of contemporary writers in the medium is not less impressive. These facts are not surprising, for composers of all times, functioning as the true producers of music,[1] always have been only too eager to make their creative abilities available to sympathetic and competent performers. They readily channel their skill and inspiration into any legitimate medium and will not hesitate to bestow their genius even upon a barrel organ, as Mozart proved to the world. Always favorably disposed to try a new form, a new combination, a new outlet or market, it is small wonder that composers found their imagination stimulated and their efforts rewarded in the young field of duo-pianism. Here was beckoning a territory which lay virtually untouched. Here was offering itself for exploration an instrumental realm which generated an ever-increasing demand for special literature with the performing musicians and drew much acclaim from the general public. As a consequence, a very substantial group of composers is found to devote an unexpectedly large amount of creative efforts to the two-piano medium. The result emerges that there actually is an abundant literature at hand although general opinion has it that the repertoire of original music for two pianos is scanty and limited.

It is one of the paradoxical aspects in the history of duo-pianism as an art form that the chief argument against its final acceptance has been based on the fallacious assumption of a prevailing lack of good original compositions. The performing and therefore most vitally interested group since long could have effectively disproved this objection. Once duo-pianists begin scanning the available repertoire, they will hardly any more incur the necessity of duplicating each other's program numbers. Instead, they will be able to rightfully claim for themselves the merit of having uncovered much beautiful and unjustly forgotten music. Such revival of neglected two-piano compositions, added to the present standard repertoire, and augmented by the constant influx of contemporary works, will stamp with the brand of absurdity the wide-spread prejudice that duo-pianism has no sufficient literature of its own.

To evidence this assertion, the investigation now proceeds to a survey of composers and their contributions to the two-piano medium. Only

---

1. Burnet C. Tuthill makes the following distinction between composers and performing artists: "In a very real sense, the performers of great music are simply the agents and intermediaries between the creators of the music and the listeners." The foregoing quotation is taken from an open letter by Dr. Tuthill on the subject of *Recordings of American Music*, published in *National Music Council Bulletin*, Volume X, Number 1, September 1949.

creative musicians of recognized standings are included because the assured quality of their work in itself implies a guarantee for the worthiness of their two-piano efforts. For convenience, the following cross-section of composers is arranged according to their nationalities, but the sequence of such national groups is arbitrary.

"Late nineteenth century and present-day composers have made enormous strides in realizing the practically unlimited polyphonic, orchestral, and color possibilities of two modern pianos." Thus writes Vera Brodsky in her essay *The Art of Two-piano Playing.*[2] No better representative for the accuracy of the foregoing statement could be found than the great Italian pianist and composer, Ferruccio Busoni. As a later exponent of the monumental possibilities of the piano which Franz Liszt had discovered for the musical world, Busoni is credited with having explored the resources of the instrument to an even greater degree than Liszt. As time marches on, the Italian master is less remembered for his enormous technique than for the many compositions and transcriptions from his pen. Four works for two pianos are among his prolific creative output. They are the delightful *Duettino Concertante, after Mozart*[3]; an *Improvisation* on the Bach Chorale "Wie wohl ist mir, o Freund der Seele"; a transcription of Mozart's *Fantasy for barrel-organ* ("Phantasie fuer eine Orgelwalze"), *Koechel No. 608;*[4] and the *Fantasia contrapunctistica.* The latter work, originally written for piano solo, represents a daring modern version of an unfinished fugue by Bach.

There are several countrymen of Ferruccio Busoni who have notably contributed to the literature for two pianos. Guiseppe Martucci wrote two original works: *Theme with Variations in E flat Major,* and *Fantasia in D minor, opus 32.* Giovanni Sgambati, a nineteenth century pioneer of instrumental music in song-dedicated Italy, arranged his *Concerto, opus 15,* for two pianos. Franco Da Venezia wrote a *Fantasia* for the two-piano literature. Mario Tarenghi contributed to the medium a number of original compositions. They include *Eight Variations on the Minuet Theme, opus 99,* of Robert Schumann (Tarenghi's own *opus 40*); *Nine Variations on Prelude XX by Chopin* (Tarenghi's *opus 68*); and *Prelude and Fugue in G minor.* Gino Marinuzzi composed a *Partita* in A minor.

The Spanish composer Manuel Infante added to the literature the frequently performed *Trois danses andalouses* and a suite entitled *Musiques d'Espagne.* His famous countryman, Manuel de Falla, likewise was active as a propagandist for two-piano art, more especially for the convenient

2. A. E. Wier, *The Piano,* p. 351.
3. Transcribed from the Finale of the Piano Concerto in F major by Mozart.
4. For additional comment on this work, see also Chapter IV, *Mozart.*

dissemination of orchestral music through the expedient of this medium. On May 24, 1911, de Falla played in London at one of the concerts organized by Franz Liebich. One of the program numbers then was Debussy's *Iberia,* arranged for two pianos by André Caplet; the work was performed by de Falla and Liebich.[5]

Among Swiss composers, Josef Joachim Raff must first be named. Raff attained a prominent place in German music life and exerted a powerful influence. His works for two pianos include a *Chaconne, opus 150;* a *Fantaisie, opus 207a;* and a *Tarantella, opus 82.* Another Swiss pianist-composer was Charles Samuel Lysberg, a pupil of Chopin, who endowed the repertoire for duo-pianists with several Fantasies on motives from Mozartean operas and with a symphonic idyll entitled *Les bruits des champs, opus 134.* The eminent Hans Huber evidently was very interested in the two-piano medium. His *Improvisations* (Etudes on an original theme), *opus 64,* and as many as three *Sonatas* (constituting the opus numbers 31, 121, and 126) represent a substantial addition to the literature. Huber's countryman, Werner Wehrli, wrote *Variations and Fugue on a Jolly Song, opus 18.* The noted Swiss pianist, Emile Robert Blanchet, composed a *Ballade, opus 57,* for two pianos.

The small neighboring country of Switzerland, Liechtenstein, is the home of Josef Rheinberger, a powerful musician and composer who contributed generously to the repertoire for two pianos. His works in this idiom are *Duo in A minor, opus 15; Sonata in C minor, opus 122;* and *Duo* (after the suite for organ, violin, violoncello and string orchestra), *opus 149a.*

The Austrian pianist Gustav Satter who became well-known in the Americas through repeated concert tours, and whose compositions drew the commendation of Berlioz, enriched the list of original two-piano literature with not less than six of his works. The Moravian Ignaz Bruell added three compositions, including a *Sonata in D minor, opus 21.* The Bohemian master, Bedrich Smetana, joins the array of famous names among the composers for two pianos with his *Sonata in E Minor.* The Hungarian pianist-composer Stephen Heller who belonged to the Parisian circle of Chopin, Berlioz and Liszt, likewise ranks in the repertoire for two pianos with his *Tarantella, opus 85.*

Edvard Grieg must first be mentioned among the Scandinavian composers to whom the literature of original two-piano music is indebted for their contributions. Grieg's major work in the medium is an extended composition, the *Romance with Variations, opus 51.* Christian Sinding is

---

5. J. B. Trend *Manuel de Falla and Spanish Music,* p. 65.

noted for his *Variations in E Flat Minor, opus 2,* and for the *Duets, opus 41.* Selim Palmgren wrote the Suite *Maskenball, opus 36.* Thomas Dyke Acland Tellefsen, a pupil of Chopin, composed a *Sonata, opus 41.* The Danish musician, Ludwig Schytte, who studied with Louis Rée, one of the pioneers in the two-piano field, paid tribute to his teacher by writing two concert pieces, *Carnival and Festival March, opus 115.*

Of the many English, Irish, and Australian composers who went on record in the two-piano medium, Charles Hubert Hastings Parry comes first to mind; he composed a *Grand Characteristic Duo* in E minor. Arthur Somervell wrote *Variations* on an original theme and the symphonic variations *Normandy.* Cyril Scott contributed *Lento, opus 35,* and *Theme and Variations;* in these works, Scott exploits every sonority of which the two-piano medium is capable and displays the exotic harmonies and irregular rhythms which are features of his work. Charles Villiers Stanford, Ernest Walker, George F. Boyle, Algernon Ashton, Ralph Vaughn Williams, York Bowen, and many others have employed the duo-pianistic idiom in their creative work. The youngest generation of English composers likewise is very active in this field: Arthur Bliss has written a *Concerto for Two Pianos and Orchestra.* Arnold E. Trevor Bax is the composer of a number of two-piano pieces, including *Moy Mell, The Poisoned Fountain, Hardanger, The Devil That Tempted St. Anthony,* and *Red Autumn.* Bax also wrote a *Sonata.* Arthur Benjamin's *Carrabean Suite* is set for two pianos; well-known is his *Jamaican Rumba.* Benjamin Britten contributed several works to the literature, including *Mazurka Eligiaca,* dedicated to the memory of Paderewski; *Soirees Musicales,* a suite after Rossini; *Scottish Ballad* for two pianos and orchestra; and—in 1940—*Introduction and Rondo alla Burlesca.*

Ranking among the earlier Russian composers, Michael von Asantschewsky has written a *Festival Polonaise, opus 12,* for two pianos. Alexander Adolfovitch Winkler is the composer of *Variations and Fugue on a Theme by Bach, opus 12.* The mighty Anton Rubinstein also added to the original literature with his *Fantasia in F, opus 73.* The German-Russian Eduard Schuett wrote for the medium in his characteristic style. It is Anton Arensky who has especially endeared himself to all lovers of two-piano music by composing as many as five *Suites* for the combination; they are marked with the opus numbers 15, 23, 33, 62, and 65. Suite No. 2 is entitled *Silhouettes,* and opus 65 is in canon form. Probably the most popular of all original two-piano pieces is found in the first suite, opus 15; it is the famous *Valse.*[6]

6. For comment on this work, refer to Book III, *The Literature,* Chapter XXIII, *The Standard Repertoire.*

Indubitably the most important Russian contributor to the literature of two-piano compositions is Sergei Rachmaninoff. He devoted several major creative efforts to the medium and enriched the repertoire with two extensive *Suites, opus 5* and *opus 17.* These suites of which the first bears the title *Fantaisie,* rank in the front line of the standard literature. Indispensable to all serious duo-pianists, they contain a wealth of beautiful writing, showing Rachmaninoff at his best, both in the masterly realization of the piano idiom and in the projection of the spirit of late Romanticism.[7]

Cesar Cui composed *Trois Morceaux, opus 69,* for two pianofortes. Sergei Ivanovitch Taneiev likewise wrote in the medium as is evidenced by his *Prelude and Fugue, opus 29.* Alexander Glazunow also contributed an original work, entitled *Fantasy, opus 104.* Reinhold Glière is the composer of *Six Morceaux, opus 41.* Several other Russian born composers like Stravinsky, Levitzki, and Babin will be referred to in connection with the two-piano music produced in their adopted country.

The Polish pianist, Ignaz Friedman, added to the repertoire for duo-pianists his *Suite opus 70.* His landsman, Alexander Tansman,[8] composed an original *Carnival Suite* and also made a two-piano transcription of his *Sonatine Transatlantique;* the last named work was originally written for piano solo. Although Polish born also, Leopold Godowsky will be referred to in a later paragraph because he became prominently identified with musical activities in this country. The Polish-Silesian Moritz Moskowski added three of his characteristic pieces to the repertoire, and Joseph Wieniawski, a brother of the famous violinist, further augmented the literature with his *Fantasy, opus 42.*

A great number of distinguished names is encountered among the host of Germans who composed for two pianos. Again, it will be found surprising to notice that so many of these famous and highly respected creative musicians were interested in the medium. One cannot but express wonder why their works should remain unheard, and amazement must be voiced that most of these compositions seem to be ignored in their very existence by contemporary duo-pianists. To begin with the enumeration of some exponents among German composers and their two-piano works, there is Robert Volkmann with his *Variations on a Theme by Handel, opus 26.* The Schumann disciple, Theodor Kirchner, wrote several original compositions, including *Variations, opus 85,* and *Waltzes, opus 86.* Karl Reinecke who during his youth was intimate with Mendelssohn and Schu-

---

7. For analyses of the Suites, op. 5 and op. 17, see Book III, *The Literature,* Chapter XXIII, *The Standard Repertoire.*
8. Tansman, after 1940, settled in the United States.

mann and who remained a powerful influence in musical affairs throughout his life, ranks with no less than a dozen two-piano compositions, both works originally written for the medium and transcriptions from his compositions in other forms. To the original group belong his *Andante and Variations* (after the model of Schumann), *opus 6; Impromptu* on a motif from Schumann's "Manfred," *opus 66; Variations* on a Sarabande by Bach, *opus 24b; La Belle Grisélidis,* Improvisations on a French Folk Song of the 17th Century, *opus 94; Improvisations* on a Gavotte by Gluck, *opus 125; Four Pieces* (Etude, Minuet, Scherzo in canon form, Allegretto), *opus 241;* and three *Sonatas,* one with the opus number 240 and two more under opus number 275. To this wealth of original music for two pianos, Reinecke has added a number of transcriptions such as *Duo, opus 216a* (after the octet for wind instruments), and *Pictures from the South, opus 86* (arranged from the original for two hands). He also made several two-piano condensations of his orchestral works, like *Festival Overture, opus 148;* the symphonic variations *Zur Reformationsfeier* (based on Luther's Chorale "A Mighty Fortress"), *opus 191;* and the Overture to Klein's drama *Zenobia, opus 193.*

A name probably unknown to most duo-pianists is that of Salomon Jadassohn. Once a celebrated theorist and composer, he wrote for two pianos his *Chaconne, opus 82.* The German-Russian Nikolai von Wilm contributed several works to the literature; among these compositions are sets of *Variations, opus 64,* and of *Waltzes, opus 72,* besides a number of other pieces. Ferdinand Thiériot is the author of a *Concerto* for two pianos and orchestra, *opus 77;* he composed for the medium three additional works containing two pieces each. Gustav Adolf Thomas figures in the realm of original two-piano composition with his *Fuga eroica, opus 12.* The versatile Adolf Bernhard Vogel wrote *Andante and Variations, opus 14.* Adolph von Henselt provided two-piano settings of two of his compositions. Paul Schumacher of Mayence composed in the idiom several preludes and fugues as well as variations. The works by Anton Urspruch *(Variations and Fugue on a Theme by Bach, opus 13),* Adolf Ruthardt *(Sonata quasi Fantasia, opus 31),* and Georg Alfred Schumann *(Variations and Fugue on a Theme by Beethoven, opus 32)* all added substantially to the literature of original two-piano music. Emil von Sauer is also to be mentioned, as is Hermann Zilcher. The latter contributed his *Symphonie, opus 50,*[9] which is *not* an arrangement of an orchestral work, but represents an original two-piano composition; the title is suggestive of the composer's symphonic conception of two-piano potentialities. The eminent Max Bruch wrote for the medium his *Phantasie in D minor, opus 11.* In 1915, Bruch

---

9. Composed in 1925.

added to the literature another work which was especially designed for the Sutro sisters whose friend he was; the title of this composition is *Double Concerto, opus 88*. Three original works for two pianos come from the pen of Julius Weismann. They are *Nine Variations, opus 64; Partita, opus 107;* and *Sonatine "Ille terrarum," opus 122*. Another respected name among German composers is that of Hugo Kaun; he is listed in the repertoire with his *Suite im alten Stil, opus 81*, and with an additional *Suite, opus 92*.

The genius and the accomplishments of Max Reger still are appreciated by comparatively few. This lack of recognition is somewhat similar to that which prevails in the symphonic field with regard to Anton Bruckner. Yet, Reger was one of the most conspicuous composers of recent music history. He is notable for the gigantic dimensions in which many of his works are cast. Emotionally and intellectually, these compositions are representative of the depth of his musical insight. The enormous workmanship and monumental conception which are chief characteristics of this late genius in German music life, find their full release and expression in several works which Reger composed for two pianos. His chief contribution in this idiom, entitled *Introduction, Passacaglia, and Fugue, opus 96*, is written in a masterly manner which understands to match the doubled resources with the height and depth of the musical conception.[10] Reger's *Variations and Fugue on a Theme by Beethoven, opus 86*, constitute another original work for two pianos; the composer subsequently orchestrated this score.[11] The reverse procedure was followed by Reger in his *Variations and Fugue on a Theme by Mozart, opus 132*; this work appeared first in its orchestral instrumentation before it was transcribed for two pianofortes.

In addition to the contribution made with his own compositions, Reger enriched the two-piano literature by producing an excellent transcription of the *Goldberg Variations* by Bach. Through the expediency of this score, he enabled many music lovers to become more closely acquainted with Bach's wonderful composition. Further two-piano transcriptions made by Reger include two excerpts from Richard Wagner's orchestral music, the *Meistersinger Prelude* and the *Tannhäuser Overture*. Reger's pupil, Hermann Unger, apparently shared his master's interest in the medium; he composed *Kammervariationen, opus 8*, for two pianos, a set of chamber variations on an own theme.

Towering over the musical scene of France for many decades was the

10. For additional comment on this work, see Book III, *The Literature*, Chapter XXIII, *The Standard Repertoire.*
11. Paul A. Pisk in *Handbuch der Musikgeschichte* by Guido Adler, Vol. II, p. 1017.

personality of Camille Saint-Saens. He took a very active interest in duo-pianism, being himself particularly fond of this ensemble form and attributing to it high value. Like several of his distinguished colleagues, Saint-Saens also was one of the friends and sponsors of the Sutro sisters. In his prolific output, not less than ten works for two pianofortes are to be found. They include foremost original compositions like the monumental *Variations on a Theme by Beethoven, opus 35,* which for generations have occupied a prominent position in the standard repertoire.[12] Among other original two-piano works by Saint-Saens are his *Polonaise, opus 77;* the exciting and virtuosic *Scherzo, opus 87;* and *Caprice Arabe, opus 96.* The best known of his numerous transcriptions from orchestral scores is that of the famous *Danse Macabre, opus 40;* the work is hardly less effective in the two-piano idiom. Saint-Saens has also written a delightful and humorous *Carnival of the Animals* (Carnaval des animaux, Grande Fantasie zoologique) in which two pianos are used to figure conspicuously in the proceedings.[13]

A famous Frenchman belonging to the same period was Benjamin Godard; he demonstrated his interest in the two-piano combination by writing two works for it. Charles Marie Widor, more generally known as a distinguished organist and organ-composer, likewise employed the medium for his *Suite Concertante.* Other composers of the French school who contributed to the original literature, include the Belgians, Theophile Ysaye and Charles W. de Bériot. Ysaye, the brother of the famous violinist, wrote *Variations in E minor, opus 10,* while de Bériot, the son of the equally noted violinist, Charles Auguste, composed a two-piano *Sonata opus 61.* Gabriel Fauré is represented in the idiom with his *Fantaisie,*

12. For analysis of this work, refer to Book III, *The Literature,* Chapter XXIII, *The Standard Repertoire.*

13. Ernest Hutcheson makes extensive mention of this work in his book *The Literature of the Piano,* (pp. 271-272). Hutcheson writes:

"The piece, composed for two pianos and a small group of orchestral instruments but playable by two pianos alone, is one of the wittiest skits ever penned, so unique that I make no apology for giving some space to it. Saint-Saens indulges in bare-faced but amazingly clever imitations of animal sounds and movements—the lion's roar, the crowing of cocks and cackling of hens, the donkey's bray; the fleetness of wild asses (Hémiones) and the sluggishness of the tortoise, the uncouth gambols of a waltzing elephant, and the eccentric leaps of the kangaroo. These antics are relieved by numbers of real beauty—the notes of a cuckoo coming from deep woods, the sweetly confused sounds of an aviary, a suggestion of an aquarium, and the gliding swan (cello solo). The 'animals' include two pianists who interrupt the proceedings to practice the dullest imaginable finger exercises, scales, and thirds, and a group of Fossiles humorously represented by three old French tunes and Saint-Saens's own Danse macabre. By a marvelous touch of fun the poor elephant is made to waltz to the Dance of Sylphs of Berlioz and a fragment from Mendelssohn's Midsummer Night's Dream music. The tortoises crawl along in exaggeratedly slow tempo to two volatile themes from Offenbach's Orphée dans l'enfer. The Finale brings the animals together in a Noah's Ark parade."

opus 111. The women composers have a capable exponent in Cécile Chaminade who added to the repertoire a number of workmanlike compositions which are characteristic of her style and still appeal to lovers of the particular musical salon type.[14] Of greater consequence as a composer is Florent Schmitt who composed *Three Rhapsodies, opus 53.* Charles Martin Loeffler transcribed his symphonic score *A Pagan Poem* for two pianos, and Emmanuel Chabrier likewise employed the idiom for a condensation of his familiar Spanish Rhapsody *España.* Chabrier seems to have favored the two-piano combination for he also wrote three original *Valses Romantiques* for this medium. Often considered French, but actually Venezuelan by birth, Reynaldo Hahn contributed a total of four works to the literature.

The leader of the French impressionists, Claude Debussy, left an early original work for two pianos, the tone poem *Linderaja.* This composition is of less importance than his subsequent addition to the literature, the suite *En Blanc et Noir,* a work from the composer's last creative period.[15] Debussy also made a masterly two-piano transcription from the orchestral score of his symphonic poem *L'Après-midi d' un Faune;* regardless of the idiomatic change, the arrangement retains the atmospheric quality which distinguishes this model of impressionistic music. Another contribution to the literature was made by Debussy when he arranged for two pianos Robert Schumann's *Six Etudes in canon form.*

Debussy's great contemporary and compatriot, Maurice Ravel, composed a two-piano score entitled *Les Sites Auriculaires;* he also made special transcriptions of his orchestral masterpieces *Rhapsodie Espagnole, La Valse,* and *Bolero.* In the two-piano versions, the same stunning brilliance and finish are achieved which distinguish these works in their symphonic originals. In the repertoire of duo-pianists, the names of Ravel and Debussy have frequently come to be used in conjunction, because of the former's two-piano arrangements of Debussy's three orchestral *Nocturnes (Nuages, Fêtes* and *Sirènes).* These transcriptions which are often performed on the concert programs of leading teams rank with the most felicitous two-piano writing of the entire literature.

Of other modern French composers, mention is due to Eric Satie who composed *Three Pieces in the Shape of a Pear.* Satie is especially important because of the influence which he exerted upon a progressive group of younger composers who called themselves *Les Six.* Several members of this circle have made notable contributions to contemporary two-piano

---

14. For comment on *Andantino* by Cécile Chaminade, see Book III, *The Literature,* Chapter XXIII, *The Standard Repertoire.*
15. For analysis of this work, refer to Book III, *The Literature,* Chapter XXIII *The Standard Repertoire.*

music. The eminent woman composer of "The Six," Germaine Tail-leferre, wrote a suite *Jeux de plein air* as well as a concerto for two pianos; the latter is scored with the accompaniment of an orchestra and a chorus. Francis Poulenc, another representative of *Les Six,* likewise wrote a concerto for two pianos and orchestra which has achieved many public renditions.[16] Robert Casadesus, who himself propagates two-piano art in concerts together with his wife Gaby, is the composer of *Dances Méditer-ranéennes* as well as of a concerto for two pianos and orchestra. A further concerto in the same category was written by Jean Françaix.

Another native of France and also a member of *Les Six* is Darius Milhaud who has professed an especially strong interest in the two-piano medium throughout his career as a composer. This predilection is mainly testified by his *Scaramouche Suite* which within the few years since its creation has already become a stronghold of the literature.[17] Further original two-piano scores by Milhaud include *Le Bal Martiniquais,* [18] the suite *Les Songes,* and *Carnaval à la Nouvelle Orleans.* In addition, the composer wrote a concerto for two pianos and orchestra. Notable among Milhaud's two-piano transcriptions from his symphonic scores is a recent work entitled *Kentuckiana.* Another composition by Darius Milhaud, *Le Boeuf sur le Toit,* originally also was cast into two-piano form;[19] the primary score then was orchestrated. Thus another example is provided for the ready interchangeability of the duo-piano and orchestral media, and of the reciprocal metamorphosis frequently resulting therefrom.

---

16. For analysis of this concerto, see Book III, *The Literature,* Chapter XXIII, *The Standard Repertoire.*

17. For a discussion of the work, refer to Book III, *The Literature,* Chapter XXIII, *The Standard Repertoire.*

18. An interesting analogy to the working method of Brahms, as far as the employment of the two-piano medium in a central position between primary and final form of a work is concerned, can be observed in the evolution of *Le Bal Martiniquais.* After the liberation of the French West Indies in 1943, the Governor of Martinique sent Milhaud some poems expressing the people's joy over the regained freedom. Several old folk tunes came along. Utilizing this material, Milhaud first made a suite for piano and voice, entitled *La libération des Antilles.* The composer relates on the further procedure:

"It was the collection of these tunes on which I had just worked that gave me the idea of a two-piano work entitled *Le Bal martiniquais.* I thought these two pieces could be orchestrated. As a matter of fact, following the *Suite Française* which is based on French folk tunes, it makes a normal suite to end my little fantaisie on folk tunes of the French Empire."

This information was given to Bagar and Biancolli for their book *The Concert Companion;* it is found on page 452 of that work.

19. Later on, the composer used the music for a farcial pantomime about the happenings in an American bar during the time of the prohibition. The writer of the pantomime, Cocteau, closely followed the humorous implications of the two-piano music which contains an abundance of jazz elements and Latin-American rhythms.

Darius Milhaud now lives and works in the United States, one of a multitude of foreign-born composers who have made their home in this country. Many of these distinguished personalities have become naturalized citizens and are prominently identified with the musical life of America. Yet, the definition as to who represents an American composer or, rather, the analysis of qualifications which classify a composer as American, remains a controversial subject.

In keeping with the genesis and development of the nation, it appears only logical that a definite line of demarcation cannot and should not be drawn. The processes of continuous amalgamation, mutual absorption, and fertilization which are singular traits of American life, defy the establishment of autocratic categories, particularly cultural or artistic. The answer to the inquiry whether a foreign-born composer may or should be called American, after his official naturalization, must be left to the individual himself. His decision most likely will be based upon the degree of his assimilation and chiefly on his personal attitude towards the very concept of Americanism. Only the individual confronted with this situation knows the manifold considerations entering into the problem. However, once he has made Americanism a working principle for himself, the claim for his classification as an American composer will be forthcoming as an outgrowth of the material substance and essential character which are reflected in his music.

At any rate, it is a large and important group of composers who, to a greater or lesser extent, have become a part of the musical tradition in America. The line extends far back to the days when the first musicians arrived from Europe in quest of new opportunities, chiefly economic. Many came only to visit; but some, and subsequently more and more, stayed on. Theirs was success and recognition, and then a home. Reciprocating with loyalty, they became the first shareholders in the musical culture of the New World.

Again the present survey needs to be confined to those more important composers who have shown an active interest in duo-pianism. They include, to begin with, the Austrian-born Wilhelm Karl Ernst Seeboeck, the German-American Wilhelm Berger, and Polish-born Sigmund Stojowski. Louis Victor Saar, of Dutch extraction, was especially devoted to the two-piano medium in which he wrote original as well as transcribed music. The Rhenish composer, Johann Heinrich Bonawitz, becoming identified with the musical scene of America for some time, contributed a concerto for two pianos to the literature. Leopold Godowsky, the eminent Polish born pianist, edited a two-piano version of his charming *Alt Wien* which is now one of the most popular pieces in the entire repertoire.[20] Godowsky also composed a *Contrapuntal Paraphrase on Weber's Invitation to the Dance* and two cadenzas to Mozart's *Concerto in E flat major* for two pianos.

Among the many noted composers who have arrived from Europe more recently to make America their home, the Jewish-Swiss Ernest Bloch must be listed with his *Evocations;* he transcribed this score for two pianos from the original symphonic suite. The late Béla Bartók, a modern exponent of Hungarian music, contributed to the literature his highly significant *Sonata for Two Pianos and Percussion.* Bartók afterwards edited an additional version of the same work, now employing, besides the two solo pianos, the accompaniment of an orchestra.[21] Mario Castelnuovo Tedesco, a native of Italy, likewise appears strongly interested in the two-piano medium, both for original composition and as a form of arrangement. The Bohemian, Jaromir Weinberger, has made a masterly transcription for two pianos from the orchestral score of the genial *Polka and Fugue,* contained in his opera *Shvanda.* An important *Concerto* for two pianos and orchestra was composed by Bohuslav Martinu who was born in Czechoslovakia.[22] Music in a much lighter vein is the *Valse Tzigane* by Mischa Levitzki; the composer who is of Russian descent, himself transcribed the piece for two pianos. Percy Grainger, a native of Australia, also appears to be partial to the medium, for he has provided two-piano versions for a large number of his characteristic pieces.

Paul Hindemith is German born, but he has been a resident of the United States since over a decade. Held to be one of the greatest of living composers, he has written a *Sonata for Two Pianos (1942)* which forms an important part in the contemporary literature.[22]

Another vital force in modern music is embodied by Igor Stravinsky, of Russian extraction, who also made his permanent home in this country. It is Stravinsky who has composed an epoch-making *Concerto per Due Pianoforti Soli* in which he links to the early tradition of the concerto form. The work thus aspires to materialize, in a contemporary counterpart, the same ideals to which Bach adhered in his own works for two

20. See Book III, *The Literature,* Chapter XXIII, *The Standard Repertoire.*
21. For description of the composition, see Book III, *The Literature,* Chapter XXIII, *The Standard Repertoire.*
22. For comment on the work, see Book III, *The Literature,* Chapter XXIII, *The Standard Repertoire.*

claviers.[23] Stravinsky also has written a *Sonata for Two Pianos*. More-over, he has transcribed his *Scherzo à la Russe,* originally scored for Paul Whiteman's orchestra, into the two-piano medium. This piece constitutes a genuine *tour de force* for duo-pianists. With its vigorous rhythms and melodies of nationalistic character, the scherzo recalls the famous dances in the score of Stravinsky's *Petrouchka* ballet.

Turning to the native American composers, the survey soon meets with such deans of domestic music as Daniel Gregory Mason and Charles Gilbert Spross who composed several original two-piano compositions. One will expect to find the name of Edward MacDowell listed in this group of contributors, considering his great interest and achievement in the pianistic idiom. For some unknown reason, however, MacDowell failed to endow the literature with an original composition for two pianos. Nevertheless, there is a record of MacDowell's employment of the medium for purposes of expediency. It is known that he drafted his first concerto in a version for two pianos and thus presented it to Franz Liszt who was always pre-pared to extend generous assistance to young, aspiring composers. Law-rence Gilman describes MacDowell's experience as follows:[24]

> ". . . the visit to Liszt, which he had dreaded, was a gratifying surprise. That beneficent but formidable personage received him with kindly courtesy, and had Eugen D'Albert, who was present, play the orchestral part of the concerto which MacDowell had brought with him in manuscript, arranged for two pianos. Liszt listened attentively as the two young musicians played it through,—not too effec-tively,—and when they had finished he commended it in warm terms. 'You must bestir yourself,' he warned D'Albert, 'if you do not wish to be outdone by our young American'; and he praised the boldness and originality of certain passages in the music, especially their harmonic treatment."

23. Stravinsky himself has given expression to the ideas governing this significant two-piano composition:

> "The concerto logically presumes a rivalry between several instruments, called concerted, or between a single instrument and an ensemble opposed to it.
>
> "Now this conception of the concerto is not applicable in works bearing the name nor has it been for a long time. The concerto has become a work for solo instruments without competition, where the role of the orchestra generally finds itself reduced to an accompaniment.
>
> "In the four concertos I composed, I adhered to the earlier formula. To the principal concerted instrument, I opposed, in my orchestral ensemble, either sev-eral instruments or whole groups, themselves concerted. Thus I safeguarded the principle of competition.
>
> "In the same way that the most natural conception of an accompaniment is of a harmonic order, concerted rivalry by its nature requires the contrapuntal order. It is this last principle that I have applied to my new work where the two pianos, of equal importance, compete with one another and thus assume a concerted role. And it is precisely this that has permitted me to give to my work the qualification of concerto."

24. Gilman, *Edward MacDowell.*

MacDowell's friend and colleague with whom he roamed the forest hills near Wiesbaden, was Templeton Strong. The latter composed *Drei sinfonische Idyllen, opus 29,* for two pianos. Other native Americans to augment the literature include Edward Burlingame Hill who wrote four original *Jazz Studies*[25] and also a *Scherzo* for two pianos and orchestra; Henry Cowell with his *Celtic Set*; John Powell who transcribed some of his compositions for the medium; and George Gershwin with two-piano versions of his *Second Rhapsody* and of the variation set *I Got Rhythm.*

In still another group, it is found expedient to combine a number of the younger American composers, including both the native and foreign-born. Their common denominator at this time lies in the fact that all have given attention to duo-pianism as a creative medium. Lukas Foss composed a set of three original pieces. Anis Fuleihan[26] is represented with a *Toccata* as well as with a *Concerto* for two pianos and orchestra. Both Roy Harris and Harl McDonald likewise have written concertos for two pianos and orchestra. Homer Simmons is very active as a composer in the two-piano medium, as are David Guion and Abram Chasins; the latter is noted for his brilliant treatment of the idiom. A *Ballade* for two pianos and orchestra, after the old English poem "King Estmere," is the major contribution to the literature by Leo Sowerby. Burnet Tuthill, the composer of the orchestral rhapsody *Come Seven,* also arranged the score for two pianos. Original works as well as transcriptions have been added to the repertoire by Aaron Copland.[27] The literature was further enriched by composers such as Frederick Jacobi who produced a setting of biblical excerpts in the novel combination of voice and two pianos.[28] Charles Haubiel, Norman Dello Joio, Morton Gould, Vittorio Rieti, Alexi Haieff, John Cage, Paul Bowles, and Amadeo Roldan all belong to today's vanguard of composers; each of them has evidenced his interest in the two-piano medium by devoting a share of his creative work to the idiom.

A large percentage of all works comprising the two-piano literature

---

25. For comment on these pieces, refer to Book III, *The Literature*, Chapter XXIII, *The Standard Repertoire.*

26. Fuleihan, although born on the Island of Cyprus, is generally regarded as an American composer, for he has made his home in this country, and it was here that he received most of his musical training. He now is professor of piano at Indiana University.

27. Copland's *Birthday Piece* (*On Cuban themes*) for *Two Pianos* was performed by Leonard Bernstein and the composer at the twentieth anniversary concert of the League of Composers in Town Hall, New York, on December 9, 1942.

28. *From the Prophet Nehemiah:* Three Excerpts set for voice and two pianos. The premiere of this work was given by Marjorie Lawrence in collaboration with Dougherty and Ruzicka, on December 9, 1942, in New York, at the same concert which was mentioned in the preceding footnote.

were especially written by their composers for a particular combination
of duo-pianists, and most teams of professional repute have been so
honored with compositions intended for and dedicated to them. But there
are also such members of famous concert teams who themselves rank as
noted composers. While they have often excelled in various other media
of composition, it is their contributions to the two-piano literature which,
as may be expected, bear the stamp of first-hand familiarity with their
métier. From Louis Rée to Victor Babin and Celius Dougherty, there
exists a distinguished line of duo-pianist-composers. Of the more recent,
Rudolph Gruen, Lee Pattison, and Harold Triggs are to be mentioned,
each of whom has written in the smaller forms. Ernest Hutcheson is the
composer of a two-piano *Concerto* and also of a *March* for two pianos and
string orchestra. Representative of the younger native Americans, Beryl
Rubinstein has produced a *Suite* for two pianos, consisting of four sections
(*Prelude, Canzonetta, Jig, Masks*), "a gaily-rhythmed and amusing piece"
(Hall).[29] Victor Babin, who is one of the most versatile composers among
duo-pianists, wrote *Six Etudes;*[30] a *Concerto;*[31] *Three March Rhythms;*
and *Three Fantasies on Old Themes*. All these compositions add materially to the original literature for two pianos. Previous mention was
already made of Robert Casadesus who composed *Dances Méditerranéennes*
and a *Concerto* for two pianos and orchestra. Celius Dougherty, well-
known as a composer of successful songs, wrote for the medium of his
concert profession a *Nautical Sonata* the music of which is based on sea
chanties.[32]

The enumeration of some representative duo-pianist-composers brings
this survey to a fitting close. The purpose of the foregoing paragraphs
has been to demonstrate the active interest which composers at large have
taken in the two-piano medium. For a more exhaustive representation of
the available repertoire, the reader is referred to the Appendix *Original
Two-Piano Music* which is contained in Chapter XXIV of Book III, *The
Literature*. On the basis of the evidence submitted, it will be agreed that
.the supposed lack of original compositions in the realm of two-piano
music, as it has sometimes been asserted by the uninformed, in reality is
non-existent. Instead, students and artists are confronted with a reservoir
of material which is most substantial both in volume and quality. If the
fallacy concerning a scarcity of original literature could persist at all,
the blame for this illusory condition must be laid mainly to the duo-

29. For analysis of this suite, see Book III, *The Literature,* Chapter XXIII, *The Standard
     Repertoire.*
30. For comment, see Book III, *The Literature,* Chapter XXIII, *The Standard Repertoire.*
31. Premiered in London, 1937; in Chicago, 1939.
32. The work was premiered in New York, 1944.

pianists themselves. With a few laudable exceptions,[33] they apparently fail to scan the libraries and older catalogues. Instead of depending, season after season, on the same time-honored repertoire items, they could easily enough create sufficient demand with publishers to re-issue many a long-forgotten score. There is little doubt that publishers will readily comply with such requests. It is therefore the task of all serious duo-pianists, and indeed their privilege, to conduct the fascinating search for those numerous items of the extensive literature which seem to have fallen into oblivion almost as soon as they were created.

Music needs to be played and heard, and performance is its chief promotion. Considering the successful careers of so many practitioners in the field, there certainly must be a nucleus of artists who are interested in scholarship and methodology. The results of their organized research will quickly abolish one of the most absurd prejudices ever to stifle a young art. Their findings and demonstrations will effectively disprove some popular misconceptions on duo-pianism which exist, as Appleton and Field remark,[34] with "those musical eclectics who insist that (a) there is little literature for the combination, except transcriptions; and (b) that it has no status as an art form."

As far as the rank of duo-pianism as an art form is concerned, it appears hardly necessary at all to take a stand; for if beauty is said to be its own excuse, it assuredly also can be its own defense. Whatever implication has been made in regard to insufficient literature, this chapter should have dispelled that careless derogation. Moreover, it will have revealed the abundance of material which actually prevails and is at the disposal of all two-piano devotees. But even if the existing repertoire should be absorbed and exhausted in years to come by the continuing upsurge of the movement, new composers already are creating the standard works of tomorrow. More sympathetic to the medium than ever before, they will not fail in satisfying the demand. It is the constantly increasing popularity of duo-pianism which provides composers with the stimulus and encouragement so important for all creative work.

May this be called just wishful thinking? To answer any doubt, here is an eloquent example: When duo-pianists Gold and Fizdale gave their annual New York concert on November 14, 1948, the program consisted, with the exception of Mozart's *Sonata in D major (K. 448)*, entirely of

---

33. To quote one of these, it is Pierre Luboshutz who states:
    "The two-piano four-hand repertoire is not nearly as limited as appears at first glance, and my wife and I in the fifty engagements we play each season, are able to present as many different programs as the average solo pianist plays for his audiences in the course of a year's recitals." Luboshutz, *The Two-Piano Recital.*
34. *Is There a Two-Piano Dilemma Today?,* "Musical Courier," August 1947.

compositions written especially for this team and then given their first performance. The singular event produced the following new works: *Sonata* by Marcelle de Manziarly; *Suite Champêtre* by Vittorio Rieti; *Concerto for Two Pianos, Winds and Percussion* by Paul Bowles; *Valse Lente* by Germaine Tailleferre; and *Carnaval à la Nouvelle-Orleans* by Darius Milhaud. The concert was a feat of enterprise and vision and it may well be that it will go down in the annals of duo-pianism as a memorable occasion.

Composers are practical people. Like everybody else, they do not like to invest their time and efforts for a cause in which they do not believe. They are unwilling to entrust their genius, that priceless possession, to a medium unsuited to their inspiration. If composers enlist duo-pianism to become one of their creative channels, they thereby sanction the art. In turn, as long as duo-pianism develops within the precincts of creative music, the medium always will attract composers as its heralds.

Were it not composers who first became its prophets?

CHAPTER XI

THE EXTENT AND THE TREND

1. THE EXTENT

Duo-pianism in 1950 has assumed commanding proportions. Not only are there many artists of the highest caliber who devote their best energies to this ensemble form; not only are there numerous composers who are busy creating new works for the genre; but there is also a large number of additional functions which have considerably widened the scope of the entire field.

These new applications of the art of two-piano playing have far exceeded the confines of its original aspirations which principally revolved around the cultivation of an independent ensemble art for the use at home and in public concert. Up to this time, only the aspects of artistic performance and composition have been considered, and indeed it is these primary factors which have been chiefly instrumental in creating and nurturing a tradition of duo-pianism. In the following paragraphs, brief attention will now be given to a number of additional utilizations of the two-piano medium. To be considered are the various employments which have been given to the idiom for other purposes and seemingly have proved themselves as suitable expediencies. These applications are indicative of the variety of practical possibilities inherent in the medium and of the full extent of the duo-pianistic territory. After observing the general character of the movement, it will then be possible to draw some conclusions in regard to the present trend and the expected future.

The following illustrations are chosen at random and demonstrate the broad level of application which duo-pianism has found in this day.

The opera *Down in the Valley* by Kurt Weill was chosen for performance in a student production at the Chicago Musical College in 1949, Rudolf Fellner conducting. Technical limitations prevented the employment of an orchestra. In substitution, a two-piano score was secured upon special commission. The effect obtained is said to have been entirely satisfactory.

At the New York premiere of the same work, staged by the Lemonade Opera in Greenwich Village, again the small orchestra called for by the composer could not be assembled, but what a critic termed the "very clever arrangement for two pianos by Paul Aron" remedied the situation.

In *Music News,* issue of April 1949, editor-in-chief Dr. Hans Rosenwald reports on an opera workshop presentation of Donizetti's *Don Pasquale.* Part of the criticism reads:

> "Credit must go to musical director Edwin Jespe for an excellent job from the piano so that the whole work had fluency and imagination. One can be doubtful as to the usefulness of presenting 'Don Pasquale' without an orchestra: *sans orchestra an arrangement of the score for two pianos would conserve more of its flavor.*"

Mia Slavenska and her ballet troupe are traveling with duo-pianists Henrietta Pelta and Joseph Barish. The musical backing provided by the two-piano team amounts to what critics call "accompaniments of orchestral proportions." The pseudo orchestra plays an overture preceding the dance presentations, and also furnishes entr'act music; the continuity thus remains unbroken, and the special atmosphere of an evening of grand ballet is successfully simulated with only two pianos in the orchestra pit. This example is representative of a pattern in that many ballet troupes now employ duo-pianists for musical support. The substitute is so much less expensive than an orchestra that the very existence of the group may be due to this economy. Moreover, the two-piano combination offers distinct advantages regarding the frequency of rehearsals. It can also be said that the incisive quality of the piano tone is unequalled for the supply of rhythmic precision in certain phases of ballet routine.

Lately, much ballet music has been written for two pianos rather than for a large orchestral apparatus. It is the economy of the medium which evidences itself as a strong incentive to choreographers. It has already been shown that many works with orchestral instrumentations have been reduced to two-piano scores in order to make their more frequent performances possible. Sometimes, however, the reverse transition takes place. An interesting case in point is furnished by the music to the ballet creation *New Dance* which was composed by Wallingford Riegger for Doris Humphrey. The original version which had only the functional objective of providing ballet accompaniment, was written for one piano, four hands. Afterwards, Riegger remodelled the composition to become a concert piece for two pianos, in which form it was introduced by Luboshutz and Nemenoff at one of their Carnegie Hall recitals. Finally, the Finale of the erstwhile ballet music was orchestrated, and as a symphonic score it has found entrance into the repertoire of several orchestras.

Duo-pianism has made its way into the Little Theatre, into Opera and Ballet. At any rate, theatergoers are no longer surprised to see two pianos in the orchestra pit or on the stage. Nor is the substitute of detrimental consequence. To the contrary, many listeners consider a good two-piano team as preferable to a mediocre orchestra. In like tenor, Luboshutz and Nemenoff express their opinion as follows:[1]

"From the purely musical standpoint, two-piano work approaches most closely to orchestral values of sonority and color. Its tonal possibilities are infinite. In schools, or communities, that lack an adequate orchestra, it is quite possible to duplicate orchestral richness by means of two pianos. Indeed, two virtuosi who perform a truly polished arrangement of a Mozart operatic overture, let us say, or a symphonic excerpt, can achieve a more correct and more satisfying effect than an unpolished orchestra."

Whether or not the sonorities of two pianos actually are preferable to orchestral effects, however "unpolished," probably remains subject to controversy. There is no doubt, however, that the combination can be used in good stead when there is no orchestra available. A valid example are the programs of the Society for Private Musical Performances in Vienna, a group founded in 1918 upon the suggestion of Arnold Schoenberg. This society has as its aim the clear and well-rehearsed performances and frequent repetitions of modern compositions from Strauss and Mahler to the present, so that artists and music lovers may be enabled to acquire an intimate knowledge of contemporary works. With no orchestra at the disposal of the group for the rendition of symphonic works in their original form, two pianos have frequently been employed to give such compositions a hearing. The argument in behalf of the two-piano medium becomes especially noteworthy in this case, because duo-pianism is now deliberately elevated above the function of a mere substitute to the rank of a true gauge for abstract musical values inherent in a composition. The following interesting passages are quoted from a statement by Alban Berg outlining the purposes of the particular society:[2]

". . . the necessity becomes a virtue. In this manner it is possible to hear and judge a modern orchestral work divested of all sound-effects and other sensuous aids that only an orchestra can furnish. Thus the old reproach is robbed of its force—that this music owes its power to its more or less opulent and effective instrumentation and lacks the qualities that were hitherto considered characteristic of good music—melody, richness of harmony, polyphony, perfection of form, architecture, etc.

1. *The Art of Piano Ensemble*, "The Etude," January 1941, p. 5.
2. Nicholas Slonimsky, *Music Since 1900*, p. 545.

"A second advantage of this manner of music-making lies in the concert style of the performance of these arrangements. Since there is no question of a substitute for the orchestra but of so rearranging the orchestral work for the piano that it may be regarded, and should in fact be listened to, as an independent work and as a pianoforte composition, all the characteristic qualities and individualities of the piano are used, all the pianistic possibilities exploited. And it happens that in this reproduction—with different tone quality—of orchestral music, almost nothing is lost. Indeed, these very works, through the sureness of their instrumentation, the aptness of their instinctively chosen tone-colors, are best able to elicit from the piano tonal effects that far exceed its usual expressive possibilities."

Among the many compositions thus propagated by the society were works such as *La Mer* and *Three Orchestral Nocturnes* by Debussy; *Don Quixote, opus 35,* and *Symphonia Domestica, opus 53,* by Richard Strauss; *Passacaglia for Orchestra, opus 1,* by Anton von Webern; and *Kammersymphonie* by Franz Schreker.

In addition, original works for two pianos were pioneered on the society's programs, such as *Introduction, Passacaglia and Fugue, opus 96,* by Max Reger. The objectives and methods of this group deserve imitation on the widest plane. The two-piano medium is capable to make accessible and thereby to subject to appreciative processes an abundance of orchestral compositions which will otherwise be condemned to oblivion.

Motivations similar to those of the Viennese group seem to govern the policy of the Chicago Manuscript Society. This association is devoted not only to the performance of deserving works of obscure contemporary composers, and of such music of today's better-known composers which has not received ample attention, but includes into its project also any significant music of other epochs which has undeservedly disappeared from the concert repertoire. The working idea of this project could easily become instrumental in bringing to new life much of the forgotten two-piano music which was referred to in the preceding chapter.

To continue with the discussion of further applications, the survey now turns to the field of the oratorio in which the two-piano combination likewise is functioning as an adequate instrumental accompaniment. The contrapuntal complexities of the orchestral scores by Bach or Handel are exceeding the possibility of a correspondent representation when condensed to only one piano. Given over to two instruments, however, the significant voices can be treated with independence, and the general texture gains immeasurably in clarity and dynamic range.[3]

The same pattern of two-piano expediency can be observed on the largest scale with choir groups and glee clubs in general. For a long

3. In the annual performances of Handel's *Messiah* by the Lewis and Clark High School Choir of Spokane, two pianos are regularly employed for the instrumental portion of the score, and a fully satisfactory rendition of the work is thereby achieved.

time, choral conductor Fred Waring of "Pennsylvanians" fame has employed duo-pianists Morley and Gearhart on his nation-wide radio broadcasts. Although their two-piano art is frequently featured in special program numbers, the chief function of the team is that of assisting the glee club with its performance. Mixed voices and keyboard ensemble blend and balance well, as was already realized by Brahms when he wrote his *Liebeslieder* waltzes for vocal quartet and piano duet.

Radio logs generally abound in programs of two-piano music. In the preparation of this survey, an examination has been conducted involving typical broadcast schedules on a transcontinental scale. The particular investigation was mainly based on the weekly radio calendars of the *New York Times* and the weekly program guide of station *KDFC*, Sausalito, California (San Francisco region). Over a two-year period, during the seasons of 1948 and 1949, an average of two programs each week was found to be entirely devoted to two-piano music. In many communities of regional importance, local two-piano teams have been sustained on radio programs for considerable lengths of time.[4]

Considering that the program directors of the broadcasting industry react with the greatest sensitivity to the musical wishes of the people, the frequency of radio programs containing two-piano music is an unfailing barometer of the popularity enjoyed by the medium. As a result, various high-ranking network programs under commercial sponsorship have been noted to employ two-piano teams.[5] It is the awareness of its drawing power in business advertising which perhaps most strikingly attests to the great attraction exerted by the duo-pianistic idiom.

Another industry which also has recognized the popularity of two-piano music, are the recording companies. There is available a wide selection of recordings played by the leading duo-pianists, and a steady stream of new releases is forthcoming from the manufacturers.[6] A large percentage of compositions in the standard repertoire can now be heard on the phonograph. Whereas Wier's compilation of recordings for two pianos, dating from 1941, contained a mere thirteen items,[7] less than a decade later there exists a representative cross-section of two-piano

---

4. Hans and Rosaleen Moldenhauer, duo-pianists of Spokane, Washington, began a weekly half-hour broadcast of two-piano music over *KGA* in December 1943. The program, presenting music of a serious type and complete with extensive annotations, has since been sustained without interruption and at this writing is in its seventh consecutive year. *KGA*, a 50,000 kilowatt station, extends in range over the states of Washington, Idaho, Montana, Oregon, Utah and Northern California.
5. Chesterfield, Westinghouse, and other sponsors.
6. An extensive listing of recordings in the two-piano medium is found in Book III, *The Literature*, Chapter XXV, *Recorded Two-Piano Music*.
7. A. E. Wier, *The Piano*, pp. 447-448.

literature in recorded form, and the total amount has risen to hundreds of selections.

Much two-piano music which has been written and recorded, is of the lighter type. Sometimes, an accompaniment of various rhythm instruments is added to the two pianos, and a new variety of dance music has thereby been inaugurated. The entertainment field has generally seized upon the two-piano medium which seems to possess perennial novelty appeal and other qualities to make it a lasting attraction. For some time, the two-piano combination has found its way into the orchestras of revues and broadway musicals, into vaudeville and night club. Several leaders of popular orchestras have since years employed duo-pianists in their ensembles; Paul Whiteman is one of these conductors, and Ferde Grofé once was a member of his two-piano team. Morley and Gearhart, serious and recognized artists of the concert stage, have found it compatible with their musical standards to work for one of New York's fashionable hotels in nightly appearances. Whittemore and Lowe were featured as stars in close to 750 performances of an all-Navy musical and played for nearly a million service men and women during their years of enlistment in the Navy. In England, Rawicz and Landauer have reached the top level of popular acclaim, spreading the repute of the art to thousands after thousands. José and Amparo Iturbi gave the opportunity of a first acquaintance with duo-pianism to probably more people than was accomplished by any other single agency; they effected this service to the art through the medium of their two-piano performances in motion pictures.

From the entertainment field with its commercial aspects, the survey is turning to the functions of duo-pianism in the broad territory of educational endeavors. Two-piano teams have long been popular with music clubs of all types. *Pan Pipes,* the sorority magazine of Sigma Alpha Iota, recently devoted an entire issue to an appreciation of duo-pianism.[8] Besides paying homage to several internationally famous teams of which the women members are connected with the sorority, many duo-pianists of regional or local importance were also enumerated. The number of such teams who are practicing the art on a semi-professional or purely social level is legion. Their existence is a measure of significance for the appeal exerted by the medium, and their function in fostering and promoting the art is of vital importance.

There are also many active two-piano teams in local music teachers' associations; they afford the opportunity of ensemble work among colleagues and give variety to the programs of membership meetings. A special duo-piano club was organized in Miami Beach, Florida; possibly

8. The issue of February, 1949.

it is the first association entirely devoted to this form of ensemble.

In the planning of most music festivals, large or small, it has become necessary to reserve a full division to the flock of aspiring duo-pianists. Competition in all age groups is keen, and adjudicators are frequently heard to comment on the usefulness of ensemble work and the refreshing musical experience which can be found in two-piano activities.

In answer to the increasing demand, and at the same time providing further stimulation of interest in the art, many music schools and conservatories are now offering regular two-piano ensemble classes. The Juilliard School of Music in New York City and the Cornish School in Seattle, to mention only two institutions at opposite coasts, both list a special course in duo-pianism as part of the curriculum.[9] Chicago even boasts of a piano ensemble training school, devoted entirely to the development of piano teams including those of orchestral dimensions.

In a previous paragraph, the frequency of two-piano music on the air lanes was referred to as an accurate barometer of its popularity. An equally reliable indication for the spread of duo-pianism can be found in a survey of the market for printed compositions. Publishers are announcing new issues of two-piano music in steadily increasing numbers. These releases include both original works and arrangements; their difficulty ranges from the highest technical standard all the way through the intermediate grades down to the level of beginners. The carefully considered grading of the printed literature implies that two-piano playing has found entrance into the home and teaching studio as much as into the various branches of public performance. Acclaimed by artists and amateurs alike, it has become a definite and highly specialized form of musical activity and expression.

Characteristic of the attention which is accorded to the field by commercial publishing houses, are the opening remarks to *A Catalog of Two-Piano Music* which was issued by J. Fischer & Bro., New York, a few years ago. The preface reads as follows:

> "The popularity of two-piano playing has increased to such an extent in recent years that there is available today more literature for this field than ever before. In addition to the concert stage and radio studio, where many excellent artist teams are performing daily, interest in piano ensemble has asserted itself also in the home and schools. Particularly in the latter has it been used with success, for it has served as an incentive to the younger pupils as a splendid means of developing a sense of active participation in music with a resultant greater interest and appreciation."

The educational aspect of duo-pianism is perhaps the most important

---

9. The two-piano class at Juilliard is conducted by Appleton and Field; the instructors at Cornish are Stephen and Patricia Balogh who have promoted the medium also through weekly radio broadcasts of two-piano music.

of all its functions. The presence and frequent employment of a second pianoforte in the teaching studio has become the rule rather than the exception. Progressive educators have recognized the additional instrument as a valuable aid in the process of instruction and therefore are making it a permanent fixture in their set of pedagogic tools. The usefulness of the second piano as an expedient for the purposes of demonstration,[10] and the opportunity to provide the pupil with the benefits of piano ensemble work, are topics reserved for discussion in a later chapter.[11] A body of leading piano instructors, as it is represented by the Faculty membership of the National Guild of Piano Teachers, attests to the many and varied two-piano activities which can be coupled with the professional life of the successful pedagogue. To be sure, it is from the educators that the chief stimulus and support in duo-pianistic respect must come to the young. Pupils need guidance and inspiration in this ensemble form which presents a challenge in its complexity of mechanical aspects and in its basic demand of *esprit de corps.*

It only remains to investigate the extent to which duo-pianism has penetrated into the musical life of the average amateur. Fundamentally, music belongs into every home; it is within the family unit that there lies its most applicable and rewarding function. Again, of all types of home music by far the most satisfying is that of ensemble playing in the companionship of family members and friends. It is no mere accident that so many professional two-piano teams had their beginnings in such informal social gatherings when the future duo-pianists still cherished as a pastime what afterwards was to become their art.

For all amateurs, one of the greatest benefits of two-piano playing is the acquaintance with the best of musical literature which can be gained through this medium. Unhampered by the exacting routine of concert stage and teaching studio, the music lover will derive continual pleasure and find an inexhaustible source of learning in the many available arrangements from masterworks of the symphonic and chamber music literature. These condensations for two pianos usually do not present any undue difficulties and therefore may be attempted by average players. They are, on the other hand, thoroughly adequate in their reproduction of the original.[12]

It seems suitable to conclude this brief survey of the extent of duo-

10. Already fully realized, for example, by Chopin, the teacher.
11. See Book II, *Nature, Applications and Problems,* Part C, "The Educational Medium," Chapter XXI, *Pedagogic Applications.*
12. A representative selection of such arrangements can be found in Book II, *Nature, Applications and Problems,* Part C, "The Educational Medium," Chapter XXII, *Pedagogic Materials.*

pianism with an example from everyday's music life. Reference is made
to a recent issue of the professional magazine *Northwest Music Review*.[13]
In a short routine report on a month's concert life in one typical city
(Portland, Oregon), the numerous activities in the piano ensemble field
are strikingly accounted for.[14] In proportion to other concert events, the
medium of duo-pianism figures conspicuously in its frequency. The Junior
Symphony orchestra of Portland gave a performance of the C minor
Concerto for two claviers by Bach. A local music school premiered a two-
piano suite composed by the director of the institution. The University
of Portland presented "good-to-look-at and excellent-to-hear" duo-pianists
Appleton and Field on the university's cultural program series. The civic
chamber music group, Collegium Musicum, in a single concert programmed
a Bach concerto for two claviers and another for three claviers. Again
it is to be emphasized that all four presentations of two-piano music occurred during a one-month period in a city of average size.

The tremendous rise in popularity, and the continuing expansion of
applications, are observed by the professional adherents of duo-pianism
with diversified expressions of their gratification. Dougherty and Ruzicka,
for instance, account for the development as follows:

"For the public, the exhilaration of the new sound and the spectacle
of double keyboard technique provide aural as well as visual interest.
All the new literature for two pianos has proved irresistible to pianists,
and all music schools are endorsing and encouraging the art of two-piano
playing."

Over a decade ago, in 1939, Silvio Scionti commented on the trend
of the movement with these words:[15]

"The present very marked revival of interest in two-piano playing is a development rather than a sensational outburst of enthusiasm resulting in a fad."

Time has proven the foregoing statement to be correct. It has also born
out to the fullest measure what Josef and Rosina Lhevinne propounded
even earlier, in 1933, with the following inducement to the art:[16]

"The possibilities of entertainment and instruction, both to the performers and
their hearers, are virtually limitless."

What in 1933 may have appeared as propagandism, turned out to be
a prophecy. Despite the current upsurge of interest in the medium, and
notwithstanding the broad field of applications which two-piano music
has since found, the prognosis of the Lhevinnes holds true even now, and
the possibilities of duo-pianism still appear limitless.

13. March-April, 1949.
14. The particular news item is found on page 10 of said issue.
15. *The Fascination of Two-Piano Playing*, "The Etude," September 1939, p. 567.
16. *Four Hands That Play As Two*, "The Etude," December 1933, p. 809.

2. THE TREND

The time has come to summarize and to conclude. It has been observed how, in this day and age, the combination of two pianos is encountered from the concert hall to the teaching studio, from the glee club podium to the pit below the ballet stage, from the radio station to the night club. Where the almost universal presence of a single piano since generations has come to be regarded as commonplace, the pairing of keyboards and the resultant doubling of resources create a new fascination in the instrument. Two-piano music is inciting a novel experience in abstract sonorities, but it is also provoking the awareness of a team-born discipline unheard of and not even expected in solo performance. Such is the status of today (1950) when duo-pianism appears as one of the last frontiers on the musical scene, still holding out challenge and opportunity for the pioneer.

Duo-pianism, according to all signs, has become a function. But what of the future? Is the attraction of the medium caused by a quickly fading novelty appeal, and is the present popularity of the art merely an ephemeral vogue? Does the call of this "last frontier" lead into a blind alley and eventually to a dead end?

There is, it can be most emphatically maintained, no reason for doubt in the actuality of duo-pianism as a living art, nor in its equality as a member in the ranks of other instrumental music. There is, furthermore, no cause for concern over the future development of the medium. Indications are that the rise of popularity with performers, composers, pedagogues, and listening audience will continue towards a culmination point not as yet to be estimated. The present momentum of the movement will carry it onward to that destination. At the same time, a most important symptom makes itself noticed. It demonstrates more poignantly than any other argument that duo-pianism is here to stay. While the general trend is still pointing forward and upward, a nucleus of *tradition* has quietly come into formation. The stakes of the art are now securely grounded in the system of musical culture; therefore, *perspective* becomes possible for the first time. For it is only when the extent of a movement encompasses both its historic past and the actuality of its present existence, that a speculation may be attempted in regard to the trend which already is shaping its future influence.

In the fall of 1949, duo-pianists Appleton and Field gave a series of three Town Hall recitals entitled "Two Pianos Through Four Centuries." The concerts were announced as a survey of original music from the earliest known compositions for two virginals through the writings of

Stravinsky, Bartók, Hindemith and other contemporaries. This project represented the first professional undertaking of its kind on record. The artists themselves set forth their purpose in a joint statement which was worded as follows:

> "Although ensemble piano playing has achieved a new peak of popularity within recent years, with multiple keyboard combinations among the most heavily booked of all concert attractions, there has been a regrettable tendency to stress stunt value and to regard the ensemble of two or more pianos either as a means of dressing up for greater popular appeal music conceived originally for a solo instrument, or as a means for more economical presentation of works intended for the orchestral medium. Thus the distinguishing characteristics of the specialized art of duo-pianism have come to be obscured, and it is seldom realized that this art has a four centuries' tradition of its own, with a substantial literature representing the recognition of the world's greatest composers of its unique range of sonorities and tonal effects. Our purpose in giving this series of three survey concerts at Town Hall is to remind students of the piano and the piano music public that four-hand piano playing is no mere stunt act, but an independent art form that has inspired original masterpieces in all the great schools of composition and thus fully justifies from a purely artistic standpoint, aside from all other considerations, the popularity it is now enjoying and the challenge which it presents to the creative musical genius of today and tomorrow."

Nothing can demonstrate the consolidation of an art form better than a comprehensive review of the historic course which it has transgressed. The parade of four centuries of two-piano music implies so great a breadth of scope, that the inquiry into the past inevitably must indicate the rounding out of a cultural evolution.

A tradition of duo-pianism has come into being and is further consolidated with each passing year. Tradition is conducive to perspective. A striking evidence of the reflections and practical consequences brought on by both tradition and perspective, today is furnished in the very existence of a harpsichord ensemble which confines itself to performances of the music written for the ancient instrument and consequently is specializing in a comparatively narrow segment of duo-keyboard history.

Manuel and Williamson are these duo-harpsichordists who have set themselves a task as difficult as rewarding. Their repertoire concentrates on Couperin, Bach, and Mozart and sometimes includes the composers on the borderlines of harpsichord writing. The fact of their successful and by now established association was conditioned by the general broadening of interest in the two-piano field; only the recent upsurge of the art could render the specialization in a particular branch or period possible. Analogous examples in the piano solo field are provided by the many Bach or Beethoven or Chopin specialists. The appearance of a two-harpsichord team, specializing in the earliest literature, probably also results from the repeated revivals of interest in the harpsichord idiom generally. Many performers now are devoting themselves entirely to the ancient medium, and modern composers like de Falla and Poulenc have written new music for it. This renewal of interest is significant because of its connotations and implications. Several aspects of a philosophical nature make the harpsichord indeed a "modern" instrument. It must be remembered that the pianoforte, while repressing the harpsichord by its arrival, really never replaced it in acumen to express certain aesthetic sentiments. The fundamental differences between the pianoforte and the harpsichord were already aptly pointed out by Saint-Saens who witnessed an earlier attempt to bring the harpsichord back into its own. In his *Musical Memories*, Saint-Saens wrote as follows:[17]

"The harpsichord has been revived of late so that it is needless to describe it. It lacks strength, and that was the reason it was dethroned in a period when strength was everything. On the other hand, it has distinction and elegance. As the player can not modify the intensity of the sound by a single pressure of the finger—in which it resembles the organ—like the organ, with its multiple keyboards and registers, the harpsichord has a wide variety of effects and affords the opportunity for several octaves to sound simultaneously. As a result, while music written for the harpsichord gains in strength and expression on the modern instrument (the pianoforte), it often assumes a deceptive monotony for which the author is not responsible."

Manuel and Williamson have taken on the mission of performing the works for two claviers by Bach, his predecessors and successors, on the same instruments for which they were originally conceived. The presence of these duo-harpsichordists brings truly historical depth to the entire field, and it renders duo-pianism that distinction which adheres to all tradition. In a striking manner, evidence is given of the age-honored existence of keyboard ensemble art, and of the active interest shown to it by the most accomplished harpsichordists of their time who since have lived on as the most eminent composers of all times. Can any reference to the "novelty" aspect of duo-pianism find a more forceful refutation?[18]

Appleton and Field, with their survey of four centuries of keyboard

17. pp. 173-174.
18. Philip Manuel, of Portugese and British descent, was born in Minnesota. Following graduation from Grinnell College where he studied in both the academic and music departments, he went to Vienna and later to London. After a period of teaching in the University of North Dakota, he established himself in Chicago, where he has become known as organist and harpsichordist.
    Gavin Williamson, of Scotch descent, is a native of Winnepeg. His musical activities took him to Minneapolis, Boston and Chicago, where he became known as an accompanist for many of the world's most renowned singers. His teachers include Palmer Christian in organ, Victor Heinze and Ethel Leginska in piano, and Wanda Landowska in harpsichord. He also did special work in Paris and London.
    Since their debut as duo-harpsichordists, Manuel and Williamson have been heard in all the key cities of this country, both in concert and on the air. They appear frequently with the Chicago Symphony Orchestra and they specialize in authentic performances of ancient music with an ensemble which includes strings, flutes, oboe, and singers.

ensemble music, and Manuel and Williamson, as duo-harpsichordists, are rounding out the historic picture, if only by bringing into relief the series of changes which have taken place in the process of duo-pianistic evolution. From the consideration of the past, and from the actuality of the present day, the inquiry now needs to turn into the future. There cannot be but wonder what causes underlie the popularity of duo-pianism, placing the art on so broad a fundament and giving it propulsion for the continuing expansion. The urge for an inquest is aroused concerning the motives and stimuli which have produced the results at hand and must affect the future course.

Paul Bekker points out that "history is not a collection of dates and incidents and so-called facts, but the great life process of mankind, which we may comprehend, not by looking at it as a kind of historical costume parade, but only by trying to recognize the forces which control it."[19]

The generations of this century live in an age of quest for a new community of human association. Whatever political and economic forces were reflected in the manifestations of art during the Romantic period, they have since run their course and are replaced by new ideologies and new experimentations. As a consequence, musical tastes likewise are pronouncedly turning away from the connotations of Romanticism which, in quintessence, has represented and encouraged the more or less pathological indulgence in the affairs of the individual. In the system of aesthetic philosophy of the nineteenth century, such pathological qualities were considered indispensable for the creation of a work of art. Literary monuments attesting to this tendency are numerous, such as Goethe's *The Sorrows of Young Werther* and Hoelderlin's *Hyperion*. The individual artist necessarily found himself involved and engulfed by this ideology; inevitably, he was placed into marked contrast to other individuals.

After the passing of the *fin de siècle*, however, there occurred again a marked shift of emphasis, a breaking away from the self-indulgence of the individual and an orientation towards the more impersonal attitude of a group. It stands to reason that the subjective element can never be abolished in behalf of the objective, or vice versa. Rather it is by the degree of weight given to either attitude that the character of the whole is determined.

Igor Stravinsky, generally identified as a representative of the objective trend in musical composition, fully realizes the crucial problem of balance and expresses it concisely in the following words:[20]

19. Bekker, *The Story of Music*, p. 20.
20. *Subjective and Objective* by Igor Stravinsky, as told to Sol Babitz, *Music and Dance in California and the West.*

"The mere fact of the individual's existence is a guarantee of subjectivity; the creative problem is to *objectivise* the subjectivity."

The present period in art is becoming increasingly critical toward the manifestations of the subjective element, and individuals are taught to be self-effacing. This doctrine is but "the reaction which always comes when some older form of art passes into its hypergrotesque stage. Then the call for simplicity sounds suddenly from some new direction."[21]

To the composer, this postulate means categorically "to strip the music of unnecessary instruments (for essential sound) and unnecessary notes (for essential form)" (Stravinsky). The *neue Sachlichkeit* or "new objectivity" is expounded and propagandized by leaders like Hindemith, Milhaud, and Stravinsky. They and the phalanx of contemporary composers agree that the "over-emotionalized music of the nineteenth century has caused the new composer to react in the direction of cleanness and simplicity which may be deceptive because of the rhythmic and musical complexity contained." (Stravinsky)

The course of the composer therefore seems clear. Once again he is becoming the prophet of his age, by shaping musical history long *before* perspective denotes it as such, unrecognized and unrewarded perhaps in his own time, but true to the voice of his vision.

For the interpretative musician and particularly for the soloist, the quality of objectivism in attitude and behaviour is always difficult to achieve. Indeed, it is in the state of loneliness that subjectivism calls loudest for expression. The soloist is accountable only to himself in his every aggression and reticence. Mechanically and aesthetically, he is his own lord. By contrast, any form of ensemble averts the danger of excess in that individual tendencies are modified by mutual control, and a common denominator needs to be arrived at to make the team a working unit.

True, the organ and harpsichord soloists still perform on the same classic instruments as they had been designed and developed for the requirements of the Classic period; but these solo players take meticulous care to display the same classic style which is demanded from them by the unquestionable authority of tradition. The pianoforte, however, came into being as the special and ideal musical medium for Romantic expression. "It is the romantic instrument in an inclusive sense" (Einstein). Highly responsive to the slightest inflection, the pianoforte is suited to speak the language of subjectivity with infinite nuances which react to, and correspond with every shade of emotion. It is a perfect vehicle for

---

21. Paul Bekker, *The Story of Music*, p. 98.

the most individualistic rendition of music. Considering that this capacity in truth is the explicit purpose for which the instrument was developed to its present perfection, the solo performer of today must find it increasingly difficult to ignore the natural properties of the pianoforte and to satisfy his audiences with the self-effacing, objective attitude which is the tendency of this time. Logically, the momentous question arises: Does the pianoforte, this ideal medium for the projection of human sensitivity into music, face a future in which it must stand forlorn as a *solo* instrument?

In the realm of pianoforte art, it is duo-pianism which answers the postulates of today. The same approach to objectivity which eludes the solo pianist, becomes at once obligatory for the combination of two performers. The call for emotional restraint and simplicity is fulfilled. In place of the egocentric attitude characterizing the typical soloist of romantic concepts, there now appears a common will, fusing the dualism of personalities into one single agency which controls and directs both mechanics and ideology until they blend in perfect accord. Here is piano music fundamentally different from that which is produced by the soloist or supplied by that humble subordinate, the piano-accompanist. Duo-pianism is rational, precise, efficient, tempered, impersonal because of its collectivistic character, streamlined to present-day, yet classic ideals, expressing aesthetic sentiments without sentimentality, conforming to the principle of "new objectivity" and aiming for a common unity in music through the synthesis which only ensemble playing can give.

In duo-pianism, the same type of community spirit is alive which created, after the First World War, the genre which has since been termed *Gemeinschaftsmusik*. This category is distinguished from the usual orchestral styles in that every voice now has an importance of its own. The partners being on equal footing, they form a new community in which new joy is found. A trend toward polyphonic styles is collateral; it can be effectively materialized in duo-pianism which constitutes the smallest ensemble form as far as the number of players is concerned, yet renders possible a maximum employment of interwoven voices.

It resolves that duo-pianism is fulfilling the principal requirements of this mechanical age: The medium presents both an apparatus of technical complexity and precision, and it offers the orientation toward new objectivity. If José Ortega y Gasset finds the most generic and characteristic features of new art "in the tendency to dehumanize art,"[22] he means much the same. In the place of passions, he looks for aesthetic sentiments: "It

22. *The Dehumanization of Art*, "The Symposium," April 1930.

was necessary to root out private feelings from music, to purify it by an exemplary objectification."

The English critic Edwin Evans looks at the first thirty years of the twentieth century as a period of experimentation during which "it has performed its function of providing a sufficiency of new expressive resources. It has yielded a profusion of new material none of which has been fully exploited, and much of which has scarcely been developed."[23]

Duo-pianism is one of these new expressive resources. It is not a recent medium by any means, but the art, repressed and neglected for a full century by the individualistic tendencies of an age of solo pianism to which it had to be foreign, now stands recognized, acclaimed, and *needed* in the development of a new community life and in the promotion of a new social attitude. Duo-pianism contains that "profusion of new material" into which the musician of today wants and needs to merge if he, too, is to become a full member of his generation and, being an artist, a historian of his time. For "when individuality has been exploited to the limit of its possibilities, the desire for a common unity grows up once more."[24]

Duo-pianism, combining the physical resources of two modern instruments and fusing the minds of a community of players into one common direction, has the strength to meet the Tomorrow of Music. The tendencies of this ensemble form, inherent in apparatus and manipulation, indeed are actively shaping the trend. Duo-pianism like all art has become a *symptom,* and thereby is fulfilling its mission to life and to the history of the ages.

---

23. *Stocktaking,* 1930. *Music and Letters,* January 1931.
24. Paul Bekker, *The Story of Music,* p. 247.

BOOK II

NATURE, APPLICATIONS, AND PROBLEMS

CHAPTER XII

DEFINITIONS

1. WHY TWO PIANOS?

At the outset of any general discussion of duo-pianism, this question will inevitably arise. Mostly it is posed quite casually, but sometimes it betrays profound insight. Why two pianos? The solo piano with its properties of mechanism and sonorities seems to offer a sufficiently wide range of tonal resources and an adequate volume of intensity and dynamic shading, to make it appear entirely self-sufficient as a medium of expression. Music written for the pianoforte, like that for the organ, replete with harmonic richness and contrapuntal complexities, is singularly capable of producing a fully independent musical performance.

Another question which readily suggests itself, asks for the incentives because of which the pianist should sacrifice the freedom of emotional expression which is his in solo performance to the apparent necessity of discipline and restraint which has to govern any partnership. This obvious call for cooperation and for compromise in duo-piano ensemble from the beginning hampered the development of this branch; as early as in Mozart's time, this factor proved obstructive to the full acceptance of the combination.[1]

From the purely personal point of view, there is no doubt that the privilege of absolute freedom will need to be abandoned, or at least greatly modified, when two pianists join forces for ensemble playing. The compensation must therefore be commensurate to encourage the prospective disciple of two-piano art, and it must in addition contain certain incentives which make duo-pianism actually preferable to solo playing.

1. See quotation of Jahn's statement in Book I, *The History*, Chapter IV, *Mozart*.

The physical reasons for the combination of two pianofortes lie in the realm of mechanical propensities peculiar to the instrument, while the motivating causes for the association of two pianists can be found in the emotional disposition common to most any human being.

To be specific, these factors are on the mechanical side the great range of sonorities of the pianoforte, with all its coloring and tonal balance, which must receive an inadequate representation by the only ten fingers of one performer and can find a more complete realization in the employment of twenty fingers. As to the psychological motive, the quest for companionship undoubtedly is the chief stimulus of the entire social life and system. If musical performance, according to the consensus of opinion, is an emotional outlet for the individual, ensemble playing offers the added inducement of companionship. In the words of the late Dr. Preston Ware Orem:[2] "There is no joy in music like playing with others," which means to say that the greatest satisfaction of self-expression derives from the awareness of rapport and resonance with others.

As to physical aspects, a short discussion of the pianoforte as an instrument seems in place at this time. The eighty-eight pitches fixed by the keyboard provide a wide range of semi-tones which Dr. Preston Ware Orem[3] has classified as "four distinct registers, although the points of demarcation are not rigidly distinct."

Dr. Orem describes these registers as follows:

"The topmost register is that 'glassy' or brilliant one . . . the vehicle for all the music-box imitations from Poldini to Liadoff; and still useful for a variety of purposes. . . . Then comes the melodic or the treble (as you please) register. In spite of Chopin's fondness for tunes in this register, we are inclined to distrust it, it is so likely to be submerged by too heavy accompaniments in other registers. . . .

"The next might be named the baritone register, the one so much preferred by Franz Liszt for the delivery of so many melodies, both original and transcribed; one recalls at once the famous *Love Dream* and Wagner's *Evening Star*. . . . This register is of use in delivering melodies or counter-melodies, and in backing upon strengthening melodies assigned to other registers. And now our final register is the bass, the real bass."

Considering the length of the keyboard, it appears evident that these four definite choirs of the pianoforte can never be simultaneously employed by the only ten fingers of one performer. While it is true that *tutti* effects may be desirable at few occasions only, there still will be many instances when three of the registers should be in action, or when the tonal material is so distributed that its spacing becomes a physical impossibility for execution by two hands. A practical approach to the problem suggests itself through the medium of four-hand playing on one

2. *About Pieces for Two Pianos*, "The Etude," LVI, September 1938, page 565.
3. *All About Four Hand Music*, "The Etude", LVI, February, 1938, p. 76.

keyboard, and indeed this could be the logical solution as far as the mechanical exploitation of keyboard sonorities is concerned. This reasoning, however, fails to take into account the human psyche, in that four-hand playing on one piano makes for a one-sided distribution of *primo* and *secondo* parts, arresting as if it were each performer to either the treble or the bass registers. This limitation or confinement rarely produces the best results, musically or personally. Ruthardt[4] writes: "One will have noticed that four-hand playing is ineffective in the concert hall for the reason that it cannot afford sufficient room to the individuality of the players." The essence of this statement is not limited to performance on the concert stage. Four-hand playing, popular as it is as a piano ensemble because of its convenience, does not compare in satisfying results with playing on two instruments. This becomes readily evident as soon as original one-piano, four-hand music is performed on two keyboards. At once each individual experiences distinctly greater ease and freedom. This statement is acknowledged by Josef and Rosina Lhevinne who write:[5] " . . . four-handed playing upon two pianos . . . is of greater interest to us than four hands at one piano. Musically, its scope is richer. And, from the point of view of the playing itself, the players have greater freedom, for each one can draw upon both bass and treble, and each one is master of his own pedaling."

The greater convenience attending the employment of only *one* instrument is, of course, to be realized; however, the debate at this time does not aim for convenience, but at the attainment of the best results. Where the manipulation of four hands on one keyboard meets with physical restrictions which bring about interference with interpretative freedom, two pianos are affording each player with greater liberation through the equal allotment of resources. An increased autonomy for the performer personally results, as well as greater musical flexibility, in that the bass and treble parts can now be interchanged at will.

In the argument in behalf of two pianos, four hands, versus one piano, four hands, a few pertinent remarks coming from Luboshutz and Nemenoff[6] are quoted in the following. They write:

"Two-piano playing is as different from ordinary duet playing (four hands at one piano) as it is from solo work. Its ultimate beauty lies in the richness of sonority and volume released by the two instruments, and this can never be duplicated on one alone. Also, when working at one piano, the two players sit too close for complete freedom. Again, one plays the Primo (or important) part while the other takes the Secondo (or obbligato) throughout the entire duet, a circumstance which

4. *J. C. Eschmanns Wegweiser durch die Klavier-Literatur*, edited by Adolf Ruthardt, Preface to Chapter XII.
5. *Four Hands That Play As Two*, "The Etude," LI, December 1933.
6. *The Art of Piano Ensemble*, "The Etude," January 1941, p. 5.

nullifies the possibility of balance between the voices. And, lastly, the technical resources of the two players at one piano are decidedly limited. Four-hand duets are very pleasing to hear, and they provide a measure of ensemble training which is decidedly better than none at all; still, in order to explore the fullest possibilities of piano ensemble work, two pianos are just twice as valuable as one."

The value referred to lies chiefly, in addition to all other possibilities, in the opportunity for antiphonal effects provided by two pianofortes. Antiphony indeed is one of the greatest advantages of the art; it is the *concertante* style of playing which has elevated duo-pianism to become a true ensemble. The character of antiphonal treatment is pointed out in the following paragraph from the pen of Dr. Preston Ware Orem who thus considers the resources of two pianofortes:[7]

"For two orchestras, as it were, comes first the antiphonal aspect. Like many Greek derivatives, the word antiphonal has a wide meaning: not even musical, necessarily; two anvils might be beaten antiphonally; or even echoes might be considered antiphonal. And two orchestras? Well, good old father Bach showed us how to manage those; and of antiphonal choruses there are a multitude. Two pianos are susceptible of many such effects, almost inexhaustibly so. And, by the way, there is a symphony for double orchestra, *The Consecration of Tones* by Ludwig Spohr, classic violinist and pedagog, that is well worth the study of any profound musician. If two orchestras can conduct a colloquy, how much more readily two pianists?"

The antiphonal employment of the two instruments then would appear to be one of the primary objectives for the combination. There would be no incentive whatever in the duplication of what one piano can perform alone, for

". . . the piano is a 'home orchestra' . . . but two pianos are two orchestras, and the older writers found this out at a very early date; the great Bach himself excelled in music for two (and even more) harpsichords. But the piano has its own peculiarities; outside of its own interior it is not an instrument of sympathetic vibration; two pianos do not react, one upon the other; and, in a way, this has some advantages. A multiplicity of pianos played in unison is hardly worth while; we may, in a measure, increase the noise but not the true sonority." (Dr. Preston Ware Orem.)[8]

To the foregoing statements may be added the remark that nothing will more falsify the essential nature, purpose and meaning of two-piano art than playing the same solo piece on two or more instruments, or any other similar approach to mere multiplication. Mechanical precision then is degenerated to a stunt, and artistry becomes absurdity.

If we accept the theory that four hands on two pianos can accomplish more mechanically and musically than two hands on one piano may do, the further hypothesis will soon be deducted that three, four or more performers and a corresponding number of instruments accordingly should

7. *About Pieces for Two Pianos*, "The Etude," September 1938, p. 565.
8. *About Pieces for Two Pianos*, "The Etude," September 1938, p. 565.

be capable of attaining the proportionately greater results. This reasoning proves erroneous, however, in that, regardless of the number of instruments and players employed, there still are only eighty-eight fixed tones available for textural employment. Because of harmonic laws, only a fraction of the total amount of tones can be used at any one time. Consequently, duplications of individual tones are certain to occur as soon as more than two performers are at work. Aesthetically, the result will be negative; practically, it is likewise futile.

Ruthardt opposes the larger ensembles with the following pungent remarks, combining his refutation with a recommendation of the two-piano medium:[9]

"Je mehr Klavierspieler zusammenwirken, z.B. zu 6 und 8 Haenden, desto aufdringlicher verletzt den feineren Musiksinn ein unertraegliches Geklimper, Gehacke, und Gepolter, und dies selbst auf den besten Instrumenten. Dagegen sind gute Kompositionen fuer 2, ausnahmsweise 3 Klaviere, wo an jedem Fluegel *nur ein* Spieler sitzt und die ganze Klaviatur zu beherrschen vermag, hoechst anregend, lohnend, und leider nur noch zu selten. In dieser Gattung, die sogar ueber das vierhaendige Spiel zu setzen ist, liesse sich noch viel Schoenes teils schreiben, teils bearbeiten."[10]

Following Ruthardt's verdict, a good many authorities have formulated their negative attitude in regard to the massing of pianofortes beyond the number of two. Among the more recent experts of piano ensemble, it is Silvio Scionti who states:[11]

"When the number of pianos is increased, the opportunity for artistic effects is diminished accordingly. The giant ensembles, say from ten to a hundred pianos, while entertaining from the standpoint of a 'stunt' and of creating an interest in the instrument itself, do not provide an easy opportunity for rehearsals and cannot realize all that two pianos can achieve in the way of a finished product."

Notwithstanding the reasons which speak against the employment of more than two pianofortes, the popularity of massed instruments is great. The "show" element certainly provides much of the attraction. The First Piano Quartet, to cite only one case in point, is achieving triumphs both in concerts and on the airlanes. In April 1949, the ensemble even received the coveted Peabody Radio Award for outstanding meritorious public service. While the First Piano Quartet might be the first permanent organi-

9. *J. C. Eschmanns Wegweiser durch die Klavier-Literatur*, Sixth Edition by Adolf Ruthardt, Preface to Chapter XII.
10. In free translation, these interesting remarks read: "The more pianists collaborate, for instance with six or eight hands, the more obstrusive becomes the intolerable strumming, banging, and noise making which is hurtful to the finer senses for music, and this even when the best instruments are used. By contrast, good compositions for two, and in exceptional cases for three pianos, (where only one person sits at each piano and thereby is able to reign over the entire keyboard) are highly stimulating, satisfying, and regrettably only much too scarce. In this category which is to be placed even above four-hand playing, much beautiful music could still be written, be it by original composition, be it by transcription."
11. *The Fascination of Two Piano Playing*, "The Etude," September 1939, p. 602.

zation of its kind, the idea of assembling four pianos is, it should be mentioned, not a recent one. The reader only needs to look at the evidence of the earlier literature to realize that the temptation to group numerous instruments and players together has been everpresent since the pianoforte was perfected. Karl Czerny, for instance, published a *Quartet Concertante* for four pianofortes, opus 230, as early as 1825 through Diabelli's firm, and he had a *Second Grand Quartet Concertante,* opus 816, printed by Cranz in 1851. Czerny even arranged, as a special commission, the overtures to *William Tell* and *Semiramide* by Rossini for eight pianos, four hands each! This record of thirty-two hands performing simultaneously on eight pianofortes was equaled in the *Caprice Concertante* by Willem Coenen (published 1879, Novello). Adolfo Fumagalli has as his opus 90 a *Grand Fantasia Militare* for four pianos (published ca. 1880, Ricordi), and Alfred von Livonius arranged Richard Wagner's *Meistersinger* Prelude for three pianos, twelve hands (published 1888, Schott). The examples just mentioned are only a few of the strenuous efforts which from time to time have inflated the capabilities of the pianoforte.

In this connection, a quotation is inserted from a concert report which was written [12] for *Music News,* issue of May 1949:

"On March 28, the First Piano Quartet made a popular hit. The Quartet undoubtedly is composed of capable and enthusiastic musicians, but the artistic value of their cause remains questionable. Where four hands on one, or more conveniently on two keyboards certainly can procure a richer texture of sonorities than two hands can do, the addition of a third or fourth pianoforte cannot but provide duplications or else burdening embellishments or detracting counter subjects. . . . Thus, with all mechanical precision of the ensemble, and in full regard of the stunning show which it provides, the question needs to be raised whether the First Piano Quartet is pioneering a new art form or must be considered a meteor of musical vaudeville."

During this controversial issue, reference needs to be made to the fact that Bach wrote several concertos for three and four claviers. At once it must be observed, however, that the design of these concertos is entirely contrapuntal and so transparent in texture that the cumulative results never approach the massive effect of a homophonic chord passage in the piano *solo* works of a Liszt or Rachmaninoff. The economy of texture employed and the linear tendencies of the contrapuntal voices place these works by Bach on a level of tonal effect very different from what might be expected in a concerto for three or four pianos with orchestral accompaniment.[13] Moreover, it must be remembered that there exist im-

---

12. By the author.
13. A modern parallel to Bach's ideals may be found in Isidor Philipp's *Concertino in A for three pianos without orchestra,* a product of typically French refinement and artistic economy of which Hutcheson writes that it is "to be admired for its euphony, skill and effectiveness."

portant differences between the sonorities of Bach's instruments and our modern pianofortes. In the following excerpts from comments on a performance of Bach's *Concerto in C major for Three Pianos and Orchestra* by the Minneapolis Symphony Orchestra, these differences are referred to, and stress is also laid on the different meaning which the term "concerto" held for Bach, as compared with the present-day conception of the form:[14]

> "Bach's instrumental resources were essentially unlike those of today. . . . The incisive brilliancy of tone of the clavecin, for example, cannot be even remotely approximated by the modern piano. With this difference goes a corresponding difference in the conditions of performance; it would have amazed and horrified Bach to have thought of having his preludes or concertos played in huge halls to audiences numbering thousands.
>
> "Nowadays a concerto for three pianos and orchestra suggests something monumental, above all in volume of tone. Bach's C major concerto, however, was written for three 'claviers' (in German the word was applied to both clavichords and clavecins) accompanied by two violins, viola and 'continuo', the last-named indicating the figured bass played by the lower strings, the clavi-cembalo, or both. Furthermore it must be remembered that the word 'concerto' has been so far perverted from its original and proper meaning—which it still had in Bach's time—that it has come to imply almost the exact opposite of what it once meant. Today a concerto is a solo performance against an orchestral background; in Bach's period it was literally a concerted playing of various instruments, one of them, or a group, having a more prominent obbligato part, but the main burden of the music resting with the whole ensemble."

It can also be said that only in his C major concerto for three claviers Bach gave equal prominence to each instrument, whereas the D minor concerto subordinates the second and third pianos to the first. A similar situation prevails in the *Concerto for Three Pianofortes and Orchestra* by Mozart, *K.242,* which is another classic example of the multiple piano concerto. This work was occasioned by the commission of a wealthy patroness who desired to play it together with her two daughters. In due time, it became Mozart's conviction that the concerto did not gain from the employment of a third piano; the latter, in the composer's own realization, merely served as accompaniment. Consequently, the third piano was outruled in a later revision of the work. Mozart then reduced the score to the more satisfactory combination of *two* pianos.

To conclude, and by way of summarization, these are some salient physical factors which place duo-pianism into advantage over all other types of piano performance:

1. The eighty-eight fixed tones with their various sound registers cannot be fully exploited by the only ten fingers of one performer.

2. Duet playing, four hands on one keyboard, stifles the freedom of the players by confining them to either "high" or "low" register.

---

14. Minneapolis Symphony Orchestra *Notes,* Season 1923-24.

3. More than twenty fingers cause the overburdening of pianoforte resources, in that the latter remain confined to eighty-eight tones regardless of the number of instruments.

4. Four hands on two pianofortes make possible the employment of all mechanical properties. Freedom is assured to each pianist.

The psychological motives of duo-pianism, more specifically its personal incentives and advantages, are reserved for discussion in the following group of chapters, entitled "The Artistic Medium."

At the close of this section stand the remarks of one observer who comments on the advantages of duo-pianism as follows:[15]

> "To pianists, one of the most intriguing and satisfying of musical forms is that of the duo-piano. For ensemble playing of this type does more than merely blend and enhance tonal strength; all of the harmonic color and depth of the keyboard, the rich and inexhaustible possibilities of this noble instrument, are exploited here to their fullest."

2. THE APPLICATIONS

From the history of two-piano playing, three principal applications of the art have emerged. They will now be used as basic types for classification. These categories are the *artistic* (pertaining to performance), the *creative* (original composition and transcription), and the *educational*.

The place of duo-pianism as an artistic genre by now is uncontested. Performers agree on being inspired by the semblance of orchestral heights which can be achieved, and by the flight of their coupled imaginations. At the same time, audiences are attracted by the richness of tone blending and by the precision of the concerted team work.

The composer and arranger finds in duo-pianism a creative medium *par excellence,* capable of revealing new sonorities, with enlarged polyphonic and antiphonal possibilities.

As to the educational application, pedagogues have come to realize at an early time that two-piano playing possesses a decided constructive influence. All phases of musical discipline can be demonstrated and applied more directly and more suggestively with the aid of a second piano. The team spirit in the pupil arouses his sense of responsibility and consideration, and indeed excites his greater alertness and resultant coordination. Most important, two-piano playing gives the teaching procedure impetus and inspiration, with invaluable psychological results.

The principal assumptions derived from the foregoing definitions will now become the points of departure for further discussion. These hypotheses are, in short, that duo-pianism offers to performers and composers

---

15. From the program notes to *A Two-Piano Recital,* RCA Victor Album DM 1047.

of music a field of artistic activity in thought and expression to be found in no other instrumental combination; furthermore, that two-piano playing is a method of musical instruction, providing immediate and practical educational benefits.

Through these three distinct applications, duo-pianism becomes a vehicle for

1. the performer, as an original medium for artistic expression;
2. the composer, as an original medium for creative thought;
3. the educator, as an original medium for instruction.

3. THE PROCEDURE

In the discussion of each separate field, extensive reference will be made to the opinions and statements of accepted authorities as they have come to the knowledge of the author through one or more of these channels:

1. Oral statements during interviews.
2. Written contributions in answer to questionnaires.
3. Printed communications on the subject.

Of particular interest, no doubt, will be found the direct quotations of answers given in reply to the specific inquiries generated by the project of research. These statements come from a cross-section of authorities on the given topics. During the investigation conducted preliminary to the present dissertation, a large group of duo-pianists was consulted, representing the highest professional rank. A nucleus of leading composers and eminent pedagogues likewise was invited to share in the discussion. Their contributions form a large part of the contents of this book on the "Nature, Applications, and Problems" of duo-pianism.

The opinions of the authorities will be found to be in agreement with each other on many points, if with modifications here and there. On other topics, the widest contrast of attitude and approach can be noted to exist. On several details of the research matter, a bewildering variety of findings confronts the reader. The sum total of reactions received adds up to the realization that it is difficult to establish generalities in such matters of approach and procedure as were subjected to investigation. Many problems must remain open to individual analysis and negotiation, because important psychological subtleties need to be taken into account from case to case. While there will be a certain amount of evidence and agreement, and a corresponding number of norms concluded therefrom, several salient phases of this complex matter at this time are eluding the attempts to arrive at a doctrine. In these instances, opposing statements will need to be left standing without compromise or decision in behalf of one or the other viewpoint. As long as both artistic and popular success are attained beyond any doubt, these authorities are certainly entitled to their individual beliefs and practices. The old maxim of the purpose sanctioning the means employed, finds again its confirmation in the variety of duo-pianistic methods.

To the casual observer, the awareness of different practices will be interesting in itself. For the student, the comparison even of apparent antitheses will be helpful. He will be enabled to select for himself the approach best suiting his inclination and disposition, his technical and nervous equipment, and the specific case of his two-piano partnership. He must remember that it is often difficult to distinguish between, and to select from, the many existing "methods" of solo performance; and he should expect that the matter becomes doubly vexing and crucial when two pianists face individual as well as collective problems for solution.

In the face of this situation, it must also be realized that the very nature of a problem *per se* involves the possibility to advance several and varying theories for its negotiation. This choice of approach, coupled with curiosity, indeed constitutes the very challenge of inquiry into the basis of phenomena. In our specific case of investigation, it must further be kept in mind that many phases of artistic activity are life processes of an ever-creative and pro-creative nature. Their character defies tabulation and eludes finality. They largely belong into the realm of aesthetic philosophy.

Therefore, it is proposed to conduct this survey in the manner of a *symposium,* one in which the writer merely attempts to channel the discussion into an unbiased system of observation. Rather than acting as arbiter, his role will be that of the moderator. Impartiality becoming the keynote, all answers are listed in alphabetical order of the names of their contributors; any semblance of strategic placement or grouping will thus be avoided.

The purpose of the following chapters then largely exists in the location, in the establishment, and in the enumeration of problems connected with duo-pianism. According to the multitude of opinions expressed, the answers to each problem will be of comparative rather than general significance. Yet, it is the seeking out, the finding, and the formulating of a problem that ultimately promotes the progress of a culture. Only if existing problems are eyed with open-mindedness, and their solution is attempted rather than relegated to subconscious reaction, that vital phase in the eternal quest for truth is entered during which attitudes occasionally may conflict. Taking for granted sincerity of purpose on the part of all concerned, such disagreement, however perturbing at the moment, eventually will bring about accord and benefit, and ultimately will insure accomplishment.

Part A: Duo-Pianism, An Artistic Medium

INTRODUCTION

Two-piano playing as a vehicle for expression will first be considered among the various manifestations of duo-pianism. Expression is the ultimate fulfillment of emotional life in every form; the need for expression underlies all types of communication. This is why the primary discussion is devoted to that branch of duo-pianism which will attract and affect by far the greatest number of devotees: the field of *performance*. The consideration of the creative and educational media which also are provided by the duo-pianistic idiom, will follow in subsequent chapters.

CHAPTER XIII

PARTNERSHIP

1. REASONS AND INCENTIVES

a. The Quest for Companionship

The reasons for becoming a duo-pianist, if this term will be permitted here for usage in the singular form, are manifold. They may be of a purely psychic nature. Very often a musician, although well equipped technically and musically, finds himself temperamentally incompetent or too nervous for solo work. Such conditions can be tempered or modified, and lacking nervous composure often is restored, in partnership with a fellow musician. Many of the pitfalls by which some pianists find themselves hampered in solo activities, like exaggerated emotionalism or undue reticence, and frequently lacking self-confidence, can be remedied through the association with another person.

Some accomplished pianists actually are abashed at playing alone. It is the quest for companionship which underlies so many attitudes and utterances in human behaviour that indeed it appears to be one of the basic motivating forces in life. While loneliness of thought or action might develop the greater individual strength, it lacks the wholesome values of companionship which lie in educational discipline, in unselfish coordination, and sometimes subordination, all of which are necessary adjustments in the social intercourse with others.

But will not duo-pianists of necessity lose their individualities when merging into an ensemble? To this obvious question Dougherty and Ruzicka offer as their answer:

"Duo-piano playing does not differ from other forms of enterprise demanding teamwork. It takes flexibility on the part of the individual to merge himself for the good of the team, just as in football or basketball. The brilliance of a player is sometimes sacrificed for the good of the team; at other times the field is his."

b. Romantic Attachment

The presence of a romantic attachment between the partners has frequently been the extra-musical cause for the formation of a two-piano team. The degree of intensity governing this motivation eventually consolidates or terminates the association. Many of the most distinguished ensembles have thus originated and, by way of their marital bliss, have attained so complete a synthesis of personal life and musical experience that the artistic result can be spoken of as a form of musical mating. A large percentage of the greatest teams, past and present, fall under the husband and wife classification.

c. Professional, Economic, Social, and Other Opportunities

There are, of course, many other reasons and incentives besides the nervous, temperamental, or romantic, for joining forces in a two-piano partnership. In fact, practical considerations of a purely professional, economic, or social kind cause the majority of teams to come into being. Typical examples from the history of the art are the ensemble activities of Bach and Mozart. The former played on multiple claviers with his sons or with friends solely for purposes of edification, study, or instruction. For Mozart, the incentive of his duo-work with Frl. Aurnhammer plainly was that of a teacher-student relationship, in this case fermented to the highest aspirations by the pupil's excellence. The raison d'être and the basis of their ensemble, however, remained economic.

The greater number of the present-day duo-pianists no doubt join together in view of financial opportunities. Today, in 1950, there are eight leading concert teams in the field, touring the United States under the management of the two major concert agencies. One of these teams relates that their earnings run from $500.00 to $1000.00 per concert, and that the average number of recitals during a regular season amounts to 45. There are, however, teams which play as many as 75 engagements in a concert season. The average net earnings, after deduction of traveling expenses and commissions, compare favorably within the economic structure of the musical profession. The financial compensation which can be attained indubitably provides a major incentive to pianists at a time when solo performers crowd the field in a bitter struggle for recognition and livelihood.

The positive attitude with which concert teams in the field look at the economic opportunities of their profession, is reflected in the answers which were received to the question:

"How do you consider the financial possibilities of two-piano playing in
    (a)   concert-recital
    (b)   on the air lanes (commercially sponsored)?"
Here are some of the comments:

Appleton and Field: " (a) Concert-recital. Limited but not unrewarding, depending on one's standard of taste and meaning. (b) Air-lanes. Enormous, provided one waives the aforementioned."

Bartlett and Robertson: "This entirely depends on the success of any particular team. It is quite possible for a successful team to earn a good living either in concert or on the air."

Dougherty and Ruzicka who responded to the question during an interview hold this opinion: "No prediction as to economic opportunities is possible. There are definite opportunities in small communities without orchestra, for Little Theatres, Ballets, Choirs, etc."

Gold and Fizdale: "Possibilities in concert: good; on the air-lanes: better financially but worse aesthetically."

Morton Gould writes the following: "There have been periods when two-piano teams have been successful commercially on the air. This varies with particular conditions. Concert hall teams can be quite successful but, generally speaking, this is a very limited field from a commercial point of view."

Rosina Lhevinne observes: "Popularity of two-piano playing is remarkably expanding."

Morley and Gearhart: "Two-pianos appears to be a very popular form of concert entertainment. . . . Up to the present, there has been less exploitation of two-pianos on the radio than in concert. Occasionally sponsored locally in a small way, two-piano teams find an occasional outlet in the national network field as guest artists. Television may open up entirely new possibilities."

Vronsky and Babin, interviewed on the same question, state: "Quality must come first, overruling financial considerations."

Whittemore and Lowe write: "The financial possibilities of two-piano playing have not been realized, nor will they be until the medium is as popular at the box-office as the *name* singers and instrumentalists. However, it is encouraging to note that in many, many cities the duo-pianists are *out-drawing* many performers whose fees are twice as much."

Social motives, sometimes with an intermingling of professional aspects, are numerous. Women's clubs frequently feature some duo-pianists from within their own membership, and in local music teachers' associations the opportunity for the formation of a two-piano team leads to many fine and enduring combinations between colleagues. Fraternity members furnish a strong contingent of the younger teams; evidently, the stimulus for ensemble playing is particularly prevalent within the music fraternities. Fellow students on the grade and high school levels derive much incentive from two-piano work; it holds out the challenge of an original endeavor and gives the feeling of special accomplishment. Then there are the countless amateur teams of functional if fluctuating significance. Some of these associations are ephemeral in their existence, while others prove stable; the attainments of some amateurs can be measured only by the amount of pleasure which the players themselves derive from their team work, while others achieve more absolute standards and may gain as much as local or regional recognition. Last but not least, the two-piano unit offers a source of congeniality and deep enjoyment to family members: Husband and wife, brother and sister, parent and child always make for a logical combination which can provide a feature in the social life of the home.

2. CHOICE OF A PARTNER

A question of primary nature and of greatest consequences is to be decided upon at the very beginning of all duo-pianistic activity. This problem involves the choice of a partner. Personal factors like that of sex, age relationship, and congeniality are to be considered.

a. Sex

Obviously, there are three combinations possible as to sex, namely those of 1) two men, 2) two women, and 3) man and woman. Opinions as to preferability are varied, and probably prejudiced, according to the particular type of combination which was consulted on this subject.

Appleton and Field consider as the most advantageous combination of two-piano partners that of an independent, not married couple: " . . . naturally, since we are the only unmarried two-piano team. Seriously, however, we feel that the less interjection of personalized reaction between the members of the team, the better. Although, actually, we feel the composition of the teams is not an important factor unless one wants to consider visual aspect: the way a man and woman look together as against a combination of two people of the same sex. Unimportant in any case."

Rae Robertson (Bartlett and Robertson) answers to the question concerning sex preference: "It doesn't matter as long as the partners are musically sympathetic."

Humorously, Dougherty and Ruzicka ventured this edict during an informal interview: "Men quarrel less." In their opinion, the combination of Bauer and Gabrilowitsch ranks superior to any other, confirming their theory that a team of men will be most successful.

To Gold and Fizdale the combination as to sex "makes no difference."

To Morton Gould, the problem seems baffling. Laconically, he writes: "I do not know the answer to this one. I would say that it depends on the people."

Rosina Lhevinne relegates the question to the prime requisite that "most important is musical affinity." On the issue proper, she has a pertinent experience to relate:[1]

> "I would like to mention an amusing change that took place in the attitude of the managers and impresarios who urged us to use different names. They thought it would stimulate interest if the public were to speculate, 'who is he to her—and who is she to him?' Gradually this attitude changed completely and many times the newspapers would emphasize the fact that we were husband and wife, and comment on some particular little attention Mr. Lhevinne would show me on the stage."

Although Pierre Luboshutz and Genia Nemenoff do not think it absolutely mandatory that duo-pianists be married, they believe marriage is a distinct advantage. They consider music and marriage as two subjects so closely interwoven in their lives as to form a single unit of public and private perfection.

Though they do not go mystical on the subject, the Luboshutzes believe that a duo-piano team must be physically attuned. "All people, particularly married people and above all musical married people, get vibrations from one another—call it transference of thought, mental telepathy, what you will," says Pierre Luboshutz. "It makes duo-piano playing a constant source of wonder and delight."

Morley and Gearhart prefer "married couples" of duo-pianists, forming a husband and wife combination themselves.

Dorothy R. Sinnitt, the member of a team which consists of two women, nevertheless gives preference to "a married couple for convenience in practicing."

Vronsky and Babin are in solidarity with the beliefs of Mr. Robertson and Mme. Lhevinne. Miss Vronsky declares categorically that "sex does not enter," and Mr. Babin adds that "prerequisite is the harmony of the emotional musical life of the partners."

Whittemore and Lowe feel prompted to the following opinion: "Two women players seem to have an inexplicable disadvantage with audiences. All other combinations seem equally well received."

While attitudes on the subject are far from unanimous, it would seem that the husband and wife combination, because of its very nature, offers

---

1. *The Spirit of Ensemble,* "Pan Pipes" of Sigma Alpha Iota, February 1949.

greater likelihood for enduring existence. Of husband and wife teams
can further be said, more than of any other partnership, that the state of
personal compatibility finds itself directly and accurately reflected in the
degree and colorit of the musical achievement. In favor of this combination stands also the great convenience for frequent rehearsals at practically all hours. To the general public, the husband and wife team now
appears almost traditional. When *Newsweek* published an article on duo-
pianists,[2] the first remark of the item read as follows: "To be a successful
duo-piano team, it is advisable—though not obligatory—to be married."

b. Age Relationship

As to age relationship, two distinct opinions are prevailing with the
authorities: One view maintains that differences in age between the partners do not matter; the other holds that approximation of age is
advantageous.

The following are some of the comments which were received on the
question concerning the age difference in the grouping of duo-pianists:

Appleton and Field write: "Psychologically, it would be advantageous
to have two people in the same intellectual, emotional, and chronological
relation."

Bartlett and Robertson believe: "Partners of roughly the same age
would be more likely to be musically sympathetic, having most likely had
the same musical influence during the formative years."

Dougherty and Ruzicka say: "Too great a difference is to be avoided."
Mr. Ruzicka vividly recalls a teacher-pupil team in which the partners
were forty years apart in age.

Gold and Fizdale state: "No preference for age relation."

Morton Gould follows the same opinion.

Rosina Lhevinne also feels that age relationship "is not of first importance."

Morley and Gearhart agree with this viewpoint.

Whittemore and Lowe, however, hold the other opinion: "The ages
of the partners should be as close as possible, so that the maturity of
expression will be at the least variance."

c. Congeniality

Regardless of sex or age relationship, an *a priori* congeniality of the
partners indubitably is the *conditio sine qua non* for the formation and
operation of a successful team. Granting any two candidates all other
prerequisites of competence, the quality of mutual compatibility remains
the final and most crucial factor of ensemble playing. In fact, personal

---

2. *Twenty That Strike as One,* issue of December 27, 1943.

congeniality needs to be the fundament of all other necessary qualifications; its absence, or lack of cultivation of this binding element, will cause the neglect of proper cooperation and the resulting failure of the ensemble. Mutual satisfaction and enjoyment in two-piano work must come through complete sympathy with one's partner and through evident respect for the opinions of the companion. Reciprocatory tolerance and courtesy will soon lead to openmindedness and the willingness to admit one's own mistakes. These are basic requirements if the association is to be a lasting and fruitful one. Furthermore, the maintenance and further development of such harmonious rapport becomes a prime task for all duo-pianists.

3. Individual Qualifications

Sometimes underestimated in its importance, but of far reaching influence, is the cultural background of each partner. Evidently, an agreement of standards and tastes will preclude many misunderstandings and promote unanimity of purpose. For the same reason, the musical education of the colleagues preferably should be of a similar character. If wide differences in training and in the appreciation of musical values exist, it may be difficult for both partners to work together with mutual understanding and the confidence derived therefrom. The amount and type of technical equipment likewise should be approximately on a par, and agreement in the mechanical aspects of piano technique will greatly simplify the collaboration.

The duo-pianistic ideal in technical as well as in every other respect is that of organic integration. It is difficult to conceive how partners, when individually professing themselves to different methods or styles of piano playing, will arrive at cohesion technically. Much the same holds true in regard to the musical ideology which needs to be on a common denominator of outlook and maturity.

What they consider the requisites for a good piano ensemble is summed up by Dougherty and Ruzicka in the following words:

"A good basis for ensemble playing of any kind is a common approach and conception of music in general. If this can be fortified by similar technical training, so much the better."

If these conditions are met, much time will be saved in the solution of technical problems as well as in the establishment of interpretative concepts. If, on the other hand, wide discrepancies exist as to phrasing, pedalling, touch, tempo, style, and the many nuances of interpretation, disagreements cannot but arise, the mutual adjustment is hampered, and an ill-balanced ensemble will be inevitable.

Of all basic requirements, one of the most important is the harmony of musical tastes. Temperamental differences, on the other hand, can be reconciled. For instance, the scholarly attitude of one partner, expressing itself in emotional self-restraint and in an intellectual approach to music, may blend well with its temperamental opposite which pronounces freedom of feeling and improvisational abandon. Miss Nemenoff, of the Luboshutz and Nemenoff team, has an appropriate remark to make in this connection:

"Just as good marriages depend not only on unanimity, 'two hearts that beat as one,' but also on the counterpoint of the two personalities, the full flowering of the individual nature of each, so must a two-piano team combine perfect unity with complete artistic freedom."

The same line of thought apparently is the tenor of a pertinent statement which Beryl Rubinstein made in a letter to the writer: " . . . two pianists with different styles make a more interesting ensemble than two with identical or similar styles."

Compatibility rather than equality of temperaments is evident in the work of many accomplished teams. Of Pierre Luboshutz and Genia Nemenoff, for instance, it is said that the theory of the attraction of opposites, sometimes denounced by psychiatrists, has worked out to perfection for these duo-pianists, who in some ways are as different from one another as the sun is from the moon.

4. INFERIORITY, SUPERIORITY, AND SUPPLEMENTATION

In the formation of a team, the question will arise whether it is necessary for the two pianists to be equally skilled. To this, Dougherty and Ruzicka say: "Yes, not only does two-piano playing demand virtuoso display on each individual's part, but the playing of each pianist is a constant reflection of the other."

A different opinion is voiced by Vera Brodsky, a member of the Brodsky and Triggs combination, who makes the following statement:[3]

> "Each member of a team need not of necessity be an expert solo pianist; it must be remembered that in two-piano playing as in all other forms of ensemble, it is necessary to fuse the parts into one complete whole. The technical problems offered by a large part of the duo-pianistic repertoire are moderate because the main difficulties presented are divided between the two instruments. Of course there are several compositions requiring advanced technique, but for the most part, the most representative examples of two-piano literature can be performed by pianists with moderate technical ability."

An examination of the bulk of two-piano literature will bear out the correctness of Vera Brodsky's statement.

---

3. Wier, *The Piano*, pp. 339-340.

Pierre Luboshutz meets with the question of skill on entirely different premises: "Good duo-pianists are born, not made" he says. "It is a special gift. Any two virtuoso pianists won't necessarily make a good duo-piano team." The history of duo-pianism is rich with examples to illustrate this last observation.

Even when cultural, musical, and personal qualifications have been brought upon a common denominator, there will still remain certain marked inferiorities or superiorities distinguishing one individual from the other in the various phases of their ensemble work. If it has been stated by a high authority that "two-piano work should not be undertaken because of the inferiority, pianistic or otherwise, of one of the partners," such inferiority is nevertheless likely to exist in certain respects whenever pianists are joining in ensemble.

Instead of inferiority or superiority, it is preferable to call this condition a *difference* by some degree. A striking case in point is furnished by the experience of Rosina Lhevinne.[4] Although an honor graduate of the Conservatory and an accomplished pianist herself, she considered her own status as so far below the level of eminence held by her illustrious husband, the late Josef Lhevinne, that she resigned from solo performance altogether. However, in their successful joint career as duo-pianists, she evidently was not possessed by the same complex of inferiority; their team work, at any rate, never showed a trace of existing differences in individual competence or attainment.

It is in the very difference of individual abilities and in the mutual supplementation of technical and musical assets that the greatest opportunities of the ensemble are discovered. Indeed there is little purpose in duplicating, and thereby deluding, the undisputed excellencies of two solo virtuosos. This practice exactly was the historic fallacy of the Grand Duo and the reason for the long-lasting stagnancy of duo-pianism as an art form. There is no room for a star virtuoso in a two-piano team deserving of the name. The technic of each partner must match or complement the other so closely that the two cannot be distinguished by ear or eye. In the formula of Pierre Luboshutz, this is a paradoxical secret: " . . . for while good duo-piano playing must sound like the performance of a single artist, still there must be nothing mechanical or monotonous in the technical feat of perfect adjustment of the two partners."

Only when there predominates the realization that the aimed-for attainment of the greatest sum total of excellencies lies in the reconciliation of individual deficiencies and assets, duo-pianism arrives, through the full

4. See Book I, *The History*, Chapter VIII, *The First Golden Era.*

measure of mutual supplementation, at the deepest meaning of the truism that in unity there lies strength. Possibly the greatest reward which two-piano playing can offer to its disciples, is the awareness that it is so "intimate a form of art, and depends greatly upon close communion, deep mutual understanding and respect, a careful complementing of one another's special gifts" (Luboshutz).

The blending of two individualities each of whom contributes the maximum of his capabilities at the proper place and time, is the outstanding characteristic of a good two-piano team.

5. THE PROBLEM OF LEADERSHIP

But what about the problem of leadership which can be expected to exist and therefore demands its clarification in even the smallest ensemble, like the pairing of pianists? Is there the need for a "boss," and how can the individuality of each teammate be safeguarded so that there will be no misproportion of authority, but rather a maximum of autonomy within that recognized and unavoidable interdependence of all association?

This problem of leadership which at one time or another must become acute in any ensemble combination, from all reports seems to offer no difficulty at all to professional teams. Accomplished duo-pianists deny the need of a "boss." A few individual comments may be of interest.

Bartlett and Robertson simply say: "Problems must be worked out together."

Dougherty and Ruzicka deny the absolute necessity of a boss; on the caustic side, they add that in many teams there should be one.

Morton Gould in his reaction discloses deep insight into this personal problem and meets it with the advice of mutual supplementation. He writes: "It is only natural that the partners should have different assets and defects. The constructive approach would be to use the respective assets of both people."

Rosina Lhevinne sees no need for a leader "if partners are well matched."

Luboshutz and Nemenoff elaborate on the same viewpoint with the following remarks:[5]

"... pianists who intend to play together over any length of time must make certain they possess those spiritual sympathies that enable them to think and even to breathe together. They must know each other well—each other's thoughts, tastes, habits. And this knowledge must lead to an ever increasing personal congeniality. If you quarrel with a person, if your every thought pulls in opposition to his, the chances are that you will never agree with him at the keyboards, either!"

Morley and Gearhart place the problem into comparison with political

5. *The Art of Two-Piano Ensemble*, "The Etude," January 1941.

principles: "Both tyranny and democracy have their advantages and drawbacks. Neither is ideal."

Dorothy R. Sinnitt believes in "a very flexible relationship with each one amenable to suggestions from the other."

Vronsky and Babin also repel the very thought of dictatorial leadership in a two-piano association. In an interview, these duo-pianists declared that they have formed a habit to discuss all occurring differences and problems at length and at leisure. Eventually, the most convincing suggestion for the solution of the difficulty is adopted, whereupon the problem usually proves to have been successfully negotiated.

Whittemore and Lowe formulate their answer to the question of leadership as follows:

" . . . the ideal partners will have equal maturity artistically; this will not, and should not, permit *one* to 'boss' the other. However, there must be a 'give and take,' but this must never be confused in the minds of the partners *or* of the audience with 'leading' by one or the other. And even this so-called 'give and take' must never be permitted to obtrude on the large musical picture or concept."

Obviously, there is no recipe or guarantee available for an ever-present duo-pianistic congeniality. On the other hand, the potential threat of an absolute leadership should be analyzed and arrested as soon as it is noticed; it must be prevented from ever becoming acute. Dictatorial practices, according to the consensus of authoritative opinions, have no place in duo-pianism. The problem rather becomes comparable to the question of leadership in a republic. *Res publica* here means the common interest in the best realization of the musical purpose. However, since a final authority is indispensable for every concern of public interest, such power, even in as small a partnership as that of duo-pianists, will need to be assigned to the most convincing opinion which emerges from the thorough discussion of any controversial issue. Thus, no absolute or *a priori* authority is ever invested in any one member of a two-piano team, but all leadership becomes incidental to whatever superiority of approach momentarily provides the solution of existing problems.

Therefore, the call is again one for supplementation, this time of mental powers. This process becomes both challenging and educational for the partners; it makes, moreover, for good sportsmanship so essential in all group activities. As to authority itself, the word loses its personal connotation and exerts itself in the abstract.

Taking a realistic outlook, it is only normal that differences of opinion at times should arise. In this event, all criticism needs to be stated dispassionately and objectively, so that no feeling of an individual quest for hegemony will suggest itself. In fact, any attempt to impose one will upon the other is a serious danger signal in a combination which depends for its success on the commonly exerted effort. The deliverance from any difference of opinion must either come through a mutually satisfactory decision made in free and fair discussion, and strict adherence to it thereafter, or through a compromise agreed upon by the partners. The latter ability, namely to settle a problem by mutual concessions, is an absolutely essential quality among teammates. Actually, it is in the difference and exchange of ideas that even richer results are produced. The stimulation provided through this constant alertness to the manifold ensemble problems is much greater for the members of a team than could be found by the individual pianist in solitary work.

These then are the watchwords for the duo-unit: Courtesy, tolerance, free discussion, compromise, adherence to the decision agreed upon. It should always be remembered by the partners, and it will thus be sensed by the listening audience, that the perfection of the ensemble is the ultimate goal and not the personal display of the individual. The glory of duo-pianism is manifest in the idea of the *team,* not in the principle of the "leader."

CHAPTER XIV

PRACTICING

ANALYTIC VERSUS SYNTHETIC PROCEDURES

1. SEPARATE AND JOINT PRACTICING

The reasons for joining in a two-piano partnership have been laid clear. The choice of the partner has been made after due consideration and in the best judgment. Individual qualifications match well. Both partners pledge to aim towards the greatest sum total of assets through mutual supplementation. The problem of leadership has been discussed and agreed upon to mutual satisfaction.

All these become preliminary assumptions before the newly-formed team of duo-pianists is ready to face the first important question of an entirely practical nature. How to practice? More specifically, what proportion and type of the practicing should be done individually by each partner, and what amount of joint rehearsal is necessary for the two-piano ensemble proper?

These questions will now be given an airing by several authorities. Again a variety of methods becomes apparent.

Appleton and Field practice "Separately, to learn things. Together, when we know them."

The same procedure is followed by Bartlett and Robertson. Mr. Robertson reveals: "We do all the mechanical part of our practice separately— learning notes, working at difficult passages, making a general study of the complete score away from the piano, etc. Then when we are practically note-perfect and know the whole score we work together on ensemble."

In some variance to this practice method stands that of Dougherty and Ruzicka:

"New compositions are first read through on two pianos to establish an interpretive conception. Then the technical problems and memorizing are worked out separately. Then the parts are brought together and constantly readjusted until the desired end is reached."

In an interview with the writer, Dougherty and Ruzicka went on to explain that they first "weed through" a new piece many times, sometimes even proceeding to the degree of memorizing the composition. Each of the pair then frequently practices by himself. On tours, they keep up their mechanical drills by means of a dummy keyboard which can be used in train compartments and in hotel rooms.

Gold and Fizdale state that they practice "almost always together."

Rosina Lhevinne relates that she believes in "practice together mostly for ensemble purposes." Mme. Lhevinne also places emphasis on this postulate:[1]

"Regular ensemble rehearsals are 'sine qua non' of two-piano playing; otherwise no accuracy of performance or unanimity of expression can be achieved."

Luboshutz and Nemenoff express their opinion on practicing methods as follows:[2]

". . . it is always advisable for duo-pianists to practice together,—not merely to *rehearse* together when all is in readiness, but to do their actual *practicing* together. Scales, thirds, sixths, octaves, trills, arpeggios, technical exercises, all these should be practiced by the two partners in unison. And each one should listen carefully to his own performance as well as to his partner's! This builds not merely technic alone, but the surety of cooperative technic which must lie as a reserve fund behind every piece. In learning the pieces themselves, the partners should prepare their individual parts separately, working at technic and rhythm until both are clean, and fluent enough to avoid trouble when combined. But interpretively, the parts should be practiced together."

Morley and Gearhart, in reply to the question of how they practice, come forth with a "Sorry, the answer to this is a volume." In explanation, they term the problem "one of the most important aspects of the field, to which we have given years of trial and error. Impossible to set down briefly or hastily. In length, we seldom practice as much as three hours a day; never more. On tour we are lucky to average six hours a week."

Vronsky and Babin discussed this phase during an interview with the writer. Miss Vronsky took issue in stating that "the more the pianists are individually developed, the more valuable they are as partners," an

1. *The Spirit of Ensemble,* "Pan Pipes," February 1949.
2. *The Art of Piano Ensemble,* "The Etude," January 1941.

opinion which would speak for a great amount of separate practice. Mr. Babin contributed an explanation of their approach to compositions which are new to them: They first play together. A vision of the whole is needed for the general conception, just as the conductor cannot come to know the context of an orchestral composition from a trombone or other single part.

Whittemore and Lowe are in favor of doing most of the practicing together. They describe their working method in the following manner: "85 percent of all our practice is together (quite in contrast to most teams, we discover). Even the learning process, while slower, we feel is much more effective together. Our particular interest in transcribing (which we do *together* . . . one does *not* write out both parts) requires this approach."

The consensus of opinion advises as the best procedure to first read jointly through a composition which is intended for study. A conception of the functions and characteristics of each component part can thus be obtained, and the decision for its most advantageous assignment will thereby be facilitated.

In this connection, it should be emphasized that the designations "Piano I" and "Piano II" in two-piano scores are in no way indicative of the greater or lesser difficulty or importance of either part. These terms are merely used for the purpose of distinction. It is a mistaken notion that Piano I represents the leading part and that Piano II assumes a subsidiary role. This wide-spread fallacy should be avoided. All well-written two-piano music allows an equal share of participation to the performers. Negotiating the portion assigned to him, each player finds himself *paris inter pares*. Nevertheless, a scrutiny of each composition which is about to be undertaken for study, will reveal certain peculiarities in regard to technical, formal, or other traits, and the assignment of the individual parts should be decided upon only after due consideration of the respective adaptabilities of the companions. While offhand each pianist may appear sufficiently proficient to cope with either part, their particular distinction in some pertinent respect will very often render them the logical executant for a certain requirement and thereby imply the assignment.

In any event, careful discrimination in the selection of parts is of far-reaching importance. Any amount of time given to this deliberation will therefore be well invested.

Sometimes it may also be found advisable to exchange certain fragments

or sections of a composition between the partners. Such transfer is beneficial if by it the dispositions and abilities of the players can better be
realized, and if—as a consequence—the ensemble can thereby be improved.
Diligent experimentation in this direction is apt to solve many problems
which may have arisen during practice. The objection that by such interchange of parts the original score is not being adhered to, has no basis.
It is the perfection of the musical entity for which both partners must
forever be striving; in the synthetic projection of a two-piano ensemble
the interior distribution of parts remains irrelevant as long as the effect
of unified mastery is achieved.

After the first reading of the composition and after assigning each part,
the character of the work will in most cases determine the further practicing method. In the case of a piece which technically proves within easy
reach of the players and musically is self-evident, the learning process may
well be accomplished with a number of joint rehearsals. More often, however, complexities of structure, phraseology, tempo, climax and other
factors will require detailed analysis, discussion, and the mapping out of
a common strategy. The time invested in conscientious intellectual preparation will greatly accelerate the synthetic process.

Technical problems, however small, are liable to disrupt the ensemble rehearsal and therefore should be worked out in separate practice. Difficult
passages, even after they have been mastered individually by each partner,
should be practiced together so slowly that their every detail may be heard
by the players. The organism of all two-piano ensemble will benefit in
soundness if it is allowed to grow gradually and without undue acceleration. The element of speed in performance will hold no hazards if the
concepts of studied security and full insight into the complexities of the
score are at its roots.

Frequent repetition of simultaneous passages will bring about the solution of ensemble problems in cohesion and balance. Such reiterations
must be undertaken with patience and perseverance on the part of the
players who individually may not incur any difficulty at all in the particular passage.

2. Proportion of Emphasis on Mechanics and Aesthetics

A question which is quite generally met with during rehearsal, will
also arise in the practicing procedure of every two-piano ensemble. The
problem is the following: How much stress should be applied to the
mechanics of the learning process, i.e. to the elements of articulation?
In turn, how much attention is to be given to the *aesthetics* which involve
the factors contributing to artistic finish?

The manifold implications of this problem are developed at length in the answers with which the authorities have reacted to the question.

Appleton and Field think that "a great deal" of stress should be placed upon the mechanics, "although, generally depending on the intricacy of rapid passages played together. However, we have found, after our years of playing together, less and less need to spend undue amount of time on these." As to the aesthetic aspects, the duo-pianists apply to them a great deal of attention. "More, however, in a didactic fashion since this gives us the framework of our musical conception."

For the team of Bartlett and Robertson, Rae Robertson acts as speaker on this problem: "One must first get a general idea of the musical content of the work, then one should concentrate rather on the mechanical side (without, however, entirely forgetting the other). When more or less note-perfect, one can then cease to worry about the mechanical and study the artistic rendition, structure, tone-color, etc."

Dougherty and Ruzicka make no conscious separation between mechanics and aesthetics during their practice sessions. They rehearse none without the other and are convinced that each is helping the other.

The same opinion, somewhat modified, is expressed by Gold and Fizdale. They believe "the more stress on both the better. More attention to mechanics at first and to aesthetics later."

Morton Gould, like Dougherty and Ruzicka, is convinced that "both must go together."

Rosina Lhevinne holds the same belief. She writes: "Equal attention must be given to all elements involved." For "younger players and casual teams" Mme. Lhevinne gives this more detailed advice which, beyond its stated extent, contains some practical directions of general value:[3]

". . . the partners must discuss and agree upon the dynamics, balance, expression, and phrasing, keeping in mind as in solo playing great respect for the composer. In the beginning of study of a new composition both players must read the score together to decide which part is best adapted to the talents of each one. After that, the partners should analyze the structure and character of the composition to decide on the best method of interpretation. Analysis of form, tempos, climaxes, will help greatly, and of course each player must practice his part separately, mastering the technical problems alone. The joint rehearsals should be employed principally in conquering ensemble problems."

While the foregoing remarks pertain mainly to mechanical aspects, Mme. Lhevinne, in collaboration with her late husband, also has opened vistas for the proper approach to the aesthetic subtleties of musicianship

---

3. *The Spirit of Ensemble*, "Pan Pipes," February 1949.

in two-piano performance. Josef and Rosina Lhevinne thus have expressed
their conception of duo-pianistic philosophy:[4]

> "That, too, is the first thought to bear in mind in approaching playing on two
> pianos. We must not let ourselves fall into the error of regarding mere piano
> playing as a goal in itself. It is but one means of expressing musical thought.
> It is not enough simply to strike correct keys. Even before he seats himself at
> his instrument, the performer must devote careful study to his score, weighing
> phrases, balancing statements, setting off themes in contrast to each other, dis-
> covering the pattern and the plan of the unified whole which the composer wished
> to present.
>
> "If this is true of any sort of piano playing, it is doubly true of two-piano work,
> with its richer inter-weaving of thematic material. Taking an adequate playing
> technic quite for granted, one of the most important parts of ensemble playing is
> done away from the keyboards, in this delicate preparation of thematic adjustments."

Morley and Gearhart who, like so many of their colleagues, find themselves pressed for rehearsal time, have adopted the following attitude:
"Ideally the two practices should interlock. In actual practice we spend
much more time on the mechanical aspects, when time is limited, as it
usually is. In our case, this does not seriously affect performance, and may
even result in a more fluidly spontaneous aesthetic result."

To Vronsky and Babin "all technical questions are always subordinate
to the artistic aim," a principle which would indicate strong emphasis
on aesthetic penetration and polish during their joint rehearsals.

Whittemore and Lowe express their belief in inter-dependence of the
two aspects when they write: "Mechanics and aesthetics are too interrelated in our learning process to permit us to make proper proportionate
estimates."

Again it has been learned that theories and working methods vary with
different teams. A similar diversity of opinions will continually be encountered throughout this discussion of duo-pianism as an artistic medium.
As has been pointed out previously, the status of each authority in itself
justifies the individual practice recommended. In keeping with the stated
purpose of this symposium, it is impossible to suggest any one prescription as preferable to the other. This decision of choice remains the
responsibility and essential opportunity of all practitioners in the field.

3. *Gestalt* PSYCHOLOGY

Without intending to trespass the boundaries to which this dissertation
of duo-pianism is confined, a short reference to the theories of *Gestalt*
Psychology is made at this time. This system of mental operations enters
into the processes of learning (to which the subject of practicing belongs)
as much as into the realms of general attitudes, of thought and emotion,
like acting, striving, reproduction, and so forth. According to *Gestalt*

4. *Four Hands That Play As Two*, "The Etude," December 1933, p. 809.

Psychology, all these subject matters do not consist of independent elements, but are determined in a situation as a whole.

For illustration, two excerpts from *Gestalt Psychology* by Dr. Wolfgang Koehler are quoted in the following. In the chapter devoted to *The Properties of Organized Wholes*, the author writes:[5]

". . . the reader will readily understand that talking about a 'disturbing' factor in the case of 'thinking' presupposes a definite dynamical whole, as it does in sensory experience. There is no meaning in the word without it. Whoever is slightly acquainted with musical theory will recognize at once that a tone cannot have the character of the 'tonic' without belonging to a larger musical whole, in which it plays a definite role; of course, the same is true of the leading tone, which has its strong dynamical properties in the definite key of a sequence of tones, and not independently."

". . . there are temporal *gestaltqualitäten* as well as spatial ones, since the definition applies to the specific properties of a melody, to its 'major' or 'minor' character, for instance, in the same way it does to the 'angularity' of a figure. Finally, seen movement as a whole may have a *gestaltqualität* which is temporal and spatial at the same time. This is the case in the aspect of a definite form of dancing and in the characteristic movement of animals, such as 'jumping' or 'creeping.'

"At this point a general remark about terminology may be useful. For von Ehrenfels the new characteristic properties themselves were objects of outstanding importance; he was more interested in them than in those segregated parts of the field which exhibit the best examples of *gestaltqualitäten* as their properties. In the German language however—at least since the time of Goethe, and especially in his own papers on natural science—the noun "gestalt" has two meanings: besides the connotation of 'shape' or 'form' as a *property* of things, it has the meaning of a concrete individual and characteristic entity, existing as something detached and *having* a shape or form as one of its attributes. Following this tradition, in *gestalttheorie* the word 'gestalt' means any segregated whole, and the consideration of *gestaltqualitäten* has become a more special side of the *gestaltproblem*, the prevailing idea being that the same general type of dynamical process which leads to the formation and segregation of extended wholes will also explain their specific properties. Here the main stress is laid upon a characteristic type of process. This indeed, is the most general concept of *gestalttheorie*: wherever a process dynamically distributes and regulates itself, determined by the actual situation in a whole field, this process is said to follow principles of *gestalttheorie*. In all cases of this type the process will have some characteristic which exists in an extended area only, so that a consideration of local points or local factors as such will not give us full insight into the nature of the process. From this viewpoint, even the segregation of circumscribed wholes becomes one more or less particular, though highly important, case among the various possibilities which are included in the most general idea of self-distribution and self-regulation, and in consequence the concept of *gestalt* may be applied far beyond the limits of sensory fields. According to the most general definition of *gestalt,* the processes of learning, of reproduction, of striving, of emotional attitude, of thinking, acting, and so forth, may be included as subject matter of *gestalttheorie* insofar as they do not consist of independent elements, but are determined in a situation as a whole. Quite apart from psychology the same will be true of ontogenetic development, and other biological events, wherever they show the definite marks of self-distribution and self-regulation."

5. *Gestalt Psychology,* Chapter VI, p. 222 and pp. 192-194.

The deduction from this theory for the special problems here discussed would imply that in duo-pianism self-distribution and self-regulation will take place in joint rehearsal rather than in separate practice; in Koehler's words, the latter would constitute "a consideration of local factors," which will not yield full insight into the nature of the composition. Self-evident as this conclusion may appear, the continuing necessity for individual practice should be taken into account whenever there arises an obstruction to *Gestalt* in form of a mechanical or technical difficulty. Such impediments indeed require the "consideration of local factors" and must be given the isolated attention of the individual confronted with the obstacle.

Before closing this discussion on practicing, the fact remains to be stressed that an absolute requirement for success in two-piano playing, as in any other form of ensemble performance, is regular and consistent rehearsal. Accuracy of detail and unanimity of expression cannot be arrived at otherwise. A daily association of the duo-pianists will lead to the welding and blending of concepts and styles much more organically than sporadic rehearsals can ever accomplish; even though the daily practice session may be comparatively short, its regularity will maintain the momentum and safeguard the trend of study.

To the appropriate question "How much time should we spend on rehearsals?", Silvio Scionti proposes this answer:[6]

"As much as is at all possible. It takes hours, days and months of indefatigable labor at the dual keyboards to conquer the difficulties that stand in the way of beautiful coloring, rhythms, and dynamics. The players must learn to listen to each other so acutely that, with years, something resembling a kind of mystic musical telepathy is developed. At all times, the ear must be intensely alert."

The ear, more especially the inner ear of "musical telepathy" depends on the highest degree of sensitivity; the latter faculty can be brought out and developed into something of a routine experience only by daily contact. The large percentage of husband and wife teams indubitably is due to this realization in the wake of which the convenience for numerous and regular practice periods is but the outward manifestation. At any rate, duo-pianists will need to arrange for an ample and consistent rehearsal routine if a truly mature and polished ensemble is their goal.

---

6. *The Fascination of Two-Piano Playing*, "The Etude," September 1939, p. 567.

CHAPTER XV

MECHANICS AND AESTHETICS

1. Accuracy

As soon as the practice routine as such has been agreed upon by the partners, the details of the formative process present themselves in bewildering number and variety. Technical difficulties in the learning of a two-piano composition run the gamut of conceivable problems. But the foremost component to be cultivated is always that of accuracy which takes into account all indications of the printed or written score.

The need for accuracy is so self-evident, and its importance has been stressed so universally, that the mere emphasis on this principal element of all good performance is held sufficient at this occasion. Some appropriate statements on the subject by Josef and Rosina Lhevinne may, however, help to underscore the necessity and the scope of accuracy:[1]

"Simply to follow a score sounds easy enough; and yet it implies a life's work of precision, of careful alertness to the smallest details of note values, of phrasing and of melodic statement. Then, only after preparation such as this, is one given the possibility of expressing the message of the music to the utmost of one's powers.

"The musical and technical preparation for two-piano playing is not in any way different from ordinary piano playing. It is simply more precise, more accurate, more orderly. Naturally this must be so, lest the fractional part of a second's divergence in time or the faintest difference in shading blur an effect which should stand out meaningful and clear."

2. Signal Systems

In two-piano playing, inasmuch as it is a form of ensemble activity, the necessity for a definite signal system arises with the inception of the first practice session. The employment of signals becomes obligatory in all instances when missing contact would endanger the precision and balance

1. *Four Hands That Play As Two,* "The Etude," December 1933, p. 809.

of the entire unit. At the beginning of the performance, for instance, mutual observation must be established as an indispensable requisite. This postulate is raised for simultaneous starts as much as for compositions in which one of the players begins before the other. The feeling of attention, readiness, and unanimity of purpose cannot be present unless the eyes of the performers meet even before the first tone is sounded.

In simultaneous beginnings, the signal to start is given by one of the pianists who for this special purpose assumes the function of conductor. The indication to commence may be made by a slight nod of the head; the latter beforehand is raised very lightly. The antecedent upward movement is serving as "preparatory beat"; its duration sets the tempo, and its gesture marks the character of the music to follow.

The starting signal can also be given by a decisive motion of the arm or shoulder. In any event, the accuracy of the attack will depend both on the concentration of the players before the start and on the clarity of the sign itself. While this and all other signals must be sufficiently distinct for the partner, they should be almost imperceptible to the audience. The expedient of intentness is the best aid towards realization of this important objective.

Further signals during performance may be either necessary or desired for precision in simultaneous chord passages, for security in the rounding-out of phrases, and for coordinated release at the end of the composition. Constant alertness and assiduous watching will soon limit the amount of indispensable signalling devices to a minimum. For *fermata* signs, other holds (*tenuto*) and so-called silent bars, a definite number of beat units or fractional beats should be established and counted silently by each partner. The number and duration of such silent beats must be in proportion to the line of musical thought. If properly fitted into the general tempo, these additional counts will insure the synchronization of intent and action and give the impression of freedom and spontaneity.

The same plan is also particularly useful in simultaneous *recitativo* passages which, if perfectly executed, represent a distinct accomplishment of team work and provide one of the most stunning effects with audiences, because of the illusion of declamatory freedom which is obtained from the smooth rendition of such *recitativo* sections.

Generally speaking, the feeling of reliability and solidity in ensemble playing should not depend on an elaborate system of signals. The less signs become necessary, the better. In this field of endeavor, as in any other, experience will be the best teacher. While frequent looking at one's partner is giving the assurance of mutual concentration, while intent listening to each other is revealing the composite inner structure of the music, it depends on the growing understanding and confidence to eventually accomplish an entirely invisible transference of thought by the exercise of the will alone.

In the following paragraphs, a series of comments is enumerated as they were given by the members of this symposium in response to the question:

"How do you signal (a) beginnings (b) entrances (c) endings?"

Appleton and Field make the statement that they signal "imperceptibly and depending on the phrase construction. These might be described as up beats with the merest movement of the body; lifting of the hands above the keyboard as in up beat or as a phrase ending."

Bartlett and Robertson have reduced their signal system to a minimum. They write: "A little nod of the head for a beginning is the only signal necessary. The rest must be done by feeling together and by work in rehearsal."

Dougherty and Ruzicka likewise subscribe to the policy to signal at the outset only. They find it advisable that one and the same player should always give the starting sign. As to the latter, Dougherty and Ruzicka do not reveal the exact nature of their signal. They say: "Many piano teams adopt the simple means of indicating the beat with the nod of the head, in the manner of a conductor. We have found, through years of experience, that intuitive feeling is our surest guide."

Gold and Fizdale, in their own words, solve all signal problems summarily "by breathing together."

Morton Gould is more specific on the issue. He states: "When a team has been working together, the natural physical preparation to begin is sufficient. Entrances, endings, etc. can be indicated by head or body motions or, in really compatible ensemble playing, the actual sound of the phrase."

Rosina Lhevinne likewise would like to see signalling limited to openings only. She writes: "For synchronization of attack a slight nod of the head is permissible." Her advice for all further contact between the duo-pianists is thus expressed:[2]

> "The most important factor in achieving good ensemble, lies in each musician's listening constantly and intently to the other's playing as well as his own. A feeling of unity and understanding is established between the partners by looking at one another whenever required during the performance."

All authorities agree on the importance of simultaneous attack. Analyzing this problem which presents one of the greatest difficulties to duo-pianists, Luboshutz and Nemenoff write:[3]

2. *The Spirit of Ensemble*, "Pan Pipes", February 1949.
3. *The Art of Piano Ensemble*, "The Etude," January 1941.

"When two violins are played together, the very mechanics of the attack serve as an aid to precision. The technical formation of a down-bow and an up-bow can be followed, and thus the players are subtly assisted in keeping together. There is no such mechanical attack on the piano; there is nothing to be heard in pressing down a key except the resulting sound—and then it is too late for the other partner to come in, even though he be but a millimeter of a second behind!"

As his approach to the problem, Guy Maier (Maier and Pattison) issues this recommendation:[4]

"Starting signals are given by one pianist who raises his head slightly, like a conductor's upbeat, and then lowers it for the 'attack'. For one of the pianists to wink his eyes at the other for a starting signal—as actually happened in a case I know— is too risky."

The signal system of Morley and Gearhart is described by the duo-pianists as follows:

"When necessary, (a) beginnings are signalled by a slight nod. (Over years this nod has a tendency to become imperceptible.) (b) entrances do not require a signal (c) endings are mutually 'felt'; occasionally we have recourse to a number of silent (invisible) counts or beats, but these are not strictly metronomic always. Call it osmosis."

E. Robert Schmitz contributes to the discussion his opinion that signalling is to be done by "the performer who has thematic material."

Dorothy R. Sinnitt believes that the signal problem can be met "by careful preparation and counting in practice, and by slight gesture in performance."

The practice of Vronsky and Babin stands in agreement with the theory voiced by E. Robert Schmitz. Signalling, according to Mr. Babin, depends on the complex of sounds. The player having the primary part is in charge of giving the signal, exactly as the players in a string quartet are alternately assuming this task, when the thematic material passes from one instrument to the other.

Whittemore and Lowe, like Gold and Fizdale, have developed a system which appears to the outsider somewhat occult. They reveal: "Our method of musical attacks is founded upon *breathing* and employs absolutely no visible signalling. The 'how' is unique and something we feel unable to explain concisely. We do know that it can offer absolutely no distraction to an audience."

3. TEMPO AND RHYTHM

In duo-pianism, the problems of tempo, including its fluctuations, and of rhythm are so closely interrelated that they are here considered together.

Getting off with the proper tempo is no stumbling block to those who have carefully rehearsed at the mutually agreeable rate of speed. If at all necessary, the duration of the silent preparatory beat, i.e. the timing of

---

4. *Two-Piano Ensemble*, "The Etude," February 1938, p. 87.

the opening signal, will serve as a gauge for the attentive partner. One should listen to the other especially intently during the first few counts so that fluctuations of tempo, caused by nervous differentiations, can quickly be eliminated.

During the period of study and preparation, disagreement may sometimes occur regarding the proper rate of speed to be adopted. Any such difference of impulse or opinion needs to be decided or compromised upon in the same spirit of cooperation which must prevail for the settlement of all other problems of interpretation. During public performance, however, any considerable deviation from the established basic tempo, if caused arbitrarily by either player, amounts to nothing short of a reckless breach of the confidence invested in the partnership. The entire perspective of all other details is abruptly changed by an overthrow of the accepted rate of speed, and a complete distortion of the rehearsed ensemble will be the inevitable result. Possibly the greatest damage of the escapade, however, lies in the severe impairment of mutual confidence which is the most indispensable factor in all two-piano association.

Steadiness of tempo must continually be observed. However, the speed should never be regulated by heavy accents on the downbeats. A potential danger in any ensemble performance is caused by the anxiety of the participants to stay together. Through concentration on the melodic and harmonic flow of the music, by listening and anticipating, each partner will consolidate with the other in outlook and aspiration. All anxiety will be dispelled, and rhythmical ease will overcome mechanical weightiness.

Playing on two pianos offers a certain temptation to exaggerate the rate of speed, partly because of the mutual support and the resulting feeling of security inherent in the combination, partly because of the fact that in a faster tempo ensemble can be much more easily maintained than at a slow rate of speed. The tendency of playing too fast needs to be curbed, however. Paramount among the reasons for this requirement is the largely polyphonic texture of two-piano music. The various voices with their individual outlines and phrases cannot be discerned from each other if undue speed destroys the possibility to properly trace them. Duo-pianists do well to remember, therefore, that they are mostly in much greater danger to play too fast than too slowly.

One of the truly crucial factors in musical performance deals with the complexities of rhythm. In two-piano work, which offers a pronounced opportunity for cross-rhythms, this most subtle of musical elements must be regarded with even greater discrimination.

The proper projection of the rhythmic currents can be likened to giving music its blood stream. While only a sensitive feeling for rhythmic flexibility can completely overcome the taint of mechanical precision in two-piano art, a number of practical directions may assist in the initial adjustment and will be useful as controlling devices thereafter.

Eye, Ear and Hand are known to correlate in the production of all types of piano music. Two-piano playing requires the even greater activation of those faculties which enable the performer to look and to listen. The degree of excellency in team-work actually depends on the amount to which these abilities are being developed. Good ensemble can be achieved and maintained only if each partner listens constantly and carefully to the slightest nuances of tempo, rhythm, dynamics, and timbre on the part of his colleague. He must possess the alertness to immediately detect every shading and to instantly attune himself to any situation. These abilities which require unusual power of coordination and responsiveness, eventually may develop beyond the awareness of what the partner presently is doing into an intuitive knowledge of what he intends to do next. The fluctuations of impulses and nuances, the rhythmic waves of individual initiatives are equally alluring to observe in a well-adjusted pair of duo-pianists as they are, to use a comparison, noticed in the interplay of body movements with a well-matched pair of dancers.

In addition to the most acute listening, the assiduous employment of the eyes is of infinite help. Looking at each other establishes contact beyond the physical realm into spiritual dimensions. By the frequent meeting of the eyes a sense of unity is created, and from it harmony and assurance are derived. If this feeling of mutual understanding is distinctly present, a complete agreement in the treatment of *rubato, ritardando,* and *accelerando* will be forthcoming. It can be said quite generally that the excellence of a team is readily evidenced by the proportion, line, and duration which are given to tempo changes like *ritardando* or *accelerando.* On the other hand, if these fluctuations of speed are left to chance or momentary impulse, a ragged ensemble must be the outcome, in that the two performers most likely will have different notions about the passage.

In summary: Mutual observation and constant vigilance furnish the key to correct ensemble. In the sharing of responsibilities during this incessant concentration, the Ear and the Eye are equally important aids. The goal ultimately may be reached in a state of clairvoyance where the final triumph over all aspects of mechanism is achieved.

The synchronization of tempo and its fluctuations and the meaning of rhythm offer fascinating problems to duo-pianists. The simple question:

"How do you treat *ritardando* and *accelerando?*"

was used as a point of departure into the subtleties connected with the entire tempo and rhythm complex. Each *accelerando* or *ritardando,* when jointly executed by a pair of pianists, represents the act of speeding up or slowing down at an exact ratio. How to arrive at that ratio? This problem was submitted to the authorities who are reaching a remarkable amount of agreement on the methods for solution.

Appleton and Field master the difficulty "by a synonymity of musical intention which results for us, at least, in plastic ritardandos and accelerandos."

Bartlett and Robertson suggest a similar approach to the hazards of tempo changes:

"This cannot be arrived at by any other means than by listening carefully to one's partner. By long association and much rehearsal one gradually comes to anticipate what the other is going to do."

Dougherty and Ruzicka meet the problems of tempo and its fluctuations "by feeling and intuition."

To Gold and Fizdale the treatment of *ritardando* and *accelerando* is a "question of taste."

Morton Gould writes on this subject: "Basically, the solution is for both performers to have the same musical values as regards retards or acceleration."

The same opinion is expressed by Rosina Lhevinne who relegates this question to the necessity of reaching "mutual understanding at the rehearsals."

Luboshutz and Nemenoff place the emphasis on what *not* to do when writing:[5]

". . . there must be nothing mechanical in adjusting the interpretative variations of tempo. As soon as a *rubato* or a *ritardando* sounds mechanically calculated, the art of the performance is gone."

The same duo-pianists find their answer to the problems of tempo and tempo changes in the perfection of rhythmic unanimity. They state:

"Two-piano work requires the utmost precision of rhythm. The two partners must begin absolutely simultaneously, they must hold each note for exactly the same duration of time. Hence, all *tempi* must be discussed in advance. It is well, also, for each player to count to himself while he plays. There is no need for counting aloud; indeed, this is often disturbing; but each must bear the responsibility for perfect rhythmic unison. Awareness and practice are the best 'helps'."

Guy Maier alludes to the same crucial feature of rhythmic perfection when he admonishes all duo-pianists:[6]

"They must strive for an impeccable, alluring rhythm, since this is the most important attribute of good two-piano playing. . . ."

5. *The Art of Piano Ensemble,* "The Etude," January 1941.
6. *Two-Piano Ensemble,* "The Etude," February 1938, p. 87.

Morley and Gearhart negotiate all tempo fluctuations by intuition. They relate: "Simplest way of answering is that we 'feel' them. We do not indicate by visual signal."

Dorothy R. Sinnitt subscribes to the same approach. She suggests to treat tempo "the same way you would in accompanying, by *feeling* the ensemble."

Vronsky and Babin, interviewed on the problem, consider it one of the most difficult in duo-pianism to cope with. Miss Vronsky urges "Listen!" Victor Babin, in a mixture of humor and seriousness, voices his credo in the matter thus: "We pray to God. But you must help God!"

Whittemore and Lowe take up the question of *ritardando* and *accelerando* in duo-piano performance with the following statement: "These present no problem when the pianists think alike musically. A musical unanimity of rhythm and 'line' will, and should, encompass *any* of the expressive aspects of a performance."

Whittemore and Lowe at the same time are very concerned over the problem of rhythmic subtlety. They write: "The enormous physical obstacle in the way of the expression of true beauty in any piano playing lies in the method in which the sound must be produced: namely, to play (to strike *sic*) vertically and yet produce a horizontal musical 'line'. If this basic articulation of beauty is admittedly difficult for a *soloist,* consider then how the problem doubles (even quadruples) in intensity when applied to two pianists attempting to play simultaneously!"

Their basic tenet for the solution of this very problem is formulated by Whittemore and Lowe as follows:

"A disciplined coordination of body and emotional rhythms in the process of any musical articulation seems to us the only foundation on which can be built a subtle, elastic, effortless yet rhythmically-integrated ensemble playing. This approach enhances and gives freedom to the artist's expression of his own musical understanding and personality."

4. PHRASING

Whereas all matters of phrasing are left to the pianist's erudition or caprice in solo performance, this phase of rendition needs to be closely synchronized in two-piano work. Attack and release of simultaneous phrases require the highest precision of execution. The ensemble must be subjected to absolute discipline before, because of and through such training, the freedom of joint phraseology can be achieved. Eventually, the pianists will be "breathing together," like members of a well-trained vocal ensemble.

5. PEDALLING

The area of mechanical problems in two-piano playing is further extended with the subject of pedalling. Considering the duplication of instrumental resources, it is only logical to assume added opportunities as well as responsibilities for the executants. Therefore, pedalling in two-piano playing becomes considerably more of a discipline than in solo performance.

All details of phraseology, no matter how well thought out in the minds of the partners, regardless of how well performed by the hands of the players, can be rendered ineffective if the pedalling fails to be properly correlated. It is furthermore to be realized that the error in pedalling of only *one* performer will mar the impression of the entire passage.

On the other hand, a perfectly synchronized duo-pianistic pedal treatment is providing the performance with an enormous plasticity of musical form in line and texture. The various types of pedal applications, especially simultaneous and syncopated pedalling, need to be agreed upon according to their appropriateness in each instance. Generally, an attitude of careful discernment should attend the working out of pedal problems as much as the experimentation with other phases of mechanics.

Sureness in the final pedal release, at the very end of the performance, is especially important. A number of beats, or fractions thereof, should be agreed upon during which the pedals are jointly to be held. Some gesture, as an additional signal for final release, may be helpful. A decided backward thrust of the head or shoulders will serve adequately for this purpose. Exactitude in closing together is as vitally important as the simultaneous start; therefore, the foot needs to be trained as much as the hand to obey the command of the mind in the impulse of termination.

Generally speaking, pedalling in two-piano playing offers greater hazards than in solo performance, but a rich compensation for this danger element lies in the widely increased scale of sonorities. To seek out these new experiences in *Klang* must be left to the curiosity and taste of the players. Experimentation and good judgment will bring many rewards in this branch of duo-pianistic mechanics.

Before closing the discussion on pedalling, a few practical hints from authoritative sources are to be quoted. The particular directions are recommended by Luboshutz and Nemenoff and by Guy Maier, respectively. The former state in regard to the topic:[7]

"Duo-piano pedaling is somewhat different from solo pedaling, in that the greater sonority of the two instruments augments the danger of blurring. Thus duo-piano pedaling must be a trifle lighter and a great deal more careful. The marked indications should be watched with utmost care, and variations from them should be

7. *The Art of Piano Ensemble*, "The Etude," January 1941.

carefully discussed. There can be no individual liberties in work that depends upon two! A solo pianist may draw a certain advantage from heavy pedaling (provided he knows what he is doing!) but duo-pianists must exert alert watchfulness that an intended 'effect' does not result in catastrophe."

The advice of Guy Maier on the same subject follows herewith:[8]

". . . In rapid pieces with scale, arpeggio or finger passage work, the pedal is employed much less than in solo playing, in fact the best advice I can give you at such times is to use no pedal at all, and to play lightly non-legato or semistaccato. On the other hand, in slow sustained pieces like the *Coronation Scene* from 'Boris,' or Debussy's *Afternoon of a Faun,* even more pedal can be used than is possible in solo playing. In fact, one of the fascinations of two-piano playing is the pedal experimentation made possible with the two sounding boards and dampers."

6. DYNAMICS

The slightly malicious notion is sometimes encountered that "two pianos make twice as much noise as one." While a doubling of dynamics by the two instruments appears physically possible, such duplication of mere force is, of course, not the objective of duo-pianism. It is true, however, that the combination of two instruments opens up a range of dynamic shadings twice as resourceful as that of the solo piano. This advantage implies once more new potentialities and duties for conscientious performers.

With the extremely large scale of intensity which two pianos are affording, a complete scheme of dynamic gradation must be worked out. An important principle which applies to any well-understood and psychologically effective performance is: *One* climax only! The particular highpoint of a composition needs to be carefully determined, although musicians would hardly ever go wrong in locating this moment of the greatest emotional impact. Each additional climax is apt to produce only an anti-climax. The delicacy of the softest passage needs to be rehearsed as assiduously as the brilliance and power of the loudest. Within these extremes, the players will meet with an inexhaustible scale of shadings and colors.

Dynamic mastery in duo-pianism is as difficult to achieve as the control of tempo and rhythm. This fact, too often overlooked, is impressed upon the student of two-piano art by Luboshutz and Nemenoff who state the following:[9]

"In difficult passages that must be played simultaneously (a series of chords or runs for both instruments), the students should work for unison of sonority and volume, as well as of speed and rhythm. It is not enough to play the same notes and come out on time! Volume must be identically adjusted, and the thematic voices must always remain in their proper places. This requires much musical suppleness and flexibility—and even more careful practice!"

8. *Two-Piano Ensemble,* "The Etude," February 1938, p. 87.
9. *The Art of Piano Ensemble,* "The Etude," January 1941.

Guy Maier (Maier and Pattison) is very explicit in his directions for dynamic adjustment in two-piano performance. He writes on this subject:[10]

"Each pianist must halve his solo dynamics if the resulting amount of tone is to be satisfactory. This is very hard to do; for instance, if *piano* is called for, each pianist must play *pianissimo*, if *forte*, each must play *mezzoforte*, and so on. This is almost impossible to achieve unless the performers play by memory, with the piano racks down, listening every instant to the quantity of their tone. To be made acutely conscious of this exaggerated dynamic scale is of the greatest value to the pianist, not only in ensemble but also in solo playing. If, to produce a *pianissimo*, he must play so lightly as to be practically inaudible, he will gradually double his dynamic range.

"The difficulty of playing softly enough is illustrated in the following story. My colleague and I (years ago) were practicing a passage of that favorite old war horse, the Arensky *Waltz* in which he had the tune, accompanied by my piano in soft scale passages. We repeated it several times—each time with my partner's emphatic request that I play the embroidering passages softer. Evidently, I failed miserably, for the air in the practice room soon became blue! His exasperation finally gave way to the sad realization that it was impossible for me to play *pianissimo* enough. But, since hope springs eternally, he patiently said 'Well let's try it just once more.' This was so successful that he burst out—'There! That was perfect! Why can't you always play it that way?' Meekly (but triumphantly) I answered, 'You see, I didn't play my passage at all that time, I just 'made believe' by playing on the tops of the keys!' From which you will deduce that in two-piano playing it is always the other fellow who plays too loudly; often it is annoying if you can hear him at all.

"On the other hand, the team must be wary about its *fortes* and *fortissimos*. Only one or two *fortes* should be permitted in each piece, and certainly not more than one *fortissimo*. When (and if) this is required, it should burst forth brilliantly like a shooting rocket, and subside as quickly. But (I say it with a resigned sigh) duo-pianists will probably still continue to disregard this advice, and we shall be everlastingly irritated by those players whose sole color is a hard, rusty-wired *forte*. Heaven preserve us from the clan!"

To summarize: The most common danger in the dynamic treatment of two pianos arises from the over-statement of volume. The greatest opportunity, on the other hand, lies in the beauty of sonorities which may be obtained from the twin keyboards through judicious shading and blending. Mere force resulting from the exaggeration of dynamic resources defeats the art of duo-pianism, but in tasteful dealing with the increased scale of tonal tints and colors the two musicians may enlarge the horizons of their mastery without end.

7. TONE BLENDING AND BALANCE

The realm of dynamics is closely connected with another complex of problems, involving both mechanical and aesthetic aspects of duo-pianism. This further subject matter deals with the blending of tonal materials and the balance of ensemble. The applications of the traditional textures in the tonal web—monophony, polyphony, and homophony—assume new significance in the medium of duo-pianism because of the identity of in-

---

10. *Two-Piano Ensemble*, "The Etude," February 1938, p. 87.

struments employed. It is the sameness of timbre which confronts the partners with vexing problems. The uncertainties condense to alternatives such as this:

"Should two-piano playing sound like *one* piano, or should there be antiphonal (choir) effects at work?"

In the following answers to this question, opinions will be found to be widely differing. As a matter of fact, the present problem appears to be one of the most provocative.

Appleton and Field deny that the two pianos should sound like one. They hold that "the very basis of ensemble playing depends upon relating one instrument to another. In the case of two-piano playing, the specific 'two piano sound' should be achieved."

Bartlett and Robertson modify their own attitude from time to time, in accordance with the musical texture involved. This is what they write in answer to the problem:

"In certain kinds of music, for instance music which is harmonic in structure rather than contrapuntal, it is important that the two pianos should blend in one homogeneous sound (which you might call 'sounding like one piano'). In contrapuntal music, however, differences of tone-color should be employed and orchestral effects can be obtained."

Dougherty and Ruzicka likewise make the character of their approach depending on the texture of the particular score.

Gold and Fizdale, on the other hand, express the definite view that duo-pianism "should sound like an ensemble, not one piano. Antiphonal effects have the same validity that they have in solo piano. No more."

Morton Gould subscribes to the same opinion when he asserts: "If two pianos sound like one piano, other than in the coordination, then there is not much point to the medium."

Rosina Lhevinne counters this problem with an answer which could well stand as a universally valid definition of two-piano playing as an art form. Mme. Lhevinne states: "Figuratively the synchronization must be as in one piano performance, but literally the gamut of effects becomes wider than is possible on one piano."

Luboshutz and Nemenoff come forth with a detailed exposition of their ideas and ideals of tonal blending and balance in two-piano art when they write:[11]

"Two-piano work requires special adjustments of tone. We ourselves have experimented much to determine what our own tonal ideal should be. When we first began playing together, at the time of our marriage, . . . we both believed that, to facilitate the effect of complete unison, our pianistic tones should approximate each other as closely as possible. But after a year of study along these lines,

11. *The Art of Piano Ensemble,* "The Etude," January 1941.

we arrived at a different conclusion. The value of duo-piano work, after all, lies in its orchestral richness—and orchestral richness, in its turn, depends upon the variety of instruments which forms it. What makes an orchestra so superlatively satisfying is just the fact that there are violins, flutes, oboes, not sounding *like* each other, but blending their individual differences, and adjusting to the distribution of the thematic voices. That led us to a complete reversal of our earlier idea of tonal approximation. From then on, we tried to adjust our individual piano tones, not to each other, but to the orchestral balance of the voices in our music. Sometimes in a symphony, a theme may be stated and then repeated by a flute; in such cases, we try to make our tones sound as much like each other as possible. But at other times, a theme may be stated by a flute and repeated by an oboe; in such cases, we try to duplicate the tonal variations that make for added color. Since the two pianos have no difference in timbre (contrary to the distinct difference in timbre of the various orchestral instruments), these variations of tone must be achieved entirely by the volume and color of the pianists' touch. Hence, the duo-piano partners should possess a knowledge of instrumentation and orchestral effects, as well as tonal coloring on the keyboard."

Should two-piano playing sound like one piano? Morley and Gearhart answer: "Yes and no, depending upon the musical concepts to be communicated."

E. Robert Schmitz subscribes to the same attitude which allows for flexibility of treatment "according to score."

Victor Babin (Vronsky and Babin), in opinions expressed during a personal interview, approaches the question on the platform of aesthetical considerations. To his mind, the most important expedient towards the achievement of tonal perfection is to make the two instruments the single agency of the composition. This principle does not necessarily suggest that duo-pianism should sound like one piano, but the postulate implies that a single agency must insure plasticism of musical performance. In this connection, Victor Babin offers practical advice to obtain a satisfying balance of two-piano sound. He refers to the degrees of relationship which distinguish the ingredients of chordal structures, and thereby propounds one of the greatest problems in musical performance generally. The lowest and highest tones of the chord must be made to stand out. When two pianists simultaneously play *forte* chords without differentiation between the chord members, the net result is chaos. Only if the elements which must predominate are recognized as such and given plastic shape in relation to the other tones, only then the duo-pianists, according to Mr. Babin, really are "together."

Whittemore and Lowe are elaborating, with thoughts of their own, on a viewpoint which was expressed in the foregoing discussion by Mme. Lhevinne. Confronted with the problems of tonal blending and balance which arise through the combination of two pianofortes, they submit this statement:

"To capitalize on these very assets and to combine them into the expression of real musical beauty is the challenge in the field of two-piano composition and performance. So far as ensemble is concerned, it is naturally desirable to produce simultaneity which, in the words of the layman, 'sounds like one piano'; however, because of the color potentiality, the two instruments together should hardly ever sound *literally* like one piano. They should have a resonance of their own!

"If, in arranging for two pianos, there is concern *only* for the utilization of twenty fingers (simply because there are that many available), the end product will tend toward a 'busy-ness' which has given the field itself a black eye with many serious musicians and music-lovers. It is the realization of the capabilities and assets of the medium which will illuminate its future path musically."

Of uppermost importance in every consideration of tonal blending and balance becomes the function of the melodic line as it passes from one piano to the other. At all times, this line must be easy to trace and it needs to stand out clearly against the background of the accompaniment. The latter, because of the identity of timbre prevailing in the combination, should generally be kept even more subdued than when accompanying the melody given out by the human voice, the violin, or any other instrument of different tone color.

Bearing no less consequence in the endeavor to achieve fine balance is the cognizance of what one's partner is playing. Each pianist should read through the score of his colleague and thus become aware of the full context of the music. He will then be enabled to integrate his own share more intelligently into the composite whole. Balance is achieved not alone by aurally weighing the individual parts against each other, a procedure which indeed may at times produce a fallacious result. Rather, an equal effort is to be directed towards intellectual comprehension of the musical fabric. If this rational habit is consistently developed and faithfully adhered to, two minds may come to succeed in operating as *one* agency. Musical intent and performance will eventually reach that happy equilibrium of unity, variety, and proportion which epitomizes all true art.

The tonal quantity and quality of the melodic line is to be full and sonorous, yet plastic and clearly defined. The performer of the melody for the time is to be given the freedom of the soloist. As has already been emphasized, the most careful adjustment of the accompaniment is necessary, with a wide margin allowed to exist between the dynamic level of the melody and the total volume of the accompanying parts; this large difference becomes obligatory because of the sameness of timbre.

It should always be remembered that infinite possibilities for the achievement of new and different tonal effects are substantially inherent in the two-piano medium. The judicious examination of inner voices, of rhythmic designs, of dynamic levels, and of the manifold other details comprising a musical score will reveal that truly symphonic dimensions can be achieved in a variety of manipulations, and that this combination of instruments offers unending opportunities for experimentation.

From the foregoing general remarks on tonal blending and balance, specific questions can be deducted concerning the treatment of the individual instruments. For instance: Should there be the impression of a dialogue or conversation between the two parts, or are cumulative effects to be preferred? In the following paragraphs, the comments of several experts will be presented, dealing with the problems of the horizontal versus the vertical, of voice leading versus clusters of tone.

Appleton and Field express this viewpoint:

"In the case of polyphonic writing one would naturally expect a clear delineation of all the voices. Cumulative effect has its place when the music requires that specific kind of sonority."

The essence of the foregoing statement proves to be the consensus of opinions on this particular topic. Rae Robertson (Bartlett and Robertson) is wording his own conclusion to the problem as follows:

"This is entirely a question of the type of music. There is no question of preference in general."

To Josef and Rosina Lhevinne, the question of dialogue leading is an integral part of the general problem of tone blending and balance. These authorities state in detail:[12]

"The players must keep their ears and their minds constantly alert for the shifts of balance—must know which instrument has the important message to state, the exact second at which he passes it into the hands of his partner, which piano is to be temporarily subdued and which brought to the fore. You have exactly the same problem, of course, in the interpretation of any two-handed piece, especially in the works of composers like Bach and Brahms where an elaborate contrapuntal pattern may shift from treble, to middle voice, to bass—but the solution becomes even more delicate when it must be decided at the same second by two different people."

For Luboshutz and Nemenoff, likewise, all questions of detail significance remain inseparable from the over-all problem of proportion. In describing their approach to balance, they write:[13]

"The first step in working together is the distribution of *balance*. For the most part, there is no 'first' piano and no 'second' piano. Each instrument holds the important voice during a given number of bars, and then hands it on to the other; and this handing back and forth of the upper and lower voices requires the greatest awareness. It may be compared to the give and take—the swing and balance of a game of ball. There must be no over-playing, and no under-playing—no dropping of the ball. The listener must watch to *see* where the change of balance occurs;

12. *Four Hands That Play As Two,* "The Etude," December 1933.
13. *The Art of Piano Ensemble,* "The Etude," January 1941.

never must he hear it. Musical accuracy and awareness decide where the balance between the voices must lie, and sympathetic team-work in practicing assures smooth movement."

Guy Maier (Maier and Pattison) tenders the following suggestion for the duo-pianistic treatment of voices:[14]

> "Never try to bring out two themes at the same time. The percussive nature of the piano precludes the success of any such plan unless the melodies are widely separated on the keyboard. Only one important melodic line should be well outlined—and all else relegated to a soft, but live background."

Maier adds further practical advice for the achievement of proper tone blending and balance:

> "One of the marked differences between ensemble and solo playing is in the extra amount of bass tone required of the pianist's left hand; in other words, he is often the only 'bottom' for the other two or three hands; so, in order to make this bass rich and powerful enough, it must be played exaggeratedly loudly. Without such solid foundation, the whole structure wobbles insecurely. . . ."

Victor Babin (Vronsky and Babin), queried on the issue of the horizontal versus the vertical, believes that the decision concerning one's attitude must lastly depend on the particular score. However, he himself feels inclined to reason that the procedure of dialogue treatment would appear to be the logical and preferable course to follow, because of the sameness of instruments and consequent identity of sonorities. Blocks of sound can be procured on one piano alone, Mr. Babin argues, and two pianos therefore should mainly be made to serve the exposition and development of contrapuntal voices in a polyphonic web.

To close this section on tone blending and balance with a practical suggestion, the use of a recording apparatus is recommended. Through this instrument, duo-pianists can secure a most valuable aid in checking the accuracy of their team work, the degree of tonal balance, and the numerous other effects which go to make up their performance. Transcriptions recorded at frequent intervals during rehearsals, concerts, or broadcasts will afford the partners with the opportunity to hear themselves play together as the audience hears them. In this connection, it should be realized that each performer, from his end of the ensemble, can obtain only a distorted impression of the total effect. Recordings are ideally providing a solution to this problem which for so long has been one of the most elusory on the road to perfection. Now, through the painstaking analysis of their recorded performance, duo-pianists are enabled to trace and correct imperfections which otherwise might have gone unnoticed.

8. INTEGRATION OF ELEMENTS

In the foregoing, the discussion has been dealing with some of the

---

14. *Two-Piano Ensemble,* "The Etude," February 1938.

often perplexing details of mechanics and aesthetics in duo-pianism. An integration of elements now needs to be brought about, a synthesis in which mechanical control is welded into artistic freedom. Whereas security is a most important objective, it must still allow for the spark of momentary inspiration without which all artistic endeavor is stifled to inanimate dullness.

Resorting here again to a cross-section of authoritative opinions, it is learned that integration is achieved through a variety of theories and approaches, in fact that the concept of integration is varying with different two-piano teams. Rosina Lhevinne, for example, summarizes her views on the process of amalgamation of mechanical and aesthetical elements as follows:[15]

> "The problem of two-piano playing is exactly the same as that of all chamber music; sound musicianship, excellent ensemble, sensitiveness to proper balance, discipline, good rhythm, accurateness in note values and rest values. However, the two pianos have a problem of their own because of the similarity of tone color. The well meant praise, 'how beautifully they play together—it sounds just like one piano,' is exactly what a good two-piano team tries to avoid. The aim of the two musicians is to achieve almost the same freedom of expression as in playing alone. I say 'almost', because in two playing together there are some points of specific ensemble playing, such as synchronization of attack, precision in time and perfect accurateness in passage work, which do not allow any freedom. Otherwise, each artist should have the possibility of using his imagination, variety of tone, pedaling and phrasing. This they can do if they are confident that each partner is sensitive to all nuances of expression and will be instantly receptive to such changes, that his playing will blend with that of the other. The highest artistic goal is achieved when the two musicians can give that improvisational quality which is one of the greatest charms in the perfect ensemble."

The "improvisational quality," that highest of artistic achievements, needs to be gradually developed from a basic precept of strict discipline, according to an earlier statement which was issued jointly by Josef and Rosina Lhevinne. They then wrote:[16]

> "The polishing and orderliness of piano ensemble work is even more fun than scheming out puzzles! This, however, does not imply that two-piano work need be in any way mechanical. There is strict discipline and a strict regard for routine and order; and indeed the truly artistic individuality is the one which is built up upon these. Freedom, to be freedom, needs a foundation of technical and musical orderliness."

It is also the belief of Josef and Rosina Lhevinne that the process of duo-pianistic integration, in the final analysis, is synonymous with the problem of unified *interpretation*. This viewpoint is given a discussion of widely significant character in the following quotation:[17]

> "Music is so elusive a means of expression that ensemble work needs some sort

---

15. *The Spirit of Ensemble,* "Pan Pipes," February 1949.
16. *Four Hands That Play As Two,* "The Etude," December 1933.
17. *Four Hands That Play As Two,* "The Etude," December 1933.

of spiritual 'binder' to hold it sharply to the pattern of non-mechanical unity. You can argue about music forever without definitely proving anything. And interpretations vary not only in individuality but in type. Some musicians, for instance, use the printed text merely as point of departure for displaying an excess of their own individualism. Others—and theirs is the sounder musical philosophy—seek to hold their own egos in check, giving first place to the message of the composer— or, best of all, perhaps, to project themselves *through a faithful adherence* to the composer's thought. This, to us, is the kernel of true artistry. Too much subjectivity, too much 'personality,' and the composer is lost sight of."

The following excerpt expresses the convictions of Luboshutz and Nemenoff in the same subject matter:[18]

"The secret of good duo-piano playing is that it must sound like the performance of a single artist. A listener with his eyes closed should not be able to distinguish the boundaries of two separate performances. There must be no breaks, no unevenness, no separate attacks. On the other hand, there must be nothing mechanical or monotonous in the adjustment of the two partners to each other. To combine complete technical unison with equally complete artistic freedom is no easy task! Yet that, precisely, is the soul of duo-piano playing. That is why it remains the most difficult form of ensemble work really to master."

Luboschutz and Nemenoff proceed to explain why they regard duo-pianism as the most difficult ensemble form to master. These are some of their reasons:

"The inter-dependence of the two partners makes duo-piano playing a rather unique art. There are not enough performers (as in an orchestra) to mass up sufficient tone to cover possible slips; and there are too many to permit of the complete individualism of the solo performer. Hence, the team-work must be of the highest order, requiring that delicate combination of personal sympathy and technical equality that permits the partners to work out and to carry out their interpretations with artistic satisfaction. Such a combination is not easy to find, but where it exists, it opens the door to unsurpassed musical riches."

Silvio Scionti, another specialist in the art of two-piano playing, sums up his doctrine for duo-pianism with the following statements:[19]

"Two-piano playing of the higher type cannot be compared with solo playing. They represent two entirely different arts, with greatly different objectives. The resources of two-piano playing are naturally greater, in many particulars, than solo playing; because there are twenty fingers and two pairs of brains involved! When the two performers have arrived where the problems of a perfect artistic ensemble have been mastered to the point of becoming second nature, the possibilities for a forceful musical expression are great indeed. Here they are giving 'imagination' its full chance and justice! With the greater resources of pedal effects, tone coloring and adjustment, which two pianos offer, and with a greater technical coloring and emotional range at their command, the performers are indeed inspired to orchestral heights. Two players with distinctive and individual musical and artistic personalities will fit into this marvelously artistic scheme more forcefully and effectively than two pianists who are as much alike as identical twins."

John Thompson, the composer-pedagogue, voices a few principles of

18. *The Art of Piano Ensemble*, "The Etude," January 1941.
19. *The Fascination of Two-Piano Playing*, "The Etude," September, 1939

his own regarding the requirements for duo-piano performance. These personal comments which include additional viewpoints on a number of subjects previously discussed, are reproduced from a letter written by Mr. Thompson to Rebecca Love Entriken.[20] A pertinent contribution to the complex of duo-pianistic philosophy, John Thompson's statements read as follows:

> "All laws of ensemble playing such as quartets, quintets, orchestra or band must be observed in two-piano work; that is, each performer must submerge his own individuality to the point where it blends with the other. Even in style of playing each should try to imitate the other—a difficult chore. Perhaps this is the reason why two-piano playing on the part of two really great artists is not as acceptable as that of two artists whose style and individuality are not so marked.
>
> "Interpretation should be reached by agreement. If a difference of opinion exists, a compromise of some sort must be worked out. Or better yet—one is the conductor and the other follows the lead. This arrangement can be alternated so that each has a chance of self-expression. That is, one leads in this piece and the other in that. Of course this is subject to exception. But the big point to remember is that the performance must not be that of *two soloists* playing together.
>
> "This 'give and take' attitude is part of the fun of two-piano playing, especially where a figure is tossed back and forth between two pianos as is often the case. Where one carries the theme or *motif* the other accompanies just as one would accompany a vocalist or violinist.
>
> "Since both instruments are pianos, more attention than ever is necessary in the matter of variation of tonal quality through various touches. The general idea is to imitate the different instruments of the orchestra as much as possible, otherwise two pianos will be just twice as noisy as one."

The integration of mechanical control into artistic freedom was referred to already in the earlier discussion of analytic versus synthetic procedures during practice sessions.[21] For the blending of technical with aesthetic aspects, the earlier remarks on *Gestalt* Psychology may again be applied. In the present problem, too, the dynamical process of self-distribution and self-regulation can accomplish the aimed-for combination of elements if, beyond the localized consideration of details and above the basic quest for artistic freedom, the over-all *Gestalt* is kept in mind, that sum total of aspects which includes not only the nature of the composition, but also the character of the two-piano unit performing it.

Encountering a veritable kaleidoscope of interpretative conceptions, it is well to recall what Josef and Rosina Lhevinne consider the best method of interpretation for all artists, namely "to project themselves through a faithful adherence to the composer's thought." This attitude, if placed on a level of general application, will go far to explain the ever-fluctuating nuances in the musical net result during the performance of any given

---

20. Later incorporated in her master's thesis *Problem of the Arrangement for Two Pianos of Sedlak by Jindr. Jindrich and Prelude opus 34 No. 5, by Dimitri Shostakovich.*
21. See Chapter XIV on *Practicing*.

composition. The fact is that a musical rendition cannot be abstracted from the personalities of the performers and their ever-varying moods.

True appreciation of a musical performance therefore must include more than an ounce of tolerance with the subjective manifestations of the individual artists. As for the music itself, each composition, like the diamond, assumes as many facets as there are individuals to render it a presentation.

The art of duo-pianism, beyond all other considerations, requires foremost that uncanny precision which is one of the great fascinations for those who achieve it and those who witness it. It needs to be the kind of precision, however, which always succeeds in transcending mechanical perfection to the plane of musical expression.

The qualities of a good two-piano team are contained in a synthesis of remarkable coordination as well as of fine musicianship. Collective exactitude and individual freedom are entering into an alliance. When queried about her precision playing with Michael Field, Vera Appleton explained: "Two personalities who share experiences together in music start with what is known as basic rapport, which they refine, develop, and study. Each finally understands the moods and feelings of the other. We spend hours of practice time just to acquire the subtleties of nuances which will give our playing the free expression and flexibility of the soloist."

The achievement of this "soloistic" objective was epitomized in a phrase of the New York critic who commented on the occasion of a successful two-piano recital in Town Hall, marking the debut performance of now well-known duo-pianists:[22]

"Two artists of the keyboard who play and think as one."

9. SUPERVISION OF THE TEAM WORK

During the preceding discussion of mechanics and aesthetics in duo-pianism, the question may have suggested itself whether or not an outside authority should control the teamwork. Evidently, such supervision could prevent or eliminate much of a trial and error procedure in practice and performance. Moreover, it would protect the team, after success has been achieved, from stagnation, pit-falls, and set-backs.

It has been pointed out that, because of the identity of sonorities, two-piano playing is the most difficult ensemble form for the partners themselves to hear. Therefore, supervision of the teamwork would seem to be an immediate adjunct, be such council regularly received from a teacher or coach, be it extended during informal sessions by a musical friend who is serving in an advisory capacity.

---

22. *New York World Telegram,* on the debut of Appleton and Field.

Guy Maier holds a strong opinion on the subject when stating that " a coach or an experienced teacher is absolutely indispensable in order to achieve a well-balanced result."

In surprising contrast to this postulate, a number of teams of the highest reputation frankly declare themselves to be without the supervision of a coach. They profess, moreover, either directly or by implication, to have acquired their ensemble proficiency as autodidacts. Several other ranking duo-pianists who were consulted on this point admit that a teacher or coach may be acceptable if the partners have confidence in him.

Characteristic for an attitude frequently incurred is the following statement which was contributed by Morley and Gearhart:

"Probably we are autodidacts, although it sounds faintly degenerate. Over nine years, we have coached several times with Stravinsky and other modern composers whose new works we were about to play. Otherwise, all we can claim along this line is a few informal sessions with musical colleagues, usually string players, rarely pianists. "

Vronsky and Babin who used to play for Rachmaninoff and now frequently perform privately for authorities like Schnabel, Stravinsky, and Milhaud, declare themselves "never averse to constructive criticism." The soundness of this principle does not require elaboration.

Some teams will find it difficult or impossible to secure the assistance of a qualified coach or teacher. In this event, it probably will be best to follow the advice given by the veteran duo-pianist Guy Maier who humorously proclaims this memento:[23]

"Duo-pianists should have conspicuous signs before them in their practice rooms to admonish them incessantly to play 'More Pianissimo,' 'Semistaccato,' 'One climax only,' 'Softer,' 'Dryly,' 'Less Tone,' 'Less Pedal,' and to 'Restrain Yourself,' 'Hold Back' and 'Keep Down.' I am afraid, however, that it would take huge, glaring neon signs to make them really heed these warnings!"

10. ON THE ESSENCE OF IT ALL

One of the more frequent questions asked by pianists who become interested in two-piano work, is the inquiry as to *when* to begin playing on two instruments. There should exist a fair degree of individual advancement and accomplishment in solo playing, in addition to a solid foundation of knowledge concerning the resources of the instrument, the various branches of theory, and the commonly accepted standards of musicianship. If these preliminary conditions are fulfilled by each partner, the association will be mutually much more enjoyable and productive than if individual deficiencies stifle the team-work from the start.

Another question often incurred concerns the length of time which it may take to achieve a good two-piano ensemble. This inquiry obviously

23. *Two-Piano Ensemble,* "The Etude," February 1938.

cannot be answered with any degree of approximation. While in the presence of unusual rapport the period of initial preparation may be comparatively short,[24] all duo-pianists seem to agree that the subtleties of their team-work and the security of mutual mental reactions grow proportionately to the number of years which they play together.

Dougherty and Ruzicka share the general conviction that time is the essence and express it in the following words:

"Ensemble of any kind, like good wine, improves with time. Although playing can be adjusted in as short a time as two or three years, it really takes many years of concert experience to achieve a true unit."

It should furthermore be remembered that the degree of collective success directly depends on the amount of perpetual individual effort summoned by each partner. The team character of duo-pianism offers no escape from the necessity of continually perfecting one's personal pianistic standards. Each ensemble benefits immediately and proportionately from the self-improvement which is achieved by the individual member and contributed towards greater accomplishment of the unit.

Therefore, the partners in a two-piano team do well to keep in mind, besides and above all necessary synchronization of their respective qualities, this permanent necessity for individual effort which Leopold Godowsky once has expressed in some general remarks on the study of the pianoforte. Godowsky, a firm believer in work, submits this thought:[25]

"The fault with many students is the erroneous idea that genius or talent will take the place of work. They minimize the necessity for careful, painstaking consideration of the infinite details of technique . . . But this is not all. Individuality, character, and temperament are becoming more and more significant in the highly organized art of pianoforte playing. Remove these, and the playing of the artist again becomes little better than that of a piano playing machine."

Applied to duo-pianism, the foregoing words propound an even greater moral. The individual effort of each partner must be contributed in full to the collective endeavor; never can it be permitted to develop into an individual tendency. Not two mere technicians, but two characters and temperaments meet, agree, and aspire. They truly become team-mates, with all the generally understood implications of the term. The accumulative efforts of two pianists are directed into a common artistic projection. The ensemble, because of the very sameness of instruments, opens up rare potentialities of a two-fold musical experience, expressed through but one medium. The happy result is achieved in the full realization of the concept of Unity.

24. Such was the case, for instance, in the experience of Appleton and Field, and Whittemore and Lowe, respectively.
25. From the section on Leopold Godowsky, in *Famous Musicians of a Wandering Race* by Gdal Saleski, pp. 315-316.

CHAPTER XVI

PROGRAM BUILDING

1. DUO-PIANISM, CONCERT OR CHAMBER MUSIC?

In the building of a repertoire as well as in the choice of an individual program, every two-piano team will meet with two pronounced types of compositions, representing the categories of chamber and concert music, respectively.

This encounter with widely differing characteristics in the two-piano literature sooner or later raises the fundamental question whether duo-pianism as an ensemble form is to be classified as chamber music or as concert music. The first is said to be of an intimate nature, the second of a more spectacular character. Both types follow established laws all of their own. For instance, chamber music traditionally permits the use of printed notes as being fully conventional, and actually recommends their employment for the sake of greater ease and security during public performance. "Concert" artists, on the other hand, discard the printed score as a distracting attribute, or else feel compelled by public opinion to perform from memory. Another fundamental difference is found in the divergent characteristics of the respective repertoires; some inherent differences all but separate chamber music from other styles of composition and performance.

According to the dictionary definition, duo-pianism may under certain conditions qualify as *chamber music* in that the requirements for this particular category call for "instrumental music written in the larger forms for combinations ranging from two to ten players, having one player on a part, and designed to be heard in a small room or chamber."[1] However,

---

1. Homer Ulrich, *Chamber Music.*

the designation would have to be changed whenever the prerequisite as to larger forms is not fulfilled, i.e. whenever smaller works are under consideration which may not meet the formal reservations. The entire situation, obviously, defies any summary attribution of the medium to either chamber or concert classification. Whatever distinction can be made in specific cases, needs to unfold from the particular aspects of the individual work. It may, for that matter, also evolve from the general attitude and behaviour of a distinctly characteristic team. Probably it is a far-fetched application of the term "chamber music" when recordings of light dances by the First Piano Quartet are brought to be listed under this heading;[2] on the other hand, it would be difficult to escape or to deny the intimate "chamber" character of Schumann's *Andante and Variations*. Similarly, it appears congruent for an ensemble like the Rochester Chamber Players to include into their programs a work such as Bartók's *Sonata for Two Pianos and Percussion*[3], whereas other two-piano artists and program items intrinsically seem to oppose the chamber style, displaying a genre quite foreign to the latter's traditional norms.

The respective characteristics of the two classifications in themselves defy a concise definition. However, it would appear that concert music by and large stresses the aspects of symphonic power and generally emphasizes the more brilliant features of concertizing. By contrast, chamber music cultivates the intimate qualities of small ensemble performance and employs means of refinement to their realization. The alternative of extremes therefore ranges from showy brilliancy to quiet intimacy, with resultant implications such as extroversion and introspection, respectively.

Some top-ranking violinists and other musicians of the highest standing have found it congruous to be classified as chamber players, according to their professed preference and specialization. Certain vocalists also follow the exclusive "chamber" line, seeking repute for themselves as *Lieder* singers. The status of duo-pianism in musical art, however, at this time defies any such distinction between "brilliant" and "intimate" teams. Duo-pianists either admit no difference whatever between concert and chamber music styles, or else declare that they will pursue the respective requirements of either classification, depending on the type of composition chosen for performance.

In order to test reactions to this problem, the question "Do you consider two-piano playing to be concert or chamber music?" was submitted to a group of authorities. The following are some of the views expressed:

2. *Listen* magazine, issue of September 1949.
3. *Musical Courier*, December 1, 1949, p. 34.

Appleton and Field regard their art as "essentially chamber music, although one might refer to it as concert-chamber music."

Bartlett and Robertson contribute this statement to the discussion: "Two-piano playing is both concert and chamber music. It is chamber music in the sense that it is ensemble playing and must be approached by the performers in the same way that a string quartet rehearses together. On the other hand, the great sonorities and brilliance possible on two pianos make this form of music-making suitable for even the largest concert halls."

Ralph Berkowitz writes[4] that "the great piano duets are essentially great pieces of chamber music." He no doubt includes all important compositions for two pianos into this classification.

Abram Chasins likewise considers the duo-piano art as a form of chamber music.

Dougherty and Ruzicka prefer to make their attitude depending on the specific type of music coming under consideration. Generally, however, they feel inclined to think of two-piano playing mainly as a chamber music activity. Mr. Ruzicka maintains, moreover, that two-piano music comes to better realization in a smaller hall, and that it definitely loses in a large auditorium.[5]

Gold and Fizdale subscribe to the opinion that two-piano playing can be both chamber and concert music.

In like tenor, Morton Gould holds that "this depends on the repertoire and on the kind of playing."

Rosina Lhevinne, on the other hand, explicitly stands for classification of the art as chamber music.

Darius Milhaud, the composer, answers the question whether he considers the two-piano medium a form of chamber music with the words: "That depends what kind of music you write for two pianos."

Morley and Gearhart seem to face no problem in this matter and therefore reply with glee: "Truthfully, we are not aware of the difference, although there must be one. Thus cannot answer. Ignorance."

E. Robert Schmitz declares that two-piano playing "should be chamber music but most of the time fails to be so!"

Victor Babin (Vronsky and Babin) express the thought that the distinction between chamber and concert styles is almost obsolete in that the

---

4. *Original Music for Four Hands*, "The Etude," January 1944, p. 27.
5. This writer, while witnessing a Dougherty and Ruzicka recital, felt clearly moved to attribute to these duo-pianists the classification of the "intimate team," because of their general approach to the art which had a distinct chamber style, notwithstanding several sparkling items performed during the program.

boundaries already have overlapped. He personally tends towards classification of the genre as chamber music.

Whittemore and Lowe, on the other hand, profess this attitude: "Two-piano playing is not intimate enough to limit it solely to chamber music. We rather prefer to consider it a concert medium."

Contemplating the variety of opinions expressed in the foregoing statements, one feels drawn to the conclusion that the problem itself must be subjected to shifting degrees of emphasis, and a decision of preference derived therefrom, according to the essential qualities of the music and taking into account also the temperamental characteristics of the performing duo-pianists. Indeed, Victor Babin's viewpoint that the boundaries have overlapped, and that consequently any distinction between concert and chamber music in the two-piano medium has become obsolete, could be interpreted as symptomatic for a future in which duo-pianism will stand as a fully individual and absolute form of musical art; when it will be recognized as an instrumental combination in which the soloistic tendencies of the players are absorbed and synthesized towards a greater manifestation of pianism; when it will come to be regarded as the medium in which the qualities of refined intimacy and improvisatory freedom can at will be amalgamated with the effects of symphonic brilliance and ostentatious grandeur. Duo-pianism, instead of splitting up into diverging branches of specialization, will then represent a streamlined vehicle of universal musical expression.

2.   ORIGINAL WORKS VERSUS ARRANGEMENTS

Whatever the attitude of a two-piano team may be concerning its functions as a concert or a chamber music ensemble, the necessity of building a repertoire appears as its foremost task. Submitting to scrutiny the existing literature, duo-pianists soon become aware of the marked misproportion of usable original works through the various style periods. Comparatively few truly great compositions are available from the Classic and Romantic eras for causes which were traced during the discussion of the history of duo-pianism. By contrast, an abundance of original two-piano works from more recent and contemporary composers calls for attention. As a consequence of this misproportion, there exists the danger either of undue frequency and duplication of repertoire items from the Classic and Romantic periods, or that of ill balance in the building of a program because of too large an emphasis on modern numbers.

Many duo-pianists avert this problem of programming by resorting to the inclusion of original compositions for one piano, four hands. So much music has been written in this particular category, and so many beautiful works from this literature indeed are deserving of being heard regularly, that the procedure of including such duet works seems quite justifiable from the purely artistic point of view. In a specific pianistic aspect, moreover, all four-hand music coming to be played on two pianos, instead of on one, affords the performers with greater individual freedom, a feeling which also conveys itself upon the audience. In addition, the two sets of pedals contribute to the achievement of widely enlarged sonorities. On the other hand, there remains the awkward and unsatisfactory aspect of a strict confinement to the treble register which is imposed upon one of the performers. The latter finds himself almost entirely responsible for the rendition of melodic and other *solo* material, while the other player must contend with the bass register and mainly functions as accompanist.

To offset these disadvantages, many arrangements for two pianos have been made of music originally written for one piano, four hands. Besides providing greater individual freedom for the performers, they accomplish a more equal distribution of piano registers and musical materials between the partners. Of the numerous four-hand works by Schubert, for instance, the arrangements for two pianos by Harold Bauer and Bruno Hinze-Reinhold are notable for their effectiveness and for the service which they are rendering to Schubert's musical genius.[6]

Following the same train of thought, Guy Maier thus advises duo-pianists who are in quest of expanding their repertoire:[7]

"Why not examine some of the works written by Mozart for *one* piano, four hands? These can easily be distributed over two pianos, and make delightful novelties. Among the loveliest are the little *Variations in G major;* the *Fantasia* in F minor No. 2; and the beautiful *Sonatas* in F and C major."[8]

Another avenue in avoiding the misproportion of style periods existing in the literature of original two-piano compositions, is the employment of arrangements, transcriptions, and paraphrases. This outlet is frequently resorted to by most two-piano teams. As a matter of fact, *The International Cyclopedia of Music and Musicians,* in the edition of 1938, went so far as to state that "the average two-piano program contains a preponderant number of transcriptions, and if there has ever existed a prejudice against playing arrangements of works in other forms it has disappeared in view of the circumstance that many compositions otherwise neglected or more or less inaccessible have been revealed by transcriptions made of them as eminently justifying closer acquaintance."

This enthusiastic view of two-piano transcriptions appears to exaggerate their popularity, however, in that the majority of duo-pianists definitely prefer *original* compositions in their program building. Arrangements

6. See also Book 1, *The History,* Chapter V, *The Grand Duo,* section Schubert.
7. *The Etude,* January 1941, p. 20.
8. See also Book I, *The History,* Chapter IV, *Mozart.*

and transcriptions generally are used only as a substitute. Even in that function, they frequently are subjected by duo-pianists to the provision that they must comply with their individual standards of workmanship and style requirements.

The nature and extent of such demands made on two-piano arrangements and transcriptions, the employment of duet-music (originally written for one piano) on two instruments, and the entire complex of related problems will now be subjected to closer survey. The following paragraphs contain a cross-selection of statements in which their authors take issue with these questions:

(1) "Do you prefer original compositions for two pianos, and why?"

(2) "Do you use arrangements from other combinations and do you advocate them in your program building?"

Appleton and Field prefer original compositions "for the same reason that one would prefer original music for string quartet, trio, or any other combination of instruments." This team uses arrangements "not too often, since there are, unfortunately, few arrangements that have a *raison d'être* other than flamboyancy. As far as using them on programs, they have a strategic place depending on the type of audience."

In addition to this reply which was given as their personal commentary to the current study, Appleton and Field have elaborated on their views regarding program building in an essay, entitled *Is There a Two-Piano Dilemma Today?*[9] From this article, the following excerpts are quoted because they deal earnestly and intensively with the specific problem of programming in duo-pianism:

"On tours throughout America, we have been able to gauge, fairly accurately, reactions of the great mass of music lovers to this supposedly 'limited' music. We have played, with gratifying results, programs consisting for the most part of music originally written for two pianos . . . the response has been uniformly enthusiastic, with people expressing their gratification at 'not being played down to.' The comment most frequently heard was: 'I didn't know such music existed. Why can't we have more of it?' And there is more of it—a wealth of it—from Pasquini, Bach, Mozart, the Romantics, and the Impressionists, to our present-day composers.

"The most unfortunate thing of all is the neglect of the music for one piano, four hands, for which composers such as Mozart, Beethoven, Schubert, Mendelssohn and the moderns have written some of their most affecting works. These can be effectively performed on two pianos, with the added advantage of another set of pedals, but we see no reason why a two-piano program could not include at least one of these works for piano duet, possibly a Mozart Sonata or Fantasie, the great Schubert Fantasie in F Minor, or either the Hindemith or the Poulenc Sonata.

"It is so tiresome to hear program after program of the standard theme and variations and Romantic suites, followed by the usual dessert of trivial transcriptions.

9. *Musical Courier*, August 1947.

Ensemble playing, as well as any other art, demands a much wider frame of reference . . .

"We . . . are constantly confronted with specimens of . . . trite two-piano programs, and are asked defiantly to justify our *raison d'être* on such limited evidence. A glance at the programs presented by our progressive teams during the past few years should answer that quite conclusively. Most of these consist almost exclusively of music written originally for two pianos, with a minimum of transcriptions.

"Frivolity, such as is often found in two-piano transcriptions, has as much place in music as anywhere else, but when it becomes the *sine qua non* and threatens to be wholly identified with a specific art form, it is time to view with alarm and to examine the true state of affairs.

"This is not to say that transcriptions, *per se*, are bad. Far from it. Those of Busoni, Liszt, Ravel and a few others are masterpieces of their genre, but it is as manifestly absurd to consider these the final objective of ensemble playing as it would be to consider the same composers' transcriptions for one piano the final objective of solo playing.

"Fortunately, the trend is in the opposite direction. The serious two-piano music being written today should be sufficient to quell the fears of the most pious purists, and still satisfy the demands of those for whom music is only a source of relaxation and pleasure.

"The ambivalence implicit in this distinction is not as clearcut as it seems, since there is a definite degree of prejudice on both sides, most of it unfounded. Only through vigorous insistence on musical integrity and uncompromising courage will this be dispelled and two-piano art emerge as the true musical expression it rightfully is."

Bartlett and Robertson write in answer to the questions under discussion: "We do prefer to make the much larger part of our programmes consist of original two-piano music but have no objection to good arrangements of music suitable for transcription for two pianos. If no music had been specially written for two pianos, we should not consider it a legitimate medium for concert purposes."

Concerning arrangements, Mr. Robertson states:

"We do use arrangements to a certain extent in making programmes, but they must have certain qualifications. First, the music arranged must not, for instance, depend largely on orchestral color for its beauty. The music of Tchaikovsky or Rimsky-Korsakoff, for example, is rarely effective on the piano. On the other hand, the music of Bach loses little by transference to another medium. Also we would avoid transcriptions of Chopin for two pianos, because this music is so perfectly written and adapted for solo piano that one could only spoil it in transcription."

Inserted here are a few relevant comments on the subject of arrangements, as written by Vera Brodsky (Brodsky and Triggs) who formerly was an instructor of two-piano ensemble at the Juilliard School of Music in New York and at the Curtis Institute in Philadelphia. Miss Brodsky states:[10]

---

10. *The MacMillan Encyclopedia of Music and Musicians*, 1938, p. 1904.

"Much unacceptable controversy has been waged regarding the artistic legitimacy of transcriptions, the debaters opposed to it seeming to forget that Bach, Beethoven, Mozart, Brahms and other masters lifted the practice into the realm of art, and through it enabled the world to become better acquainted with the important literature of music. Certainly many masterpieces, the Chorales of Bach, for instance, would scarcely ever have had the opportunity of being heard by music-lovers had it not been for the piano transcriptions of Busoni, the two-piano transcriptions of the English composers, and the orchestral transcriptions of Stokowski. One has only to mention such unique modern transcriptionists as Liszt, Godowsky, Busoni, Tausig, Kreisler, Rachmaninoff, Ravel, and others, to realize how much closer the average music-lover has been brought to the world's loftiest symphonies, operas, overtures, chamber-music, and vocal and instrumental solos through their efforts.

"For general practical availability there is no better transcribing medium than two pianos. . . ."

Dougherty and Ruzicka profess their preference for original music into which they include compositions for one piano, four hands; the latter type, to be sure, they always perform on two pianos. They also use arrangements, but—in contrast to Bartlett and Robertson—definitely prefer transcriptions from large combinations, especially the orchestra, so that music of symphonic dimensions may be introduced to the smaller communities. Dougherty and Ruzicka would like to see a guiding principle in effect for all types of arrangements. This ruling should be never to extend to two pianos what can be assigned to a single instrument.

Gold and Fizdale neither use nor advocate arrangements of any sort. They build their programs entirely from original compositions for two pianos.

Morton Gould thus replies to both questions: "I do prefer *original* compositions for two pianos, because I feel that original contributions for a given medium are necessary to the growth and stimulation of that medium.

"It is possible to use arrangements from other combinations and the value is a matter of taste—both personal and aesthetic."

Rosina Lhevinne, in her approach to the issue, is holding the middle road. She prefers original compositions "when they are masterpieces." She advocates arrangements "when they are done with excellent craftsmanship."

In response to the inquiry regarding original compositions, Morley and Gearhart make this statement: "No preference. This does not mean that we have no discrimination. It simply means we do not make our judgments on the basis of original—versus—arranged."

Concerning arrangements, the same duo-pianists contribute the following comments which include an information of practical interest: "We use arrangements freely where they fit program requirements. Our program this season is roughly fifty percent arranged by us, the rest original. A question you do not ask is: 'Do we re-arrange (or better readjust) passages in *original* works to minimize technical hazards, avoid difficulties of ensemble, improve flexibility, sonority, bring out important inner voices, etc. We do, constantly."

E. Robert Schmitz declares his preference for original compositions "if they justify musically such use." He advocates arrangements "only as a substitute for original forms."

Dorothy R. Sinnitt voices the opinion that repertoire numbers used in program building can be "either original, or well arranged, as they are better adapted to the medium (of duo-pianism)."

Vronsky and Babin acknowledge a pronounced predilection for original works. To them, transcriptions mean *Ersatz*. When using arrangements at all, these duo-pianists exclusively employ their own settings. According to Mr. Babin, there are two principal avenues which can be followed when transcribing for two pianos: The first, open only to truly great musicians, demands of the transcriber that he is able to project his own fantasy into the original, a process during which an actual transformation of the work takes place. Such are the transcriptions by Liszt or Busoni. In all other arrangements, the original intentions of the composer need to be ascertained and followed painstakingly. For exemplification of this usual type of arrangement, Victor Babin points out his own scoring for two pianos of Bach's recitative and aria "Sheep May Safely Graze." According to Mr. Babin's viewpoint, the composer's essential *piano* style is to be adapted when making arrangements for two pianos. To illustrate by example: Tschaikowsky's orchestral treatment is comparatively simple; his piano writing, however, is of the virtuoso type. Consequently, when transcribing from Tschaikowsky's orchestral works for two pianos, a virtuosic scoring is to be applied. By contrast, Stravinsky's orchestrations being complex, and his piano writing appearing highly economical, transcriptions from the orchestral into the two-piano medium are to be treated with sparing means, according to the composer's *piano* style.

While approaching the problem on premises different from those held by many of their colleagues, Whittemore and Lowe share in the general concern over these issues. Regarding the preferability of original compositions for two pianos, they write:

"Ideally speaking, music written for any given medium should be preferable to 'arrangements.' However, the greater proportion of original compositions for two pianos is not of exceptional musical significance. This may be due to composers' lack of understanding of the assets of two pianos as a medium and the lack of technique in expressing ideas through this medium. There are, of course, masterpieces which are exceptions to these complaints. It would be heaven indeed if there were a large library of worthwhile original compositions."

Although fundamentally disposed towards original works, Whittemore and Lowe, because of what they consider existing limitations in the literature, become strong advocates for the use of arrangements. They deplore, in the same vein, that critics are unduly indifferent to all transcriptions. The argument of these duo-pianists, another of the original contributions to the current investigation, is quoted herewith:

"Yes, we certainly use and advocate arrangements. In fact, for our own concert needs we have created some 180 transcriptions ourselves.

"There has been a noticeable trend in the past six or eight years to advertise and to perform programs of 'original music for two pianos.' While this is obviously attempting to curry favor with the critics who loathe transcriptions *per se,* it is an unfortunate submission for teams to make, when one realizes that no one on the press has yet made a thorough, serious, constructive survey of the problems and possible solutions pertaining to the two-piano repertoire. The press is glib in its dismissal of any music listed on the printed program as a transcription rather than as an original work.

"How fortunate is the orchestral conductor! He can, with impunity, list a Ravel (or Caillet) transcription of the Moussorgsky *Pictures;* or the Debussy-Satie *Gymnopedie;* or any one of the countless transcriptions by men like Stokowski, Beecham, or Harty. As these transcriptions have become standards in the vast orchestral literature, is it reasonable to expect that, in the much more limited repertoire of two pianos, all transcriptions should be banished regardless of artistic merit and need?

"Metropolitan music critics have ceased listening to, or at least ceased writing about the qualities of any transcription. They simply ignore them. The unfortunate fact that some duo-pianists have bowed to the whims of these critics has resulted in the repetitious programming of many warhorses and in the inclusion of much inferior music merely because it was originally written for two pianos. This kind of programming hardly reflects artistic conviction on the performer's part, and it can prove deleterious to the potential growth of two-piano audiences."

In conclusion, Whittemore and Lowe sum up their attitudes towards two-piano compositions, original and arranged, as follows:

"Music originally conceived and written well for two pianos is undoubtedly the most desirable, *if* it is music of genuine worth. At the same time, the pronounced dearth of valuable repertoire for this medium notwithstanding, *any* high-minded, vital, and creative transcription which can project honestly and without distortion a musical message (which may have been written for another medium) certainly deserves to be performed and respectfully appraised."

In the existing controversy regarding original versus arranged two-piano music, one historic fact in behalf of the latter cannot be ignored: All great composers from Bach and Handel to Brahms and Stravinsky have not hesitated to make such arrangements and transcriptions of their own works and frequently of the music of others. Many of these transcriptions have gained repute in their own right, sometimes to such pronounced degree as to render oblivious the original form. Plainly then, the inner strength and virtue of an arrangement depends entirely, and no less than with an original composition, on the standards of the arranger himself. If the musical aspects of the original score are assimilated in a felicitous and artistically satisfying manner, the *a priori* condemnation of all arrangements appears prejudiced and therefore unjust. On the other hand, an indiscriminate adaptation of materials to the two-piano medium which is so frequently committed, will give continual cause to heated arguments over this issue.

From the foregoing discussion, once again a multitude of variances in conception governing the approach to the important question of repertoire and program building can be noticed. Individual theories and tastes hold reign in a field which has not evolved binding dogmas as yet. The situation fosters certain dangers, for as long as arrangements and transcriptions are being used as an integral portion in the duo-pianistic repertoire, the degree of deviation from the original medium cannot be subjected to control. Such departure rather remains a matter of personal judgment and responsibility, and varying tastes will find an unending source of controversy over the attitudes and regulations which should be established for the scoring and the rendition of arrangements.

Revealing only one such problem in the performance of an arrangement, transcription, or paraphrase, are these practical questions: Is an imitation of tone color and other peculiarities of the primary medium to be pursued in order to approximate (if not through actual sonority, so at least by way of mental association) the idiom of the original composition? Or are the essential tonal qualities and idiomatic characteristics of the pianoforte to be adapted, thereby effecting a virtual transformation of the former composition? In the latter approach, the significance of the original score is reduced to that of serving as point of departure, while the two-piano adaptation is deliberately elevated to the status of a novel and independent work.

This alternative with its implications and consequences was condensed into the question:

"In the case of arrangements, do you advocate to imitate the tone color of the original combination, or do you prefer to adopt the essential piano tone?"

Thus submitted to the authorities, the problem provoked a number of opposing views. They demonstrate the difficulty as well as the importance of this particular detail.

Appleton and Field declare themselves for adoption of "the essential tone."

A contrary opinion is voiced by Bartlett and Robertson who assert: "Certainly the tone color of the original must influence one's interpretation."

Dougherty and Ruzicka are not definite on this subject. When confronted with the elusive problem during an interview, they made only the following comment: "Great music has to get away from the instrument. It is great music regardless of the medium."

Gold and Fizdale suggest that this problem of tone color and association can be negotiated "either way."

Morton Gould is specific in writing: "I would say to project textures in terms of the piano tone."

The opposing view is presented by Rosina Lhevinne who admonishes: "Consider the originals." This advice with all its implications is based on a duo-pianistic credo which had been expressed by Josef and Rosina Lhevinne already in an earlier statement:[11]

"The first approach to four-handed playing upon two pianos is a realization of the richness of its orchestral color effects. The piano itself is symphonic in its possibilities—was it not Schumann's dream to accentuate this unique character of the instrument he loved best?—and the combination of two pianos treated as solo instruments rather than as voice and accompaniment provides a richness of medium that can scarcely be equalled."

Luboshutz and Nemenoff approach the problem with similar convictions. Their theory of duo-piano playing rests on the idea that while a piano solo is an exhibition of the pianoforte *per se,* two-piano works are not only quantitatively but also qualitatively more than that; they approach, so to speak, the function of an orchestra.

"When we first began playing together," says Miss Nemenoff, "we had an entirely different theory from that which we now follow. We believed that our piano tones should be as nearly alike as possible. But after a year of experimenting, we changed our minds. We decided that the tones

11. *Four Hands That Play as Two,* "The Etude," December 1933, p. 809.

should blend their individual differences rather than imitate each other. After all, the unique quality of duo-piano music is orchestral richness, and orchestral richness depends on the variety of instrumental tone. Violins, flutes, oboes do not sound like each other, but they blend together."

"As soon as we reached the conclusion that our music should follow the patterns of an orchestra, we changed our method of tone adjustment," continues Mr. Luboshutz. "From then on, we tried to harmonize our individual tones to make them approximate orchestral music. We try to create tonal variations that make for color. Since the two pianos are no different in timbre, these variations must be achieved by the volume and color of the pianist's touch."

Morley and Gearhart contribute to the discussion of the same problem this statement: "Whether in an original composition or an arrangement, we attempt to use the full scale of tonal effects possible on two pianos, being guided always by the inner structure of the music."

Dorothy R. Sinnitt advocates the imitation of tone color which characterizes the original setting "as much as possible."

Vronsky and Babin, according to the comments made by Victor Babin, consider as futile and consequently do not attempt the imitation of tone color of other instruments. Their basic tenet demands that the first consideration must always be given to the spiritual aspects of the original music. The next requirement is a knowledge of the particular keyboard characteristics and the special piano technique fundamentally associated with the composer of the original score. This Vronsky and Babin principal for the idiomatic performance of piano arrangements is the natural outgrowth of their viewpoint on arrangements in general.

3. SOME TYPICAL PROGRAMS

At the close of this chapter devoted to duo-pianistic repertoire and program building, it seems appropriate to reproduce a few characteristic programs, chosen at random from cosmopolitan as well as provincial concert schedules.

The first example is taken from a recital series *Two Pianos through Four Centuries* which was presented by Appleton and Field in Town Hall, New York, during the fall of 1949. The third and last program of this cycle, given on November 4, 1949, was entitled *Modern Music*. The concert consisted of the following items:

1. *Concerto* for Two Solo Pianos.................................Igor Stravinsky
2. *Sonata*...Paul Hindemith
   (four hands—one piano)
3. *Jeux de Plein Air*...Germaine Tailleferre
   Scaramouche...Darius Milhaud

4. *Sonata* for Two Pianos and Percussion...........................Béla Bartók

Another program sample from the repertoire of Appleton and Field is characteristic for the musical fares offered by this team in provincial communities. The following recital was presented in Wallace, Idaho, during the spring of 1948:

1. *Toccata*...Girolamo Frescobaldi
    (arranged by R. Berkowitz)
    Duettino Concertante, after Mozart........................Ferruccio Busoni
2. *Andante and Variations*...................................Robert Schumann
    Toccata...Anis Fuleihan
3. *Three Preludes*...George Gershwin
    (arranged by Appleton & Field)
    Serenade...Richard Strauss
    (transcribed by Chasins)
    The Blue Danube..Johann Strauss
    (transcribed by Chasins)
    INTERMISSION
4. *Brazileira*..Darius Milhaud
    Caprice Viennois...Fritz Kreisler
    (arranged by Miller)
    Etude based on Rimsky-Korsakoff's "Flight of the Bumble Bee".....Victor Babin
    Grand Concert Variations on a Theme from "The Puritans".........Franz Liszt

Two concert programs from the repertoire of Dougherty and Ruzicka are reproduced next. One lists their annual recital in New York (Town Hall, November 20, 1942); the other is a typical program from their transcontinental tours (Eastern Washington College of Education, Cheney, Washington, January 27, 1949).

I. NEW YORK PROGRAM

1. *Sonata* ....Clementi
    Andante and Variations, opus 46.................................Schumann
    (complete version restored from the original)
2. *Sonata*..Paul Hindemith
    (First performance anywhere)
    INTERMISSION
3. *Cache-cache Mitoula*...Tailleferre
    Pantomime ....Ravel
    Circus Polka, composed for a young elephant.............Stravinsky-Dougherty
    (First time in New York)
    American Dance...Henry Gilbert
    Berceuse ....Mary Howe
    (written expressly for Dougherty and Ruzicka)
    Vindabona ....Lanner-Dougherty
    II. CHENEY PROGRAM
1. *Sonata No. 1 in D*...Mozart
    (composed for four hands—one piano, performed on two pianos)
    Pastoral Interlude (from "Christmas Oratorio")........................Bach
    Allegro Brillant, Opus 92....................................Mendelssohn
    (composed for four hands—one piano, performed on two pianos)
2. *Andante and Variations, Opus 46*................................Schumann
    INTERMISSION

3. *Two Second Avenue Waltzes*..Rieti
    (1) To Phyllis
    (2) To Elsie
   Scherzo à la Russe..Stravinsky
   Pantomime from "El Amor Brujo"
   Fandango...de Falla-Dougherty
    (Dance of the Miller's Wife) from "The Three Cornered Hat"
4. *Rosenkavalier Waltzes*......................................Richard Strauss

    Gold and Fizdale gave the following recital at the Detroit Art Institute on April, 1, 1949. The program is indicative of the policy of repertoire followed by these duo-pianists.

1. *Sonate* (1947)..Marcelle de Manziarly
   Suite Champêtre (1948)..................................Vittorio Rieti
2. *Concerto* for Two Pianos Alone (1947)..........................Paul Bowles
INTERMISSION
3. *Sonata in D* (K.448)..............................Wolfgang Amadeus Mozart
4. *Valse Lente* (1948)....................................Germaine Tailleferre
   Carnaval à la Nouvelle-Orleans (1947)..................Darius Milhaud
    (All the contemporary music on this program is dedicated to Gold and Fizdale.)

    A typical Luboshutz and Nemenoff program shows this standard of selection:

1. *Now Comes the Gentle Savior*..Bach
    (arranged by Luboshutz)
   Variations on a Theme of Beethoven.....................Camille Saint-Saens
2. *Suite No. 2*..Sergei Rachmaninoff
INTERMISSION
3. *Scaramouche* Suite...Darius Milhaud
4. *Tambourin Chinois*...Fritz Kreisler
    (arranged by Luboshutz)
   Lark...Michael Ivanovich Glinka
    (arranged by Luboshutz)
   Waltz from the "Golden Mountain".....................Dimitri Shostakovich
    (arranged by Luboshutz)

    From the repertoire of Vronsky and Babin, two programs follow. The first lists the recital which the duo-pianists presented in a city of provincial status (Spokane, Washington, February 2, 1949). The Stravinsky concerto then was heard for the first time by concert audiences of that city.

1. *Fantasia*...Georg Philipp Telemann
    (arranged by V. Babin)
   Sonata in D Major (K.448)...Mozart
2. *Concerto per Due Pianoforti Soli*...................................Stravinsky
INTERMISSION
3. *Rondo, Opus 138* ("Our Friendship is Constant")....................Schubert
    (originally written for one piano, four hands, and so performed)
4. *Etude No. 3*...Victor Babin
   Pour l'Egyptienne..Debussy
    (originally composed for one piano, four hands; performed on two pianos.)
   Waltz, "Eugene Onegin"..Tschaikovsky
    (arranged by V. Babin)

The other program was delivered by Vronsky and Babin on July 15, 1949, on the occasion of the Goethe Bicentennial Convocation and Music Festival at Aspen, Colorado. It will be noted that the duo-pianists opened and closed each of the two groups with an original composition for two pianos, playing a four-hand piece on one piano in between. No arrangements or transcriptions were used. The program of the concert, built along conservative lines, follows:

Andante and Variations, Opus 46..................................Schumann
Rondo, C major, Opus 3...Weber
Sonata, D major (Koechel 448).......................................Mozart
INTERMISSION
Variations on a Theme of Joseph Haydn, Opus 56b...................Brahms
Notre Amitié Est Invariable, Opus 138............................Schubert
Concerto Pathétique, E minor..Liszt

By contrast, the programs of Whittemore and Lowe prominently display many arrangements. The following recital was given by the duo-pianists on February 25, 1948, in Carnegie Hall, New York:

1. *Sonata, D minor* (for two claviers)..........................Pasquini-Danckert
   Grande Sonate, Opus 30, in B flat major...........................Schubert
2. *Variations on a Theme of J. S. Bach, Opus 81*.....................Max Reger
   (transcribed for two pianos by Whittemore & Lowe)
   INTERMISSION
3. *Sonate* (1918)..Francis Poulenc
   (for one piano, four hands)
   Nana ....Manuel de Falla
   Alborada del Gracioso.....................................Maurice Ravel
4. *Dance Divertimento*..Kent Kennan
   Falling in Love with Love..Rodgers
   The Continental...Conrad
   Bolero ....Ravel

CHAPTER XVII

PERFORMANCE

1. Introduction

In this survey of duo-pianism as an artistic medium, some salient aspects have by now been considered. The discussion thus far has transgressed the component problems of partnership, of practicing, of mechanics and aesthetics, and of program building. The logical sequence now leads to the subject of performance, a topic dealing with that complex of factors which in duo-pianism, as in other fields of enterprise, stands as the goal of every effort and marks both the proof and culmination of all aspiration.

Musical performance in itself is an *experience,* one which needs to be lived rather than written about. The subtleties of countless detail observations, the "atmosphere" of a recital cannot be reproduced by words. The title of this chapter may therefore seem presumptuous. What the present section does mean to include, are several considerations of a practical nature, such as will arise before and during performance, carrying direct and sometimes decisive import on the degree of success. Once again, the subject matter includes both aesthetic and mechanical aspects, although the latter make up the greater portion of the discussion.

2. Memorizing

Inevitably one of the first and deepest impressions made by any performer upon his audience derives from the aspect whether his rendition is given from memory, or whether the notes are being used. From the days of Liszt on, the practice of playing from memory became a vogue and soon a compulsion for soloists; for its essentiality, a great number of reasons have been promoted.

The situation in two-piano performance should appear somewhat dif-

241

ferent. For all types of ensemble music, and more specifically for all forms of chamber music, the use of the printed notes is the custom rather than the exception. The motives underlying this almost universal practice are obvious; sufficient reason for precaution is the great individual share which each part forms in the whole and the resulting fact that the failure of one component in the ensemble can destroy the entire unit.

Following the almost general convention observed in the various branches of chamber music, the use of the printed score would appear advisable also for duo-pianists, and could accordingly be justified in public opinion. Indeed, the hazards of performing from memory in as exacting an ensemble form as that of two-piano playing raise the question whether such undertaking can be held responsible in general practice. The fact of the matter is, however, that most concert teams in the field consistently perform from memory. Professional duo-pianists at large profess themselves either to similar motivations as they are cited in behalf of memorized solo performance, or to reasons intrinsically connected with the special technic of two-piano performance.

To once more test reactions, the questions "Do you perform from memory?" and "Is the use of printed music permissible?" were submitted to a group of practitioners in the field. The following paragraphs contain some of the answers received on this vital issue.

Appleton and Field write: "Yes. We perform from memory for the simple reason that the use of music constitutes an actual and psychological barrier between us. We feel, however, that the use of music is certainly permissible."

Identical in essence is the opinion voiced by Bartlett and Robertson. Mr. Robertson states: "We perform from memory, because we feel more comfortable that way, but I see no objection to playing from the book, if the performers are nervous about their memory and feel happier with the notes."

Dougherty and Ruzicka took issue with the questions under discussion during an interview. They likewise advocate performance from memory. It is their feeling that playing from the printed music "robs." All professional duo-pianists whose public appearances they ever attended performed from memory with this one exception: The team of Bauer and Gabrilowitsch habitually used the notes during their concerts. Mr. Ruzicka's stated conviction that Bauer and Gabrilowitsch represent the finest combination ever to have existed, makes his own tenet in regard to memorized performance appear in a somewhat paradoxical light.

Gold and Fizdale consider the use of the music "inadvisable" and themselves always perform from memory.

Morton Gould gives this answer to the questions under consideration: "When I used to perform, it was done both ways—from music or memorized—the important thing is the performance, of course."

Rosina Lhevinne, in response to the current inquiry, submits the following statement: "Performing without the music is very much preferable because it assures a more finished performance and gives more possibility of unity."

The same conviction is worded more fully in Mme. Lhevinne's essay *The Spirit of Ensemble*[1] from which the following excerpt is quoted:

"For public performances it is very advisable to play without music. In this way, one can devote his entire attention to watching and listening to the other; it also provides a wider freedom of expression. For reliable and musicianly memorizing one should adopt the same intelligent methods as in playing alone. One should use the aural, visual and tactile memories, knowledge of the harmonic structure, key changes and modulations."

Guy Maier categorically advises duo-pianists that "they should, of course, memorize all their pieces."[2]

Morley and Gearhart, in taking issue with the question of memorized performance, include the important factor of audience appeal. They write:

"We play everything from memory, at concerts. In radio, for a very small percentage of performances (say, one out of thirty) we have used music. We feel we do not perform as well, using music. Others may achieve *their* best results reading from score. Considered from a visual point of view (of the audience) using music detracts from the effectiveness of a concert. This is perhaps an unfortunate reflection on our state of culture, but is nonetheless an important consideration for those whose livelihood is made through public performance."

In like tenor, E. Robert Schmitz, as a concert pianist, explicitly advocates memorized performance; he considers the use of the music as liable to objection.

Vronsky and Babin, on the other hand, regard the playing from music as permissible. However, they do believe that a composition is really known by the performers only when it is played from memory. According to their own experience, a greater effect is produced emotionally, and there results also the feeling of special accomplishment, whenever a memorized performance is achieved.

The same essence of thought is expressed in the answer contributed by Whittemore and Lowe. These duo-pianists write: "Yes, we perform

1. *Pan Pipes*, February 1949.
2. *Two-Piano Ensemble*, "The Etude," February 1938, p. 87.

wholly from memory and believe that it is almost a requisite for any artist's complete freedom of expression."

Notwithstanding the fact that the consensus of the foregoing comments proclaims an almost unqualified preference for memorized performance, the question remains in how far professional two-piano teams merely are following the pattern set and adhered to by soloistic custom. Even while duo-pianism defies a definite classification as chamber music, it is to be wondered whether the art does not have in common with that category the particular features of small ensemble playing. One of these special aspects is the proposition that, through the greater reassurance provided by the employment of notes, undivided attention may be devoted to purely aesthetic qualities of the performance. It is of more than casual significance that Bauer and Gabrilowitsch, hailed by many as the greatest two-piano ensemble of music history, always performed from the printed score. Outstanding musicians which both of them were, it can hardly be assumed that the memorizing process would have presented to them an unusual obstacle. Their decision to make use of the notes in their appearances as duo-pianists rather was based on an axiom governing the performance of all chamber music: Complete security in mechanical detail excites the greater susceptibility for artistic inspiration.

It is also worth noting that a number of the very same duo-pianists who by principle declare themselves to be in favor of memorized performance, have used and will use the printed music occasionally for a variety of motives. Such reasons may include insufficient rehearsal time, unusual complexities of modern scores, and the like. Fundamentally, there seems to be a partial return to the formerly universal practice of performing from the book. Even renowned solo pianists like Myra Hess and Leonard Shure courageously are setting the pace in this direction. The critics[3] have voiced no objections in view of the superior musical projection achieved in the particular instances. Downes goes so far as to state that "it has long been not only a tradition, but a fetish, that every soloist should play from memory." In the two-clavier field, duo-harpsichordists Manuel and Williamson always perform from notes, be it for the practical considerations previously advanced, be it because of the particular interpretative element of style consciousness adhering to their specialized activities; it is to be recalled that the music composed for their historic instruments during that period was generally expected to be rendered from manuscript or printed score.

On the other hand, there are several definite reasons to discourage the

3. Olin Downes on Myra Hess in the *New York Times,* January 23, 1949; *Musical Courier* on Leonard Shure in the issue of December 15, 1949, p. 20.

employment of notes. One of the physical disadvantages is found in the fact that mutual visibility between the duo-pianists will be considerably obscured when the music stands are up. Another detriment is the necessity for page turning which may cause apprehension and temporary distraction from the musical line; it also often renders unavoidable the actual omission of some ingredients of the score. Furthermore, audience reaction being what it is in this day and era, it will continue to constitute an impelling reason for many artists to decide in behalf of memorized performance. As long as most teams in the concert field are adhering to the practice of rendering their recitals entirely from memory, a change in public attitude can hardly be expected. As a matter of fact, a special effectiveness does and always will derive from memorized performance, because it impresses with an improvisational quality which in its turn conveys a feeling of freedom to the listening audience.

From the discussion pro and contra memorized performance the following summary may be drawn: Providing that both partners are equally secure in their retention of musical and mechanical elements, the dismissal of the notes will assuredly better enable them to devote their entire attention to listening and watching during performance and thereby to achieve a higher standard of precision. Whether or not the duo-pianists can also better interpret without music, will depend on the degree of their mental, visual, and muscular memory, each of which may weaken or fail at any moment. In view of the risks incurred, every performance from memory, all other factors being equal, is a distinct accomplishment. Its basis lies in nervous stamina much of which can be developed only from repetition and experience.

In the act of memorization, duo-pianists follow the customary avenues, with additional attention devoted to such phases as are peculiar to the two-piano medium. Some of the latter are the entrances occurring in the individual parts, extended rests, the significance of each separate detail in the constellation of the organic whole, and even the idiosyncracies of one's partner which must be anticipated and coped with if they are likely to occur at certain strategic points. As a matter of precaution, each player should possess sufficient familiarity with both component parts of the composition so that, in an emergency, he may be able to carry on *alone* with a synthesis of the music until the partner has recovered from his lapse of memory.

Entirely aside from all debatable issues concerning memorization, the only valid criterion of judging any musical rendition must remain the standard of the performance itself. Evidently, safety should always become the first choice, if the alternative is one of security versus improvisational abandon. On the other hand, if an accomplished performance evidences both assurance *and* freedom, it matters little whether this success is achieved through memorization or by the expedient of using the notes. For it is in the desire to attain the best musical result that all aspirations must ultimately agree.

3. INTUITION DURING PERFORMANCE

The problem of freedom coupled with security which figures so prominently in the subject matter of memorized performance, also enters into the aspects which deal with the play of intuition during a public recital. This particular phase of interpretation relates to the amount of flexibility permissible during concerts; more specifically, it determines the degree of intuition allowed to enter into the actual performance. The quality of flexibility here is opposed to that of mechanical precision, and intuition is contra-distinguished from the concept of rationalism.

It is to be assumed that the basic strategy of performance has been worked out in every detail. The duo-pianists agree as to tempo, interpretative direction, dynamic nuance, and every other conceivable factor of rendition. They furthermore understand that each partner is expected to adhere to the general plan as it has been determined by frequent discussion and mutual agreement during the hours of rehearsal.

Now the performance itself is in progress. It may become a mere routine execution of the composition, or it may develop into an interpretation which seems essentially different from any previous experience with the same work. The excitement of playing in public may cause one of the partners to forget or disregard former agreements; as a result, there will be the loss of mutual support, the breakdown of poise and confidence, and the instantaneous disappearance of balance in the ensemble. Such accidents, while generally disconcerting and mostly disastrous during the particular performance, nevertheless must be accounted for with tolerance; their simple excuse derives from the fact that they are not intentional and that they are caused by nervosity.

Of quite different nature are such liberties which a partner takes during the performance with full intent and purpose. Perhaps he feels inspired to some particular impulse and wishes to deliberately deviate from the rehearsed scheme. His is a difficult alternative to face between discipline and inspiration, the first assuring the security of routine, the second promising artistic freedom. The antitheses of rationalism and intuition, of intellect and emotion, have always ranked among the most momentous problems confronting the performing artist. This alternative looms even more conspicuously in any ensemble form, and it becomes a most difficult issue in the highly sensitive apparatus of two pianofortes and the nervous adjustment of their players.

Rationalism substantially will produce a mechanical and therefore inanimated performance, but it insures safety and precision. Intuition essentially is synonymous with spontaneity and abandon; it can carry, on wings of music, the performers to heights of artistic flight previously not realized, but it may also suddenly disrupt the pre-conceived principle of order and lead to chaotic confusion.

Like all artists, duo-pianists agree that flexibility is vitally necessary and that mechanical playing must be avoided. At the same time, they are keenly aware of the hazards which attend spontaneous playing, endangering the best laid plans of rendition and upsetting the performance entirely if too much liberty should be taken by either of the partners.

The problem under discussion was condensed into the question:

"Do you advocate or deny intuitive playing on the part of the performers during concerts?"

When thus presented to the collaborators in this investigation, the problem proved to be one of the topics most delicate to approach.

The following is the theory advanced by Appleton and Field: "Intuition certainly plays an enormous role after the general structure has been conceived and delineated. Without it, it would be hard for us to conceive of two-piano playing as a form of musical projection."

Dougherty and Ruzicka likewise are pronounced in their conviction that intuition must have full sway on the concert stage. In their opinion, it elevates the act of performance to the function of a rite. Always training their sensitivity in the direction of new intuition, these duo-pianists have experienced that sometimes even physical influences like, for instance, the acoustics of the hall produce artistic inspiration.

Gold and Fizdale also advocate intuitive playing, with the reservation that it must be "subject to a well thought-out conception."

Morton Gould expresses a similar attitude by delivering a concise formulation of the real problem. Gould states: "Good performing in any medium is a combination of intellect and intuition."

Rosina Lhevinne considers "intuitive playing possible only after a long period of common association."

The essential qualities of intuitive performance are defined by Josef and Rosina Lhevinne as follows:[4]

"Ensemble playing is at its best only when the players are in sympathy with each other, when they are able to think and feel in common . . . the most sensitive

4. *Four Hands that Play as Two,* "The Etude," December 1933, p. 809.

performance of this kind results only when the players enjoy that friendly sympathy with each other that enables them to understand each other's faintest nuancings of thought, even before they are expressed. This does not mean that they need necessarily agree on every point! But they must be able to follow each other in their habits of musical thought. Often, in our own concerts of two-piano music, a change of acoustics, a change of hall, even a change of mood, have demanded sudden alterations in our work which would have been impossible for people who were not accustomed to 'sense' together."

This ability to "sense together" develops with many duo-pianists into a subconscious reaction. It represents the psychic element in the organism of the team. Although only rarely referred to and very vaguely expressed, the fact of its existence is acknowledged by the most accomplished practitioners of the art. Pierre Luboshutz, for instance, maintains that he and his partner, Genia Nemenoff, would always "be together" even if they played in different rooms. "Before Genia starts to play," Mr. Luboshutz states, "something happens inside of me and I know what she will do—even when she tries to tease me with a trick."

Morley and Gearhart have coined a special term, "controlled spontaneity," to describe their own attitude in regard to this problem. They elaborate on the topic with the following contribution to the present symposium:

"One of the greatest pitfalls of the two-piano medium is the natural tendency toward rhythmic inflexibility, whose result is often monstrously mechanical, like a player-piano. Paradox though it may sound, we strive for a 'controlled spontaneity.' This requires a large mutual capacity for quick adjustment; this capacity is of a motor-reflex type, I believe, since intellectual response would take many more microseconds than are available for adjustment in rapid passages."

E. Robert Schmitz points out that intuitive playing can be permitted "only after conscious mastery of the composition involved."

Silvio Scionti is an emphatic advocate of flexible playing during two-piano performance. In humorous vein, he writes:[5]

"Two-piano playing, that suggests just the mechanical, naturally must be avoided, no less than the curse of Hades! Precision there must be, of course, but anything which suggests wheels, levers, cams, bolts or gears, would support the old saying, 'What is worse than one piano? Two pianos!' And I would add another bit of advice, 'Burn up the instruments and assassinate the players.'"

Dorothy R. Sinnitt expresses her experience with the following statement: "I do not see how two performers could play successfully together unless they did use their intuition and innate musical instincts, and *feel* the music together."

---

5. *The Fascination of Two-Piano Playing*, "The Etude," September 1939, p. 602.

When Miss Vronsky (Vronsky and Babin) was interviewed on the question whether the sway of intuition during concert performance is to be advocated or denied, she answered in behalf of artistic inspiration with these words: "You can hardly prevent it." Miss Vronsky added, however, that in all desirability of an inspired performance, it should be established between the partners *who* may play freely *when*.

Whittemore and Lowe condense their attitude in this terse statement: "We both advocate intuitive playing (within reasonable limits, based on sound musical taste)."

In duo-pianism, like in all other ensemble forms, the ultimate wisdom is derived from a sub-conscious reaction among the partners. The attainment of any superlative accomplishment in team work, and the degree of sensitivity to which the psychic element can be activated, depend largely on the length of time over which ensemble playing is extended. In the consensus of authoritative opinions, time is the essence without which there cannot prevail the utmost familiarity with the partner's mental disposition as well as pianistic behavior. As the colleagues become increasingly familiar with each other's musical style, in all its manifest charactcristics and secret utterances, their experience in playing together will develop into a sense of freedom. This feeling of liberation gradually can extend its boundaries, commensurately to the growing degree of familiarity which attunes the pianists to each other. Whichever amount of mutual adjustment may eventually be attained, it is this factor which determines the quality of flexibility during performance commonly called "freedom of expression." In duo-pianism, this necessarily can never be an absolute freedom, but must remain what has been termed in the foregoing a "controlled spontaneity," in that the intellectually conceived and carefully rehearsed general interpretative plan needs to stay the solid foundation from which all nuances of expression emanate and receive their propulsion. This probably is in essence the same thought which Silvio Scionti has expressed with quite different words:[6]

"Ensemble playing, that is, playing together with precision, must be mastered and forgotten, just as one masters the technic of the piano itself. Not until this occurs can there be any emotional beauty."

Scionti's statement can be accepted in the sense that discipline and precision in ensemble performance are mental operations of which accomplished players are only subconsciously rather than consciously aware. Once these mechanical processes may be "forgotten," the conscious mind becomes free for the play of own moods and for the sensitive reaction

6. *The Fascination of Two-Piano Playing,* "The Etude," September 1939, p. 602.

to the moods of the partner. In this constant exchange of artistic ideas, new inspiration finds its perpetual fertilization and animation.

In the art of duo-pianism, freedom can become a reality if psychic unity and singular unanimity of expression are accomplished. This achievement is only possible through understanding, anticipating, and complementing one another's every subtlest nuance. The perfect attuning of two individuals to the interplay of their emotions, the readiness to give and take at all times, the taste and discriminating judgment which know when to assert and when to yield—all these component qualities raise the perfectly amalgamated duo-pianistic unit above the status of a highly developed mechanical apparatus. From a mere vehicle for musical rendition, two-piano art then may rise like the Pegasus of true poetic inspiration. In the perpetual quest for expression, a reconciliation between rationalism and intuition eventually can be brought about. It is in the synthesis of intellect and emotion that artistic balance is to be found, and with it the happiness of the creative human being.

4. STAGE PRESENCE

A purely theatrical aspect of any two-piano performance, but one of rather great importance, is the stage presence of the duo-pianists. In view of the particularity of this combination in which each partner carries equal prestige, a system of entrance and retreat to and from the stage needs to be agreed upon and adequately rehearsed, so that this part of the performance will appear well coordinated. Showmanship heightens the dramatic effect attending musical performances like those of the pure theatre; its meaning and consequence actually sets the final seal on all artistic presentation.

Military rigidity obviously needs to be avoided. On a hot summer evening, one pair of pianists actually could be observed to open the buttons of their jackets at exactly the same moment when they were sitting down to play, and to close the same with split-second precision when they were getting up to acknowledge the applause! Equally conspicuous in stage behavior are disorderly casualness or awkward uncertainty.

If the duo-pianists are man and woman, the former naturally follows the latter while entering the stage. If the team is composed either by two men or two women, the taller person goes behind the smaller, as if by suggestion of a natural etiquette. It is very important that both partners take their seats at about the same time. After finishing the performance, contact again needs to be established between the team-mates who will then simultaneously rise from the piano benches and, in acknowledging the applause, together take their bow; by doing so, the partners will exert the impression that the applause is accepted collectively rather than individually.

Whenever an announcement needs to be made from the stage, be it to serve as special comment on a particular program number, be it to make known the names of encore pieces, the partner best versed in public speaking should be chosen for this task. The colleague who meantime remains seated before his piano, will give the speaker his full attention as if he were one of the audience. Etiquette implies that in a team made up by members of both sexes the male partner would be the logical person to act as announcer.

5. INSTRUMENTS AND ACOUSTICS

One of the great physical obstacles in the way of duo-pianistic practice and performance is as old as the art itself. This difficulty is offered by the tedious necessity to assemble two pianofortes. The average living-room, for reasons of size and appearance, is hardly suited for conversion into a piano storehouse. This prosaic fact indeed remains the chief hindrance in the way of bringing the piano ensemble into every home. Moreover, two instruments of the upright type are less suitable than two grand pianos, a further reason to render this combination a rather exceptional musical equipment for the home. In the teacher's studio, however, two pianos are frequently met with; since generations of pedagogues, the second instrument has become a valuable tool for demonstrative instruction; in addition, it offers the opportunity for occasional ensemble practice.

It is mentioned in passing (although the reference may appear self-evident) that the two pianofortes need to be kept in exact tune with each other; any discrepancy in pitch will tend to seriously impair the acuteness of ear and sensitivity to color. Two or three tunings annually will be sufficient in most cases provided the pianos remain standing in the same locality and are not exposed to wide fluctuations of temperature. The tunings, incidentally, will assist in the mechanical upkeep of the instruments.

The following discussion centers especially on the needs of regularly performing duo-pianists with professional standing. For their purposes, the choice of instruments is of the greatest consequence in that all meticulous adjustment of ensemble work can be rendered ineffective by a severe discrepancy of tone and action in the individual pianos. Identity of make and size will furnish the best combination theoretically advisable. A close similarity in size and action ranks next in desirability, so that each partner may deal with an approximately equal amount of mechanical resources in his instrument. If possible at all, duo-pianists will avoid that dreaded combination of instruments in which one possesses a clear, glassy and brittle action, while the other has a dull, dim or mellow tone. Wide differences in size between two grand pianos also will cause an almost unsurmountable detriment in the endeavor to attain good tonal blending and to match dynamics. A partial adjustment can be effected by assigning the more brilliant instrument to the player with the lighter touch or more subdued tone, while the performer endowed with the more powerful style must cope with the duller piano. An equalization can further be accomplished through experimentation with the piano lids which are used as regulators of tonal volume, as will be pointed out shortly.

At any rate, insistence on a good match of pianofortes is advisable. For the requirements of concertizing duo-pianists, the two instruments need to be tuned together on the day of each performance.

While the assemblance of well-matching instruments often still presents a major problem, duo-pianists at least do not have to face any more a situation similar to that which confronted Thalberg and Gottschalk in 1857 when they appeared together in New York. These world-renowned artists then felt obliged to bring their own European-made grand pianos with them across the Atlantic ocean, Thalberg using an Erard and Gottschalk a Pleyel.[7] Incidentally, the pianists found the domestically manufactured Chickering grand pianos so satisfactory that both adopted them for their further use, especially since the foreign-made instruments suffered a great deal from the changes of the climate.

In our modern age of transportation, some duo-pianists are resorting to the mode of travel by car and trailer, carrying in the latter two grand pianos along on their trans-continental concert tours. At least two well-known teams (Bartlett-Robertson and Whittemore-Lowe) have dedicated themselves to this type of transportation which they find to be both efficient and pleasant.[8] The following is a quotation from an account of the "caravan" which Bartlett and Robertson are using for cross-country trips:[9]

"To the Chrysler Town and Country model sedan which they use, is attached a 7'x 5' trailer (Spen-Brooklyn) in which the pianos are strapped to the walls, upended, with the legs removed. Between them is space for clothing bags to be hung from the ceiling. This eliminates the necessity of having dress clothes pressed before each concert.

"This modern variation on the 'gypsy life' saves Bartlett and Robertson the annoyances of constant travel, such as catching trains, making connections in out-of-the-way places, waiting for porters, taxis, etc., and eating at station lunch counters. . . .

7. Richard Hoffman, *Some Musical Recollections of Fifty Years*, p. 131.
8. Among the more recent teams in the field, Alfred and Herbert Teltschik travel by truck, carrying their two grand pianos with them.
9. *Musical Courier*, March 1, 1949.

"Their chauffeur and maintenance man is Miss Bartlett's brother, former RAF Flight Lieut. Arthur Bartlett, who throughout the war was maintenance supervisor of bomber squadrons. His wife accompanies the caravan and attends to food purchases and other necessities of life on the road. . . .

". . . . the trailer . . . carries 2,700 pounds, the pianos weighing 900 lbs. each. Furniture movers are arranged for ahead of arrival; in college towns these chores are usually performed by students."

Whittemore and Lowe, who employ their own truck van with driver, are not less enthusiastic over their solution of the instrument problem. They write:[10]

"For many years we trouped around using whatever pianos could be obtained in the town or shipped in from outside. But rarely did the two pianos ever really match, or blend. Can you think what it would be like for a violinist to perform on a different instrument each concert he played? Or, to take it out of music specifically, what about the 'pro' tennis-player, a new racket in his hand every match, one to which he was completely unaccustomed? Certainly even the solo pianist who cannot have his *own* piano has immense difficulties readjusting to the peculiar quirks and vagaries of the various instruments he is obliged to use. But those selfsame difficulties, for a piano team, are literally quadrupled, considering that the two performers must both play and sound alike!

"So it was that the truck idea was born. And since the very first concert to which we 'rolled our own', . . . we have had reason only to rejoice that we made the decision and tackled the problem in this fashion.

"From the outset we had anticipated a normal amount of difficulty, but fortunately we have had nothing but gratifying results, both for ourselves artistically and for the various cities in the matter of convenience to them. Naturally we feel that the standard of our performance is now much higher, and as a challenge it now depends upon *us*, not the fallibility of local pianos. Such a challenge serves automatically as a stimulus to an artist. There are no alibis now!"

The most recommended position of the instruments for practice and on the concert stage is that of having their curves fit together, with the keyboards on opposite ends and, consequently, with the performers facing each other.

This arrangement places both members of the team into full view of

10. *Two Grand*, issue of January-March, 1949.

the audience and assures the greatest ease of mutual observation between the partners. As a courtesy to their public, duo-pianists should exchange instruments at several prearranged occasions during the concert perform- ance, so that the audiences on the far sides of the hall will be enabled to observe each player at closer range. What is only a device of show- manship for some performers, is extended by other two-piano teams into an experiment in tonal balance. Luboshutz and Nemenoff profess to be always upset when audiences think that their alternation of pianos during recitals is a stunt. Pierre Luboshutz thus explains the reason for this frequent exchange of instruments: "Whichever of us is going to play the treble part takes the piano whose treble section is nearest the audience. This makes for better balance in two-piano music." This reasoning, how- ever, would apply only to such two-piano music in which a decided separa- tion between treble and bass registers characterizes the parts, such as will occur if duets written originally for one piano, four hands, are executed on two instruments.

Clear visibility between the performers is the prime requisite in any contemplated placement of the instruments. The vision should not be materially obscured even when printed notes are used and the music racks are up. In playing from memory, it is advisable to remove the note stands entirely. This measure will assist the faculties of watching and of listening to perform their tasks even more acutely.

Sometimes, the size or shape of the room will necessitate an arrange- ment wherein the keyboards are placed parallel and next to each other. In this position of the instruments, contact between the performers can be maintained only through watching each other's hand, wrist, or arm movements while the meeting of the eyes now proves impractical. The parallel placement of the keyboards becomes compulsory in the event that two upright pianos are being used. This arrangement actually offers certain advantages during the practice of difficult ensemble passages. It is also of decided helpfulness for the purposes of demonstration, especially in the process of instruction.

Where only one grand piano and one upright instrument are available, the position again must be determined with the prime objective in mind that the performers need to see each other as readily as possible under any given conditions.

In the array of factors contributing to a successful performance, the acoustics of the hall form an important ingredient. Concert artists at large now are devoting an increasing amount of attention to the problems of acoustical phenomena. A recent issue of the *Journal of the American*

Musicological Society[11] contains a significant article by Arnold M. Small, entitled *The Partnership between Music and Modern Acoustics*. The author traces a number of distinct relationships between areas in acoustics and music. He treats particularly of the importance of acoustics within the two-way communication system between performer and listener. Included in the essay are several new branches like psycho-acoustics (sensory-perceptual aspects of hearing), physiological acoustics (neurological events associated with hearing), and electro-acoustics (infusion of principles and practices of electronics and associated fields into the main stream of acoustic theory and practice). The essay lays open a large field of potentialities entering into a musical performance from the purely scientific point of view. It is therefore advisable for all musicians to examine more closely this much-neglected physical aspect of their artistic renditions, in that acoustical properties always must attend and largely influence the production of music.

Duo-pianists, to continue with the specific survey of factors entering into a two-piano performance, will do well to test beforehand the acoustics of the hall in which they are going to give their recital. The pianos must be moved into the auditorium several hours before the concert because the metal and wood of the instruments need to warm up to room temperature even before they can be properly tuned. Physical laws of expansion and contraction require this consideration.

The volume of sound is influenced, and therefore can be regulated, by the position of the piano lids. If the top of the piano standing closest to the audience is removed, and the cover of the piano in the back of the stage is fully raised, the latter will act as a sound reflector for both instruments. This arrangement is frequently met with, but there are also many duo-pianists who prefer to remove the lids from both pianos.

Ultimately, the criterion of tonal balance in each particular situation must decide which combination of the many possible adjustments of the two piano lids is to be chosen. Some of the influencing factors are the height and shape of the stage, the acoustical conditions of the hall, the size of the audience, the mechanical characteristics of the instruments, and the general tendencies of the pianists including their chosen program. With all these and other details in view, the arrangement of the instruments should be scrupulously attended to. Failure to do so may cause the best rehearsed ensemble to lack in true balance. On the other hand, conscientious regard for acoustical properties always contributes to greater effect in musical performance.

---

11. Vol. II, No. 11, Summer 1949.

6. Duo-Pianism, a Medium to Artistic Happiness

During the investigation of the various aspects connected with this survey, one more question was posed along with the others which provoked a wide divergency of reactions. The inquiry read:

"Does two-piano playing give you a wider range of artistic expression than solo performance?"

Submitted quite *à propos,* this question frankly admits idle curiosity as its sole motivation. The replies which were received will be quoted without further commentary. While some of the answers possibly prove to be anti-climactic, they nevertheless form a logical conclusion to this chapter on "Performance", and with it to the entire realm of "Duo-Pianism, an Artistic Medium."

Appleton and Field, in their reaction to the foregoing question, deny that they derive a greater musical experience from duo-pianism. They state that the art gives to them "merely a different facet of musical expression, as does all ensemble playing."

Bartlett and Robertson also disavow finding a wider range of artistic expression in duo-pianism than in solo performance. Mr. Robertson's reasoning is, however, altogether different from the aforementioned viewpoint. He writes: "The literature for solo piano is so large and varied that no one could ask for a wider range of artistic expression."

Dougherty and Ruzicka answer the question in the affirmative: According to their experience, duo-pianism is yielding a wider gamut of musical expression than can be derived from solo performance.

Gold and Fizdale likewise find richer musical rewards in two-piano playing than in solo work.

Morton Gould, on the other side, denies the superiority of duo-pianism over solo performance as far as expressive power is concerned.

Rosina Lhevinne is contained in her judgment of this question. She states: "Two-piano playing adds to the scope of musical development."

Morley and Gearhart distinguish between personal and mechanical aspects of duo-pianistic opportunities. To the inquiry whether two-piano playing gives a wider range of expression, they answer: "Personal-intuitive expression: no. It does offer a wider variety of textures, colors, contrasts, and makes possible the performance of musically more complex structures than is possible in solo."

Vronsky and Babin elevate the question from the specific into the general. Their edict therefore becomes an abstract directive for all aesthetic endeavor: "The greatest artistic happiness derives from the greatest artistic achievement. The medium itself is secondary."

Whittemore and Lowe confirm this dogma from their own end with the statement: "Two-piano playing, ideally, should give as wide, but no wider, range of artistic expression."

The following thought may serve as summary and conclusion: Duo-pianism as an artistic medium does not rival with other media for superior powers of emotional expression. Beyond doubt, however, two-piano art "adds to the scope of musical development" (Lhevinne), and it can serve as an implement to achieve "the greatest artistic happiness" (Babin). With Happiness considered the end in itself, the medium towards its realization admittedly carries only subordinate significance. Nevertheless, the claim of duo-pianism in the system of musical art is that of exercising a practical and independent function in the quest for the common goal which lies in the greatest artistic achievement. Duo-pianism thus ranks as a fully appointed agent in behalf of those who through it are aspiring towards artistic happiness.

Part B: Duo-Pianism, A Creative Medium

CHAPTER XVIII

THE CHALLENGE

1. INTRODUCTION

"The growth in popularity of two-piano playing has as its basis not only the expanding music consciousness of America and the consequently greater opportunities for the performer, but, more importantly, the ever growing additions to the literature by recent or contemporary composers. Reger, Bartók, Stravinsky, Hindemith, Milhaud, Poulenc, Martinu, Bennett, Copland and Fuleihan, to name a few, have by significant contributions indicated their awareness of the potentialities of this medium.

". . . The more important of these . . . compare more than favorably with the large works being written today for the solo instrument. Nor are these mere musical *esoterica* to be played only for the initiated 'few.'·'

The foregoing quotation from an article *Is There a Two-Piano Dilemma Today?* by duo-pianists Appleton and Field[1] compellingly leads from the problems of the performing musician to those of the creative artist, the composer.

As a matter of basic fact, it is the composers who are chiefly responsible for the present-day growth of duo-pianism as an art form. When, during the current investigation, Bartlett and Robertson were queried: "Why do you believe in the two-piano medium for artistic expression?," their telling answer was:

"The fact that most of the great composers have written music for two pianos, and that at no period in musical history has there been greater activity creatively in this (e.g. works by Stravinsky, Hindemith, Milhaud,

---

1. *Musical Courier,* August 1947.

Bax, Britten, Copland, etc.) is more than sufficient grounds for belief in the medium as a form of artistic expression."

Concert patrons at large have gradually come to realize that the two-piano repertoire is far more extensive than was generally believed and that it contains literature on the plane of the world's greatest instrumental masterpieces. "The activities of contemporary composers have done much to acquaint the concert-going public with the unique qualities of duo-piano music; Stravinsky, Martinu, Wallingford Riegger, Nicolai Lopatnikoff, Harl McDonald, Poulenc—these are but a few of the many distinguished modern composers who have contributed to the rapid artistic growth of this medium."[2]

The discussion will now center on an investigation of the two-piano combination as an instrument for the expression of original musical thought. This proposition is formulated under the title:

Duo-Pianism, a Creative Medium.

From the beginning, it is emphasized that it cannot be the intention of this limited section within the over-all survey of duo-pianism to deliver a compendium of the techniques of composition applying to the two-piano idiom. Based on both the endowment of creative genius and the acquisition of skill in the handling of tonal materials, the craft of musical composition is too universal an ability that it could not be adapted readily to any medium. The student of composition must resort for basic information to the many text books which are available; the prospective composer in the two-piano idiom, moreover, will try to acquire a first-hand familiarity with the medium through practical experimentation and by the study of existing masterworks. The following essay is intended only as a treatise of some principles particular to the idiom; in consequence, it is proposed as a general introduction rather than as a specialized technical discussion.

2. ACCEPTANCE AND RESERVATIONS

Composers react largely to the economic laws of demand and supply. Like in other branches of music, this axiom is found to hold true in the field of duo-pianism as a creative medium. The processes leading to productive stimulation always have been similar, although the demand for compositions in earlier centuries was caused and governed to a great extent by the invention and perfection of new instruments for which a suitable literature was needed. Composers then came more often than not from the ranks of the leading performers, and the reputation of their artistry as executants frequently surpassed that of their creative talents.

---

2. According to a statement by Luboshutz and Nemenoff.

Nowadays, the composer belongs to an established and specialized profession of its own. Economic considerations rank as a highly important incentive for musical composition, and the commissioning of new works frequently is the first stimulus for their creation.

The appearance of so many two-piano teams in the field and the popular success accorded to duo-pianism as an art form, as they are witnessed today, would have stimulated the composers of any generation to write profusely for this instrumental combination. It is therefore not surprising that almost unanimous acceptance by professional composers is accorded to two-piano scoring as an absolute medium, and that to an unheard-of extent creative efforts now are devoted to or channeled into this idiom.

The tenor of the foregoing statement is reflected in some of the replies which were received from established composers in answer to the question:

"Do you believe original composition for two pianos to be an individual creative medium?"

Abram Chasins says: "Certainly." Celius Dougherty and Morton Gould fully agree. Darius Milhaud is emphatic in stating his own: "Yes, of course." Livingston Gearhart and Victor Babin also regard two-piano instrumentation as an original idiom for the projection of musical creativeness.

The acceptance of the medium by the composers is, however, not entirely without a voice of reservation. An attitude of strong skepticism is expressed by Beryl Rubinstein, one of the younger exponents of the American composer. Because of his successful activities in the two-piano field, both as performing and creative artist, Rubinstein's viewpoint should be expected to be prejudiced in behalf of the medium. Surprisingly enough, this is not the case. In this forum of qualified opinions, Beryl Rubinstein will now propound the argument which he has prepared especially for the present discussion:

"I do not believe that two-piano playing is a basic form of ensemble. This belief is borne out by the fact that the great composers, from Beethoven into our present time, gave comparatively little attention to it. Their reasons for not writing more extensively for two pianos are not entirely clear, but it may be conjectured that they felt that an instrument so complete within itself required no amplification, and that the lack of tonal variety between two pianos made writing for them redundant.

"It will be observed that ensemble works involving piano and other instruments are largely antiphonal in nature. Such antiphonal writing is effective because of differences in tone color. When applied to two pianos it appears to me to lose point. The greatest praise that can be given two-piano playing is to say that you cannot tell one piano from the other, in which event why have two. One can certainly tell the difference between the playing of a melody by a violin, and by a piano. This leads one to say that two pianists with different styles make a more interesting ensemble than two with identical or similar styles.

"There can be no doubt that a tremendous knowledge of piano technic, and a penetrating understanding of two-piano writing-technic is required in order to write successfully for two pianos. It is with a good deal of reluctance that I question whether many of our contemporary composers, particularly Americans, know how to write effectively for one piano, much less two pianos.

"There are perhaps a dozen great and near-great works written originally for two pianos. This is rather sparse literature for serious musicians.

"All the foregoing seems to sound rather pessimistic from the point of view of a long career. I think a survey would show that most two-piano teams have had short careers. On the other hand, two-piano playing can be most enjoyable, both from the performer's and the listener's point of view. It is undoubtedly a great boon for the study and analysis of symphonic literature.

"Perhaps future composers can devise a new approach to the technic of two-piano writing, so that there will be, not merely a mass of tones cascading relentlessly from the instruments, but an ensemble of fine-textured and delicate quality. I made some such endeavor in my Two-Piano Suite. Composers should keep in mind that it is not the number of notes, but the disposition of them that is of peculiar importance in writing for two pianos. Of course, that is true of any composing, but because of the terrific problem of tonal distinction, it becomes a paramount issue where two pianos are involved."

3. SYNOPSIS

The true status of the art of composition for two pianos must be evaluated from a short survey of its historical development. A synopsis of events will show the process of evolution which the medium has undergone in its relationship to the composer.[3]

It needs to be remembered first that for Bach the combination of two claviers was a matter of expansive experimentation. His governing approach, practical as the man himself, was that of study or instruction. Partial to contrapuntal complexities, he saw in the assemblage of two keyboard instruments the opportunity and challenge of knitting a greater number of voices into the polyphonic web. To Bach, two (and more)

---

3. For more exhaustive information, refer to Book I, *The History*.

claviers afforded the suitable medium for his aspiration towards monumental musical abstractions.

Next to be recalled are the many kaleidoscopic changes in the history of music, its instruments, styles, textures, forms, economical and philosophical motivations. There is the advent of Mozart, the rise of the gallant style, the beginning of the public concert with its practical consequences. There comes the outbreak of the Revolution, political and artistic, catapulting Romanticism into full command and raising the individual to its sole minister. The pianoforte becomes the ideal vehicle of the typical soloist of Romantic concepts. Duo-pianism temporarily appears perverted in the caricature of the Grand Duo. Eventually, an altogether new function for two-piano writing is inaugurated by Brahms; to him the medium provides a laboratory of experimental composition, the two-piano score often serving as a first sketch and blue-print for subsequent symphonic expansion.

Still another function is devised by Czerny, Brahms, and Liszt when works written for a large orchestral apparatus are reduced to performance on two pianos and thus become readily accessible to students and amateurs of symphonic literature. This practice since has been widely utilized, with modern composers like Debussy, Ravel, Weinberger, Stravinsky, and Milhaud continuing to employ the medium for the same purpose. The two-piano condensation achieves uncontested superiority over the *Klavierauszug*[4] for one piano, two hands, because the latter is physically incapable of doing justice to the orchestral original. From Brahms to Milhaud, a reversal as well as supplementation of practical aspects in the employment of duo-pianism is thus observed, all confirming the inherent symphonic qualities of the medium. Lastly, the present trend again points to the purity of design as well as abstraction of musical matter which have been Bach's ideals and for which two pianos offer a logical instrumental combination.

The amount of attention given to the medium by almost every major composer from Couperin to Stravinsky leaves little doubt that the idiom as such presents an absolute creative channel, one which is attractive for both artistic and practical reasons. Moreover, duo-pianism by now holds its rightful place in the ranks of instrumental forms by virtue of a time-honored existence.

Josef and Rosina Lhevinne at one time have formulated their views regarding the real opportunities of composition in the two-piano field in an article entitled *Four Hands That Play as Two,* published in 1933.[5]

---

4. "Piano extract," H. M.
5. *The Etude,* December 1933.

In this essay, they clearly point out the challenge confronting the composer who intends to use duo-pianism as his creative vehicle. Their definition of the technic and ideology of two-piano scoring has governed composers as early as Bach; with it they also anticipate an outline of the principles which since have found materialization in works like the *Concerto for Two Solo Pianos,* composed by Igor Stravinsky in 1935.

This is what the Lhevinnes have then stated:

> "There is an immense field awaiting the composer who can adjust himself to writing for pianos while thinking symphonically. An orchestral approach means more than simply an abundance of notes laid on with an over-generous hand! It requires an arrangement of materials so that each part shall contain the weight and the content of solo subjects. It requires a realization of the fact that there is no accompaniment, no 'second' piano, but two solo instruments."

If the term "orchestral" is accepted to apply to the resources of a solo pianoforte, and if two such "orchestral" instruments are combined to sound together "symphonically," then indeed the expediency of the two-piano medium is realized unmistakably, with its particular challenge and as a true artistic goal.

CHAPTER XIX

THE FIELD

COMPOSING FOR TWO PIANOS

The composer devoting himself to the two-piano medium is meeting with an extended field of applications. In a survey of the various possibilities, eight distinct categories of composition can be recognized within the realm of two-piano music. These classifications include

(1) Original compositions for two pianos, four hands, without accompaniment.

(2) Original compositions for two pianos, four hands, with ensemble.

(3) Original compositions for two pianos, four hands, representing the composer's own arrangement or transcription of one of his works originally written for a different medium.

(4) Arrangements.

(5) Transcriptions.

(6) Paraphrases.

(7) Added second-piano parts.

(8) Concerti with second-piano parts, the latter representing a condensation from the orchestral score.

A brief comment on each of the forenamed eight types will follow. The first group—*Original compositions for two pianos, four hands, without accompaniment*—for obvious reasons appears as the most natural form of creative effort in the medium. It is also the most desirable because, in this category, the absolute character of duo-pianism as an expressive force is realized. The standard products of this classification occupy a place in musical literature entirely of their own, which means to say that these works in their primary effect are not subject nor comparable to any other. For illustration of this statement, and for identification of the category proper, it may suffice to mention a few prototypes such as Mozart's Sonata in D (K. 448), Saint-Saens' Variations on a Theme by Beethoven, the Haydn Variations by Brahms, the two Suites by Rachmaninoff, Stravinsky's Concerto for Two Solo Pianos, and Milhaud's Scaramouche Suite.

The second classification of two-piano works—*Original compositions for two pianos, four hands, with ensemble*—includes

(a) Concerti for two pianos and orchestra.

The Concerto No. 2 in C Major by Bach, Mozart's Concerto in E flat (K. 365), and the many concerti for two pianos and orchestra written in more recent times all belong to this group. Also included may be Saint-Saens' Carnival of the Animals, although this example represents a border case because of the obligato character of the two pianos.[1]

(b) Other ensemble forms.

Two pianos have been combined with a wide variety of instruments, producing many unusual ensemble forms such as Bartók's Sonata for two pianos and percussion instruments. An interesting combination is employed by Hans Zilcher in his "Night and Morning" for two pianos, string orchestra, and tympani. Noteworthy are also settings like Frederick Jacobi's Three Excerpts from the Prophet Nehemiah, composed for voice and two pianos; Amadeo Roldan's Curujey, "Son" for choir, two pianos, and Cuban percussion (1931); and Germaine Tailleferre's Concerto for two pianos, orchestra, and chorus. Such unusual combinations demonstrate originality and point to further possibilities.

The third group comprises *Original compositions for two pianos, four hands, representing the composer's own arrangement or transcription of one of his works originally written for a different medium.* To illustrate this classification, Bach's Concerti Nos. 1 and 3 for two claviers and orchestra are mentioned; both were transcribed from concertos originally written for two violins. Further typical examples are Debussy's own two-piano version of his symphonic poem "The Afternoon of a Faun," and Weinberger's two-piano condensation of the orchestral Polka and Fugue from his opera "Schwanda." The intentions of the composer are so completely realized in these recasts that they can justly claim the distinction of being "original" compositions. They represent the authentic reproduction of the original material by the author himself and, therefore, resulting differences in idiom notwithstanding, are fully characteristic of the composer.

The fourth group—*Arrangements*—applies to the wide open field of two-piano settings which are arranged from different instrumental or vocal media. An arrangement, in the terminology of Dr. Hans Rosenwald,

---

1. For comment on this work, see also Book I, *The History*, Chapter X, *The Composers*.

is a "transliteration." As such, it is equivalent to literal translation or transference of the original material into another medium; the latter thereby becomes in essence a rearrangement of the original cast, with the primary materials redistributed.

This objective and workmanlike procedure endeavors not to alter nor to detract; during the operation, it never adds and it scrupulously leaves the form, harmony, and general character of the original work intact.

In this connection, the reader is referred to a treatise on the subject of "Arrangement" which can be found in *Grove's Dictionary of Music and Musicians*. The particular essay, of which Sir C. Hubert H. Parry is the author, offers a general discussion of the topic as well as detailed examples. From the concluding remarks, the following excerpt is quoted in that its essence recommends itself for general adoption:[2]

> "The tendency of high-class modern arrangements is towards freedom of interpretation; and the comparison of classical arrangements with their originals shows that this is legitimate up to the point of imitating the idioms of one instrument by the idioms of another, the effects of one by the effects of another. Beyond that lies the danger of marring the balance of the original works by undue enlargement of the scale of particular parts, of obscuring the personality of the original composer, and of caricature—that pitfall of ill-regulated admiration. For however unlimited may be the rights of composers to alter their own works, the rights of others are limited to redistribution and variation of detail; and even in detail the alterations can only be legitimate to the degree which is rendered indispensable by radical differences in the instruments, and must be such as are warranted by the quality, proportions and style of the context."

The field of arrangements can be properly surveyed only in comparison with and in contradistinction to another category which includes *Transcriptions* of all sorts. This approach is, in fact, the procedure followed by many dictionaries and encyclopedias which treat of the two terms in a simultaneous discussion.[3] Much of the existing confusion derives from a certain lack of sufficient discrimination in the application of either term. On the other hand, the boundaries between the two types often appear so narrowly drawn or actually overlapping that a classification in some instances is difficult to arrive at. Mostly, however, the features of a transcription stand out clearly. They consist of greater or lesser changes in texture or harmonic idiom, resulting in a distinct modification of the original work. The characteristics of a transcription may also include extensions of the basic material in the form of preludes, interludes, and postludes, or such other additions as the arranger finds appropriate in the process of completely reworking the primary composition. The most salient single feature of a transcription, however, is the creative participation of the arranger which readily evidences itself in the general style of the finished product.

A comparison between some typical arrangements and transcriptions

---

2. *Grove's Dictionary of Music and Musicians*, Vol. I, pp. 123-124.
3. See, for instance, *Harvard Dictionary of Music*.

will quickly establish an understanding of the differentiation to be made. The two-piano setting by Elizabeth Gest of the Bach Chorale "Jesu, Joy of Man's Desiring," or Albert Renaud's two-piano version of the Minuet from the *L'Arlésienne* Suite by Bizet[4] are to be termed arrangements because they literally and faithfully translate the original media into the two-piano idiom, without change of general texture and style, and without injection of extraneous material.

By contrast, the characteristics of transcriptions are easily recognized in such editions as the one by Percy Grainger who reworked Bach's aria "Sheep May Safely Graze" into a piece programmatically entitled "Blithe Bells." Another typical example of a transcription is the two-piano version of Rubinstein's Romance in E flat by Silvo Scionti. In both settings, pronounced deviations from the original scores are encountered. These changes pertain to texture, harmony, form, and other elements of both material and idiomatic nature. Introductions and coda sections are added, and cadenzas are interspersed.

Excellent examples for the genre presently discussed are also the free transcriptions for two pianos by Abram Chasins. Objects for transcription were, among other works, the "Blue Danube" and the "Artist's Life" waltzes by Johann Strauss. So much of a metamorphosis has taken place from the original material to the transcribed version that the critic, Pitts Sanborn, feels moved to write:

"It is hard to define such works, for there is nothing quite like them. The original themes are all there. Their contours are used as guiding principles, and yet they become points of highly imaginative departure. There is the utilization of the variation form in every possible way, with the architectural aid of sparklingly suggestive introductions and thematic bridges. Through a developing series of ideas and countervoices of theme against theme, all that happens is directly traceable to the original phenomena of those beautiful themes. There is an obvious love and respect for these themes in every bar, and surely the two-piano medium has never been more completely exploited."

Setting a high standard of conception and execution not only in his transcriptions, Abram Chasins has also won distinction for a number of two-piano arrangements which he himself so classifies in contradistinction to the former; the differences between the two groups are found to be in keeping with the general principles governing each category. Chasins has made such two-piano arrangements, among others, of the mighty Passacaglia in C minor by Bach and of the lovely "Melody" from the opera "Orpheus" by Gluck.

Paraphrases, the sixth classification, deviate even more from the original

---

4. Curiously enough, Renaud himself, in the printed copy, refers to his arrangement as a "transcription," thereby proving the confusion which exists even among composers regarding this terminology.

composition than transcriptions. They frequently treat of the basic text merely as a point of departure for extensive elaboration and variation. Through the development of considerable extraneous material, they aspire and mostly amount to a free rewriting of the original work. In duo-pianism, this style of creative juxtaposition had a flowering during the time of the Grand Duo. Its characteristics may best be exemplified by the numerous paraphrases of Liszt. Among contemporary composers, Gregory Stone writes prolifically for two pianos in this genre which, generally speaking, has fallen into a certain disrepute because of its often pretentious and artificial character. However, if undertaken with artistic taste and commanded by inspiration, the result may be very satisfactory. Reference is here made to the two-piano paraphrase by Mario Braggiotti on the well-known song "Trees" by Oscar Rasbach. This phantasy is carried out so freely as to achieve a complete transformation of the original music; the latter now serves merely as the *Leitmotif* for an entirely new and characteristic musical discourse.

The following is a summary of what has been said on the complex of arrangements, transcriptions, and paraphrases: Arrangements, as their foremost requirement, need to be executed in a workmanlike manner. Therefore, the emphasis in the operation of arranging lies on the objective conception of style and on the technical skill of managing the musical translation. In the case of transcriptions and paraphrases, however, the task becomes one of personal productive participation and therefore of subjective superimposition. Here, in reality, a recreative process is taking place. The imagination of the transcriber derives such stimulation from the primary music that he ultimately transcends the barriers of material and idiomatic treatment and aspires to a transformation, metamorphosis, or even apotheosis of the original score. The transcriptions for two pianos by Maurice Ravel of the three orchestral Nocturnes by Debussy—*Nuages, Fêtes,* and *Sirènes*—amply illustrate the artistic value of such recreations, a worthiness which places the "arranger" into a position alongside the composer of the original work.

In closing, a few general remarks on arrangements and transcriptions may be allowed: The two-piano ensemble now is considered the nearest substitute for the orchestral idiom. In polyphonic textures, rhythmic designs, and dynamic resources, it closely approaches symphonic sonorities and proportions. Practically all of the standard literature for orchestra and chamber ensembles has been transcribed for two pianos either by the composers themselves or by other competent arrangers. The quality of these adaptations has kept pace with the universally growing technique of instrumentation, and many transcriptions for two pianos reach the level of thoroughly idiomatic creations. Ravel's two-piano settings of the orchestral Nocturnes by Debussy have already been mentioned as suitable examples. Such works definitely enrich the literature, and it would amount to musical chauvinism to ignore them simply because of their status as transcriptions. All great composers have been arrangers par excellence. If the fame of their name could attain sanction for their transcriptions, it appears only fair and just to let the superior quality of an arrangement or transcription be sufficient reason for its acceptance, as well as a commendation for the name of its author.

Group 7—*Added second-piano parts*—includes such music for two pianos in which one performer plays the original *solo* composition while the other renders a second-piano part which has been devised additionally. The original solo work is left fully intact, and the added part is contrived as an obligato to the former. During performance, consequently, the first pianist is acting as soloist, while the player of the second-piano part provides the counterpoint of new material which is closely patterned after the original composition.

The entire method is subject to controversy. To give the problem an airing, a number of opposing attitudes will be examined in the following paragraphs.

During a special investigation of reactions regarding the use of second-piano parts in addition to original piano solos, Victor Babin has termed the procedure "absurd."

Abram Chasins also says: "No. This is invariably poor and 'manufactured' because the second part has to be tailored to an inflexible unit."

Celius Dougherty likewise calls second-piano parts "worthless."

The opinion of Livingston Gearhart is that "such attempts usually fail. However, it can be done."

Morton Gould expresses strong skepticism when stating: "For the most part, I would be dubious of this approach."

On the other hand, Darius Milhaud considers second-piano parts an "excellent *Ersatz*."

In spite of much derogation, and sometimes violent attack, this particular type of two-piano music has held its place in practice and repertoire throughout the years, and it enjoys distinct popularity in the educational field. Several composers of note have from time to time contributed to the medium; its literature boasts, for example, the names of Czerny, Moscheles, Grieg, and Saar. Moscheles selected ten Preludes from Bach's Well-Tempered Clavier and added to them a concertizing second-piano part; the title of this work is "Melodic-Contrapuntal Studies, op. 137." Louis Victor Saar devised a set of second-piano obligatos to Bach's fifteen

Two-Part Inventions, and Edvard Grieg composed extensive second-piano parts to accompany several of the solo Sonatas and the C minor Fantasy by Mozart. These particular additions have been ardently debated, Grieg receiving both praise and condemnation for his second-piano parts which are alternately termed "most enjoyable" and "glaring examples of bad taste."

Of the opponents, Adolf Ruthardt, in his *Wegweiser durch die Klavier-Literatur*,[5] gives this verdict:

> "Es ist unbegreiflich, dass ein so geistreicher Tonsetzer wie Grieg auf die Idee verfallen konnte, einigen der besten Mozartschen Sonaten eine so ausnehmend gewuerzte, exotische Begleitung beizulegen die Mozarts Physiognomie teils vollstaendig verhuellt, teils in eine unnatuerlich fremdartige Beleuchtung rueckt."[6]

Another adverse critic is Wiktor Labunski who, in a paper entitled *Adventures in Two-Piano Arranging*[7] calls it a mistake to add a second-piano part to an existing solo-piano composition. Dr. Labunski continues:

> "It may be all right sometimes, for pedagogical purposes, to make arrangements such as Timm's second piano to Clementi's Sonatinas Opus 36. But Grieg's second piano additions to Mozart's Fantasie and Sonatas are a grave sin against style and good taste. Likewise, some existing second piano additions to Bach's Two-Part Inventions are, musically speaking, of inferior quality especially if you consider the musical quality of the Inventions themselves."

Guy Maier is even more outspoken in his condemnation of Grieg's additions to the solo sonatas by Mozart. Maier writes:[8] "I scorn them as glaring examples of bad taste; under no circumstances would I teach or play them."

There are, on the other side, defenders of this practice. Dr. Preston Ware Orem states[9] that "probably the most distinctive of such accompaniments are those by Grieg; these are most enjoyable to play; and, aside from Grieg's characteristic employment of major ninths and descending thirds of dominant chords, they do no violence to the original."

Another advocate of the medium is Silvio Scionti who writes:[10] "Of unusual interest is the second-piano part to the Bach Two-Part Inventions, ingeniously written by Louis Victor Saar. Students practicing the Two-Part Inventions will find it refreshing to try them with the additional piano."

5. Page 290.
6. "It is incomprehensible that as intelligent a composer as Grieg could fall upon the idea to add to some of the best sonatas by Mozart an accompaniment which is so extremely spicy and exotic; an accompaniment which partly obscures Mozart's physiognomy completely, and partly moves it into an unnatural and strange light." Translation: H. M.
7. *The Etude*, March 1949, page 150.
8. *The Etude*, January 1941, page 20.
9. *About Pieces for Two Pianos*, "The Etude," September, 1938.
10. *The Fascination of Two-Piano Playing*, "The Etude," September 1939, page 602.

In view of the predominantly adverse reactions from concertizing duo-pianists, it appears that added second-piano parts find their foremost utilization in pedagogical rather than in artistic pursuits. Therefore, this category will receive further discussion in a later chapter.[11]

The eighth and final group of distinct applications which appear possible in the process of composing for two pianos is that of the *Concerto*. Most standard concerti and many other large-scale piano works are written with the accompaniment of an orchestra. Of necessity, there is only a slim percentage of the many aspiring performers, and even of the professional artists, who succeed in reaching a concert appearance with orchestral accompaniment. In most cases, a second piano will have to suffice for the simulation of the orchestral portion, and in this modest but important function it has proved a satisfactory substitute throughout the years. Were it not for the second-piano "orchestra," little incentive indeed could be provided for the study of a piano concerto. The solo part, if played alone, remains a torso; its full effect and meaning can be gained, for major portions, only through the integration of the solo into the web of the entire score. Most condensations of the orchestral instrumentation into a second-piano part are doing justice to the symphonic character of the work itself as well as to the piano idiom into which it is translated. Moreover, suitable changes can readily be effected wherever the arrangement does not prove satisfactory to the executants.

While their usefulness in study seems beyond a doubt and therefore is uncontested, the employment of a second piano for the public performance of a concerto meets with a certain amount of controversy. In order to obtain definite viewpoints, the opinions of a number of ranking composers were solicited with the question:

"What about second-piano condensations from orchestral scores, arranged for the performance of a concerto?"

The reaction of Victor Babin to this question is contained in the following reply: "For study: yes; for performance: no."

Abram Chasins expresses a favorable opinion: "This can be very effective and artistically unassailable because in the Concerto, the solo instrument or instruments are originally devised to sound in cooperation with or in combat against another body of sound."

Celius Dougherty likewise advocates the practice of performing concertos with a second-piano arrangement of the orchestral part. He goes still further by stating that, in the case of a concerto for two pianos and orchestra, even a third piano can be used. This latter combination was

11. See Part C, *Duo-Pianism, An Educational Medium,* Chapter XXII, *Pedagogic Materials.*

employed to satisfaction, although merely as a necessary substitute, when Dougherty and Ruzicka gave a performance of Milhaud's Concerto for Two Pianos and Orchestra.

Livingston Gearhart regards second-piano condensations of orchestral material as "fine, but not for concert use."

Gold and Fizdale declare themselves in opposition to the practice, while Morton Gould considers the method "for the most part, not very satisfying."

Darius Milhaud, on the other hand, defends the second-piano arrangements of orchestral portions in a concerto because he again sees in them "excellent *Ersatz*."

E. Robert Schmitz extends his approval with this definite limitation: He allows for second-piano condensations "only as a substitute for original scoring."

The latter statement can readily be endorsed and generalized: It should be wholly understood that the second-piano part in concerto performance serves strictly as a substitute. It functions as a surrogate orchestra and provides the backing and supplementation without which the work would remain fragmentary. This service to the large and important literature of the piano concerto is so well rendered by the expedient of second-piano condensations that their general employment has become one of the most practical functions of duo-pianism.

The following statement expresses the acceptance of this type of composition; it is quoted from the section devoted to the "Duet" in *Grove's Dictionary of Music and Musicians*:[12] "This combination (for two pianos) is particularly successful in representing works for piano and orchestra; all the best known concertos are arranged for two pianos, and in the case of Chopin the arrangement is at least as effective as the original."

---

12. Vol. II, page 103.

CHAPTER XX

SPECIAL PROBLEMS, TECHNIQUES, AND OPPORTUNITIES

Challenged and attracted by so large a variety of possibilities for writing in the two-piano idiom, the composer soon faces a series of special problems. They involve not only the textures and devices generally related to the craft of composition, but they pertain more specifically to the scoring for two identical instruments.

It is held self-evident that an intimate knowledge of the mechanical properties of the pianoforte is an *a priori* requirement for any attempt at two-piano composition. An additional postulate is the clear vision of the artistic purpose and effect which the combination of two pianos can be made to serve. Finally, the principle of equal distribution and integration of part writing must govern the approach, lest the idea of unity between the two instruments is ignored and satisfying balance abolished from the outset.

In his endeavor to clarify the latter two objectives, the composer will come to envisage the same alternative between chamber music and concert styles which was already discussed in connection with the problems of repertoire and program building.[1] The difference in conception with which the medium can be regarded implies corresponding distinctions in approach and execution. In chamber music, the characteristics of individuality and intimacy are prominent; when regarded as a concert form, however, the two-piano combination will primarily stress the effects of symphonic dimension and orchestral proportion.

The composer needs to decide or compromise in this alternative on the

1. See Chapter XVI, *Program Building*, Section 1, *Duo-Pianism, Concert or Chamber Music?*

basis of the dictates implied by both his personal predilection and by the particular subject matter chosen for musical realization. These criteria of preference *and* occasion will provide the logical and acceptable answer to the problem from one case to the next. Darius Milhaud subscribes to this very attitude and, consequently, feels not preoccupied with the question. For him the decision "depends (on) what kind of music you write for two pianos."

Other composers, when queried in regard to the problem

"Do you consider two-piano composition a form of chamber music?", in their majority expressed an affirmative conception in this direction. Some such adherers to the belief that two-piano writing belongs into the genre of chamber music, are Abram Chasins, Celius Dougherty, and Morton Gould. Victor Babin personally is inclined toward classification of the two-piano medium under the same rubric, but he is at the same time anticipating a new orientation wherein the alternative between concert and chamber music types will be obsolete, because the boundaries of distinction already are overlapping.

The techniques of composition for two pianos employ the usual devices for the weaving of a musical fabric. Melodic and harmonic treatments draw from the textures of monophony, polyphony, and homophony. Considering the tonal resourcefulness of even a single pianoforte, the doubling of instruments at once suggests a wealth of possible combinations. Polytonality is one such field in which two pianos offer an ideal vehicle for experimentation. Likewise there exist special opportunities for unusual rhythmic designs. All types of polyrhythm, for instance, present themselves for extensive employment in two-piano writing. The execution of cross rhythms not only offers little difficulty to the performers, but adds real attraction to two-piano playing in that it drastically exemplifies the idea of rivalry on an equal basis which is the true meaning of concertizing.

Perhaps the greatest advantages in scoring for two pianos are made available by the art and science of counterpoint. All polyphonic devices which embody the simultaneous treatment of independent voices can be brought into application to their fullest extent. For while contrapuntal writing for piano solo has definite physical limitations, making difficult the projection of the polyphonic relief, the boundaries for contrapuntal activation become tremendously expanded by the now available twenty fingers on two instruments. If, by the same token, the employment of counterpoint in most piano solo composition and performance has become reduced to an esoteric discipline, in the two-piano medium it emerges anew to practical and gratifying realization.

For both technical facility and intellectual grasp, the scoring of contrapuntally complex pianoforte works will therefore call for the utilization of two instruments. Was it not the combination of two claviers which Bach chose for the materialization of an important excerpt from that greatest treatise on counterpoint ever essayed by man, The Art of Fugue?[2] This historic example for the last two hundred years has pointed the way to the true opportunities of two-piano composition and has made Bach the prophet in one more field of musical art.

Summarily, it may be said that the doubling of instrumental resources produces special advantages for the exploitation of all conceivable devices known to composers, and for the invention of new effects in treatment and sonority. In detail respects, the musical intent must command the particular means of expression. Individual taste and momentary inspiration defy preconceived formulas. To mention only one practical question concerning the technique in composing for two pianos, the inquiry was formulated:

"Do you advocate a cumulative effect, or the thinner texture of dialogue treatment?"

It was Darius Milhaud who, speaking here easily for every composer, dismissed this question with the laconic statement: "That depends on the music. Please leave possibility to fantasy—dream—unexpected."

Therefore, little can be said on the methods or recipes to be chosen in composing original works for two pianos. Here everything depends on the approach of each individual composer. The more original and unorthodox his treatment of the medium, the more significant his ultimate achievement. It is a truism that the greatest works of the greatest composers are found in little conformity with the established rules of their own time.

Fundamentally, it is to be stated that the scoring for two pianos requires infinitely greater skill than that for one piano. The medium particularly calls for a quality possessed by few, the virtue of economy. While the full range of keyboard sonorities is to be activated, this being the primary justification of duo-pianism, the musical fabric needs always to remain clear and transparent.

This policy of economy also has to apply to the process of arranging for two pianos. But arrangers and transcribers face tremendous additional problems. Not only must they be thoroughly versed in the techniques of scoring, but they also need to command a comprehensive knowledge of musical styles and possess an intimate familiarity with the various instrumental and vocal idioms. Only in the presence of these requisites the primary material can be successfully distributed over the proper registers

2. See also Book I, *The History*, Chapter III, *Bach*.

of the two pianofortes, and an adequate representation of the original work be achieved. In this connection, it is well to remember that arrangements *per se* are controversial with some critics and performers. A definite objective should always underlie the basic plan for any arrangement or transcription, both for the sake of an honest and purposeful artistic aim on the part of the arranger himself, and in view of the particular practical place which the arrangement is to assume within the literature.

During the investigation leading to the present discussion, several composers were consulted on their opinions concerning arrangements for two pianos, derived from other combinations. They all express a favorable view and strongly advocate such arrangements, if well adapted to the piano medium. This positive outlook of the composers stands very much in contrast to the purist attitude taken by some of the concertizing duo-pianists who spurn the very idea of arrangements.

Among composers, Victor Babin applies to his arrangements and transcriptions for two pianos the same principles which were outlined by him in an earlier debate of this subject matter.[3] He is convinced that arranging definitely is a composer's task, to be undertaken with the outlook and qualifications of the professional composer. Otherwise the procedure, in Mr. Babin's emphatic statement, suffers a degradation to the status of mere colportage.

Celius Dougherty reasons that transcriptions should be made only from the larger combinations, especially the orchestra. He sees no practical need for, and therefore denies the sanction to, the arrangements for two pianos from the scores of small ensembles (like songs, instrumental duos, etc.); he maintains that such small combinations can and should be heard in their original form.

One type of composition meeting with general suspicion and much opposition when arranged for two pianofortes is that of original piano solos. Suspicion derives from the assumption that existing solo difficulties are divided between the performers so that the arrangement mainly amounts to technical simplification. Opposition is based on the doctrine that a work for piano solo is self-sufficient in the form given to it by the composer. Guy Maier expresses his adverse view in this respect and points the way to more suitable fields of arranging with the following statement:[4]

> "I see no earthly reason why pieces written and *thought* for solo piano should be transcribed for two pianos, when there is such a wealth of orchestral and chamber music, songs, violin sonatas, and so on, hopefully awaiting a good arranger to make it available in this attractive medium."

3. See Chapter XVI, *Program Building*, Section 2, *Original Works versus Arrangements.*
4. *Two-Piano Ensemble,* "The Etude," February 1938, page 87.

In addition to the genres indicated in the foregoing quotation, two-piano arrangements should be encouraged of such keyboard compositions which are originally written in three parts, including all organ literature and some special harpsichord music, like the six Trio Sonatas and the Passacaglia in C minor by J. S. Bach. It is recalled that the latter works primarily were composed for a harpsichord with two claviers (manuals) and a pedal keyboard, an instrument used by organists for practice purposes at home.

It is especially the vast literature of organ works which has remained *terra incognita* for the majority of music lovers. Church organs always have been set aside for the nearly exclusive use of the professional organist, a measure prompted by the delicate technical apparatus of the instrument. Only comparatively few public organ recitals are serving the dissemination of the repertoire, and the average amount of functional organ music during the church service—such as prelude, offertory, and postlude—does not begin to probe the depths of the extensive literature.

An organ score which consists of three staves, usually covers widely separated tonal registers. It can be arranged for one piano, two hands, only with undue technical difficulties to the performer and under almost certain loss of sonorities. This is where two pianos offer a gist to the wealth of beautiful music composed for the organ. The English publication *Musical Opinion* recognized this fact when stating in a recent article:[5] "If we must have Bach's organ works on the piano, then two pianos are a far better approximation to the original than one."[6]

In creating second-piano parts, the same elements and resources are employed as are available for original writing or for arranging. Mere accompaniments of a homophonic character will be less satisfying than such second-piano additions which to a degree balance the original piano solo by concertizing with it. Rather than enforcing certain parts by their mere duplication, contrapuntal voices should be woven into the texture of the primary material. The subject matter for the added second-piano part will best be derived from the themes or motives of the original composition so that fundamental unity is secured. It hardly requires special emphasis or elaboration that the composition chosen for augmentation by a second-piano part must be studied and analyzed closely before it is subjected to amplificative measures. Any fundamental divergency in gen-

---

5. Contained in the issue of July 1948.
6. An entire recital consisting of organ works by Bach and Handel, arranged for two pianos, was given on March 14, 1949, by duo-pianists Hans and Rosaleen Moldenhauer for the Spokane Chapter of the American Guild of Organists. Also included in this particular program were the *Passacaglia in C minor* and the *Sixth Trio Sonata* by Bach.

eral concept and style will easily become disastrous to the all-important unity of musical thought.

Thematic material, whenever restated in the course of the composition, should be assigned alternately to each of the two instruments; by this disposition, the individuality of the performers will automatically produce a different projection of the phraseology which is to be reiterated. Variety of rendition, all other factors remaining unchanged, is in music as in all other arts the most important objective.

For the same reason, the literary repetitions of entire sections will yield a markedly varied effect when the parts are interchanged between the two pianists with each repeat. This method may cause additional work in writing out the score, but richer musical results will compensate for the extra effort.

Two-piano compositions should always be written, and printed, in full score, showing both the parts of *Piano I* and *Piano II* above each other. Sometimes the economy of printing each single part by itself is encountered; this method appears inadvisable because it deprives the performers of the possibility to properly study the full context of the composition. The partners must be able to easily survey the entire fabric of the two-piano score if they are to integrate their individual shares with intelligence and understanding.

The complex of special problems, techniques, and opportunities in writing for two pianos will now be subjected to further discussion by a symposium of authoritative opinions. The following comments pertain to some of the more specific aspects, especially those connected with the problems of arrangement. The broad emphasis on this latter topic will serve to complement the foregoing general remarks.[7]

The first quotation is taken from *Grove's Dictionary of Music and Musicians*[8] and pertains to the version for two pianos of opus 34 by Brahms. The evolution of this Sonata was traced historically in an earlier chapter.[9] At this time, particular attention is devoted to the analysis which Parry gives of the composition. Contrary to historical evidence which proves the priority in date of origin as belonging to the two-piano sonata, he calls the work "the arrangement by Brahms of his pianoforte quintet in F minor, opus 34, as a sonata for two pianofortes." Parry then continues with this discussion:

---

7. In addition to the quotations used in the text, the reader is also referred to the two theses on the techniques of arranging for two pianos, written by Virginia L. Bivens and Rebecca Love Entriken, respectively; further information concerning these papers is found in Book III, *The Literature*, Chapter XXVI, *Annotated Bibliography*.

8. Vol. I, p. 123.

9. Book I, *The History*, Chapter VII, *Brahms*.

". . . the main object seems to have been to balance the work of the two piano-fortes. Sometimes the first pianoforte, and sometimes the second has the original pianoforte part for pages together, and sometimes for a few bars at a time, but whenever the nature of the passages admits of it the materials are distributed evenly between the two instruments. There are some changes—such as the addition of a bar in two places in the first movement, and the change of an accidental in the last —which must be referred to critical considerations, and have nothing to do with arrangement. The technical changes in the arrangement are the occasional development of a free inner part out of the materials of the original without further change in the harmonies, the filling up of rhythm-marking chords of the strings, frequent reinforcement of the bass by doubling, and, which is especially noticeable, frequent doubling of both melodies and parts of important figures. It is this latter peculiarity which especially marks the adaptation of certain tendencies of modern pianoforte-playing to arrangement—the tendency, namely, to double all the parts possible, to fill up chords to the utmost, and to distribute the notes over a wider space, with greater regard to their tonal relations than formerly, and by every means to enlarge the scope and effective power of the instrument, at the same time breaking down all the obstructions and restrictions which the old dogmas of style in playing placed in the way of its development."

Of special interest in the present phase of this survey is an essay entitled *Adventures in Two-Piano Arranging* by Wiktor Labunski.[10] The author first emphasizes a point previously referred to:

"If we agree that arrangements for two pianos are not only permissible but desirable, the question arises—what to arrange? There is one important thing we have to remember before we make a selection of a piece to be arranged, and this is the principle that two-piano is not division, but multiplication. Therefore, I would strongly advise against a rather unsophisticated procedure of taking a solo piano piece and dividing the material between the two players. In my opinion all attempts to arrange piano solo pieces for two pianos are doomed to complete fiasco."

In the same treatise, Dr. Labunski proceeds to offer a number of directions and recommendations to arrangers of two-piano music. These practical suggestions are quoted herewith:

1. "Each individual part should be comparatively easy: arranged comfortably, without forcing the pianists into undue rushing and skipping around the keyboard. There is no doubt that things written easier sound better. Let us compare, for example, the original Liszt *Campanella* with the Busoni version: Busoni eliminates all the tough spots (of which every pianist is afraid) and substitutes new variants for them, which are extremely convenient to play, and are therefore much more effective. As an illustration of good and convenient arrangement for two pianos, I would like to point to the rapid double-notes in Rachmaninoff's *Waltz* from the 'Second Suite.' The double-notes are distributed singly between the two players, and any other arrangement would make it difficult and clumsy. Writing for two pianos is not unlike orchestrating, where you have to see that each individual instrumental part lies conveniently for the player, and is expressed in the particular idiom of his instrument.

2. "There should be a fairly equal distribution of technical passages, important thematical material and secondary things, so that there are really two first pianos. Otherwise the idea of ensemble playing is defeated. Let each of the parts alternate between different registers of the instrument, so that you won't have one of the

10. *The Etude*, March 1949, page 150.

players hopelessly stuck in the lower part of the keyboard, while the other is having a good time in the treble.

3. "Good voice leading is essential in two-piano writing. An idea started by one pianist should be continued in the same part, and not given away to the other player in the midst of a passage, unless there are special coloristic effects desired. This will lead to interesting and good-sounding 'two-layer playing,' and crossing of the parts.

4. "I would like to advise against burdening both pianists with the task of mastering the same complicated passage, because if one spends time and energy on a given difficult problem, it would be a waste for the other to duplicate the work.

5. "I would caution to be very careful about the distribution of chords, especially in forte. Simple duplication of the same chord in the same octave usually sounds bad. And incidentally, two pianos in unison *do not* sound twice as loud as one piano.

6. "When we make an arrangement of an orchestral work, it is in most cases impossible to reproduce everything that is in the orchestra score. (And sometimes there are things in the score which you see, but do not hear). Let us select the most important things, so that the arrangement does not sound thin, or over-loaded, but reflects the true spirit and character of the piece.

7. "The most important matter in the whole problem of two-piano writing is to acquire the ability of two-piano thinking, which is so different from piano-solo or orchestral thinking. Sometimes things that sound good in the orchestra will come out very pale in two-piano form, unless certain characteristically **orchestral devices** be translated into specific two-piano language.

8. "Question of style. How often this important factor has been totally disregarded by transcribers, beginning with Tausig-Scarlatti, and followed by many others! Let us respect to the utmost the original in its character, its spirit, its *style!*

9. "If we have even the very best in arrangements, they will never substitute for original good two-piano compositions. There should be more compositions comparable to Stravinsky's Concerto for Two Pianos. And, we are also in need of several good contemporary concertos for two pianos, with orchestra."

The concluding thought of the foregoing suggestions has repeatedly been stressed and was already strongly voiced in an earlier essay by Josef and Rosina Lhevinne.[11] These authorities combined their demand for more original works with a direction for the achievement of new effects in two-piano composition:

"The first need for the further development of two-piano playing is new composers, with new works which emphasize the distinctly symphonic character of the pianos. Most of the existing literature fails to do this. Rather, it treats the various themes in an easy, conversational style, permitting first one instrument and then the other to take the lead, with the result that endless repetition ensues."

"Rachmaninoff is the first, perhaps, to break away from this style of composition. Being pianistically-minded, he realizes that two-piano work must not give the listener the impression of a single thing split in two; that it must be formed as a rich unit of musical thought. So he arranges his thematic material in the pattern of a well-orchestrated whole, where treble and bass are not merely accompaniments for each other but means of achieving fuller shapes and deeper colors of tonal thought."

The necessity of economy in two-piano scoring is raised to a prime

11. *Four Hands That Play as Two,* "The Etude," December 1933, page 809.

postulate by Guy Maier who contributes to the discussion the following arguments:[12]

"I can only give you a few general, but I hope, helpful suggestions, on two-piano ensemble. First, you must always remember that the addition of an extra piano and pianist doubles your mechanical resources, giving you four arms, twenty fingers, two damper pedals, one hundred and seventy-six piano keys. And here is where duo-pianists, composers and arrangers make their first mistake—they employ all these resources too prodigally, resulting in hard, hammered quality, and opaque, muddy texture. The composers who have written best for the two-piano medium—Mozart and Saint-Saens—evidently sensed this danger, for their own works are models of restraint. If teachers and players would follow these examples of note economy, two-piano playing would be even more popular than it is. When the tones of a percussive instrument (with its pitch already inexact) are doubled, as often occurs in two-piano playing, the resulting out-of-tuneness adds to the thick, dull sound. An arranger should constantly try to shear off all such doublings—and indeed, as many other nonessential tones as possible in order to attain a texture of sufficient thinness and transparence."

While utmost restraint is the keynote of the policy just stated, Preston Ware Orem emphasizes contrapuntal elaboration as a chief advantage in two-piano writing. Dr. Orem propounds his viewpoints with obvious gusto:[13]

"Another, and most valuable, resource lies in the ability to double any part or voices; not necessarily in the octave, above or below. For instance, one player may double in the third or the sixth a melody or ornamental passage played by the other; and when this same resource is employed in the doubling of a countertheme also, we come perilously near to having to manipulate the devices of double counterpoint. Just see how it all fits in, really! And a crossing of the parts, frequently involving contrary motion, another contrapuntal device; and there we are, once again. The beauty of it is that all of these resources serve to bring within our reach passages that, on a single piano, would be either impossible, or else demand the technic of the virtuoso. And at that, one does not have to bang the life out of the instrument. From the preceding, one can gather readily that the purely vertical aspect of harmony alone will not answer in this type of musical creation. Even in an easy teaching piece, by a slight deftness of treatment we can spin a little musical web that will lift us right out of the commonplace. A composer of music is a poet in tones; and a poet, as the Greek derivation of the word informs us, is a worker, a creator, not an extemporizer. Not long ago we happened to hear a 'duo team' extemporize on a very well known American art song. By the time they had discharged their torrents of ill-assorted chromatics and other pestilential passage work, the excellent theme had disappeared entirely. One player might as well have been in New York, the other in San Francisco. We wished them both elsewhere. Music is not made in this manner. Nor is it made by taking an otherwise good piano composition and . . . arranging it (*de*-ranging it, rather) for two pianos."

Principally prominent as duo-pianists of the concert stage, but also noted for a host of arrangements, Whittemore and Lowe have formulated their experiences and beliefs with regard to composition for two pianos

12. *Two-Piano Ensemble*, "The Etude," February 1938, p. 87.
13. *About Pieces for Two Pianos*, "The Etude," September 1938, p. 565.

in the following statements. This discourse represents their special contribution to the present investigation:

"The attitude that two-piano playing is a bastard art has no real foundation. Nearly all the great composers have found pleasure in creating works for this form. It is only today that it is finding its deserved place in concert halls and with symphonies in every part of the world. If composers, and even the duo-pianists, were all constantly aware of the reality of duo-pianism's essential musical value, all of us involved would be able to make even greater strides.

"Certainly not all the works written for the medium by even the past 'greats' are masterpieces. This is partly due to the unfamiliarity of those composers (and many today!) with the possibilities musically of two pianos. It seems more important to us, (even in an arrangement), that a piece sound 'right' on two pianos than that it simply bear the signature of a well-known composer!

"Metropolitan music critics have indeed lambasted many of today's teams for the inclusion of arrangements on their programs. But it has been these very arrangements which have helped to explore the musical horizons for duo-pianism, and which have created a stimulus for contemporary composition. It is quite obvious that when a composer finds real possibilities for expression in an unusual form he is likely to be well-disposed to write in that form.

"It is regrettable that a few of the country's widely read critics listen most sympathetically to any composition written expressly for two pianos even though it may be an inferior work. By contrast, they throw up their hands in horror at any mention of the word arrangement or transcription. Yet Olin Downes, in writing of Rachmaninoff and Kreisler transcriptions, states it most succinctly by acknowledging that a transcription is a worthy addition to repertoire if it fits or becomes the instruments for which it has been arranged and is a good composition for them.

"Therefore to sum up, a good arrangement and one worthy of a place on any program is one which does not by trickery seek to imitate something that it is not, but rather carries the honest musical message of the work in an unquestionably integrated manner. For this reason, we believe that if we can put on our programs familiar or unfamiliar music which sounds to the listener as if it had been written originally for two pianos, our transcriptions and those of other arrangers are justified. If, on the other hand, the arrangement can do nothing but conjure up in the listener's mind the original or more attractive *sound* of the original, we have failed . . . and the arrangement is worthless.

"We have played (and for doing been sharply criticized even by our colleagues) many light things. But we have endeavored always to make them sound as if they were meant for two pianos, and have achieved in these, we hope, a wider scope. While we do admit that our facility with these lighter things has brought us favor with the untutored listener, we nonetheless hope that our greater contribution has been the addition to the repertoire of works important musically; viz: Schubert's *Grande Sonate* in B flat, Bach's flute *Sonate* (E flat major), Albeniz' *Triana*, Ravel's *Alborado del Gracioso*, Copland's *El Salon Mexico*, etc.

"Our greatest pride has been in introducing to the American public (to date, over one hundred performances) the monumental *Variations on a theme of Bach* by Max Reger. This is a work which has been acclaimed without dissent as one of the five greatest sets of variations ever composed for the pianoforte. Yet the almost insuperable difficulty of the work in its original form and its inordinate length had heretofore limited its hearings to a select few. The task of transcribing this giant consumed no less than two years of arduous labor to meet the artistic requirements which the work itself imposed. There has been some minor quibbling over our final decision to omit two variants and the concluding fugue. However, it is indisputable that the average recital audience throughout the country, in contrast to a symphonic audience, will receive with far greater open-mindedness a work lasting 23 minutes instead of almost 40! The unbelievable difference in response to the complete version versus the slightly cut version has been all the proof we need. The end result? We have brought to immediate success a great work by a comparatively unfamiliar genius, and this success in appeal cannot be rivaled by either the masterful Brahms-Haydn or Saint-Saens-Beethoven Variations. The recurring comment by audiences and critics alike that the Reger's expressiveness and emotional impact make it 'the greatest music (they have) heard on two pianos' not only repays us for our labors (which is quite unimportant), but gives us confidence that we are making a real contribution to the necessary expansion of pertinent repertoire and that we are on the right road in assisting the growth of duo-pianism as a genuine artistic medium."

Last, but not by any means least, to be mentioned among the opportunities which present themselves to composers and arrangers in the two-piano medium, are the available channels for utilization of their products. An inquiry into the marketableness of two-piano compositions reveals a field of great extent. Concert teams as well as radio artists are constantly in search of new material. A considerable number of prominent duo-pianists have been commissioning our leading composers to write two-piano works especially for them. In turn, the fascination of the idiom and the superior accomplishments of a veritable Galaxy of teams have induced many composers to direct their creative efforts to this medium.

The ballet which, for economic and other practical reasons, has frequently been observed to employ a two-piano team as substitute for an orchestra, provides a substantial share of the steady demand for original compositions and arrangements. The opera workshop often resorts to the same surrogate orchestra, and the oratorio likewise is finding the two-piano combination a ready tool and satisfactory expedient for its instrumental realization. All these and numerous other applications create a steadily increasing need for new two-piano scores.

One of the largest consumers of two-piano material is the branch of music education. The supply in this field does not meet the heavy demand for graded ensemble pieces, concerto arrangements, and added second-piano parts. Lastly, there remains the multitude of amateurs who in their duo-pianistic activities transgress the full extent of the literature from original works to arrangements, from salon music and "character" pieces to the symphonies of Beethoven, Bruckner, and Mahler. The particular function of duo-pianism as a guide to symphonic and chamber music literature will be further demonstrated in the chapters devoted to "Duo-Pianism, an Educational Medium"[14] in that every appreciative process largely assumes the character and importance of a study and consequently rises to the status of an educational method.

The foregoing brief survey must suffice to indicate the availability of rich markets open to composers and arrangers who may look for outlets for their products in the two-piano medium. To supplement the picture, it will now be interesting to learn from composers themselves some of their opinions regarding the possibilities of performance and publication of their works in this idiom. Another reaction of symptomatic significance is evoked at the same time by the correlated question which amount of attention composers intend to give to the two-piano medium in their future work.

Victor Babin sees for two-piano compositions "a steady interest, proportionate in amount to the publications of piano solo works." As to his own plans for future compositions, Babin does not feel preoccupied in behalf of any particular medium. He will write for two pianos, as for other forms, according to his sense of creative necessity.

Abram Chasins states: "Every one of my two-piano works has been published immediately and widely performed shortly thereafter."

Chasins, in consequence, anticipates to compose in the two-piano medium "a good deal. I intend to complete a two-piano concerto within a year. Much work has already been done on it."

_____
14. Chapters XXI, XXII.

Celius Dougherty had a moderate number of his two-piano works published. Several additional scores in the idiom are under contract and expected to appear in print. One of these still unpublished manuscripts is Dougherty's "Lulu" Suite, after music from the opera by Alban Berg. As to his intentions for the future, Dougherty is superstitious to communicate himself. He indicates, however, that he is planning a work for two pianos with ensemble.

Livingston Gearhart recognizes an "excellent market" for two-piano compositions, although he himself, for special reasons of his own, intends to give "less and less" attention to this idiom.

Morton Gould, on the other hand, considers the marketableness of scores in the medium as limited; at present, he personally devotes little time to duo-pianism.

Darius Milhaud regards the opportunities for distribution of his two-piano compositions the same "as the performance or publication of my other works." Milhaud goes on to state that the degree of his future attention to the medium "depends upon occasion, commission, etc."

This thought must be fully realized in closing. The lifeline of duo-pianism at the present time does not depend mainly on the performers of whom there are many of the highest status. It rather hinges on the contributions which must come from the creators of its own music. The urgency of this fact was recently expressed by Rosina Lhevinne who found the words adequate to the challenge and the responsibility arising to composers of today:[15]

> "The whole future of two-piano playing depends on the expansion of adequate literature, for an unbalanced situation exists now between the very limited number of original compositions and the many excellent two-piano teams. Two-piano programs now have numerous repetitions of the same limited original compositions. The rest of the programs are filled with two-piano arrangements ·adapted from other media, very few of which have great musical value . . . Though the two-piano ensemble may at the present be a vogue, it will undoubtedly become a permanent part of our musical culture when more significant compositions are written. When composers of today realize the potential value of this combination warrants their serious efforts, the art of two-piano ensemble will become an integral part of our musical heritage."

To this challenge may one more incentive be added: Whereas duo-pianism as a vehicle for performance and as an educational tool is limited to temporary and individual significance only, it is in the application as a creative medium that it assumes universal importance and assures enduring value, lasting through the ages as long as the history of the arts.

---

15. *The Spirit of Ensemble*, "Pan Pipes," February 1949, page 164.

Part C: Duo-Pianism, An Educational Medium

CHAPTER XXI

PEDAGOGIC APPLICATIONS

After the foregoing investigation of the functions which duo-pianism fulfills for performers and composers, the educational application of the two-piano medium will now be discussed. While this field of utilization is given attention only at the close of the total survey, it should at once be understood and emphasized that it is the pedagogic function of duo-pianism which, according to all educational philosophy, is fundamentally responsible for the material success and the aesthetic status of the entire field. The reason for nevertheless placing this discussion after those of the artistic and creative applications, is to make the correlation of the educational processes with all other problems of duo-pianism easier and at the same time more compelling.

In pronouncing duo-pianism an educational medium, the hypothesis is adopted that this instrumental combination provides a method of discipline and demonstration, whereby the pupil derives practical benefits from the instruction, as well as an added stimulus to his interest and enjoyment. To more concisely delineate this tentative assumption, a definition of the term "education" will be undertaken shortly.

While the literature of duo-pianism affords the reader with a few essays from the elevated platform of professional artists, the majority of practitioners has remained aloof to a theoretical penetration of their chosen

286

field.[1] Engrossed by the perpetual quest for an ever higher state of proficiency, aspirants sometimes tend to forget the origins of all attainment, those educational processes through which they have arrived at their accomplishments. Yet, whatever progress has been made in the history of man, rests on the foundation of past experience. Imparted to each new generation, this tradition of experience becomes the fountainhead from which may flow additional contributions into the channels of that vast complex system which summarily is called Education.

Consequently, there can be no serious discussion of any project without an investigation of its educational genesis. It should first be emphasized that the term "education" frequently fails to be employed literally, which is to say that its full meaning often is not understood. The latin word *e-ducere* in its exact translation signifies "to lead out." This primary deduction finds its application in that particular phase of education which follows the initial imparting of new information: The teacher then draws from his pupil the investment of previous learning. Only if the earlier instruction can be brought forth again, it is to be considered as acquired knowledge.

This constant two-way process of study and application produces the educated person, one who has been trained to be his own teacher, both in the instilling and in the leading out of information, in learning and in applying. He himself now knows to draw from the storehouse of his acquired knowledge. Education thus can be likened to an intellectual savings-plan, because it appears self-evident that nothing can be elicited from the resources of the mind under the designation "educated" that was not imparted beforehand in some form of study.

The dissemination of all such information which is expected to become knowledge, arises as the primary task of the teacher. An abundance of tools and materials are at his disposal in that the educational evolution of almost any branch of human experience and knowledge has been explored in countless specialized text books and suitable courses of study.

However, a curriculum still needs to be established for the new educational branch of duo-pianism. While we see ourselves confronted with the phenomenon of accomplished artistry, in that we are aware of the many superlative results yielded by the medium, there is no tabulated

---

1. To mention a case in point, the writer at one time interviewed a ranking concert team and found its members to be quite unfamiliar with important facts of their profession. During the conversation pertaining to the history of the art, for instance, the duo-pianists confessed that they had never heard of the Sutro sisters. Regarding the musical literature, they were ignorant of Debussy's own two-piano transcription of *L'Après-midi d'un Faune*. Concerning printed information on duo-pianism, the essays by Vera Brodsky were unknown to them.

system available of the factors composing the entity, and of the methods producing their unity.

This seems to be a foregone conclusion: Whatever elicits such superior effects must also exert a beneficial influence on any pupil using the two-piano medium as a method of music study.

It is this inference which arouses the vital interest of the teacher: Duo-pianism, an *educational* medium. It has long been recognized that any form of ensemble playing is promoting immeasurably the discipline and musical growth of the participants. It is also an accepted fact that the average pupil who devotes himself to the exclusive study of a *solo* instrument, by comparison appears less disciplined in certain respects than the members of choral groups, of orchestras, bands, or other ensembles. This condition applies to the principle of accuracy in its widest definition. It applies especially to what Johannes Brahms once jokingly called the three main essentials of music: "Rhythm, Rhythm, and Rhythm!" It entails similarly the other elementary phases of proper musical adjustment, as for instance time (meter), tempo (degree of speed), and dynamic shading, to mention only a few.

It will be interesting to observe how and to which degree the employment of two pianos furnishes the teacher with a working method to bring home these elements more easily, faster, and at the same time more thoroughly. It will be illuminating to experience the amount of participation and the increased sense of responsibility on the part of the student. The concept of accuracy could readily be made synonymous with the idea of self-discipline. It is the latter quality which is universally recognized as an ultimate achievement. The principle of self-discipline knows no more direct road to its realization than the training which is experienced by working in a group.

Experiments have shown that piano pupils of all ages as well as of various stages of accomplishment eagerly accept the challenge of duo-pianism whenever it is offered by the teacher. They respond with interest and display marked enjoyment. Their learning appears vitalized, and their progress furthered. There can be noticed the deep satisfaction of playing in the company of others. The team spirit being added to the individual initiative, no greater joy can be found in music.

Once a second piano is placed into usage as a pedagogic tool in the teaching studio, the first opportunity is immediately at hand: Demonstration by the instructor, both visual and aural, now is very much facilitated. The advantage of this method was fully realized by no other than Chopin, the teacher, to mention only one of many famous examples. Chopin employed a second piano regularly and extensively in his lessons for the purposes of exhibitive demonstration, thereby clarifying his technical and interpretative instructions.

Chopin's pupil, Carl Mikuli, has left an enlightening account of the typical lesson procedure followed by his master, and of the function of the second piano in it.[2] Mikuli writes:

"On phrasing, and on style in general, he gave his pupils invaluable and highly suggestive hints and instructions, assuring himself, however, that they were understood by playing not only single passages, but whole pieces, over and over again, and this with a scrupulous care, an enthusiasm, such as none of his auditors in the concert-hall ever had an opportunity to witness. The whole lesson-hour often passed without the pupil's having played more than a few measures, while Chopin, at a Pleyel upright piano (the pupil always played on a fine concert grand, and was obliged to promise to practice on only the best instruments), continually interrupting and correcting, proffered for his admiration and imitation the warm, living ideal of perfect beauty. It may be asserted, without exaggeration, that only the pupil knew Chopin the Pianist in his entire unrivalled greatness.

"Chopin most urgently recommended ensemble-playing, the cultivation of the best chamber-music—but only in association with the finest musicians. In case no such opportunity offered, the best substitute would be found in four-hand playing."

The last paragraph of the foregoing quotation possesses particular interest in that the popular conception of Chopin's musical style so often is an antithesis of discipline and adherence to those reglements which are the prerequisites of ensemble performance.

Besides the advantages of demonstration, a further educational opportunity derives from the use of a second piano in the simultaneous playing of passages by teacher and student. This method serves to develop evenness in rhythm and to build up stamina during a given tempo. Above all, the student will gain a greater amount of self-reassurance once he grows accustomed to the active and material assistance rendered by the second instrument. His increased confidence is conducive to better and faster coordination. Moreover, the team spirit which is coincident to all ensemble work gives him a distinct sense of responsibility as well as consideration towards the team-mate.

An early experience in two-piano work is therefore desirable for every pupil of this instrument. It will acquaint him with that higher task of getting along not only for himself, but also in collaboration with a partner. In two-piano performance, the pupil will find himself geared under the common laws of musical rendition. His striving for the quintessence of musical intelligence, summarily called "interpretation," gains compelling direction in the cooperative endeavor and avoids the many dangers of aberration which are conspicuous in all solo work.

A second piano has long and successfully been used in the study of

---

2. Preface by Carl Mikuli to *Chopin, Complete Works for the Piano, Book I, Waltzes*; Schirmer's Library of Musical Classics, Vol. 1549.

piano concertos. Through this method, the teacher, or a qualified class-mate of the student, furnishes a keyboard condensation of the orchestral score on the additional instrument. A suitable semblance of the entire work with its context, fabric, and sonorities can thus be obtained. While most piano concerti of the standard literature are the domain of advanced pupils only, it is exactly the latter who need to be given the more challenging incentives for further study. A concerto invariably stimulates the pupil to greater efforts; it spurs his ambition, and the addition of the second-piano "orchestra" noticeably increases his sense of compatibility.

There is the further opportunity at hand to effectively teach sight-reading on two pianos, a skill important to develop for any musician, yet one which is much neglected in courses of instruction. The pedagogic possibilities of duo-pianism can be extended into many additional avenues, but they all lead up to and find confirmation in the one single and most important quality which an educational method should possess: the *inspiration* to the student which must be provided by the medium of successful teaching.

In this most vital task of selecting a tool for instruction which also furnishes an incentive for the pupil, all teachers will agree. No possibility of a new approach may be overlooked or ignored, and no teaching device promising of any usefulness can be left untried by the conscientious educator.

As for duo-pianism as a method in musical pedagogy, a set of twelve questions is submitted in the following. Every piano teacher is invited to interrogate himself with this questionnaire from which stimulation may be derived towards the establishment of a two-piano workshop or, where already existing, for the even more extensive employment of this educational laboratory.

These are the questions which first had been prepared for a preliminary experimental investigation (1945) and now are to serve again the same study and the deepening of relevant knowledge on a wider scale. May the piano educator therefore ask himself:

1. Am I interested in a research of practical and psychological aspects of two-piano playing?

2. Do I use the second piano during lessons (a) ever, (b) sometimes, (c) how often, (d) regularly?

3. Do I use the second piano for the purposes of (a) demonstration, (b) simultaneous passage work, (c) ensemble playing?

4. Do I use (a) original compositions, (b) arrangements and transcriptions, (c) added second-piano parts for my two-piano ensemble work with students?

5. Do I give qualified pupils a concerto for study, with the condensation of the orchestral part performed on the second piano?

6. Do I believe that two-piano work helps me to teach, better and faster, all phases of musical discipline, especially (a) time (meter), (b) rhythm, (c) tempo, (d) dynamic shading, and (e) accuracy generally?

7. Do I experience that two-piano work brings about greater (a) coordination, (b) cooperation, consideration and team spirit?

8. Do I find two-piano playing helpful in teaching to sight-read?

9. Do I witness greater interest and enjoyment on the part of the student whenever I use the second piano in the lesson procedure?

10. Do I notice an increase in stamina (staying power) at a given tempo when the pupil is assisted by the second piano?

11. Which considerations do I follow in pairing pupils as partners for two-piano work?

12. To which amount do I use two-piano performances in student recitals? What do I notice in public reaction?

The answers of several prominent teachers who were interrogated concerning their attitude toward the two-piano medium as an educational method, are throughout positive. This group of authorities attests unanimously to the value of duo-pianism as an educational tool and recognizes its abundant pedagogic possibilities. The fact hardly needed confirmation: Since the days of Czerny and Chopin, many progressive teachers have realized the inherent educational influence of two-piano activities and have availed themselves of the medium with splendid results.

Beside the pedagogues, a number of concertizing duo-pianists and composers likewise were consulted regarding their estimation of the educational advantages of two-piano work, as evidenced by their individual activities as performers and teachers. The inquiry, formulated to the question "Does two-piano work produce educational benefit?", is answered by Appleton and Field with the following words: "Yes. Any form of art in which one has to propagandize besides functioning is, *per se,* a broadening personal experience."

Bartlett and Robertson formulate a generalization with the statement that "all ensemble playing is valuable for many reasons."

Abram Chasins expresses the belief that two-piano work is "very valuable from every viewpoint, if the teacher is careful in insisting upon individual responsibility and perfection in detail, and guarding against one player using the other as a crutch for his inadequacies."

Dougherty and Ruzicka also are convinced that duo-pianism possesses definite educational merits. However, Celius Dougherty takes occasion to warn against any duplication of the solo part on the second piano. He remembers as a most stifling early experience the habit of one teacher who insisted on playing everything in unison with him on the second piano.

Gold and Fizdale find educational benefit in duo-pianism because of "the continuous stimulation of another person's point of view." They likewise consider two-piano work of substantial help in teaching.

Morton Gould also answers in the affirmative. He writes: "I should imagine there would be many facets of music that could be helped through two-piano team work."

Luboshutz and Nemenoff are attributing to their chosen medium a high degree of educational value. They formulate their views on this subject in the following statement:[3]

> "From the pianistic standpoint, two-piano work offers splendid opportunities for the discipline of ensemble playing—opportunities rarely found by the solo pianist. Instrumental accompanying does not provide the same advantages. In such work, the piano is usually a secondary instrument, with but limited scope for feeling out the balance of alternating thematic voices (melody and obbligato). Two-piano work, then, offers a maximum of musical and pianistic advantage, and it is advisable for all piano students to investigate its possibilities."

Luboschutz and Nemenoff further specify their positive attitude regarding the educational opportunities provided by duo-pianism when they continue as follows:

> ". . . the piano student will find an excellent stimulus to precision, cooperation, and musical awareness in two-piano playing.
> "The development of two-piano teams is . . . depending upon qualities of personal sympathy and likeness of mental approach that are not easily found. But for the purpose of acquiring training in balance, rhythm, reading, and accuracy, any two pianists can profit from joining their forces at two keyboards."

Morley and Gearhart recognize in duo-pianism a "very great educational value." Livingston Gearhart, who is vitally interested in pedagogy, feels that "another volume" could be written on the topic of duo-pianism as an educational medium. In his opinion, "resources in this direction have hardly been tapped."

Of the team of Vronsky and Babin, Victor Babin voices the conviction that two-piano ensemble work is of considerable help in the process of instruction because it furthers accuracy and discipline. Miss Vronsky, in addition, attributes a therapeutic value to duo-pianistic activity. During the war years, she experimented in this direction in hospital wards for mental cases. Teaching the patient to play a simple melody, and building up the tune harmonically and contrapuntally with her accompaniment on the second piano, she found that a new sense of companionship could be

---

3. *The Art of Piano Ensemble,* "The Etude," January 1941.

aroused and that the gratification of accomplishment was frequently achieved. The piano ensemble was thus used for therapy through education.

An important problem is always presented by the inquiry which particular stage in the curriculum of studies should be chosen for the beginning of ensemble playing. This question is answered by duo-pianists Luboshutz and Nemenoff in the following tenor:[4]

"It is important to decide when two-piano work should be begun. Little beginners can be trained in it if, from the very start of their studies, they are encouraged to play short exercises and simple tunes together. At such a pliable age, anything can be learned, depending upon the wisdom of the teaching methods. But if the student has not been accustomed to duo-piano work at the very start, he should stay away from it until he has mastered enough fluency of technic and enough accuracy of rhythm to allow him to adjust both to his notes and to his partner without too much difficulty. Once the pupil is past the plastic age of early childhood, it is wiser to wait until he is no longer disturbed by technical matters (like fingering scales, passing under the thumb, counting rhythms, and so on)."

A few more contributions of general as well as specific character are here added to the discussion. The particular comments originate with some of the most highly qualified pedagogues in the field of piano instruction; their opinions and suggestions will serve to strengthen the tenet of educational benefits which are provided by the medium of duo-pianism.

An editor and teacher, Mrs. Crosby Adams attributes to the cultivation of two-piano ensemble some special advantages which are outlined in her preface to *Album of Piano Duos*.[5] The following quotation is an excerpt from this preface:

"The inspiration that comes to a young student who is privileged to interpret musical literature expressed in Duo-form, can scarcely be estimated. For this reason, more and more teachers are placing two pianos in their studios, in order that ensemble work of this character may become a part of the pupil's training and experience. . . .
". . . In Duos, each performer has the whole keyboard at his disposal, and the sweep that comes to one as he plays is exhilarating. The mutual exchange of the melodic outlines, the keener perception of the harmonic content, make for a better understanding of what true ensemble means, and work wonders in quickening the imagination, and in promoting real musical cultivation."

Bernice Frost elaborates on the opportunity to build up stamina through ensemble work. Dr. Frost, when incurring the query "Why do pupils continue to stumble in their playing, especially when they are playing easy numbers?", offers this suggestion for the development of staying power:[6]

"Duet playing is one of the best ways to overcome this habit of stopping. In

4. *The Art of Piano Ensemble*, "The Etude," January 1941.
5. Published by G. Schirmer, Inc., New York.
6. *Musical Courier*, November 1, 1949, page 24.

that case, after the pupil stops, the teacher continues to the end of the duet. The pupil may be able to start again, and even though it may be in the very last measure, there has been gained some sense of a 'follow-through.'

"Continued use of this procedure will give the pupil increasing ability to see ahead, rather than go back to the beginning. Many incorrect notes may be played in this working-out stage, but the visual training is the more important matter, and no improvement will be made until this seeing ahead is established. (The duets and solos selected for the purpose must be easy for the pupil, and tempi must be slow.)"

Practical suggestions of a highly stimulating character are offered by Wiktor Labunski in his essay *Adventures in Two-Piano Arranging.*[7] These directions pertain to the possibilities for novel technical exercises in two-piano work; they open up new opportunities not only for the drill of technique and ensemble, but also for the enlargement of pianistic sonorities.

Dr. Labunski writes:

"One of the interesting developments of two-piano work is the possibility of scale and arpeggio playing simultaneously on two pianos, without having to resort to dull unison playing. The field is extremely wealthy and virtually unexplored. From scales and arpeggios within one tonality, one can go into scale-arpeggio playing that is less conventional, sounds intriguing, and opens up new vistas in polytonal combinations akin to contemporary harmonic thinking. Without going into detail, I would like to point out several of many possibilities in this line.

1. The students play scales in contrary motion, one beginning at the bottom, the other at the top of their respective keyboards. This also can be combined with different forms of scales, for example, the one playing the scale in the octave, the other in the third or sixth.

2. Parallel motion, but not unison: for example, both students playing the scale in the octave a third or a sixth apart; or both playing in thirds or sixths an octave apart.

3. Polytonal combinations: these scales introduce new and interesting sonorities. Try, for example, to have one player play the C major scale in the octave, and the other the E major scale in the third, so that the third is placed between the extremities of the octave, ('inside' the octave). Or try the same C major scale combined with F-sharp or D major scales in thirds, respectively. It is interesting to note that scales with the equal number of sharps and flats have some affinity, and when played in thirds, contrary motion, sound interesting. Try B major—D-flat major; and, E major—A-flat major, simultaneously.

4. Arpeggios could be made interesting by having one student play a triad in root position, the other in first or second inversion, and then shift the combination one and two chord tones. There is a large number of combinations possible if you also include the dominant and diminished seventh arpeggio.

5. Polytonal arpeggios: try the combination of C major and E major triads, in all positions; or a combination of A major and F major dominant sevenths; or a combination of two diminished sevenths a major third apart (for example, B—D-sharp). Or C major root position combined with F-sharp major root, or D-sharp minor first inversion. All of these polytonal scales and arpeggios have a somewhat Ravelian coloring."

Beyond the virtually unlimited application of the second instrument which is possible during the course of instruction, the two-piano combination can find another useful employment in student recitals large or small.

---

7. *The Etude,* March 1949, page 150.

Whether or not the teacher will consider it advisable to himself assist the pupil at the second piano, or to entrust some qualified student of his class with this responsibility, must be left to his discretion; the decision in this alternative depends on manifold considerations which require mature judgment.

The success attending two-piano performances during student recitals is recorded by general observation. Audience reactions are pronouncedly favorable, and the danger of irksome monotony which sometimes accompanies a lengthy recital of piano pupils is successfully averted. Some teachers feature full-length two-piano programs in their annual recital schedule, presenting several student teams on various levels of age and attainment during the concert.

Special interest is always aroused, and a peculiar appeal is effected by the duo-piano offerings of a team formed by pupils. Much promotional usage can therefore be derived by the progressive teacher from the apparent attraction of the medium. However, the pairing of students for ensemble work demands a great deal of deliberation and sound judgment on the part of the educator. The prospective associates need to be technically and musically equalized as nearly as possible, to permit of a two-piano partnership without impediment to either pupil, and to insure balance in performance. Personal qualifications have to be taken into account as much as the pianistic and other musical equipment. More harm than good can be caused by an autocratic insistence on a two-piano combination of children who are not compatible to each other. On the other hand, if the formation of a student team is undertaken in full regard of the physical and psychological principles previously discussed,[8] the musical education of each participating pupil will gain much individual promotion through the collective enterprise. Lagging interest can be stimulated and indifference converted into enthusiasm by the expedient of occasional or regular duo-piano ensemble.

Some students are found to be particularly inspired by the medium, and actually may wish to specialize temporarily in two-piano work. Such initiative should be encouraged by teachers and parents alike, because the musical development of the pupils will be advanced in general proficiency even if their solo practice is neglected for a time.

Close observation has confirmed that two-piano teams, consisting of students on the grade or high school level, and likewise collegiate duo-pianists, enjoy pronounced popularity everywhere. They draw attention and respect at their appearances in school assemblies and music clubs,

8. See Part A, *Duo-Pianism, An Artistic Medium*, Chapter XIII, *Partnership.*

and they are favorite performers on whichever program they take part in. The distinction so conspicuously commanded by the two-piano medium may in part be the outgrowth of the recognition generally accorded to the manifestation of discipline and coordination; it is the latter qualities which obviously are chief requisites for the attainment of the flawless precision necessary even in the smallest duo-pianistic undertaking and therefore never fail to impress the most casual listener.

There is another important benefit which student partners on two pianos learn to appreciate at an early stage of their collaboration. It is the awareness of their successful adjustment to a social musical life, embodying a satisfaction which the solo pianist will rarely derive from his necessarily egocentric activities, and one which the piano accompanist in his subordinate function likewise cannot envisage. It is the integration of equal shares of individual endeavor at first, and the indivisible character of the unified attainment thereafter, which make two-piano work deserving of attributes far beyond the music-educational and emotional functions. In its basic philosophy, duo-pianism is a character builder par excellence. Here the partners, beginning on equal premises, are given equal tools and resources with which to achieve their keyboard community. The exigencies of this situation are productive of the highest types of cooperation, responsibility, and zeal.

In the foregoing, a few avenues of duo-pianism have been pointed out which may lead to a further realization of opportunities previously not apprehended in the exploration of the pianoforte and its musical domain. In summary, it is held that the activation of duo-pianism as an educational medium promises a multitude of general as well as special benefits for the student. All phases of the discipline of music can be demonstrated and applied more directly and more convincingly with the aid and through the influence of a second piano. The team spirit in the pupil deepens his sense of responsibility and solicits his better cooperation; it indeed incites his keener alertness and resultant quicker coordination. Most important, perhaps, two-piano work gives the studio routine fresh impetus and new inspiration with incalculably valuable psychological consequences.

The brief survey of the pedagogic utilization of the two-piano combination is concluded herewith although, in the words of Livingston Gearhart, "another volume" could be written on the subject of duo-pianism as an educational medium. A specialized study in this field would indeed offer a fertile research project to the music educator.

CHAPTER XXII

PEDAGOGIC MATERIALS

In the choice of suitable materials for two-piano instruction, the teacher will be guided by two main considerations. The first regard must aim for the greatest possible promotion of the pupil as a solo performer; the second thought recognizes ensemble training as an equally important goal in the musical development of the student.

For the realization of the first objective, added second-piano parts and concerti provide the most appropriate material. Notwithstanding the existing controversy, and despite the almost general rejection by professional duo-pianists and composers alike, many teachers have found the second-piano accompaniment to original piano solos useful in their courses of instruction. By virtue of their extensive employment, second-piano parts seem to be fulfilling the function which they serve: This purpose is to provide ensemble material which matches but does not encroach; material which leaves entirely intact the solo composition performed by the pupil, yet infuses the study of the work with the *concertante* and *obligato* styles of playing. While thus receiving the stimulation and the benefits of ensemble training, the disciple yet is building up his solo repertoire. Frequently, too, the interest of the student in the original composition is increased, or sometimes renewed, and an encouragement to perfect his solo part is provided, for causes intrinsically connected with the incentives derived from ensemble playing.

In favor of added second-piano parts, it may be pointed out that the history of music from the tenth to the sixteenth century gives ample justification for using known works as a basis for a new development. Therefore, the rejection which these particular materials sometimes are encountering, appears hardly justified in the historic light. Performers may be reluctant to program this type of two-piano music for public rendition, but pedagogues have come to use the genre extensively because "the modern piano teacher finds the addition of the second piano part a valuable and delightful experience for the student once he has learned the solo."[1]

Typical of such compositions with added second-piano parts are the following. The name of the composer of the additional piano score is given after that of the composer of the original solo piece. As a guide to the printed material outlined in this and the following sample groups, publishers are indicated by symbols. A key to these characters, giving the names of the respective publishing houses, is found in Book III, *The Literature,* at the beginning of Chapter XXIV, *Original Two-Piano Music.*

TITLE	COMPOSER	PUBLISHER
Menuet in G Major	Bach—Frothingham	CFS
Menuet in D Minor	Bach—Frothingham	CFS
Solfeggietto	Bach—Frothingham	CFS
Tambourine	Gossec—Elizabeth Gest	EV
Londonderry Air	Folk Song—Elizabeth Gest	EV
Dancing Doll	Poldini—Elizabeth Gest	EV

Special mention is also made of the numerous added second-piano parts which were composed by Rueven V. Kosakoff. They cover a wide selection of classics from the standard literature of piano instruction. The publishers of the Kosakoff additions[2] state in one of their commentaries regarding these particular second-piano parts: "They are written in the style and spirit of the compositions which they complement—even to the point of using thematic material from the solos; and are, in themselves, highly interesting, of teaching value, and may even be used independently of the solos."

For the convenience of the reader, a selection of well-known solo compositions to which second-piano parts by Kosakoff are available, is listed in the following:

COMPOSER	TITLE
J. S. Bach	Minuet in D minor
	Musette in D major
	Minuet No. 1 in G major
	Minuet No. 1 in G minor
	Minuet No. 2 in G major
	Minuet No. 2 in G minor
	Polonaise
	Prelude in C major
	Prelude in C minor

1. *Pan Pipes,* February 1949, page 185.
2. J. Fischer & Bro., New York.

COMPOSER	TITLE
P. E. Bach	Solfeggietto
L. van Beethoven	Albumblatt "Für Elise"
	Bagatelle, op. 119, No. 1
	Ecossaise
	Sonatina in G major
Fr. Chopin	Three Ecossaises, Op. 72, No. 3
M. Clementi	Sonatina, Op. 36, No. 1
E. Gayrhos	Etude in A minor
E. Grieg	Dance Caprice, Op. 28, No. 3
	Elfin Dance, Op. 12, No. 4
	Grandmother's Minuet, Op. 68, No. 2
C. Gurlitt	By the Spring
G. F. Handel	Bourrée
J. Haydn	Vivace
St. Heller	Curious Story, Op. 138, No. 9
	Etude, Op. 81, No. 2
	Etude, Op. 125, No. 1
	Etude, Op. 125, No. 21
	Etude, Op. 138, No. 6
F. Kuhlau	Sonatina in C, Op. 55, No. 1
F. Mendelssohn	Presto Agitato
W. A. Mozart	Rondo-Alla Turca
	Sonata in C major
G. Pescetti	Presto, from Sonata
J. P. Rameau	Tambourine
F. Schubert	Moment Musical, Op. 94, No. 3
	Scherzo in B flat major, op. posth.
R. Schumann	Allegro from Sonata, Op. 118, No. 1
	Merry Farmer
	Sicilienne, Op. 68, No. 11
	Wild Horseman, Op. 68, No. 8

Further second-piano parts are available in a multitude, covering every degree of difficulty. For complete information, the catalogues of the various publishing houses should be consulted. The foregoing examples must suffice to indicate the extent of this type of two-piano activity. In addition, reference is made to the more famous specimens of this genre which have already been mentioned in a previous discussion of added second-piano parts.[3] Such are the Melodic-Contrapuntal Studies, Op. 137, by Moscheles which constitute concertizing obligato parts to ten Preludes by Bach, selected from the Well-Tempered Clavier. Such are also the second-piano parts by Louis Victor Saar, composed additionally to Bach's fifteen Two-Part Inventions, and the accompaniments for a second piano by Edvard Grieg to Mozart's Sonatas in C major (K. 545), in F major, (K. 533 and 494), in G major (K. 189h), and to the Fantasia and Sonata in C minor (K. 475 and 457).

Karl Czerny apparently was convinced of the pedagogic value of ensemble work during piano instruction for he wrote accompanying second-piano

3. See Part B, *The Creative Medium*, Chapter XIX, *The Field*.

parts to some of his own velocity studies. In the same category, there exist also correlated second-piano parts by Adolf Henselt to the Etudes by Jean Baptist Cramer which Hutcheson calls "ingenious." Another set of accompaniments to the Cramer studies has been devised by Art Napoléon.

Many sonatinas, highly esteemed as perennial teaching materials, have likewise been provided with obligato parts, as for instance the Six Sonatinas, Opus 36, by M. Clementi for which Henry C. Timm composed the additions. Moreover, several Sonatinas by Friedr. Kuhlau have received accompaniments by Aug. Riedel (opus 18) and by Sigfr. Karg-Elert. William Lester wrote a second-piano part to the Sonata in G major, opus 49 No. 2, by Beethoven.

Practically every concerto or other large-scale work for piano solo with orchestral accompaniment has been published in two-piano score, showing the part of the soloist *(Piano I)* above a condensation of the orchestral portion *(Piano II)*. The second piano provides an adequate substitute for the symphonic element, and the feasibility of hearing the solo within the context of the entire musical fabric proves to be a decided incentive for the study of a concerto by the aspiring young artist.

Besides the large literature of the standard concerto, demanding considerable caliber of execution, there exist many concerti for less proficient students. These can be learned by average pupils with much benefit and enjoyment, and may readily receive a satisfying performance with the assistance of a second piano.

A few such children's concerti are here recommended to the attention of teachers and young students:

TITLE	COMPOSER	PUBLISHER
Kinder Concerto	Haydn-Robyn	OD
Kinder Concerto	Mozart-Robyn	OD
Concertino on Familiar Tunes	Stephen Avery	TP
Concerto in F Major	Boykin	SG
Concerto Americana	Kasschau	SG
Concerto in C Major	Kasschau	SG
Junior American Concerto	Mittler	
Concerto in C Major	Williams	SG
Concerto in F Major	Williams	SG
Concerto in A Minor	Williams	SG

Regarding a list of original compositions for two pianos, the reader is referred to Book III, *The Literature,* Chapter XXIV, which contains an extensive index of the several categories classified as original works.

Arrangements and transcriptions for two pianos exist in such great numbers and widely varying degrees of difficulty that a coverage of this vast literature here can not be attempted. The selection of suitable teaching material will present no obstacles, considering the large quantity and diversity of publications in this field. Merely for the purpose of exemplification, a graded list of a few recommended arrangements and transcriptions is offered in the following. In these two-piano ensemble pieces, each part approximates the other in difficulty, so that performers of fairly matched ability are called for. The name of the arranger follows that of the composer. Publishers again are indicated by symbols.[4]

GRADES 2 AND 3

TITLE	COMPOSER—ARRANGER	PUBLISHER
Lullaby	Brahms—Dungan	BMC
Flowing River	Chilean—O. Dungan	BMC
Six Folk Songs (The Mannes Music School Ensemble Series)	arr. by Mary Flanner	HFA
Two Country Dances— Shepherds Hey Turkey in the Straw	arr. by June Weybright	WM
Two English Folk Tunes— Oh No, John Polly Put the Kettle On	arr. by June Weybright	WM
Two Fantasies— Tumble Town Cakewalk Tumble Town Waterfall	arr. by June Weybright	WM

GRADES 3 AND 4

Minuet in D, from Suite #4 for Orchestra	Bach—Steiner	GS
Rondo in B Minor, from Suite #2 for Orchestra	Bach—Steiner	GS
Sicilienne	Bach—Maier	CF
The Teacher and the Pupil	Haydn—Maier	CFS
Allegro (Quasi Carillon)	Mozart—Maier	CF
Minuet—From Sonatina in C Minor	Mozart—Maier	CF
The Music Box	Liadow—Hesselberg	CFS
March of the Little Lead Soldiers	Pierne—Riegger	HFA

GRADES 4 AND 5

Sonata, Allegro in G Minor	Scarlatti—Gest	EV
Valse in A Major	Moszkowski—Dieter	CFS
Romance in E Flat Major	Rubinstein—Scionti	TP

It becomes the final expediency of duo-pianism considered in this chapter to combine educational benefits with a working method of exploring the gamut of musical literature. In the words of Josef and Rosina Lhevinne,[5] "it is the finest practice possible for developing reading facility as well as for making the acquaintance of new music." These indeed are the two outstanding advantages which the ensemble has to offer to the amateur: Two-piano playing leads a pleasant road to *prima*

---

4. For key of publishers, see Book III, *The Literature*, Chapter XXIV, *Original Two-Piano Music*.
5. *Four Hands that Play as Two*, "The Etude," December 1933, p. 809.

vista proficiency, and at the same time it provides inviting avenues to the treasures of the entire literature of music.

Arrangements from the master works of the symphonic and chamber music repertoire will furnish edification without end. Where the piano solo condensations of larger scores are awkward and tedious to play, and remain inadequate in their representation of the original composition, the arrangements for two pianos assume such symphonic power and such richness of sonorities that they succeed in the reproduction of the orchestral idiom and in the projection of the musical essence. Within a brief comment, *Grove's Dictionary of Music and Musicians* points out this very function of the piano ensemble as follows:[6] "A large quantity of orchestral and other music has been arranged for . . . piano duet, the comparative facility in performance making such works more readily accessible to the amateur."

For the specific purpose of indicating the extent of the literature which may be explored in the two-piano arrangements of symphonic works, the following are enumerated:

COMPOSER	TITLE OF WORK	ARRANGER	PUBLISHER
Bach, Johann Sebastian	Brandenburg Concerti Nos. 2, 4, 5, 6	Gust. Krug	BH
Bach, Johann Sebastian	The Art of Fugue	Erich Schwebsch	KA
Beethoven, Ludwig van	Symphony No. 1, op. 21	Ernst Naumann	BH
Beethoven, Ludwig van	Symphony No. 2, op. 36	Ernst Naumann	BH
Beethoven, Ludwig van	Symphony No. 3, op. 55	Karl Czerny	SIR
the same		Selmar Bagge	BH
Beethoven, Ludwig van	Symphony No. 4, op. 60	Ernst Naumann	BH
Beethoven, Ludwig van	Symphony No. 5, op. 67	M. C. Eberwein	BH
the same		Ernst Naumann	BH
Beethoven, Ludwig van	Symphony No. 6, op. 68	M. C. Eberwein	BH
the same		Ernst Naumann	BH
Beethoven, Ludwig van	Symphony No. 7, op. 92	Ernst Naumann	BH
Beethoven, Ludwig van	Symphony No. 8, op. 93	Ernst Naumann	BH
Beethoven, Ludwig van	Symphony No. 9, op. 125	Franz Liszt	SO
the same		Ernst Naumann	BH
Berlioz, Hector	Romeo and Juliet, op. 17	Otto Singer	L, UE
Borodin, Alex.	Symphony No. 1	Bessel	BH
Borodin, Alex.	Symphony No. 2	Bessel	BH
Brahms, Johannes	Serenade, op. 11	Paul Klengel	SIR
Brahms, Johannes	Serenade, op. 16	Paul Klengel	SIR
Brahms, Johannes	Symphony No. 1, op. 68		SIR, UE
Brahms, Johannes	Symphony No. 2, op. 73		SIR, UE
Brahms, Johannes	Symphony No. 3, op. 90	Brahms	SIR
Brahms, Johannes	Symphony No. 4, op. 98	Brahms	SIR
Bruckner, Anton	Symphony No. 4	Walter Magnus	UE
Bruckner, Anton	Symphony No. 7	Herm. Behn	UE
Bruckner, Anton	Symphony No. 8	Walter Magnus	UE
Chausson, Ernest	Symphony, op. 20	Geo. Humbert	ROL

---

6. Volume II, page 103, section "Duet."

COMPOSER	TITLE OF WORK	ARRANGER	PUBLISHER
Debussy, Claude	Images No. 1, Gigues No. 2, Iberia No. 3, Rondes de printemps	André Caplet	DFC
Debussy, Claude	La mer	André Caplet	DFC
Debussy, Claude	Nocturnes 1. Nuages 2. Fêtes 3. Sirènes	Maurice Ravel	J
Debussy, Claude	Printemps, Suite symphonique	A. Benfeld	DFC
Delius, Frederick	A dance rhapsody	Percy Grainger	L
Dohnányi, Ernst von	Variations on a Nursery Tune, op. 25	St. v. Kodula	SIR
Dukas, Paul	Symphony in C	Geo. Humbert	ROL
Dvořák, Antonin	Symphony No. 5, op. 95 "From the New World"	Paul Juon	SIR
Fauré, Gabriel	Pelléas et Mélisande, Suite, op. 80		H
Fournier, Paul	Toccata, op. 20 Etude symphonique		DFC
Franck, César	Les Eolides		EN, LIT
Franck, César	Redemption	Pierre de Bréville	HE
Franck, César	Symphony in D minor	J. Griset	H
Gade, Niels W.	Symphony No. 1, op. 5	Aug. Horn	K
Gade, Niels W.	Symphony No. 4, op. 20	Aug. Horn	K
Glazunow, Alex.	Moyen-âge (From the Mid- dle-Ages), Suite, op. 79		BE
Goetz, Hermann	Symphony, op. 9	Salomon Jadassohn	K
Handel, G. F.	Concerto grosso op. 3, No. 2	Gust. Krug	BH
Handel, G. F.	Concerto grosso op. 6, No. 2	Gust. Krug	BH
Honegger, Arthur	Chant de joie		SE
Indy, Vincent d'	Wallenstein, op. 12		DFC
Indy, Vincent d'	Symphony on a French Mountain Air, op. 25		H
Indy, Vincent d'	Istar Variations, op. 42		DFC
Indy, Vincent d'	Medée, Suite, op. 47		DFC
Indy, Vincent d'	Symphony No. 2, op. 57	Marcel Labey	DFC
Lalo, Edouard	Symphony Espagnole, op. 21 (for violin and orchestra)		DFC
Liszt, Franz	Two Episodes from Lenau's Faust 1. Der naechtliche Zug 2. Tanz in der Dorfschenke (Mephisto Waltz)	Fritz Stade	SUB
Liszt, Franz	A Faust Symphony		SUB
Liszt, Franz	A Symphony after Dante's Divina Commedia		BH
Mackenzie, Alex.	Burns, Second Scotch Rhapsody, op. 24	G. Alibrandi	NOV
Mahler, Gustav	Symphony No. 2	Hermann Behn	UE

COMPOSER	TITLE OF WORK	ARRANGER	PUBLISHER
Massenet, Jules	Suite, Scènes pittoresques Marche Air de ballet Angelus	Otto Singer	SO
Miaskowsky, Nik.	Symphony No. 12, op. 35		RUS, UE
Mozart, Wolfgang A.	Symphony No. 39, K.543	Otto Singer	PE
Mozart, Wolfgang A.	Symphony No. 40, K.550	Otto Singer	PE
Mozart, Wolfgang A.	Symphony No. 41, K.551	Otto Singer	PE
Mozart, Wolfgang A.	Maurerische Trauermusik, K. 477	Paul Graf Waldersee	BH
Moussorgsky, Modest	A Night on the Bald Mountain	Evstafieff	BES
Pfitzner, Hans	Little Symphony, op. 44	Otto Wittenbecher	MB
Pierné, Gabriel	L'an mil. Poème symphonique		EN
Raff, Joachim	Symphony No. 3, op. 153 "In the Forest"	Sal. Jadassohn	K
Respighi, Ottorino	The Pines of Rome; Symphonic Poem		GR
Rimsky-Korsakow, Nik.	Antar, op. 9 (Symphony No. 2)		BES
Rimsky-Korsakow, Nik.	Capriccio espagnol, op. 34	A. Schaefer	BE
Rimsky-Korsakow, Nik.	Scheherezade, op. 35	Geo. Humbert	BE
Saint-Saens, Camille	Symphony No. 1, op. 2	A. Benfeld	CO
Saint-Saens, Camille	Suite, op. 49	Gaston Choisnel	DFC
Saint-Saens, Camille	Symphony No. 2, op. 55	Claude Debussy	DFC
Saint-Saens, Camille	Suite Algérienne, op. 60		DFC
Saint-Saens, Camille	Rhapsodie d'Auvergne, op. 73		DFC
Saint-Saens, Camille	Symphony No. 3, op. 78		DFC
Schoenberg, Arnold	Five Orchestral Pieces, op. 16	Anton v. Webern	PE
Schubert, Franz	Symphony No. 7	Karl Klindworth	BH
	the same	Otto Singer	PE
Schubert, Franz	Symphony No. 8 (Unfinished)	Leop. Alex. Zellner	CRA
	the same	Otto Singer	PE
Schumann, Robert	Symphony No. 1, op. 38	Karl Burchard	BH
Schumann, Robert	Overture, Scherzo, and Finale, op. 52	Friedr. Hermann	K
Schumann, Robert	Symphony No. 2, op. 61	Jul. Otto Grimm	BH
Schumann, Robert	Symphony No. 3, op. 97	Jul. Otto Grimm	BH
Schumann, Robert	Symphony No. 4, op. 122	Jos. Sautier	BH
Scriabin, Alex.	Poem of Extacy, op. 54	Léon Conus	BE
Scriabin, Alex.	Prometheus, op. 60	Leonid Sabaniew	RUM
Smetana, Friedr.	My Fatherland 1. Visegrad 2. The Moldau	H. Trnecek	UR
Strauss, Richard	Don Juan, op. 20	Otto Singer	PE
Strauss, Richard	Macbeth, op. 23	Otto Singer	PE
Strauss, Richard	Death and Transfiguration, op. 24	Otto Singer	PE
Strauss, Richard	Till Eulenspiegel's Merry Pranks, op. 28	Otto Singer	PE

COMPOSER	TITLE OF WORK	ARRANGER	PUBLISHER
Strauss, Richard	Thus Spoke Zarathustra, op. 30	Otto Singer	PE
Strauss, Richard	Don Quixote, op. 35	Otto Singer	PE
Strauss, Richard	A Hero's Life, op. 40	Otto Singer	L,UE
Strauss, Richard	Sinfonia domestica, op. 53		BB
Strauss, Richard	Symphony of the Alps, op. 64	Otto Singer	L
Svendsen, Joh. S.	Zorahayd, op. 11	Rich. Lange	HN
Tschaikowsky, Peter	Symphony No. 2, op. 17	A. N. Schaefer	BES
Tschaikowsky, Peter	Suite, op. 43	A. N. Schaefer	PJ
Tschaikowsky, Peter	Capriccio italien, op. 45	Eduard Langer	PJ
Tschaikowsky, Peter	Symphony No. 6, op. 74	A. N. Schaefer	PJ
	the same	Otto Singer	PE

The large and rich literature of orchestral overtures likewise can be studied and enjoyed in many arrangements for two pianos. A representative selection follows herewith:

COMPOSER	TITLE OF WORK	ARRANGER	PUBLISHER
Albert, Eugen d'	The Improvisor	Emil Kronke	BB
Beethoven, L. van	Coriolan, op. 62	Leop. Langer	CRA
Beethoven, L. van	Fidelio, op. 72	Leop. Langer	CRA
	the same	Karl Burchard	SIR
Beethoven, L. van	Egmont, op. 84	Kumanin	OE
	the same	Karl Burchard	LI
Berlioz, Hector	Roman Carnival, op. 9	Otto Singer	L, UE
Berlioz, Hector	Benvenuto Cellini, op. 23	Otto Singer	L
Brahms, Joh.	Academic Festival Overture, op. 80	Paul Klengel	SIR
Brahms, Joh.	Tragic Overture, op. 81	Paul Klengel	SIR
Cornelius, Peter	Der Barbier von Bagdad	Hermann Behn	KNT
Gade, Niels W.	Im Hochland, op. 7	Aug. Horn	K
Indy, Vincent d'	Fervaal, op. 40	G. Choisnel	DFC
Joachim, Joseph	Overture to Shakespeare's Henry IV	Joh. Brahms	SIR
Liszt, Franz	Fest-Vorspiel	Rob. Pflughaupt	DEU
Mascagni, Pietro	Cavalleria rusticana	Emil Kronke	BB
Massenet, Jules	Phèdre	Adolf Beyschlag	SO
Mendelssohn, Felix	Die Hochzeit des Camacho, op. 10	Friedr. Hermann	BH
Mendelssohn, Felix	Midsummernight's Dream, op. 21	Aug. Horn	BH
Mendelssohn, Felix	The Hebrides, op. 26	Ernst Naumann	BH
Mendelssohn, Felix	Meeresstille und glueckliche Heimkehr, op. 27	Aug. Horn	BH
Mendelssohn, Felix	Melusine, op. 32	Aug. Horn	BH
Mendelssohn, Felix	Overture to the oratorio Paulus, op. 36	Friedr. Hermann	BH
Mendelssohn, Felix	Overture to Racine's Anthalia, op. 74	Ernst Naumann	BH
Mendelssohn, Felix	Die Heimkehr aus der Fremde, op. 89	Ernst Naumann	BH
Mendelssohn, Felix	Overture to Ruy Blas, op 95	Leo Grill	K
	the same	F. Hermann	BH
Mendelssohn, Felix	Trumpet Overture, op. 101	A. Horn	BH
Meyerbeer, Giacomo	Struensee	Friedr. Brissler	LI

COMPOSER	TITLE OF WORK	ARRANGER	PUBLISHER
Mozart, W. A.	Ascanio in Alba	Paul Graf Waldersee	BH
Mozart, W. A.	The Magic Flute	Ferruccio Busoni	BH
Reissiger, K. G.	Die Felsenmuehle von Estallières, op. 71	K. Burchard	SIR
Rossini, G.	William Tell	Hermann Behn	SO
Schillings, Max	Ingwelde	Hermann Behn	UE
Schillings, Max	Der Pfeifertag	Hermann Behn	BB
Schillings, Max	Symphonic Prologue to King Oedipus, op. 11	Hermann Behn	BB
Schubert, Franz	Rosamunde, op. 26	L. A. Zellner	CRA
Schubert, Franz	Two Entr'acts from Rosamunde	L. A. Zellner	CRA
Schubert, Franz	Alfonso and Estrella, op. 69	L. A. Zellner	CRA
Schubert, Franz	Fierrabas, op. 76	L. A. Zellner	CRA
Smetana, Fr.	The Bartered Bride	Emil Kronke	BB
Strauss, Richard	Guntram, op. 25	Otto Singer	OE
Sullivan, Arthur	Ouv. di ballo	A. O'Leary	NOV
Suppé, Franz v.	Poet and Peasant		GR, UE
Tschaikowsky, Peter	"1812" Overture, op. 49	Clara A. Korn	PJ
Wagner, Richard	Three Preludes: 1. Meistersinger 2. Tannhäuser 3. Tristan and Isolde	Max Reger	PE
Wagner, Richard	A. Faust Overture	Karl Burchard	BH
Wagner, Richard	Lohengrin	Gust. Sandré	BH
Wagner, Richard	The Mastersingers of Nuremberg	Hermann Behn	SO
Wagner, Richard	Rienzi	Rich. Kleinmichel	OE
Wagner, Richard	Tannhäuser		OE
Wagner, Richard	Tristan and Isolde	Alfred Pringsheim	
	the same	Hermann Behn	BH
Weber, Karl Maria v.	Euryanthe	August Horn	LI
	the same	Hermann Behn	K
Weber, Karl Maria v.	Der Freischuetz	August Horn	LI
	the same	Hermann Behn	K
Weber, Karl Maria v.	Jubel Overture	August Horn	LI
Weber, Karl Maria v.	Oberon	August Horn	LI
Weber, Karl Maria v.	Preziosa	August Horn	LI

A short selection of orchestral dances and marches, arranged for two pianos, will indicate the possibilities of gaining a closer acquaintance with this engaging genre of symphonic music.

COMPOSER	TITLE OF WORK	ARRANGER	PUBLISHER
Beethoven, Ludwig van	Turkish March from "The Ruins of Athens," op. 113	Louis Rée	L
Jadassohn, Salomon	Ballet Music in Six Canons, op. 58	Karl Reinecke	BH
Strauss, Johann	The Blue Danube Waltzes, op. 314	Joh. Reichert	STE
	the same	Christophe Le Fleming	AU
Strauss, Johann	Tales from the Vienna Woods, op. 325	Christophe Le Fleming	STE

COMPOSER	TITLE OF WORK	ARRANGER	PUBLISHER
Strauss, Johann	Wine, Woman, and Song, op. 333	Hans Immetsberger	STE
Strauss, Johann	Vienna Blood, op. 354	Willy Rehberg	STE
Strauss, Johann	You and You, op. 367	Joh. Reichert	STE
Strauss, Johann	Roses from the South, op. 388	Willy Rehberg	STE
Strauss, Johann	Voices of Spring, op. 410	Willy Rehberg	STE
Strauss, Johann	Emperor Waltz, op. 437	Hans Immctsberger	STE
Strauss, Josef	Dorfschwalben aus Oester- reich, op. 164	Hans Immetsberger	STE
Wagner, Richard	Huldigungsmarsch	Otto Singer	SO
Wagner, Richard	Kaisermarsch	Rich. Kleinmichcl	PE
Wagner, Richard	Ride of the Valkyries	Heinr. Ehrlich	SO
Wagner, Richard	Siegfried's Rhine Journey from "Götterdämmerung"	Otto Singer	SO
Wagner, Richard	Siegfried's Death and Funeral March from "Götterdäm- merung"	H. Ehrlich	SO
Wagner, Richard	Ride of the Valkyries Funeral March from "Götterdämmerung"	Otto Singer	PE

The chamber forms, from the smallest to the larger ensembles, are
known by connoisseurs to contain some of the most beautiful music in
existence. The instrumental combinations originally called for are at
times difficult or impossible to assemble. In their arrangements for two
pianos, many gems of the chamber music literature can be made accessible,
such as the following:

COMPOSER	TITLE OF WORK	ARRANGER	PUBLISHER
Beethoven, L. van	Trio in F flat, op. 8	Leopold Langer	CRA
Beethoven, L. van	Serenade, op. 8	Leopold Langer	CRA
Beethoven, L. van	Trios, op. 9 No. 1 (G) No. 2 (D)	Leopold Langer	CRA
Beethoven, L. van	Sonata, op. 12, No. 1	C. Krägen	BH
Beethoven, L. van	Quintet, op. 16	Otto Lessmann	LI
	the same	Gust. Rösler	BH
Beethoven, L. van	Quartets , op. 18	C. G. Lickl	GR
Beethoven, L. van	Septet, op. 20	C. G. Lickl	CRA
	the same	Leopold Langer	CRA
	the same	Ad. Ruthardt	PE
Beethoven, L. van	Sonata, op. 24 (F)	C. Krägen	BH
Beethoven, L. van	Sonata, op. 47 (A)	C. Krägen	BH
Beethoven, L. van	Sonata, op. 69 (A)	Leopold Langer	CRA
Beethoven, L. van	Trio, op. 70, No. 1	Leopold Langer	CRA
Beethoven, L. van	Sextet, op. 71	K. Burchard	BRA
Beethoven, L. van	Quartet, op. 74	E. Moos	FBG
Beethoven, L. van	Quartet, op. 95	Emil Moos	K
	the same	M. Balakirew	BES
Beethoven, L. van	Quartet, op. 127	Emil Moos	K
Beethoven, L. van	Quartet, op. 130	Emil Moos	K
Beethoven, L. van	Quartet, op. 131	Emil Moos	K
Beethoven, L. van	Quartet, op. 132	Emil Moos	K

COMPOSER	TITLE OF WORK	ARRANGER	PUBLISHER
Beethoven, L. van	Grosse Fuge, op. 133	Harold Bauer	GS
Beethoven, L. van	Quartet, op. 135	Emil Moos	K
Brahms, Joh.	Trio, op. 8	Otto Lehmann	SIR
Brahms, Joh.	Sextet, op. 18	P. Klengel	SIR
Brahms, Joh.	Quartet, op. 25	P. Klengel	SIR
Brahms, Joh.	Quartet, op. 26	P. Klengel	SIR
Brahms, Joh.	Sextet, op. 36	P. Klengel	SIR
Brahms, Joh.	Trio, op. 40	Max Laurischkus	SIR
Brahms, Joh.	Two Quartets, op. 51	Otto Lehmann	SIR
Brahms, Joh.	Quartet, op. 60	P. Klengel	SIR
Brahms, Joh.	Quartet, op. 67	Aug. Grueters	SIR
Brahms, Joh.	Quintet, op. 88	Otto Lehmann	SIR
Brahms, Joh.	Trio, op. 101	Max Laurischkus	SIR
Brahms, Joh.	Quintet, op. 111	Paul Klengel	SIR
Brahms, Joh.	Trio, op. 114	Otto Lehmann	SIR
Brahms, Joh.	Quintet, op. 115	Paul Klengel	SIR
Brahms, Joh.	Two Sonatas, op. 120	Max Laurischkus	SIR
Chausson, Ernest	Concert, op. 21	A. Pierret	ROL
Chausson, Ernest	Quartet, op. 30		ROL
Dvorák, Anton.	Quintet, op. 81	A. Schultz	SIR
Franck, César	Quintet, F minor	J. Griset	H
Gade, Niels W.	Noveletten, op. 29 for Trio	F. B. Busoni	BH
Glinka, Michail	Sextet, E flat	S. Liapunow	PJ
Glinka, Michail	Trio, D minor	A. Nemerowski	PJ
Hummel, Joh. Nep.	Grand Septuor, op. 74	Frz. Kullak	STE
Hummel, Joh. Nep.	Septuor militaire, op. 114		HS
Indy, Vinc. d'	Quartet, op. 45	Gust. Samazeuilh	DFC
Mozart, W. A.	Three Divertimenti K. 253, 270, 289	Eugen Segnitz	K
Mozart, W. A.	Quartets, K. 478, 493	Karl Burchard	AND
Mozart, W. A.	Quintets, K. 614, 406	S. Neukomm	HOF
Mozart, W. A.	Quintet, K. 452		BH
Mozart, W. A.	Quintet, K. 516	C. Kraegen	HH
Mozart, W. A.	Divertimento, K. 563	K. Burchard	GBR
Mozart, W. A.	Quintet, K. 581	K. Burchard	AND
Onslow, George	Quintet, op. 70	F. Mockwitz	K
Ravel, Maurice	Quartet, F major	Lucien Garban	DFC
Ries, Ferd.	Trio, op. 143	A. Michelot	SO
Saint-Saens, Camille	Septuor, op. 65	A. Benfeld	DFC
Schubert, Franz	Trio, op. 99	Th. Herbert	L
Schubert, Franz	Trio, op. 100	Th. Herbert	L
Schubert, Franz	Quintet, op. 114	F. G. Jansen	LI
Schumann, Robert	Quintet, op. 44	Wald. Waege	BH
Schumann, Robert	Quartet, op. 47	Wald. Waege	BH
	the same	Aug. Reinhard	SO
Schumann, Robert	Studies for Pedalfluegel, op. 58	Isidor Philipp	DFC
	the same	D. Yzelen	LE
Spohr, Louis	Quintet, op. 130	Noble	AU
Tschaikowsky, Peter	Trio, op. 50	P. W. Zapolsky	SIK
Weber, Karl Maria v.	Grand Duo concert, op. 48	A. Henselt	LI
Weber, Karl Maria v.	Divertimento, op. 38	F. G. Jansen	LI

As has been pointed out at an earlier occasion,[7] the literature for the organ and the harpsichord, honorable with tradition and inherent riches, can find an adequate representation through the two-piano medium. Listed here are only a few of the available arrangements; they may serve as an incentive for more intensive study of this much neglected branch of music literature.

COMPOSER	TITLE OF WORK	ARRANGER	PUBLISHER
Bach, Joh. Seb.	Selected Compositions 12 volumes	Isidore Philipp	GR
Bach, Joh. Seb.	Goldberg Variations	Max Reger	K
Bach, Joh. Seb.	Fantasy and Fugue in G minor	Otto Singer	STE
Bach, Joh. Seb.	Passacaglia	I. Philipp	DFC
	the same	Herm. Keller	STE
	the same	A. Chasins	JF
Bach, Joh. Seb.	Prelude and Fugue in A minor	I. Philipp	DFC
	the same	Otto Singer	STE
Bach, Joh. Seb.	Prelude and Fugue in D major	Otto Singer	STE
Bach, Joh. Seb.	Prelude and Fugue in D Minor	I. Philipp	DFC
Bach, Joh. Seb.	Prelude and Fugue in E major	I. Philipp	DFC
Bach, Joh. Seb.	Prelude and Fugue in G major	I. Philipp	DFC
Bach, Joh. Seb.	Sonata in E flat	Pierre von Mossin	RB
	the same	Herm. Keller	STE
Bach, Joh. Seb.	Sonatas (Trio Sonatas) Nos. 3, 4, 5, 6	Victor Babin	BO
Buxtehude, Dietrich	Toccata No. 2	W. D. Wassiliew	RUS, UE
Handel, G. F.	Concerto No. 5	Hannah Klein	JF
Mendelssohn, F.	Sonatas Nos. 1-6, op. 65	I. Philipp	DFC
Schumann, Robert	Studies for Pedalflügel, op. 56	Aug. Grueters	AND

Not only instrumental compositions, but also many vocal works of large dimensions have been arranged for two pianos and thus can be brought to the closer knowledge and frequent enjoyment of the music lover. Available are two-piano settings of such monuments of the vocal literature as the following:

COMPOSER	TITLE OF WORK	ARRANGER	PUBLISHER
Brahms, Joh.	Three Excerpts from the "German Requiem"	Fritz Stade	RB
Gade, Niels W.	Spring Fantasy, op. 23	Aug. Winding	BH
Pizzetti, Ildebrando	Canti	Maffeo Zanon	GR
Reger, Max	Requiem, op. 144b	Karl Hasse	PE
Verdi, Guiseppe	Messa da requiem	Rud. von Lichtenstein	GR
Wagner, Richard	50 Symphonic Excerpts from his Music Dramas	Herm. Behn	BH
Wagner, Richard	Selections from his Operas	Max Reger	PE
Wagner, Richard	Scene from the Rhinedaughters from "Götterdämmerung"	Julius Buths	SO

The foregoing selection of available two-piano arrangements from the

---

7. Part B, *The Creative Medium*, Chapter XX, *Special Problems, Techniques, and Opportunities.*

literature of great music does not represent by any means a comprehensive survey of the existing repertoire.[8] Rather, it was intended only as an indication of the virtually unlimited opportunities for edification which can be derived from the two-piano medium. There is this further thought: What at first are the practical means of an educational and appreciative process, eventually may shed the connotations of pedagogic material and become the source of an ultimate musical enjoyment. In this last realm, nothing distinguishes the professional musician of concert caliber from the amateur of only modest ability. To both, duo-pianism can serve as a vehicle of inspiration and thereby as an artistic medium, fully capable of expressing the concept of beauty.

If the question ever be asked "Should pianists play non-piano music?", here is an appropriate answer which Josef and Rosina Lhevinne have provided:[9]

"Decidedly they should. There is no better way of making the acquaintance of the great symphonic and chamber music works than to play them one's self. The piano library is rich—but the greatest music in the world is symphonic. And, without a personal knowledge of it, no one can hope to become a well-rounded musician."

To this voice of authority, Alfred Einstein adds his own with a statement which is even more compelling in its appraisal of the piano ensemble as a sesame to music's treasures in an all-inclusive sense. The following words of Einstein provide a fitting conclusion to this discussion:[10]

". . . arrangements . . . for two pianos . . . conquered the entire province of musical literature for the home."

Could higher recognition be accorded to any form of musical study and enjoyment?

---

8. Still expecting publication are many masterly arrangements from the instrumental standard literature, as for instance several two-piano settings by Louis Victor Saar. The latter arranged for the medium such monumental works as the *Passacaglia* and *Chaconne* by Bach, the *Concerto Grosso* in D minor by Vivaldi, and *Prelude, Adagio, and Fugue* in B minor by Giovanni Battista Martini.
9. *Four Hands That Play as Two*, "The Etude," December 1933.
10. *Music in the Romantic Era*, page 200.

BOOK III

THE LITERATURE

Chapter

CHAPTER XXIII

THE STANDARD REPERTOIRE

1. STATEMENT OF EXTENT AND CONFINES

In the process of selection, as well as during the discussion of some compositions written for two pianos, four hands, without and with ensemble, a number of criteria have been set up for guidance, such as

1. the place of importance in the history of music, and the aesthetic significance of the composition in regard to its period;
2. the rank of the composer generally, and his attention to the two-piano medium specifically;
3. the exceptional characteristics of the work, such as texture, structure, style, conception and realization of the pianoforte idiom, and technical aspects of performance;
4. the influence of the composition on the particular epoch of its creation, and its generating power;
5. the artistic success of the work and its popular acceptance;
6. the particular message of the work to the present day (1950).

Various authoritative references have frequently been employed, because it is felt that this chapter of analytic descriptions will gain by being placed on a broad platform of views and opinions. All quotations interspersed in the text are drawn from such qualified critics who have made special studies of the composers whom they are discussing.

This chapter is intended and undertaken as a representative cross-section only. The inclusion of any particular work is based on one or more of the aforementioned standards; the omission of a composition, on the other hand, does not imply its lesser importance or lack of significance. However, limitations of space need to be taken into account, and the purpose of this chapter is amply fulfilled if stimulation towards further evaluation of the existing two-piano literature is aroused.

2. LIST OF SELECTIONS

This commentary is presented in a sequence largely adhering to the evolution of style periods. Included into the discussion are the following compositions:

François Couperin: Allemande à deux Clavecins

Johann Sebastian Bach: Concerto in C major for Two Claviers and Orchestra

Wolfgang Amadeus Mozart: Concerto in E Flat Major for Two Pianos and Orchestra (K.365)

Wolfgang Amadeus Mozart: Sonata in D major for Two Pianofortes (K. 448)

Muzio Clementi: Two Sonatas, opus 12, opus 46

François Frédéric Chopin: Rondo in C, opus 73

Robert Schumann: Andante and Variations, opus 46

Johannes Brahms: Variations on a Theme by Haydn, opus 56b

Camille Saint-Saens: Variations on a Theme by Beethoven, opus 35

Cécile Chaminade: Andante, opus 59

Anton Arensky: Suite, opus 15

Sergei Rachmaninoff: Suite No. 1, opus 5

Sergei Rachmaninoff: Suite No. 2, opus 17

Max Reger: Introduction, Passacaglia, and Fugue, opus 96

Claude Debussy: En Blanc et Noir

Leopold Godowsky: Alt Wien (Old Vienna)

Francis Poulenc: Concerto in D minor for Two Pianos and Orchestra

Darius Milhaud: Scaramouche, Suite for Two Pianos

Edward Burlingame Hill: Jazz Studies for Two Pianos

Beryl Rubinstein: Suite for Two Pianos

Igor Stravinsky: Concerto for Two Solo Pianos

Béla Bartók: Sonata for Two Pianos and Percussion

Paul Hindemith: Sonata for Two Pianos (1942)

Bohuslav Martinu: Concerto for Two Pianos and Orchestra

Victor Babin: Etudes for Two Pianos

3. ANALYSES

François Couperin: Allemande à deux Clavecins[1]

This composition is found at the beginning of the "Ninth Order" or suite of Couperin's four-volume collection of pieces for the harpsichord. Contained in the second volume which was first published in 1716, it is one of the earliest known works for two keyboards to possess true signifi-

---

1. See also Book I, *The History*, Chapter II, *The Pioneers*.

cance. Bach who derived a great deal of instruction from Couperin's harpsichord style in general, may also have received some particular inspiration for his own works for multiple claviers from this composition.

The Allemande is in the key of A major. As is usual with Couperin's pieces for the clavecin, the dance form is highly stylized. This means to say that the composer's artistic imagination always was strong enough to successfully adapt the French taste for delineative dancing to keyboard presentation. Couperin's faculty in this respect was based on an instinctive sense of the technical possibilities of the harpsichord.

The ornamentation is intricate and characteristic of Couperin's idiom in which the late Baroque and early Rococo styles are welded together. The composer shows the greatest skill in combining the two parts. The richly decorated music is equally demanding on each of the performers.

If Couperin has aptly been called the "father of French piano music," because of the great importance of his pieces for the harpsichord, the duo-keyboard literature owes him a debt far exceeding the national restriction, for this brilliant and masterly early work.[2]

Johann Sebastian Bach: Concerto in C Major for Two Claviers and Orchestra

Bach wrote three concertos for two claviers and orchestra, the first and third of which are in the key of C minor, whereas the second has the tonality of C major. The latter concerto is the only one which Bach originally conceived for this combination, both C minor concerti being arrangements from their former settings for two violins, or violin and oboe, respectively.

The C major concerto is the great cornerstone of two-piano literature, resting—as if it were—in the Baroque era and supporting the entire arch of duo-pianistic history into the present, where an equivalent pillar might be recognized in Stravinsky's Concerto for Two Solo Pianos. This comparison is made notwithstanding the orchestral accompaniment in the Bach work, for "the piece sounds well for two pianos unaccompanied" (Hutcheson). As a matter of fact, the slow movement is played by the two harpsichords alone *("quartetto tacet"),* and the solo instruments also are in full command during the opening of the final fugue, the entrance of the orchestra being delayed for some time.

It is in this concerto that Bach's experimentations with the form of the clavier concerto attained a peak of excellence. His achievement is nothing short of epoch making for two reasons which David Ewen points out as follows:[3]

"In their combination of two pianos (rare for the time) the two voices become

---

2. See Illustration No. 2.
3. *Music for the Millions,* pp. 14-15.

one in a remarkable cohesion; the thematic material is assigned skillfully now to one piano, now to the other, in an inextricable communion. They are outstanding, further, because in these two concertos . . . a bold step is taken toward the concerto form of the future. A greater independence from orchestral bondage is here achieved by Bach; in the slow movement of the C major concerto, for example, the two pianos perform without any accompaniment whatever. Besides, in both concertos, Bach makes use of the cadenza, an invariable feature of the later concerto.

"The closing movement of the C major concerto is one of the most impressive fugues Bach ever wrote, a movement majestic for its architectonic construction, in which the details are presented with remarkable clarity of writing."

For a penetrating analysis of this concerto, and of the development of the concerto form generally, also refer to the quotations from Spitta's and Schweitzer's essays on this work in Book I, "The History," Chapter III, "Bach."

Wolfgang Amadeus Mozart: Concerto in E Flat Major for Two Pianos and Orchestra (K. 365)

The first movement, in E flat major, 4-4 time, is marked *Allegro*. Most of the thematic material is introduced by the orchestra and then is developed by both solo instruments and the ensemble. The character of the movement is vigorous. The principal theme opens with a downward leap of an octave; this same leap, in the identical rhythmic pattern, is to be found at the beginning of Mozart's Symphony No. 34 in C major (K. 338) and occurs also at the opening of his overture to the opera *La Clemenza di Tito* (K. 621).

The second movement, in B flat major, 3-4 time, is beautifully tranquil. The tempo marking is *Andante*. Strings, oboe and bassoon announce the main subject which soon is taken up by the pianos; the latter produce a new subject. The movement ends calmly with a recapitulation of the first section.

The last movement, marked *Allegro,* in E flat major, 2-4 time, is typically Mozartean in the treatment of the rondo form. There is a lively counterplay of musical thoughts, exchanged *ad variam* by the soloists and the orchestra. The movement brings the work to a joyous conclusion.

This gay concerto certainly bears no trace of the composer's troubles with his keyboard partner, Josephine von Aurnhammer.[4] Composed in 1780, the work was given its first performance the following year in Vienna by Mozart and Fräulein v. Aurnhammer, the young woman with whom the composer did a considerable amount of playing on two keyboards. Originally, the concerto seems to have been written with the intention that Mozart should present it in concert with his sister, Maria Anna, but there is no record that Wolfgang and "Nannerl" ever performed it together.

Mozart, for the first time, used bassoons in the orchestration of a piano concerto. As for the clarinet parts, these were not added until the second

4. See Book I, *The History*, Chapter IV, *Mozart.*

performance. The orchestration includes one flute, two each of oboes, clarinets, bassoons, horns and trumpets, in addition to strings and kettle-drums, the usual instrumentation of his time.

The concerto has held the most prominent place among its genre. To this day, it is "by far the best known and most frequently played of the handful of compositions for this combination of instruments" (Affelder).

Wolfgang Amadeus Mozart: Sonata in D Major for Two Pianofortes (K. 448)

"In Mozart's hands the piano sonata became richer and deeper in its musical content, more elastic in its form, and more sure of its direction and movement than it was with Haydn." A perfect example for this statement by David Ewen[5] is the Sonata for Two Pianos in D major which has become a most valuable component in the repertoire of original two-piano music.

This sonata is in three movements which are marked, respectively, *Allegro con spirito, Andante,* and *Allegro molto.*

The first movement, *Allegro,* has a spirited principal theme and a cap-tivatingly charming secondary subject. Brilliant passages abound in anti-phonal discourse. The texture, while mostly homophonic in kind, contains a fine contrapuntal passage at the beginning of the development section. The latter is unusually short. The movement is a piece of fluent writing, dramatic at some moments, and sprightly and vivacious at others.

The second movement, marked *Andante,* breathes "that serene and un-troubled beauty which Mozart was capable of creating with such an inde-fatigable pen" (Ewen). The melodic lines are drawn with an ingratiating warmth of feeling, and the element of sweet melancholy at all times is balanced by rhythmic poise.

The concluding movement, in *Allegro molto* tempo, has the outline of a rondo, but the spirit of the contents all but renders meaningless the mechanical aspects of formal composition. Mozart's world of expression is inseparable from his form, and this is the secret of the perfection and unity of his music. The movement abounds in Mozartean joviality and good humor.

Ernest Hutcheson terms this sonata "a masterpiece of antiphonal writ-ing" and goes on to state that it "remains to this day the best composition of its kind."

At any rate, the literature "boasts few works so felicitously written for the two instruments." Throughout the sonata, the music keeps a perfect balance between brilliance and tenderness. "It is Mozartean magic in its feeling of spontaneity, in the ebullience of its spirit, and in its joviality

5. *Music for the Millions,* p. 399.

. . . What appears to the average music lover as simplicity is, to the trained musician, the apotheosis of craftsmanship; the ability to write music that is inevitable in its logic, as inexorable as fate itself; so perfectly chiseled that not a single note is superfluous" (Ewen).

Muzio Clementi: Two Sonatas

These sonatas for two pianos are marked opus 12 and opus 46, respectively (Prosniz). Both are in the key of B flat major. The first has three movements: *Allegro assai—Larghetto espressivo—Presto;* the second consists of only two movements: *Allegro di molto* and *Allegretto, Tempo di Minuetto.*

Muzio Clementi, pianistic heir to Scarlatti and contemporary of Beethoven, compensates to some extent for the failure of his great colleague to write in the two-piano medium. Indeed, the style and sonorities of the sonatas strongly suggest the idiom of Beethoven's early works.

The pieces are fluent, brilliant, concise, yet deeply poetic in several places. They stand in marked difference to the sometimes cumbersome weightiness of the *Gradus ad Parnassum.* Ruthardt calls the smaller, two-movement sonata "most charming," an epitome which should rightly be extended to the first. If Clementi's sonatas are not to be called profound, they are always workmanlike and musically satisfying. Pratt attributes to them resourcefulness and nervous energy, and Frederick Niecks speaks of them as "important poetic achievements, the works in which he has incorporated the greatest emotional intensity possible to him, and where the virtuoso contents himself with being the servant of the idea." For students able to undertake these sonatas for two pianofortes, they will serve as "excellent preparatory material" (Dr. Preston Ware Orem).

The historical importance of the sonatas by Clementi lies in what Parry calls "the divination of the treatment most appropriate to the instrument." It was Clementi who may be said to have inaugurated the era for modern pianoforte playing and composition. His sonatas are "among the very first in which the genuine qualities of modern pianoforte music on a large scale are shown" (Parry).

François Frédéric Chopin: Rondo in C, Opus 73

This is Chopin's only contribution to the literature for two pianos, although the composer is known to have employed a second piano regularly in his teaching studio where it was used for the purpose of demonstration.

The Rondo in C was composed in 1828. Chopin then was only 18 years of age. The late opus number 73 derives from the posthumous publication of a group of Chopin's compositions which was undertaken by Fontana in 1855; the particular works were listed as opus numbers 66 to 74.

The Rondo, despite the composer's youthful age when he penned the work, is typically Chopinesque in many respects. It is an ingratiating piece, both sparkling and sweet at the same time, and saturated with aristocratic refinement. In the repertoire of original compositions for two pianos, Chopin's Rondo remains a foremost and favorite example for the genre of brilliant salon pieces.

The program notes to a recording of the work[6] contain the following reference:

> "This expression of the young Chopin breathes a freshness, an almost naive quality. Filled with the wistfulness and melancholy charm of his youth, a period untouched as yet by the bitterness and disillusionment of later years, the work permeates with delicate grace and melodic beauty. From its improvisational and expectant opening to the grand finish, it is filled with gayety. Polish rhythms, rubato changes, and enchanting modulations fill this music, while each new entrance of the rondo's captivating theme brings with it a refreshing interlude."

Robert Schumann: Andante and Variations, Opus 46

Among the great original works of the two-piano literature, Schumann's opus 46 will always rank in the first line. Aesthetically, this composition establishes a prototype for Romantic feeling in music and could well serve, beyond the purely musical realm, as a striking example for the artistic ideals of the period during which it came to life.

The Andante and Variations, written in 1843, are dedicated to Harriet Parish of Hamburg, but the composition was really designed for Clara Schumann and Felix Mendelssohn by whom it was performed on two pianos at a Gewandhaus concert in Leipzig on August 19, 1843. Originally, the piece was scored by Schumann for two pianos, two violoncellos and horn, but this combination was abandoned when the tryouts revealed a tonal balance unsatisfactory to the composer.

The entire work is encompassed within the tonality of B-flat major, with digressions into related keys occuring now and then. The variations are not numbered and are to be played continuously, with only a brief pause between the sections. From the formal aspect, the treatment is very free, and at times there is little similarity between the melodic and harmonic line of a variation and the theme. As though apologizing for this procedure, Schumann reverts several times to the original theme, almost unchanged by embellishment. The continuity thus established, he digresses again.

Although the variations merge into each other without interruption, they are well defined and therefore can easily be distinguished. Especially lovely is the quiet coda which conveys the impression of an evaporating cloud of sound. Ernest Hutcheson[7] calls the Andante and Variations "beautiful, pianistically grateful, and universally popular." Schauffler, who

---

6. *A Two-Piano Recital*—Luboshutz and Nemenoff, Duo-Pianists, RCA Victor album DM 1047.
7. *The Literature of the Piano*, page 102.

attaches a historic merit to the composition for reasons of the artistic resurrection of the variation form by Schumann[8] gives this critical comment on the work:[9]

"Despite a theme that edges ever so slightly towards the sentimental, and a final variation for which the expressive word 'dinky' might conceivably come to mind, it is a notable composition. With its subtle harmonic, rhythmic, and melodic wealth, and above all with the essence of true Schumann which it distills, the music more than makes up for those defects.

"It breathes a lofty excitement. One feels that it was written for Clara with deep love. The high spots begin with the third variation, where that Schumannian emblem, the descending fifth, is used in the same pivotal way in which it had recently been employed in the Quintet.

"There is something stirringly impressive yet tender about the slow fifth variation; and the blood leaps to the fanfaresque summons of the seventh. In both one seems to hear a long-vanished brazen voice. For this work was originally written for the bizarre co-operation of a horn and two 'cellos with the pair of pianos, before being restricted to the latter. I suppose that Schumann chose these instruments because he was so fond of the deep, rich coloring which we have often remarked. But practical considerations supervened. . . ."

The original version, scored for two pianos, two celli and horn, was given its first public hearing in the United States by Appleton and Field, on the occasion of their Town Hall concert on October 21, 1949, as part of a recital series "Two Pianos Through Four Centuries."

Johannes Brahms: Variations on a Theme by Haydn, Opus 56b

A history and general discussion of this, "the most inspired and inspiring achievement in two-piano literature," has been provided in Book I, "The History," Chapter VII, "Brahms." The work is considered by many duo-pianists and music lovers as their favorite composition in the entire realm, because of the mature splendor of musical projection, and the masterful treatment of the two instruments.

The theme is in B flat major, *Andante* tempo, 2-4 time. The eight variations are marked as follows:

I. *Poco piu animato*
II. *Piu vivace*
III. *Con moto*
IV. *Andante con moto*
V. *Poco Presto (Vivace)*
VI. *Vivace*
VII. *Grazioso*
VIII. *Presto non troppo*

The theme itself is so diversified in rhythm that the rigidity of the variation form which Brahms frames around it never becomes apparent. The first section of the two-part theme contains two periods of five

8. See Book I, *The History,* Chapter VI, *Salon, Chamber Music, Symphonic Workshop* pp. 364-366.
9. *Florestan,* pp. 364-366.

measures each. The second section begins with two phrases of four measures each and closes with an expanded period of eleven measures; the last could be sub-divided into groups of four and seven measures, respectively. This freedom of periodic structure is characteristic of Haydn, and Brahms "treats the irregularity with unfailing humor and understanding" (Hutcheson).

Beginning with this theme of great nobility, Brahms embarks on his masterly discourse of variants and transitions. The first variation is built on the last five notes of the chorale theme, those solemn tones which, to use Tovey's image, toll like a bell throughout the variation, as they indeed ring through the entire work. This first essay has an intricately rhythmed tracery which is freely woven above strong, marked phrases. In mood it is pensive and softly animated.

The second variation shows the character of a gypsy dance elaborated against decorative passages. It is marked *Allegretto* and utilizes a rhythmic figure derived from the chorale. This rhythmic figure becomes the "pulsating center around which independent melodic material is organized" (Veinus). The essence of this variation, which is in B flat minor, is of a strident sort and furnishes a beautiful contrast to the warm inspiration radiating from the third variation which is tranquil and flowing in movement.

A melancholy mood breathes from Variation No. IV. There are two gentle melodies in the minor key which are given out in counterpoint to each other; the principal theme towards the end is heard in double octaves. The composer's prescription *dolce e simplice* gives the direction for this variation, which Evans calls "highly scientific," because of the rather complicated species of polyphony which is involved. Brahms achieves here some of the most genuinely moving moments in the entire work, and it is the synthesis of the most severe constructive formalism with the flowing expression of emotion which makes this section comparable—*mutatis mutandis*—to Bach's "The Art of Fugue."

In the fifth variation, there occurs a complete change of mood which now becomes light-hearted and fantastic. There is an inversion of the initial three-note figure of the theme, and an altogether laughing and romping tonal effect. After this rather good-humored variation, contrast is again provided by the brilliant and energetic sixth which is in Scherzo form with staccato rhythm and an utterly martial character.

The seventh variation to many is "the crowning point of new melody and new lusciousness" (Tovey). The rhythm is that of a Siciliano. In its serene quiet and gracefulness, the variation is like a delicate idyl. An inversion of the melody is used as an ascending bass figure.

From the sweetness of the seventh variation, the listener is committed to the mysteriousness of the eighth. This section again is in the minor key and has an air of soft-footed suspense and forboding darkness. The theme is inverted, and it is in this variation that several differences in detail occur between the orchestral and the two-piano versions.

The Finale in itself represents a new and independent little set of variations. In B flat major and 2-2 time, it is designated *Andante*. The form is alternately labeled as that of the Passacaglia and that of the Chaconne, but there is no room to here dwell on the controversy accompanying the definitions. A modification of the first five bars of the theme serves as the *basso ostinato* which appears seventeen times as a ground-bass and, in addition, is heard repeatedly in the upper voices. Over the converted Haydn theme the music moves "through various phases of triumph and meditation" (Tovey) to an overwhelming climax as at the end the glorious St. Anthony Chorale is sounded in magnificent sonority, with its five bell-strokes tolling benediction.

Camille Saint-Saens: Variations on a Theme by Beethoven, Opus 35

It has been said of Saint-Saens, despite his great abilities as a musical craftsman, despite the quantity of his output, some of which was very fine, that he had the unfortunate faculty of assimilation. His ability to "soak up" all musical styles and to incorporate them into his own creative efforts without achieving a truly individual result, was one of the major factors in preventing him from becoming a master of the first rank. However, it is this very detriment in which there rests the strength of Saint-Saens' "Beethoven Variations." The composer was an ardent admirer and disciple of the older master and his humble devotion to Beethoven all but prevented him to assert himself in an idiom of his individual own. To the contrary, all that Saint-Saens tried to accomplish, he achieved to the highest degree. He succeeded in copying form and style of Beethoven as well as in capturing the spirit to such degree of perfection, that speaking of these Variations brings to mind Beethoven's musical world rather than that of Saint-Saens. This means to say that while in a comparable work for two pianos, the Haydn Variations by Brahms, Haydn's theme serves merely as a point of departure, the work itself bearing the unmistakable language and imprint of Brahms, in Saint-Saens' composition there is everywhere the original theme, the workmanship and the spirit of Beethoven. Could higher praise be accorded to Saint-Saens, the humble devotee of Beethoven's towering genius?!

This brilliant work is based on the Trio section of the Minuet movement from Beethoven's Piano Sonata in E flat, opus 31, No. 3. The Minuet possesses great charm and fluency and serves as an excellent vehicle for the variations which Saint-Saens has built on and around the graceful tune. His inspiration provides first for an introduction *Moderato assai,* mysterious and expectant in character. The theme proper follows, captivating in its exquisite delightfulness. Saint-Saens fairly outdoes himself in the ingenuity of the variations which follow. They are marked, respectively:

I.   *Allegro*
II.   *Poco piu mosso* (followed by a short reminiscence of the theme, "*Tempo del Tema*")
III. *Molto allegro*
IV.   *Moderato assai*
V.   *Presto leggerissimo*
VI.   *Alla marcia funebre (Allegro moderato)*

After a reiteration of the mysterious strains first heard in the introduction, there follows a masterly fugue, in *Allegro* and 2-2 time. The fugue leads into a brilliant finale of *Presto* tempo which brings the work to a breath-taking culmination as well as conclusion.

Pierre Luboshutz and Genia Nemenoff have pertinently commented on Camille Saint-Saens as a composer for two pianos. The following paragraph is quoted from the program annotations of a Luboshutz recital:

> "The famous Parisian understood composing for two pianos as no one since his time has really understood it. So well does his music fit the medium, that he has been called the Chopin of Two-Piano Literature. Grounded in the classics (Saint-Saens edited many works of the ancients), wise in his selection of material, talented and indefatigable, his products were bound to be worthy. To this background may be added his love of Oriental music. There are but a few of his compositions which are not tinged with the freshness of an Eastern flavor. In the *Variations* the Oriental cast is to be noted particularly in the section known as the *Funeral March* and the bars immediately following."

Cécile Chaminade: Andante, Opus 59

This little gem is one of a pair of short pieces for two pianos which Chaminade wrote as her opus 59, *Scherzettino* being the characteristic title of the other. Although of miniature size, this work is here included as a good example for sensitiveness, taste and charm in two-piano writing. The ease and fluency with which the voices are treated, and the perfect elegance with which the two piano parts are blended into each other, make the piece deserving of being classed among the standard repertoire.

The French woman composer, Cécile Chaminade, one of Benjamin Godard's most famous pupils, is primarily known for the light and pleasing type of her compositions. The Andante, opus 59, possesses all traits of the composer's best qualities. The main melody, given out in the piano's sonorous baritone register, has grace, allurement, and romantic sweep. The harmonies are delightful, and the total effect is one of complete unity, achieved within the wide compass of duo-pianistic sonorities.

While this is unpretentious music, players and listeners alike will find it charming. It is representative of the *salon* in the best sense of the word, which means fashionable refinement, dignified cordiality, and the most polished utterance of sentiments.

Anton Arensky: Suite, Opus 15

In the face of the revolutionary innovations which have taken place in Russia, it must be remembered that there flourished, a half century ago, an *ancient regime* which had an atmosphere all of its own. That old social order, manifested by the culture of aristocratic Russian life, has produced a Rubinstein, Tchaikowsky, Rimsky-Korsakoff, Rachmaninoff, and many others of equal merits.

Of the same group of eminent Russian musicians, Anton Arensky won fame, not only as a teacher and pianist, but also as a composer. The literature for two pianos owes to him several notable suites. Arensky, while always recognizing the two pianos as individual voices and treating them independently, at the same time understood to blend the two instruments beautifully into an artistic unit.

Essentially a miniaturist, excelling in the smaller forms of composition, Arensky's elegant and virtuosic music has become thoroughly representative of the cultural background of czaristic Russia. A great gift for melody, an easy fluidity of style, and a suave workmanship are notable characteristics of his talent.

These traits are supremely evident in what has become perhaps the most popular of all two-piano pieces, the *Valse* from the Suite, opus 15. Its charm lies chiefly in the series of graceful arabesques built around an extremely simple waltz theme—almost popular in character—which becomes transfigured under the spell of these exquisite embellishments.

The composition certainly is one of the most striking examples of salon music, moreover one which always remains free from the banality of thematic material and flimsiness in musical design that are so often the intrinsic characteristics of pieces in this genre.

Hardly less ingratiating is the *Romance,* the charming first movement of the same suite. Enchantingly lyrical in idea and gracefully developed, it also is fully representative of the artistic conception of Anton Arensky, and of the cultural age in which he lived and created.

The suite closes with a spirited *Polonaise*; its harmonic boldness is a contributing factor in the heightening of the martial effect.

Sergei Rachmaninoff: Suite No. 1, Opus 5

Although this work is one of the composer's earliest, it is distinguished by the qualities which have later characterized his most mature creations.

Rachmaninoff was only twenty years old when he wrote the *Fantasia* for two pianos, opus 5. He composed the work during the summer of 1893 while spending some time on the country estate of a wealthy Moscow merchant. He then found himself greatly encouraged by recent successes in Moscow and by the praises of Arensky and Tschaikowsky. As a consequence, the Fantasia bears a marked self-reassurance and portrays "the enthusiasm of a young composer conscious of his newly acquired mastery over the materials and the forms of musical composition."

Riesemann writes concerning the dedication of the work with which Rachmaninoff presented his musical godfather, Tschaikowsky:

> "Rachmaninoff, who loved and admired Tschaikowsky beyond everything, had decided to dedicate his *Fantasia* for two pianos, which he considered the best work he had composed during that period, to Tschaikowsky. Tschaikowsky wished to hear it, but Rachmaninoff refused to play the work to him for fear that he would mar the first impression by playing an adaptation for one piano. It was his intention to introduce this *Fantasia* to the Moscow audience during the same autumn, by playing it with Paul Pabst at the latter's concert. Tschaikowsky promised to come over from St. Petersburg to hear the work. But fate decided otherwise."

Tschaikowsky was not allowed to ever hear the composition performed; his sudden death occurred only a few weeks later.

The richness of sonorities which distinguishes this early work of Rachmaninoff, make it rank as one of his most important contributions to the literature of piano music in the widest sense. Moreover, the Fantasia easily compares with the creative products even from Rachmaninoff's best period. The suite already bears the programmatic subtitle *Tableaux* which was used later on by the composer for all his piano pieces. Each of the four movements in turn is headed by a programmatic title, further elaborated on by verses from Lermontov, Byron, Tyoutchev and Khomiakov. In the following are quoted the excerpts of poetry which gave Rachmaninoff the inspiration for his music. The quotation of the verses renders unnecessary a detailed description of the movements.

I. BARCAROLE

At dusk half-heard the chill wave laps
Beneath the gondola's slow oar.
. . . .
. . . once more a song! once more the twanged guitar!
. . . .
. . . . now sad, now gaily ringing,
The barcarolle comes winging:
"The boat slid by, the waters clove:
So time glides o'er the surge of love;
The waters will grow smooth again,
But what can rouse a passion slain!"
(Lermontov)

The music of this opening movement is lyric and highly ornamental.

II. A NIGHT FOR LOVE

It is the hour when from the boughs
The nightingale's high note is heard;
It is the hour when lover's vows
Seem sweet in every whisper'd word;
And gentle winds, and waters near,
Make music to the lonely ear . . .

(Byron)

Color and passion distinguish Rachmaninoff's musical setting of Byron's verses.

III. TEARS

Tears, human tears, that pour forth beyond telling,
Early and late, in the dark, out of sight,
While the world goes on its way all unwittingly,
Numberless, stintless, you fall unremittingly,
Pouring like rain, the long rain that is welling
Endlessly, late in the autumn at night.

(Tyoutchev)

An agonized, and deliberately agonizing, portrait of grief and despair.

IV. RUSSIAN EASTER

Across the earth a mighty peal is sweeping
Till all the booming air rocks like a sea,
As silver thunders carol forth the tidings
Exulting in that holy victory . . .

(Khomyakov)

This study on the art of the Russian bell ringers forms the brilliant finale of the suite. Riesemann writes of it:

> "The last movement contains a wonderful carillon—the first Rachmaninoff ever composed—which resembles the fanatic peal of Orthodox Church bells on Easter Sunday as closely as can be managed with the tones of a piano . . . Like many other Russian composers he was fascinated by the task of reproducing the 'irrational' sound of a Russian peal and the wonderful rhythmic intricacies produced by the practised hands of the ringers, on ordinary musical instruments, with the aid of measurable notes."

Sergei Rachmaninoff: Suite No. 2, Opus 17

This suite is in four movements: After a march-like introduction follows an elegant and brilliant waltz. The third section is a typical, highly decorated song-like movement. The principal theme of the *Tarantelle,* which forms the finale, is a genuine Italian folk-melody.

The following program annotations which accompany a recording of this work[10] may also be helpful in the study of the composition:

> "The Suite, which consists of four movements, bears the opus number 17. It is an immediate neighbor, in point of date of composition, of the popularly-known Second Concerto in C Minor, opus 18, and the beautiful Sonata for Violoncello, opus 19.
> "A characteristic of Rachmaninoff, and one which gives many of his compositions

---

10. *RCA Victor* Album M-822.

an almost orchestral aspect, is the richness . . . the fullness of the accompaniment with which he supports his melodies. Looking at one of his scores, one is greeted by pages black with notes. Indeed, there is a well-known story of a teacher who, after listening to a pupil play the C minor Concerto, remarked that he 'had left out enough notes to make an entire new composition.' This wealth of tone . . . this supporting under-structure . . . is a feature that is interesting to observe, especially in this two-piano Suite.

FIRST MOVEMENT: *Introduction*

"The Introduction begins with decisive chords in robust style that is fresh and exuberant, with a tendency toward the martial. A more lyric theme is heard later with delicate embroidery in the second piano, which works to a fine climax and then dies away, punctuated by a sharp chord in termination.

SECOND MOVEMENT: *Valse*

". . . . At the start one might expect . . . to veer into one of the popular Chopin waltzes, but this phase soon gives place to a new figure that becomes more and more involved and then swings into the main theme of the Valse. Here one piano sings a melody of heavenly beauty, deep-toned and impassioned, while the other weaves an accompaniment richly embroidered, building gradually—in true Rachmaninoff fashion—to a big climax; and then with equal graduation, receding quietly to take up once again the figure with which the waltz began. Here are delightful *rubato* passages and rhythmic features that glitter with sly humor as the music scampers along. At the very close of the Valse one is reminded of Tschaikowsky's "Troika en Traineau."

THIRD MOVEMENT: *Romance*

"If you enjoy the grace of the *Valse*, the nocturne-like beauty of the *Romance* is certain to appeal to you also. Its haunting melody, in spots similar to portions of the *C Minor Concerto*, confirms its date of composition, and lingers pleasantly in the memory.

FOURTH MOVEMENT: *Tarantelle*

"The name of this movement refers to a frenzied dance which was executed by one suffering from the bite of a tarantula. The victim danced until he fell exhausted, thereby offsetting the venom of the insect. If exceptional speed made the cure more effective, there can be no doubt of complete recovery for one who could maintain the tempo exacted of the performers in this Tarantelle . . . this tremendously agitated *finale* of the Suite."

Max Reger: Introduction, Passacaglia, and Fugue, Opus 96

Wier calls this work "titanic," a term which may be applied to the general capacity of this master, for Reger possibly was the greatest contrapuntalist of modern times. His intellectualism and sometimes pedantry have given cause to criticism, but his mental grasp and the perfection of his workmanship are beyond doubt.

The opus 96 has great breadth and power, reminiscent of the monumental organ compositions of J. S. Bach which were Reger's model. It is the very core of musical architecture from which Reger draws his inspiration. Performers and listeners alike stand awed before the mastery and scope of this powerful work which soars and towers like a Gothic cathedral in a period indulging in romantic and impressionistic tendencies. In the words of Kurt List,[11] Reger, "by harking back to both classical and

11. *Late Romanticism*, "Listen" magazine, October 1949.

Baroque ideas . . . understood to handle romantic material with a certain kind of abstraction and modernity which brought him close to the neo-classicists without actually abandoning the romantic thought."

Claude Debussy: En Blanc et Noir

This work of Debussy dates from that final period when he, no longer groping for an elusive idea, had attained to the true expression of his genius. The work makes it apparent that Debussy "did more than bring a new scale and new harmonies to the musical scheme of his time. He restored the practice of the 18th Century French composers in making music an illustrative art—program music in its most subtle and poetic aspect" (Vronsky and Babin).

The composition is remarkable for being the first creative effort which Debussy made after a period of complete sterility as a composer. This silence had been brought on by the outbreak of the First World War in August 1914. For almost a year after hostilities began, Debussy practically abandoned composition. Besides the paralyzing effect which the war had upon him, an extremely sensitive man and an intense nationalist,[12] he was already affected by the fatal illness which was to claim his life in 1918.

A letter which Debussy wrote in June 1915 to his friend Robert Godet, shows him in the act of conquering the motives of his inactivity. He so reasons with himself:

"I have come to the conclusion that, all things considered, it would be cowardice on my part to join the ranks of the disabled, and spend my time dwelling on the atrocities that have been committed, without reacting against them by creating, to the best of my ability, a little of the beauty which the enemy is attacking with such fury."

Debussy succeeded in conjuring up inspiration and creativeness by this constructive philosophy because he was able to write soon after:

"At long last, I have got back the power and, as it were, the right to think in terms of music—a thing that has not happened to me for the last year. It is, of course, not indispensable that I should write music, but it is the only thing I can do more or less well; I humbly regret my state of latent death. Now, I have been writing like a madman, or one who has to die next morning."

The first composition which Debussy completed after his recovery from the period of creative sterility, was a set of three pieces for two pianos. The original title *Caprices en blanc et noir* later was shortened to *En Blanc et Noir*.

Previously, Debussy had written a tone poem *Linderaja* in the two-piano idiom, an early work of little significance. He had also transcribed his orchestral tone poem *The Afternoon of a Faun* for two pianos, and he had arranged Robert Schumann's *Six Etudes in Canon Form* for the

12. This ardent nationalism is reflected in the second piece of the present Suite.

same combination. The medium, therefore, was well familiar to him. That he chose it again at this time, in the closing period of his development as a composer, is an interesting and significant gesture of the twentieth century pioneer of pianoforte music.

There is a wide difference in style and subject matter between the three pieces of the suite, although all of them seem to be pervaded by a general feeling of anxiety and depression, probably brought on by both the war and the composer's suffering from the illness which then had begun and caused his death within three years.

Some of the annotations to *En Blanc et Noir* by Paul Affelder[13] are quoted herewith:

"The first piece, *'Avec emportement'*, is based on a brief excerpt from the libretto for Gounod's opera *Roméo et Juliette*:

> Qui reste à sa place
> Et ne danse pas
> De quelque disgrâce
> Fait l'aveu tout bas.

"Vallas interprets this as an ironical allusion to those who shunned the 'macabre dance' of the battlefield, thereby admitting to some physical defect.

"The second piece, marked *'Lent-Sombre'*, is also definitely colored by the war. It is dedicated to the memory of Lieutenant Jacques Charlot, who was killed on March 3, 1915, and bears an inscription from François Villon's *Ballade contre les ennemis de la France*. Throughout the work, which has somewhat of a funereal and, at the same time, warlike tone, are vague references to military bugle calls and the distant rumbling of guns. A Lutheran chorale, obviously a symbol of the domineering Germans, also makes its appearance. The composer seemed pleased with this second part of *En blanc et noir*. When he sent it to the publisher in July, 1915, he wrote: 'You will see how Luther's hymn catches it for having imprudently strayed into a French *Caprice*. Towards the end a modest little carillon rings out a pre-*Marseillaise*. I apologize for this anachronism, but I think it is permissible at a time when the very pavements and the trees of the forests are vibrating to this ubiquitous song.' The following month, he sent in a slight alteration which he deemed necessary for the sake of balance in the work. 'Besides,' he commented, 'it makes things clearer, and cleanses the atmosphere of the poisonous fumes which were spread for a moment by Luther's Chorale, or rather by what it represents—for, after all, it is a fine thing.'

"The third and final piece of the set is a *Scherzando*, and has no warlike connotations. Its inspiration lies in an old poem by Charles d'Orléans, which Debussy had already set to music."

The work was introduced to American audiences by the two-piano team of Guy Maier and Lee Pattison.

Leopold Godowsky: Alt Wien (Old Vienna)

Although this short piece has been arranged by Godowsky from an original piano solo composition, it is included into this survey because of the excellence of the transference and for reason of the fact that the work has become one of the favorite miniatures in the entire literature.

---

13. Program notes to *Columbia* Masterworks, Set X-MX-241.

The two-piano version in itself is a study of taste and restraint in the distribution of thematic material between the two instruments; it is an essay in the craft of arranging executed by one of the great masters of modern counterpoint.

Godowsky, in his employment of the medium, was keenly aware of the full possibilities for sonorities and he consequently gave his works in this idiom a unique and comprehensive treatment. The texture is always rich yet transparent; the voice leading has a flowing quality and natural ease.

The composition is part of the cycle *Triakontameron,* a group of thirty pieces of picture music, pianistic in style and outstanding for graceful qualities. The lilting *Alt Wien,* in simple three-part form, derives its somewhat nostalgic character from the motto:

> "Whose Yesterdays look backwards
> with a Smile through Tears"

The two-piano score is dedicated to Vera Brodsky and Harold Triggs.

Francis Poulenc: Concerto in D minor for Two Pianos and Orchestra

Francis Poulenc is a member of the same French group of composers called *Les Six* of which Darius Milhaud and Arthur Honegger have emerged as leading figures. When the group first was formed, it stood in an open rebellion against the romanticism of César Franck and the impressionism of Claude Debussy. Their idols, guides and mentors were Eric Satie, the composer, and Jean Cocteau, the poet. They established simplicity of thought and expression as their program. As they believed that the composer should be a regular fellow who, in Aaron Copland's words, 'liked to go to night clubs like everybody else', so their music is distinguished by succinctness and a flair for popular idioms.

"The Six" shared a practical interest in the modern ballet, so much that Verna Arvey could write: "It was a sort of cult with them. Often, the flavor of lusty music-hall tunes has crept into their ballet music, but it has served only to define more clearly the moods of the moment."

Francis Poulenc has written a considerable amount of chamber music, numerous songs, and many delicately wrought piano pieces. The interest here centers upon the Concerto in D minor for Two Pianos and Orchestra for which the annotations by Louis Biancolli[14] provide a guide to listening and study:

"Composed in 1932, the Concerto in D minor for Two Pianos and Orchestra was first performed on September 5, 1932, at a concert of the International Music Festival in Venice. Poulenc and Jacques Febrier were the soloists, and Desire Defauw conducted the orchestra of La Scala, Milan. Notable in the scoring is the modest array of strings called for: eight first and eight second violins, four violas, four cellos,

14. *The Concert Companion* by Bagar-Biancolli, page 515.

and four double-basses, two flutes, two oboes, two clarinets, two bassoons, two horns, two trumpets, two trombones, one tuba, and percussion.

"Woven into the web of the first movement (Allegro ma non troppo, D minor, 4-4) are fragments of so-called 'Parisian folklore,' i.e., popular tunes, dating back several years, from the cafe-concert circuit. A pert and lively melody serves as main theme and opens the way to a host of similar *chansonettes*. These are brought together at one place in a clever web of counterpoint. A reverielike passage sets in as the first piano begins the coda (*très calme*), and the movement ends tranquilly.

"The second movement is a Larghetto, built largely from two ingratiating themes, the first of which is announced by one piano in B flat major, 2-2. At a point where the tempo quickens the two pianos join in voicing the second subject, in A flat major.

"Poulenc's melodic gifts are perhaps best shown in the Finale, which opens Allegro molto (2-2, 3-4), with a passage for two pianos very much in the style of a toccata. The dominant theme of the movement then appears in a march announced by both pianos and violins. There is a peaceful interlude, and Poulenc returns to his favored *cafe-concert* mood with a sheaf of gay new strains. The march theme is back (*Agité*), now worked up to a fierce climax. Finally, one of the 'hit-tune' motives is reviewed and raised to a sharp fortissimo, and the Two-piano Concerto ends on a note of brilliance."

The essence of this music is analyzed by Emile Vuillermoz with the following statement: "There is in Poulenc's music an ingenuity, a gaiety, and a freshness that seem always to have an undercurrent of folklore at the base. This art delights in plunging its roots into the popular soil of marching songs and nursery tunes."

Darius Milhaud: Scaramouche, Suite for Two Pianos

With Darius Milhaud, one of the most significant and most prolific composers of our time joins the array of contributors to the duo-pianistic repertoire. Milhaud's interest in the two-piano medium is considerable and he has frequently chosen it for both artistic and practical considerations. This is to say that he regards creative expression in the idiom as fully original; on the other hand, he often resorts to two pianos for an adequate representation of orchestral thought, using the combination as the closest substitute when an orchestra is not available.

The working method of Milhaud, who is an exponent of the "French Six," is described in an intimate manner by Paul Collaer in his biography of the composer.[15] From this book, an excerpt is quoted in which Collaer refers to the origin of techniques which have characterized Milhaud's music for many years:

"One evening, one of those beautiful summer nights in Provence, . . . we were walking in a quiet street which led from the Cours. It was at the beginning of our friendship. We stopped a moment before the door of Saint-Sauveur, a few steps from the 'Burning Bush', and I asked him, 'What was it, Darius, that led you toward polytonality; how could you have heard it before you wrote it?'

" 'Well . . . it's hard to say. . . . I don't know whether you will feel it. . . . When I found myself in the country, at night, immersed in silence, looking at the sky,

15. *Darius Milhaud*, p. 63.

it seemed to me at once that I felt coming toward me from everywhere, from every part of the sky, from under the earth, rays or movements; and all these rays bore a music, each one different, and that infinity of musics intersected, continuing to scintillate, but remaining distinct. It was an extraordinary feeling. Since then I have always sought to express that emotion, those thousand simultaneous musics that came upon me from everywhere. . . . ' "

A glance at the scores of Darius Milhaud confirms that the composer's search for the "thousand simultaneous musics" is still going on. While his melodies, *d'allure populaire,* are essentially diatonic, they are combined time after time with others in just as diatonic patterns, but with totally different tonal implications. Polytonal combinations, each part distinct in itself, are encountered frequently. But it is seldom the momentary comingling of sounds which gives his music its distinctive flavor; the character of his melodies is of greater importance. H. H. Stuckenschmidt considers "the impersonal style of objective melody" Milhaud's native heritage. "The characteristic, logical nature of the style permits the greatest simplicity of detail. Milhaud's melodies are, in fact, unpretentious to an almost primitive degree. There are long stretches of pure diatonism which contrast with contrapuntal deviations from tonality to produce a most pronounced harmonic tension."

The foregoing remarks[16] are the analytic reflection of Milhaud's general style. They are well illustrated by the particular work from the composer's wide range of productivity which has become part of the duo-pianistic standard repertoire. An expert in the treatment of two keyboards, Milhaud conceived his "Scaramouche" suite as a wholly original contribution to the two-piano literature. Scaramouche means "clown," and the title proves to be well projected by the essence of the music, which suggests the theater or the ballet, with plenty of surface glitter in evidence. The first movement, marked *Vif,* is full of gaiety and humor. With its rhythmic vivacity and continuous surprises, it rollicks along in sheer exuberance, giving a lively portrait of clownish funmaking. *Modéré,* the second movement, breathes a quiet melancholy coupled with fancy in mood. There is the atmosphere of a cradle song. Contrapuntal devices enhance the impression of refinement and sovereign workmanship. An element of lucidity pervades this music which makes it typically French. And, more specifically, there is again the feeling of the "thousand simultaneous musics" which the composer senses in this miniature as much as in his most expansive works. The result brings about delicate harmonic clashes with their peculiar Milhaud flavor.

The finale is entitled *Brazileira.* It is based on the Samba, a popular Brazilian dance-rhythm, which impressed the composer during a visit to

16. Based on program notes by Halsey Stevens, *Symphony Magazine,* Los Angeles Philharmonic Orchestra, March 31-April 1, 1949.

Brazil. This movement, with its emphasis again placed on fun, is a flashy and dashing showpiece giving more than a hint at popular appeal.

As a matter of fact, the entire composition has all the characteristics and the attraction of a popular work. It bears out to the fullest extent the words which Paul Collaer places at the end of his biography of Darius Milhaud:[17]

> "Dans le cadre de la musique française, succédant à Debussy et Ravel, Milhaud est actuellement la personnalité dominante. Après que les derniers feux d'artifice de l'Impressionisme eurent été tirés, il a rendu a la musique française la puissance dramatique et lyrique. Il a réalisé sur le plan le plus élevé la synthèse des sources d'inspiration les plus authentiquement populaires et des aspirations les plus nobles."

The synthesis of truly popular material with the noblest aspirations has always been the crucial problem for the creative artist, and the achievement of the few select.

Edward Burlingame Hill: Jazz Studies for Two Pianos

These four studies were written over an interval of several years, from 1922 to 1938. During the same period, the jazz idiom stimulated many other composers and found its most popular exponent in Gershwin; the latter's work, however, does not compare with the seriousness of intention and the deft craftsmanship of Edward Burlingame Hill's studies for two pianos.

"Jazz has reared its head to be mimicked and adorned in the . . . Jazz Studies for Two Pianos. . . . The composer has extracted its bouquet." These are the words used by George Henry Lovett Smith in his essay on the composer.[18]

Inspired by the art and popular success of Maier and Pattison, the composer also wrote a Scherzo for two pianos and orchestra.

Beryl Rubinstein: Suite for Two Pianos

This work demands particular attention in the present survey in that the composer has stated a very specific and concise formulation of his attitude towards the two-piano medium. This special contribution is quoted in Chapter XVIII, "The Challenge," of Book II, "Nature, Applications and Problems," Part B, "The Creative Medium."

Rubinstein is entirely aware of the particular difficulty of writing for two pianos, "because of the terrific problem of tonal distinction" which makes it more necessary than in any other combination to "keep in mind that it is not the number of notes, but the disposition of them that is of peculiar importance in writing for two pianos."

Beryl Rubinstein was born in Athens, Georgia, on October 26, 1898.

17. *Darius Milhaud*, page 237.
18. *Modern Music*, November-December 1938.

His studies which were begun with his father at the age of six, eventually took him to Ferruccio Busoni. He concertized extensively as a pianist, appearing in the role of soloist with most leading orchestras. With his friend and colleague Arthur Loesser (born August 26, 1894), Beryl Rubinstein formed a two-piano team, and their collaboration lead to distinct achievement and outstanding acclaim in this field. It was that successful duo-pianistic career which prompted Rubinstein to compose his Suite for Two Pianos. The work was brought into existence in the short span of only two months; it was written in the early spring of 1939. Of the composer's own remarks on his suite, the following are quoted:[19]

" . . . the dearth of older masterpieces for two pianos is a boon, for it means that the need for two-piano works is imperative . . . It only remains for the contemporary composer to bestir himself in this direction. However, a rather special knowledge is required for the creation of worth-while, and at the same time, effective two-piano music. One must possess more than a casual acquaintance with piano technic and piano sonorities. . . .

"For some years I have experimented with two-piano writing with no great satisfaction to myself. It is only recently that I have discovered what sounds well on two pianos and what pitfalls must be avoided in order to obtain certain expected effects. I think I have succeeded reasonably well in carrying out my ideas in this Suite for Two Pianos.

"There are four pieces in the Suite—Prelude, Canzonnetta, Jig, and Masks. The Prelude, Jig, and Masks are all in a modified rondo form. The Canzonnetta is in an extended song form.

"The *Prelude* has no programmatic connotation. It is light and gay in character.

"The *Canzonnetta,* as its name implies, is on the more melodious side. The first melody is completely unhampered by contrapuntal devices. The second melody, even when it reaches its big climax, remains consistently lyrical.

"The *Jig* could not but have a Celtic flavor. The subject matter of the fast parts is so characteristically jig-like that one may readily imagine having heard it before; or that feeling may be accounted for by the fact that Irish tunes are so definitely Irish and nothing else.

"*Masks* calls for a little more extended comment. The title itself was arrived at only after many others had been discarded. I believe it to be an apt one. My Masks are not ballroom masks but rather more imaginative and barbaric in type. The middle part may savor a little of 'sweet' popular music but that is just a mask too. The chief interest in the piece is rhythmic. It is almost entirely in seven-eights, with here and there a five-eights, or an occasional three-fourths. The cross rhythms are not always easy of execution, although after practice they seem quite natural.

"Both pianos are equally important in the Suite. In fact, scarcely anything happens in one piano which the other piano does not duplicate at one time or another."

Beryl Rubinstein's idiom and style are difficult to classify. He seems fond of modern effects such as polytonality and polyrhythm. At the same time, he adheres rather closely to traditional formulae of harmonic and structural principles. His textural treatment reminds of the ideals of French impressionism.

---

19. From program notes to *RCA Victor* record album DM 784.

Igor Stravinsky: Concerto for Two Solo Pianos

This work joins the literature for two pianos as a modern show piece, stunning with virtuosity and brilliance. The concerto is in four movements which are marked, respectively: *Con moto; Notturno; Four Variations; Prelude and Fugue*. The first movement is an *allegro de sonata*. The nocturne employs in a single movement features frequent in eighteenth century *Nachtmusik* and *cassations*. The prelude and fugue is preceded by variations upon two motifs recurring in the prelude; the first motif serves as the subject of the fugue which is in four voices.

Stravinsky composed the concerto in 1935 shortly after his second American concert tour. The work was first performed by the composer and his son, Sviatoslav, in Paris on November 21, 1935.

The two pianos are employed with marked economy. While the concerto possesses the predominant qualities of power and drive, there is yet a good deal of lyricism in evidence. The quintessence of Stravinsky's approach to the two-piano medium, and its originality, remains his emphasis on percussive and rhythmic writing.

> "With this extraordinarily impressive and intricate work, Igor Stravinsky joins a distinguished roster of composers who wrote concertos without orchestra. The list includes Schumann with his Piano Sonata in F Minor which is subtitled 'Concerto without Orchestra' and Bach with his Italian Concerto for solo harpsichord—these in addition to the many Seventeenth Century musicians who composed concertos without orchestra for organ and for harpsichord.[20]
> "Stravinsky's Concerto for Two Pianos has many remarkable features, not the least of which is that in no sense is one of the pianos a solo instrument and the other an accompanying factor such as the orchestra may be said to be in the classical concerto. The music for both instruments is of equal importance; and the music for both is vigorously pianistic, emphasizing the percussive rather than the legato qualities of the instrument."[21]

Stravinsky's own commentary regarding his work is given in Book I, "The History," Chapter X, "The Composers."

A penetrating essay on this concerto has been written by Edward Tatnall Canby; from this discourse, the following passages are quoted:[22]

> "The Concerto is without orchestra, for the two pianos alone. It thus joins a singular list of 'orchestra-less' concertos, since the earliest use of the form, that includes such notable works as Bach's Italian Concerto and the Schumann Piano Sonata in F minor, subtitled, 'Concerto without Orchestra'. Clearly the use of the term in this manner calls attention, via the title, to features of the music that set it off from other works for solo instrument. In Bach's case it is easy to hear that the Italian Concerto (when played on the intended harpsichord) is not only similar in

---

20. The Concerto Pathétique by Franz Liszt is a precedence in the *two-piano* literature, and a still earlier example can be found in the second movement from the Concerto in C major for two claviers by J. S. Bach, a section in which the orchestra remains silent and the two solo harpsichords perform alone.—H. M.
21. From the program notes to *Columbia* record album ML 4157.
22. Program notes, *Vox* record album 634.

style to other Bach Concerti with orchestra but, thanks to the possibilities of registration on the instrument's two keyboards, shows a consistent division into 'solo' and 'tutti' music, corresponding to the solo—or solo group—and the orchestra. Indeed, concertos for single compound-keyboard instruments, harpsichord or organ, were so common in Bach's day that we can scarcely define the concerto of the time as a work involving orchestra at all. In the Schumann 'Concerto without Orchestra', a century later, there is no detailed allusion to specific solo and orchestra sounds. But the concept of a big bravura piece, brilliant, massive, organized formally on a large scale with the characteristic lengthy sonata form first movement is essential to the 'grand concerto' style from Beethoven on. The Schumann work is a kind of public piece, a work for imposing musical occasions, laid out on what might best be called symphonic lines, (note, too, the Symphonic Etudes of Schumann, for piano alone) in contrast to most of his other piano music, which is personal, intimate, true 'chamber' music. It is possibly in this last sense that Strawinsky himself uses the term, concerto. His is a large, impressive piece, containing a wealth of musical material that clearly places it beside his larger orchestral works in the pure-music category, the Piano Concerto, the Piano Capriccio and the Symphonies. It also seems likely that Strawinsky refers, in the term Concerto, to a kind of *concertante* effect, as of numerous soloists within an orchestra; that is plainly evident in this music. Numerous works for actual orchestra of similar intention have been written in recent years; notably the Dumbarton Oaks Concerto of Strawinsky, the Concerto for Orchestra of Bartók, the Capricorn Concerto of Barber. The transfer to the piano, as in both Bach and Schumann, is in this sense merely an incidental change of medium.

"And yet what an extraordinary conception of two-piano music this is! There is, of course, no sign of any use of the two pianos, one as a 'solo', the other as 'orchestra', as some might expect; nor has Strawinsky, in Mozart fashion, distributed *solo* and *tutti* passages equally between the two. Even the concept of Brahms, of an over-all orchestral brilliance (as in the two-piano version of the Haydn Variations, opus 56b) is hardly Strawinsky's idea. In this concerto, in spite of its relationship to works of an orchestral nature, in spite of the abovementioned *concertante* complexity of inner voices, of planes and levels of prominence and accompaniment, the music is nevertheless no imitation of the orchestra—simply because it is the purest idiomatic piano writing. Every effect here, however novel, is essentially pianistic.

"The Strawinsky piano idiom is utterly original, in a sense revolutionary. As far back as 'Petrouchka' the composer was using the piano primarily as a rhythmic percussive instrument. Already he had side-stepped one of the oldest piano traditions, that piano tone is properly *legato* and hence melodic. Granted that, with the aid of the human imagination, piano writing can give (and long has given) a fine impression of *legato*. Yet the piano tone, lingering in the imagination, most assuredly dies in the physical reality! The present Concerto is the end-result (one can scarcely imagine a farther development) of some twenty years of thought and practice in piano writing on Strawinsky's part, animated throughout by the new conception of a literal treatment of the piano according to its actual sound—in particular as a means of projecting rhythm, a rhythm, we must note, that is found elsewhere only in the realms of piano 'hot jazz'; boogie-woogie, the negro blues. It is surely important that the technical means Strawinsky uses are those common in these areas— the rapid wide skips in the treble range, *arpeggio*-like; the persistent, *staccato* accompanying rhythms in the bass; perhaps most noticeable of all, the rapidly repeated single tone (à la hurdy-gurdy), used both for rhythmic strength and to prolong the actual, not the imagined sound (a striking feature of boogie-woogie music). Not that any necessary connection is implied, we must add hastily, between jazz styles and the sound of Strawinsky's own music! His definitely does not sound like jazz. It embodies, rather, his own personal use of similar technical methods, perhaps first observed in the jazz world, but adapted strictly and without the slightest compromise to the special Strawinsky idiom. His 'Ebony Concerto' is a fine case in point—the misconception that, because it was written directly for a popular band, Woody Herman's, it would sound like popular music led to some red faces on the part of those who ballyhooed it with much advance publicity in the big-time entertainment media. As the gentlemen should have expected, the work sounded like Strawinsky, jazz instruments or no. And thus with the present two-piano style.

"Perhaps the most unusual aspect of this score is the complete integration of the two pianos into a single performing unit. There is scarcely a passage in which either piano assumes individuality. The music is inextricably interlocked throughout; there are even passages where the musical ideas, as printed, run across the page from one piano part directly into the other, as though for some incredible four-handed virtuoso! One can merely conjecture the difficulties this extraordinary technique places on the two performers, individuals each, who must act as one. No team of duo-pianists not thorough-going musicians could survive the rigors of preparation, measure by measure, that must here be required—since it is virtually impossible even to play one piano part by itself, much less 'memorize' it without regard to the other piano.

"Let us say, finally, that far from a lack of pianistic sense in such writing, the opposite is true. So incalculably well versed is Strawinsky in this, his own technique, that, once the strangeness of the scoring—which at times is baffling even to watch—has worn away, the music lies, relatively speaking, under the hands. If one is ready to read 'upside-down', with the bass line as often as not at the top of the score, the treble at the bottom, if one will follow simple diatonic lines hither and yon, leaping wildly on the page from one piano staff to the other; if one is finally persuaded that these indescribable concatenations of written trills and scales and glissandi, black on the page, can in fact come forth simply and naturally in the actual playing—then this amazing two-piano writing is as simple and effective as a score of Mozart. . . ."

Béla Bartók: *Sonata for Two Pianos and Percussion*

The sonata under discussion is a significant work from one of the most important modern composers. There exist two versions of this composition. The first is the "Sonata for Two Pianos and Percussion." In the alternation, with an orchestral accompaniment added, the work is entitled "Concerto for Two Pianos with Orchestra."

The piano parts of the two versions differ in but a few instances from each other. The instrumentation for the original scoring with percussion instruments includes:

2 Pianos	Cymbal suspended
3 Timpani	Pair of Cymbals
Xylophone	Bass Drum
Side Drum with snares	Triangle
Side Drum without snares	Tam-Tam

This music is full of difficulties and problems, both from the technical and musical aspects, the latter being entirely characteristic of the idiom peculiar to Béla Bartók. The logic of the work concentrates on the exploitation of rhythmical features, and never before have rhythm and percussion entered into so close an alliance. With this rhythmic emphasis as the dominant feature, color is provided by the variety of percussion instruments.

The composer has given specific instructions for the grouping and for the treatment of the various instruments. He advises that one of the pianists should coach and lead the entire ensemble when the work is performed without orchestra.

The stunning piece was premiered in its sonata version in Basle on January 16, 1938. The performers included the composer and Ditta Pásztory, his pupil and wife, at the pianos; Fritz Schiesser and Phillip Ruehlig handled the percussion section. The occasion for the first performance was the Tenth Anniversary Concert of the Basle Group of the Swiss section of the International Society for Contemporary Music.

The work was later played in London at a concert of the International Society for Contemporary Music. Performances in Brussels, Amsterdam, Paris, Zuerich, Luxembourg, Budapest, and Venice followed. The American debut rendition took place at a session of the New Friends of Music in the Town Hall auditorium, New York, on November 3, 1940. Again the composer and his wife were the duo-pianists, with Saul Goodman and Henry Denecke, Jr. assisting as percussionists.

Immediately after the American premiere, the composer decided to expand the sonata into a concerto, and he completed the new version the following month. Bartók then wrote:

> "It seemed advisable, for certain technical reasons, to add orchestral accompaniment to the work, though, as a matter of fact, it gives only color to certain portions of the work. The two-piano and percussion parts remain practically unchanged, except for some of the climactic parts which are now taken over from the two pianos as tuttis by the orchestra."

The orchestral version employs the conventional instrumentation of woodwinds, brass and strings. A celesta is added. The debut performance of this version was given by the New York Philharmonic Symphony under Fritz Reiner on January 4, 1943. The parts of the duo-pianists again were assumed by Mr. and Mrs. Bartók.

Louis Biancolli gives the following analysis of the composition:[23]

> "The three-movement work opens with a brooding slow passage leading to the main section (Allegro molto) in rhythmically barbaric and energetic style. The second theme of this movement appears in many contrapuntal combinations. The middle movement is a Lento ma non troppo, with an A-B-A sectional division. In the rondo-like finale (Allegro non troppo, 2/4) the xylophone gives out the relatively extended chief theme. Throughout the composition, percussion instruments often play solo roles. There is wide rhythmic variety and striking counterpoint, besides daring effects of grouping and color. Also apparent is Mr. Bartók's well-known flair for utilizing short themes, especially in his piano music. These are handled with typical contrapuntal boldness. However, one or two longer themes crop up, notably

---

23. *The Concert Companion*, page 23.

in the finale, in which the xylophone states a sustained melody. The primitive and folkish quality felt in Mr. Bartók's earlier music marks much of this work too."

Bartók died in 1945, and the two-piano sonata-concerto was to remain one of his latest compositions. It also is, in the words of Ernest Hutcheson, one of his "most debatable." Winifred Glass rises above the existing controversial opinions with the off-hand remark[24] that "the Bartók sonata for two pianos and percussion is not just an array of tones but expression of spirit. . . ."

Paul Hindemith: Sonata for Two Pianos (1942)

In lieu of an opus number, Hindemith often uses the year in which a work was composed for its classification. This procedure has a definite advantage: it enables the student to place the work into perspective with the creative development of its composer.

Hindemith, prolific in almost every realm of musical form, is regarded as one of the greatest living composers; some believe him to be the greatest. His idiom is distinctive; its characteristics are thorough workmanship (especially in his mastery of so-called linear counterpoint), vitality, and clarity of thought.

Hutcheson calls Hindemith's sonata for two pianos "very difficult, but rewarding; its creative power is great and the final fugue magnificent."[25]

The movements of the work are 1) *Chimes (Maestoso)*, 2) *Allegro*, 3) *Canon (slow)*, 4) *Recitative*. The last section is based on a poem of an anonymous author, living c. 1300. The title of the poem which is contained in "The Oxford Book of English Verse" is "This World's Joy." Literary subject matter and musical essence combine to make this movement thoroughly representative of Hindemith's style.

This sonata is published as a facsimile of the composer's own manuscript.[26] The score is meticulously neat and can be read easily. It would seem as if through this procedure a more immediate contact with the author's intentions was provided.

Bohuslav Martinu: Concerto for Two Pianos and Orchestra

This concerto was composed by the Bohemian-born Martinu at New York. Its completion occurred on February 23, 1943, and the premiere took place in Philadelphia during the same year, on November 5. In the first performance, Pierre Luboshutz and Genia Nemenoff were the duo-pianists, and Eugene Ormandy conducted the Philadelphia Orchestra.

On the occasion of the premiere, the composer contributed the following statement to the program book:

"I have used the pianos for the first time in the purely 'solo' sense, with the

24. *Music News*, October 1949, page 14.
25. *The Literature of the Piano*, page 312.
26. Associated Music Publishers, Inc., New York; Schott & Co., Ltd., London.

orchestra as accompaniment. The form is free, it leans rather to the Concerto grosso. It demands virtuosity, brilliant piano technique, and the timbre of the same two instruments calls forth new colors and new sonorities."

Milôs Safránek who wrote a biography of the composer, [27] gives this comment on the two-piano concerto:

> "The concerto is in three movements, and is of predominantly rhythmical character. The first (*Allegro non troppo*) contains many ingenious and colorful effects in the combination of the orchestra with the two pianos. The second movement (*Adagio*), which is without any time signature, is more poetic in character, and includes cadenzas for both pianos. The last movement is a brilliant Rondo in dance rhythm."

The two solo pianofortes are accompanied by an orchestra of the following instrumentation: Two flutes, two oboes, two clarinets, two bassoons, two horns, two trumpets, two trombones, kettledrums, bass drum, cymbals, side drum, tambourine, gong and the usual strings.

In essence, the work exposes the general characteristics which Paul Nettl ascribes to Bohuslav Martinu, the composer:

> "His dominating principle is to attain, above all, clear thematic development and a transparency of melodic line on a foundation of absolute music. . . . The feeling for rhythmic variety and architectural composition is certainly one of the inheritances of Czech musical culture . . . We find in his work no vague, nebulous writing; the tone is always decided, transparent, and clear. Sometimes we find surprising tone effects. Equally admirable is his sense of workmanship and style."

Victor Babin: Etudes for Two Pianos

In a set of twelve etudes, the composer covers various problems peculiar to the technic and musical idiom of two-piano playing. As the member of a famous team, Mr. Babin brings to this undertaking the profound understanding and long experience which are his after dealing with the medium over many years.

The basic plan for the etudes is contrived with originality, and the individual ideas are brilliantly exposed. The work can be considered equivalent in conception to the more famous cycles of concert etudes in the realm of piano solo compositions; it opens vistas for the most original treatment of the two-piano combination.

Of the twelve etudes, a set of six has been published. They are marked:

Etude No. 1. *Tempo Giusto, Con Fuoco*
Etude No. 2. *Adagietto Cantabile*
Etude No. 3. *Veloce*
Etude No. 4. *Vivace* (Based on "Flight of the Bumble Bee" by Rimsky-Korsakoff)
Etude No. 5. *Quasi Una Siciliana*
Etude No. 6. *Allegro Molto, Dramatico.*

---

27. *Bohuslav Martinu, the Man and His Music.*

CHAPTER XXIV

ORIGINAL TWO-PIANO MUSIC

1. *Extent and Confines*

The following list of compositions for two pianos, four hands, is governed by the prerequisite that the music be *original* with the composer. Under this criterion, the catalogue comprises three categories:

1. original compositions for two solo pianos, four hands;
2. original compositions for two pianos, four hands, with ensemble such as full orchestra, string ensemble, percussion, voice, and other combinations;
3. authentic versions for two pianos, four hands, including such arrangements and transcriptions which were edited by the composer of the original score himself (as for instance Debussy's own two-piano version of his orchestral "L'Après-midi d'un Faune," but *not* Ravel's transcriptions of the orchestral Nocturnes by Debussy).

Excluded from this compilation are all types of other arrangements, transcriptions, and paraphrases, as well as two-piano versions of concertos and added second-piano parts.

Within the confines established in the foregoing, a collection of broad proportions is attempted. The author refrains, however, from the inclusion of definitely antiquated material such as is found in many salon pieces and operatic fantasies. Also omitted are the ephemeral specimens from the repertoire of popular dance music.

As to the standards governing the compilation of the following list, reference is made to a statement which was formulated by Prof. Dr. Wilhelm Altmann in the preface to one of his noted catalogues.[1] In the

---

1. *Verzeichnis von Werken fuer Klavier, vier-und sechshaendig, sowie fuer zwei und mehr Klaviere.*

particular foreword, Dr. Altmann stresses the difficulty attending the compilation of any such lists; inevitably, a dilemma arises when the desire to be comprehensive meets with the necessity of concentration; it is the latter which usually enforces a certain amount of elimination. The author of the present catalogue wishes to subscribe to the following words of Dr. Altmann:

"Every selection is, of course, more or less subjective; I refuse, however, the assumption that a work for which one looks in vain in this index is considered inferior by me. On the other hand, no guarantee for truly artistic value is given for any work which has been included in this catalogue."

The symbol given after the title of a composition is indicative of the publishing house from which the music may be secured. The following key of publishers will serve as a guide; it is arranged in an alphabetical sequence of the symbols used and may facilitate the obtainment of items which the reader wishes to procure.

2. KEY TO PUBLISHERS

A	Edwin Ashdown	London
ALS	G. Alsbach & Co.	Amsterdam
AMC	Advanced Music Corporation	New York
AMP	Associated Music Publishers, Inc.	New York
AND	Johann André	Offenbach-Leipzig
APS	Arthur P. Schmidt Co.	Boston
ART	Artaria	
AU	Augener, Ltd.	London
AX	Axelrod Music	Providence, R. I.
B	Ernst Bisping	Köln
BB	Ed. Bote & G. Bock	Berlin
BE	M. P. Belaieff	Leipzig
BEL	Belwin Inc.	New York
BES	W. Bessel (Breitkopf & Härtel)	Paris-Leipzig
BGE	Bach Gesellschaft Edition	
BH	Breitkopf & Härtel	Leipzig
BMC	Boston Music Co.	Boston-New York
BO	Boosey & Hawkes	London-New York
BOM	Bomart Music Publications	Long Island City, N. Y.
BOS	Bosworth & Co.	Leipzig-Vienna-London
BRA	Julius Brauer	Braunschweig
BRMC	Brashear Music Co.	Boston
BRT	Baerenreiter-Verlag	Kassel-Wilhelmshöhe
BTH	B. Tuthill (published by composer)	Memphis, Tennessee
C	A. & G. Carisch	Milan
CBO	Charles Bordes (published by composer)	Paris
CE	J. & W. Chester	London
CF	Carl Fischer, Inc.	New York
CFS	Clayton F. Summy Co.	Chicago
CH	C. A. Challier & Co.	Berlin
CO	Costallat & Cie	Paris

CPL	Chappell & Co.	New York
CPS	The Composers Press	New York
CRA	August Cranz	Leipzig-Bruxelles
CUR	J. Curwen & Sons	London
D	Ludwig Doblinger	Vienna-Leipzig
DE	Delkas (Elkan-Vogel)	
DEU	Deutscher Musikverlag Robert Ruehle	Berlin
DFC	Durand Fils Cie	Paris
DRE	Drei Lilien (Challier-Birnbach)	Berlin-Halensee
DS	deSantis	Rome
E	Elkin & Co.	London
EF	E. F. Fromont (Elkan-Vogel)	Paris
EL	Ernst Eulenburg	Leipzig
EMB	Edward B. Marks Music Corp.	New York
EN	Enoch & Co.	Paris
EV	Elkan-Vogel Co., Inc.	Philadelphia
F	Forlivesi	
FBG	Robert Forberg	Leipzig
FIN	Fink	Linz
FO	Foetisch frères	Lausanne
FR	Friedrich Wilhelm Froehlich	Berlin
G	Emil Grunert	Leipzig
GAL	Galaxy Music Corp.	New York
GAY	Gay and Teuton	Paris
GBR	Wilhelm Gebauer	Leipzig
GD	Goodwin and Tabb	London
GGH	Henri Gregh et fils	Paris
GH	Gamble Hinged Music Co.	Chicago
GIL	Gilbert	Chicago
GO	A. Goll	Vienna
GR	G. Ricordi and Company	New York
GS	G. Schirmer, Inc.	New York
GUT	Albert J. Gutmann (Universal Ed.)	Vienna
H	J. Hamelle	Paris
HA	Hampton (E. B. Marks)	New York
HAI	Julius Hainauer	Breslau
HAIN	Hain Verlag	Heidelberg
HAY	Ch. Hayet	Paris
HB	Harcourt, Brace and Co.	New York
HC	K. F. Heckel	Mannheim
HE	Heugel & Cie	Paris
HFA	Harold Flammer	New York
HH	Heinrichshofen	Magdeburg
HME	Hudebni Matice Umelecke Besedy (publishing house of Czecho-slovakian composers)	Prague
HN	Wilhelm Hansen	Kopenhagen-Leipzig
HOF	Friedrich Hofmeister	Leipzig
HR	Harms	New York
HS	Carl Haslinger	Vienna

HTH	Ludwig Hoffarth	Dresden
HU	Hug & Co.	Zürich-Leipzig
IMC	International Music Co.	New York
J	Jean Jobert	Paris
JC	John Church Co.	Cincinnati
JF	J. Fischer & Bro.	New York
JO	Jost	
K	Kistner and Siegel	Leipzig
KA	Georg Kallmeyer	Wolfenbuettel
KNT	C. F. Kahnt	Leipzig
L	F.E.C. Leuckart	Leipzig
LA	Lafleur	
LE	Alphonse Leduc	Paris
LEE	Leeds Music Corp.	New York
LI	Robert Lienau	Berlin-Lichterfelde
LIT	Henri Litolff	Leipzig
LM	Henri Lemoine & Cie	Paris
M	Murdoch, Murdoch & Co.	London
MB	Max Brockhaus	Leipzig
MC	Mercury Music Corp.	New York
ME	Max Eschig	Paris
MI	Mills Music Co.	New York
MU	Willy Mueller	Heidelberg
MY	Bela Mery	Budapest
N	A. Noël	Paris
NE	Paul Neldner	Riga
NOV	Novello, Ewer & Co.	London
OD	Oliver Ditson Co. (Theo. Presser Co.)	Boston
OE	Johannes Oertel (until Oct. 1941 Ad. Fuerstner)	Berlin- Grunewald
OL	Olivier	
OUP	Oxford University Press	London
P	W. Paxton & Co.	London
PE	C. F. Peters	Leipzig
PJ	P. Jurgenson	Moscow-Leipzig
PM	Praeger & Meier (Schweers & Haake)	Bremen
POP	Popular Melodies	
R	Gebr. Reinecke	Leipzig
RAH	D. Rahter	Leipzig
RB	J. M. Rieter-Biedermann (C. F. Peters)	Leipzig
RE	Ries & Erler	Berlin
RMC	Robbins Music Corp.	New York
RO	A. Robitschek	Vienna
ROE	Fr. Roerich, Nachf.	Vienna

ROL	Rouart, Lérolle & Cie.	Paris
ROT	C. M. F. Rothe	Leipzig
RU	Carl Ruehle	Leipzig
RUM	Russischer Musikverlag	Berlin-Paris
RUS	Russischer Staatsverlag	Moscow-Leningrad
S	Salabert (A. Z. Mathot)	Paris
SC	Alfred Schmid Nachfolger	Munich
SCH	Edwin Schuberth & Co.	New York
SCU	Fritz Schuberth, Jr.	Leipzig
SE	Maurice Senart (Salabert)	Paris
SF	Sam Fox Publishing Co.	New York-Cleveland
SG	Schroeder and Gunther	New York
SI	Bernhard Siegel	Berlin
SIK	Hans Carl Sikorski	Berlin-Leipzig
SIM	Carl Simon (Breitkopf & Härtel)	Leipzig
SIR	N. Simrock	Leipzig
SL	Schlesinger (Robert Lienau)	Berlin
SO	Schott Söhne	Mainz-Paris-London-Brussels
ST	Albert Stahl	Berlin
STE	Steingräber-Verlag	Leipzig
SUB	J. Schuberth & Co.	Leipzig
SWH	Schweers & Haake	Bremen
T	Tischer & Jagenberg	Köln
TP	Theodore Presser & Co.	Philadelphia
UE	Universal Edition (C. F. Peters)	Vienna-Leipzig
ULL	Ullmann	Reichenberg (Sudetenland)
UM	Universal Music Co.	Chicago
UR	Fr. A. Urbánek & Sons	Prague
V	Volkwein's Music Publishers	Pittsburgh
W	Wood Music Co.	London-New York
WB	Whitney Blake Music Publishers	New York
WE	Otto Wernthal (Robt. Lienau)	Berlin-Lichterfelde
WM	Willis Music Co.	Cincinnati
WOO	Charles Woolhouse	London
WU	Wunderhorn-Verlag	Köln
Z	Wilhelm Zimmermann	Leipzig

3. LIST OF ORIGINAL TWO-PIANO MUSIC

ABORN, LORA
Fugue in Yellow
Rhapsody for two pianos and
orchestra
ADAMS, ERNEST HARRY
Arab Dance   APS
Rondo Mignon   APS
Ice Carnival (Valse Chromatique)   APS
The Toy Doll   APS
AISBERG, JOSEPH
Capriccio Hebraique, opus 20
ALBERTI, H.
Fatinizza de Suppé, Fantaisie
brillante   SO
ALOIZ, LADISLAV
Nine Variations, Finale and Fugue,
opus 28   PJ
ANSON, HUGO
The Lonely Sailing Ship   OUP
ARCHER, VIOLET
Three Sketches
ARENSKY, ANTON
Suite No. 1 for Two Pianos,
opus 15   GS
Suite No. 2 for Two Pianos,
opus 23 "Silhouettes"   PJ
Suite No. 3 for Two Pianos,
opus 33   PJ
Suite No. 4 for Two Pianos,
opus 62   GS
Suite in canon-form,
opus 65   GS
ASANTSCHEWSKY, MICHAEL VON
Festival Polonaise, opus 12   K
ASCHER, J.
Guillaume Tell, Grand Duo
Concertant   SO
ASHTON, ALGERNON
Suite, opus 50   RE
Toccata brillante, opus 144   L
AUBERT, LOUIS
Suite, opus 6 (Suite Brève)   DFC
AUSTEN, THOMAS
Keel Row, Northumbrian Folk
Tune   GAL
BABIN, VICTOR
Six Etudes   UM
  1. Tempo giusto con fuoco
  2. Adagietto cantabile
  3. Veloce
  4. Vivace (based on Flight of
    the Bumble Bee)

  5. Quasi una Siciliana
  6. Allegro molto, dramatico
Concerto for Two Pianos and Or-
chestra (under contract with)   AU
Three March Rhythms (Military-
Funerial-Processional)
Three Fantasies on Old Themes   AU
Hebrew Slumber Song
The Piper of Polmood
Russian Village
BACH, JOHANN CHRISTIAN
Sonata for Two Claviers in G,
opus 15 No. 6   SO, STE
BACH, JOHANN SEBASTIAN
Concerto No. 1 in C minor for two
claviers and orchestra   PE
Concerto No. 2 in C major for two
claviers and orchestra   PE
Concerto No. 3 in C minor for two
claviers and orchestra
Two fugues for two claviers, from
"The Art of Fugue"   BGE, PE
BACH, KARL PHILIPP EMANUEL
Concerto in E flat for Two Claviers
and Orchestra
Concerto in F major for Two Clav-
iers and Orchestra
4 Kleine Duetten fuer 2 Klaviere
(unprinted)
BACH, WILHELM FRIEDEMANN
Two Concertos (Sonatas) for Two
Solo Claviers, in D and F   OUP, PE
Concerto in E flat major for Two
Harpsichords and Orchestra
Duetto (Sonata in F major)   BGE
BACHRICH, ERNST
Variations on a Theme of Beetho-
ven, opus 8   GO
BACON, ERNST
Burr Frolic   AMP
Suite to the Children
Wastin' Time
Kankakee River
The Sky's the Limit   DE
BACON, ERNST with
LUENING, OTTO
Coal Scuttle Blues   AMP
BADINGS, HENK
Baletto grotesco   UE
BAIRSTOW, EDW.
Variations on an original Theme   OUP

BALOGH, ERNO
Peasant Dance   JF
BALUTET, M.
Suite Charactéristique   N
BARD, VIVIEN
Fiesta   CFS
BARKER, CLARENCE
Fantasie symphonique   SCH
BARKLA, N.
Miniature Suite   OUP
BARTÓK, BÉLA
Sonata for Two Pianos and
Percussion   BO
(Exists also in a version entitled
"Concerto for Two Pianos with
Orchestra")
Rhapsody   AMP
Mikrokosmos
BATE, STANLEY
Three Pieces   AMP
  1. Prelude
  2. Pastorale
  3. Rondo
BAUDISSIN, SOPHIE GRÄFIN WOLF
Variations on an own Theme,
opus 8   CH
BAUMER, CECIL
Grotesque   GAL
Minuet, Melody and Gavotte   GAL
BAUSSNERN, WALDEMAR V.
Duo   STE
BAX, ARNOLD E. TREVOR
Moy Mell (or: The Happy Plain)   CE
The Poisoned Fountain   M
Hardanger (Dance, dedicated to
Grieg)   M
The Devil that tempted St.
Anthony   M
Red Autumn   M
Sonata   M
BAZELAIRE, PAUL
Chasse, Scherzo   LE
BEACH, AMY MARCY (Mrs.)
Suite, founded upon old Irish
Melodies   JC
Variations on Balkan Themes,
opus 60   APS
BEECHER, CARL
The Jester, for two Pianos   OD
BENJAMIN, ARTHUR
Jamaican Rumba   BO
Carrabean Suite
BENNETT, ROBERT RUSSELL
Tema Sporca Con Variazione
(Dirty Theme and Variations)

BEREZOWSKI, NICOLAI
Fantasia, opus 9, for two pianos and
orchestra (Reduction for two pi-
anos by composer)   AMP
BERGER, WILHELM
Variations in E minor, opus 61   SIM, BH
BERGT, AD.
Sonata, opus 1   PE
BÉRIOT, fils, CHARLES W. de
Sonata, opus 61   H
BERKELEY, LENNOX
Capriccio   CE
Nocturne   CE
Polka   CE
BERNERS, LORD
Chinoiserie
BIBL, RUDOLF
Scherzo, opus 57   MB
BIEHL, ALBERT
Eight Duos, opus 128   SIM, BH
BIERMANN, H.
Marche Triomphale, opus 20   APS
BILBRO, MATHILDE
Two Country Sketches   GS
BLANC, ADOLPHE
Sonatine concertante, opus 64   LM
BLANCHET, EMILE ROB.
Ballade, opus 57   ME
BLISS, ARTHUR
Concerto for Two Pianos and Or-
chestra   OUP
BLOCH, ERNEST
Evocations (transcribed from the
symphonic suite for orchestra)   GS
BLUMENFELD, FELIX
Capriccio, opus 4
BOISDEFFRE, RENÉ de
Scherzo-Serenade, opus 9   HE
BONAWITZ, JOHANN HEINRICH
Concerto for Two Pianos   GS
Duo on Gounod's "Faust"
BONIS, MELANIE
Variations   ME
Scherz-Valse   LE
BORDES, CHARLES
Rapsodie Basque   CBO
BOSE, FRITZ v.
Duo, opus 13   K
BOWEN, YORK
Arabesque, opus 119   CF, OUP
BOWLES, PAUL
Concerto for Two Pianos, Winds,
and Percussion
Sonata for Two Pianos   GS

DEMUTH, NORMAN F.
Rhapsody   OUP
Bolero   OUP
Habanera   OUP
DENNÉE, CHARLES
Danse Moderne, opus 9, No. 1   APS
Russian Dance, opus 16, No. 1   APS
DEPROSSE, A.
Andante with Variations, Intermezzi
   and Fugato, opus 22   SCU
DESTENAYE, E.
Chorale and Fugue, opus 20   H
DISTLER, HUGO
Sonata concertante, opus 1   BH
DONATH, GUST.
Prelude and Fugue in D major   LI
DOUGHERTY, CELIUS
Nautical Sonata, music from Seas
   and Ships (under contract with)   GS
DOUILLET, PIERRE
Sarabande and Variations, opus 21   BH
DRIVER, PERCIVAL F.
Variations on an Original Theme   BO
DUMAS, L.
Fantaisie   GR
DUNGAN, OLIVE
Tropic Night Suite   CF
   1. White Jasmine
   2. Enchantment
DUPARC, HENRI
Prelude and Fugue in A minor   ME
DURAND, A.
Chaconne, opus 62   CF
DUSCH, ALEX v.
Sonata in C minor, opus 13   HC
DUSSEK, JOHANN LADISLAUS
Concerto for Two Pianofortes and
   Orchestra in B flat, opus 63
Sonata for Two Pianos in E flat,
   opus 38   HS
Duos for Two Pianos, opus 11
Duos for Two Pianos, opus 36 (with
   Horn ad. lib.)
DUTEIL D'OZANNE, J. A. JOS.
Suite Carnavalesque   CO
DUVERNOY, JEAN BAPTISTE
Feu Roulant, opus 256   EMB
Don Juan Fantasie, opus 284 (on the
   Serenade from Mozart's opera)
ECKART, FRIEDRICH
Kontrapunktische Variationen,
   opus 7   HAIN

EGGELING, G.
La Capricieuse, Valse, opus 120   APS
EIGES, K.
Suite Pastorale, opus 20   RUS
EILENBERG, ROB. BRAUN
Andante and Variations (quasi fan-
   tasia), opus 24   W
ELKUS, ALBERT
On a merry folk-tune   JF
ELMORE, ROBERT
Swing Rhapsody   JF
ENDERS, HARVEY
Russian Picnic   GS
ENESCO, GEORGES
Variations, opus 5   EN
ERDMANNSDOERFER-FICHTNER,
PAULINE
Thema mit 9 Umspielungen
   (E minor)   G
ERLER, HERMANN
Prelude and Gavotte, opus 32   RE
Menuett, opus 33   RE
EVANS, EDWIN
Grand Sonata appassionato, opus 26   LA
FARJEON, HARRY
Rhapsody, opus 70   GD
Vignettes, opus 72 (Tone picture;
   Pastoral reverie)   P
FARNABY, GILES
Piece for Two Virginals (Fitzwil-
   liam Virginal Book)   OUP
FAURÉ, GABRIEL
Fantaisie, opus 111   DFC
FERGUSON, HOWARD
Partita   BO
FISCHER, ERNST
Zwei Klaviere plaudern (3 Stuecke)   HH
FISCHHOF, ROBERT
Trois Scènes aragonaises   D
Variations and Fugue on an original
   Theme   HE
FISHER, ERNEST
Skidding Along (Glatteis)   SO
Perpetuum mobile   SO
Dancing Masks   AMP
Marabu   AMP
FLEISSNER, OTTO
Polonaise Brillante   APS
FLORIO, CARYL
Easy Sonatina   SCH
FLUEGEL, ERNST
Duo, opus 40   R
Vier Original-Duos, opus 14   SIM, BH

KAUN, HUGO
Suite im alten Stil, opus 81   HH
Erste (märkische) Suite, opus 92   z

KEENAN, GERTRUDE
Country Dance   CF

KEENEY, WENDELL
Spanish capriccio   JF

KELBERINE, ALEXANDER
Londonderry Air   GS
Song of the Volga Boatmen   GS

KELLER, WALTER
Prelude and Fugue, opus 10   GIL

KELLOGG, KAY
Rojo Y Negro   HFA
Turkey in the Straw, American
Folk Song   HFA
Valse Pavonine   HFA

KELLY, F. S.
Theme, Variations, and Fugue,
opus 5   SO

KENNAN, KENT
Dance Divertimento:
Promenade—Air de Ballet—Jig

KERSBERGEN, J. W.
Variations and Fugue on No. 1
from "Erks Liederschatz," opus 5   RE

KETTERER, E.
Grand Caprice Hongrois, Etude de
Concert, opus 7   SO
Marche Orientale, opus 92b   SO

KHATCHATURIAN, ARAM
Three Dances
Suite   LEE
  1. Ostinato
  2. Romance
  3. Fantastic Waltz

KIRCHNER, THEODOR
Polonaise in F
Variations on an own theme,
opus 85   HOF
Waltzes, opus 86   PE

KLEIN, JOHN
Three Dances   AMP
  1. Jig Waltz
  2. Stoop Dance
  3. Whirl

KNORR, IWAN
Variations and Fugue on a Russian
Folk Song, opus 8   BH

KOECHLIN, CHARLES
Suite, opus 6   LE

KOUCEN
Sonatina

KOUNTZ, RICHARD
The Sleigh, à la Russe (arranged by composer)   GS

KOWALSKI, HENRI
Salute à Pesth, Marche hongroise
de concert   SO, GS

KRAMM, MAX
Chatterbox
The Village Fair   GH

KRAUSE, ANT.
Sonata in E, opus 17   BH

KRONKE, EMIL
Symphonic Variations on a Nordic
Theme, opus 14   STE
Suite, opus 42   SO
Little Suite, opus 73   K
Concert Variations, opus 80 (Sym-
phonic Ballade)   L
Lyric Pieces, opus 94   K

KUESTER, HERBERT
Excentrik-Fox   FR
Gazellen-Fox   FR
Tanz-Fantasie   FR
Meeres-Melodie   FR

LABOR, JOS.
Capriccio Big Ben   UE
Fantasy on an Original Theme,
opus 1   UE
Scherzo in the form of a canon,
opus 2   UE

LACK, THÉODORE
Duo Symphonique, opus 65   IM
Sonatine, opus 129   HE
Marquise, Menuet, opus 271   APS

LAHEE, H.
Duo sur Stabat Mater de Rossini   SO

LAMPE, WALTHER
Theme and Variations, opus 2

LANDRY, ALBERT
Valse des Mouches   MC

LA TOMBELLE, F. de
Fantaisie   CO
Prelude and Fugue   DFC

LAURISCHKUS, MAX
Three Duos, opus 7b   SIR, BH

LAWNHURST, VEE and
POLLOCK, MURIEL
Table d'Hôte   POP

LAZARUS, GUSTAV
Three Pieces, opus 39   SIM
  1. Ländler
  2. Scherzo
  3. Valse Lente

O'NEILL, NORMAN
Variations and Fugue on an Irish
Theme, opus 17   SO
ORE, HARRY
Variations and Fugue on a Theme
by L. v. Beethoven, opus 10   NE
PACHELBEL, HIERONYMUS
Toccata for Two Claviers
PAGANUCCI, A.
Valse Débonnaire   GS
PALMGREN, SELIM
Maskenball, opus 36 (Suite)   LI
PALS, LEOPOLD van der GILSE
Sonata in E minor   BES
PARLOW, EDMUND
Three Pieces, opus 84   K
    1. Bolero
    2. Notturno
    3. Waltz
PARRIS, ROBERT
Sonata in Four Movements for Two
Pianos
PARRISH, CARL
Valse Viennoise   JF
PARRY, CHARLES HUBERT
HASTINGS
Grand Characteristic Duo in E minor   BH
PASQUINI, BERNARDO
14 Sonatas for Two Claviers (writ-
ten in figured bass)   NOV, BRT, DFC
Of these published and edited
2 Sonatas (G minor, F major) ed-
ited by F. Boghen   DFC
Sonata in D minor, edited by W.
Danckert   BRT
the same, edited by J. S. Shedlock   NOV
PATTISON, LEE
The Arkansaw Traveller, Old Fid-
dler's Tune   GS
PAVIA, I. L.
Polka Viennoise on a Theme by
Johann Strauss   OUP
PELZ, WILLIAM
Sentimental Rhapsody   JF
PENNARIO, L.
March of the Lunatics   LEE
Fireflies   CFS
PERL, MATTHIAS
Konzert-Walzer   FR
PERSICHETTI, VINCENT
Concertino (arranged by composer
from original for piano and or-
chestra)   EV
PESSARD, EMILE
Suite pittoresque   LM

PETERS, RUDOLF
15 Variations on an own Theme,
opus 10   SIR
PETYREK, FELIX
Six Concert Etudes   UE
Toccata and Fugue, (Mixolydian)   UE
PFEIFFER, GEORGES
Variations artistiques, opus 90 b
(transcribed from piano, 2 hands
by composer)   H
Sonata, opus 65   GGH
PHILIPP, ISIDOR
Caprice   GS
Feux Follets
PHILLIPS, DONALD
Concerto in Jazz   MI
PICK-MANGIAGALLI, RICCARDO
Humoresque, opus 35
PIETSCH, EDNA F.
Prelude   JF
PILLNEY, KARL HERMANN
Divertimento, opus 2
PINTO, OCTAVIO
Scenas Infantis (Memories of
Childhood) 5 pieces (transcribed
from piano solo)   GS
PIRANI, EUGENIO
Fantasia in D minor, opus 87   LI
Etude de Concert, opus 51   SL
Gavotte, opus 34   CF
PISK, PAUL A.
My Pretty Little Pink (southern
folk tune)   LEE
PIXIS, JOHANN PETER
Variations on "The Hugenots,"
opus 137   GR
Grand Variations militaires, opus 66
POLDINI, EDOUARD
Study on the Impromptu, opus 90,
No. 2, by Schubert   HAI
POLLOCK, MURIEL
Hispana   GS
PORTNOFF, MISCHA
Brief Flirtation (Un flirt éphémère)   JF
March of the Imps (La marche des
lutins)   JF
Playful Leaves (Feuilles folâtres)   JF
Sentimental Parting (Adieu senti-
mental)   JF
POULENC, FRANCIS
Concerto for Two Pianos and
Orchestra
Sonata for Two Pianos (or One
Piano, Four Hands)   CE

POWELL, JOHN
  Natches-on-the-Hill; Three Virginian Country Dances, opus 30,
  bis .... GS
  Rhapsodie Nègre .... GS

POZZOLI, E.
  Tarantella .... GR

PRICE, FLORENCE B.
  Three Little Negro Dances .... TP
  Hoe Cake
  Ticklin' Toes
  Rabbit Foot

PUETTER, HUGO
  Duo Concertante in C sharp minor .... MU

RAASTED, N. O.
  Variations and Fugue on a Theme
  of D. Buxtehude, opus 14 L

RABAUD, HENRI
  Divertissement sur des Chansons
  Russes .... EN

RACHMANINOFF, SERGEI
  Fantaisie (Suite) opus 5 .... IMC
    1. Barcarole
    2. "Oh night, oh love"
    3. Tears
    4. Easter
  Suite No. 2, opus 17
    1. Introduction
    2. Valse
    3. Romance
    4. Tarantelle

RAFF, JOSEF JOACHIM
  Chaconne in A minor, opus 150 .... CO, PE
  Fantaisie in G minor, opus 207a .... K
  Tarantelle, opus 82

RAMEAU, JEAN PHILIPPE
  Two Portraits from Concerto No. V
    1. Mme. Cupis
    2. Mme. Marais

RAVEL, MAURICE
  Les Sites Auriculaires
  Rhapsodie Espagnole (transcription)
  La Valse (transcription) .... DFC
  Bolero (transcription) .... DFC

RAVINA, JEAN HENRI
  Grand Duo sur l'Opéra Euryanthe
  de C.M. v. Weber, opus 9 .... SO
  Souvenirs de Russie, Grand duo,
  opus 64 bis .... SO

REBIKOFF, VLADIMIR
  Cauchemar, opus 26

RÉE, LOUIS
  Variations and Fugue on an Original Theme, opus 14 .... FBG
  Suite Champêtre, opus 21 .... RO
  Scherzo, opus 32
  Two Concerti

REGER, MAX
  Variations and Fugue on a Theme
  by Beethoven, opus 86 .... BB
  Introduction, Passacaglia, and Fugue, opus 96 .... BB
  Variations and Fugue on a Theme
  by Mozart, opus 132a (transcription from orchestra) .... PE

REICHARD, A.
  Waltz Suite, opus 94 .... SIM

REICHEL, BERNHARD
  Bourrée .... STE

REINECKE, KARL
  Andante and Variations, opus 6
  (after the model of Schumann) .... HOF
  Impromptu on a Motif from Schumann's "Manfred," opus 66 .... AMP, BH
  Variations on a Sarabande by Bach,
  opus 24b .... SUB
  La Belle Grisélidis, Improvisations
  on a French Folk Song of the
  17th Century, opus 94 .... BH
  Improvisations on a Gavotte by
  Gluck, opus 125 .... PE
  Duo, after the Octet for Wind Instruments, opus 216a .... K
  Festival Overture, opus 148 (arr.
  by composer) .... BH
  Zur Reformationsfeier (Variations
  on Luther's Chorale "A Mighty
  Fortress"), opus 191 .... FBG
  Pictures from the South, opus 86
  (arr. from original piano solo) .... CF, RB
  Four Pieces, opus 241 .... RB
  Etude
  Minuet
  Scherzo in canon form
  Allegretto
  Three Sonatas
    1. In F major, opus 240 .... PE
    2. In G major, opus 275
    3. In C major, opus 275 .... HOF
  Overture to Klein's drama "Zenobia," opus 193 .... BH
  (arr. by composer)

REINHARD, AUG.
  Waltz Suite, opus 94 .... SIM, BH

REINHARD, B. FRANÇOIS
Waltz Suite, opus 24
RENÉ, C.
Reflets du Nord, Suite OL
REPPER, CHARLES
The Dancer in the Patio BRMC
REUSS, AUG.
Fantasie, opus 42 T
RHEINBERGER, JOSEF
Duo in A minor, opus 15 H, K
Sonata in C minor, opus 122 (also
for 4 hands)
Duo, opus 149A (after the Suite
for organ, violin, violoncello,
and string orchestra) K
Cantilene and Fugue, opus 148
RIEGGER, WALLINGFORD
New Dance (arranged by composer
from original four-hand, one pi-
ano score)
RIES, FERDINAND
Duo pour 2 pianos, opus 142 SO
Sonata, opus 32, in B flat major
Trio for Two Pianos and Harp
RIETI, VITTORIO
Second Avenue Waltzes
Suite Champêtre
RIETSCH, HEINRICH
Fantasy in F minor FBG
ROENTGEN, JULIUS
Scherzo, opus 33 ALS
Ballade on a Norwegian Folk Mel-
ody, opus 36b SIM
ROLDAN, AMADEO
Curujey, "Son" for choir, two pia-
nos, and Cuban percussion
ROPARTZ, J. GUY
Pièce (B minor) DFC
ROSCHER, JOSEF
Fantasy, opus 114 ROE
ROSELLEN, HENRI
Grand Duo sur Norma (d'après
l'Op. 21) SO
ROSENBLOOM, SYDNEY
Variations and Fugue on an orig-
inal theme, opus 16 AU
ROSENHAIN, JACQUES
Fantasia appassionata, opus 40
(Grand Duo, also for piano and
harp) HOF
ROSENTHAL, MANUEL
La Belle Zelie, Suite for two pianos
ROSENWALD, HANS HERMANN
Sonata for Two Pianos

ROSSLER, RICHARD
Variations on a Folk-Song, opus 29
RUBINSTEIN, ANTON
Fantasia in F, opus 73 SIM, H
RUBINSTEIN, BERYL
Suite for Two Pianos GS
Prelude
Canzonetta
Jig
Masks
RUDORFF, ERNST
Variations in E, opus 1 BH
RUTHARDT, ADOLF
Sonata quasi Fantasia (in one
movement), opus 31 K
SAAR, LOUIS VICTOR
Gavotte Intermezzo from Three
Love Episodes, opus 75, No. 2 CF
In Old Vienna, an arrangement of
a Viennese folk tune OD
SAINT-SAENS, CAMILLE
Duo, opus 8, (d'après les Duos pour
Piano et Orgue) DFC
Caprice Héroique, opus 16
Variations on a Theme by Beet-
hoven, opus 35 DFC, GS
Danse Macabre, opus 40 (tran-
scription) DFC
Polonaise, opus 77 DFC
Scherzo, opus 87 DFC
Caprice Arabe, opus 96 DFC
Carnival des Animaux, for two pi-
anos and orchestra
Fantasy and Fugue, Chorale, Scher-
zo, Finale EF
Le Rouet d'Omphale (transcrip-
tion)
SAMUELS, W. G.
Fiesta
SATIE, ERIC
Three Pieces in the Shape of a
Pear
SATTER, GUSTAV
L'Union, Morceau de Salon,
opus 73 SO
Trois Morceaux Lyriques (Marche,
Chanson, Dance), opus 81 SO
Trois Romances sans Paroles,
opus 82 SO
Poème, opus 87 SO
Tarantelle de concert AND
In der freien Natur, opus 77
(Wald-, Wasser- und Blumen-
geister) HTH

Tango at Midnight from Suite
"Partita Americana"   JF
Alice in Wonderland, Modern
Suite   JF
   The Duchess (Passacaglia)
   The Gryphon and the Mock
    Turtle (Minuet)
   The Queen of Hearts (Gigue)
   The Cheshire Cat (Cake Walk)
   The Dormouse (Sarabande)
   The Lobster Quadrille (Reel)
Phantasmania (transcribed from
orchestra)   GS
SIMON, ANTONY
Deux Morceaux (Mélodie, Danse)   PJ
Petite Suite, opus 63   PJ
SIMON, C. P.
Variations libres   HAY
SINDING, CHRISTIAN
Variations (in E flat minor),
opus 2   HN
Duets, opus 41   HN
  1. Andante
  2. Deciso ma non troppo allegro
SINGER, OTTO
Andante with Variations, opus 1   BH
SISTERS JEANNE MADELEINE and
FRANCIS TERESE
Prelude
Legend
SMETANA, BEDRICH
Sonata in E minor (Kàan)   HME
SOMERVELL, ARTHUR
Variations on an original Theme   AU
Normandy, Symphonic Variations   AU
SOWERBY, LEO
Ballade for two pianos and or-
chestra (after the old English
poem "King Estmere")
SPIES, CLAUDIO
Sonata for Two Pianos
SPONER, ALFRED v.
Novelette, opus 16   RB
SPROSS, CHARLES GILBERT
Valse Caprice   TP
STANFORD, CHARLES VILLIERS
Serenade, opus 17   BO
STAUB, VICTOR
En Valsant, Valse mignonne,
opus 18   APS
STAVENHAGEN, BERNHARD
Caprice in C major (arr. by the
composer)   HB
Menuetto Scherzando, opus 5, No. 3

STEIBELT, DANIEL
Duos for Two Pianos   BH
STEPHENS, CHARLES EDWARD
Duo concertant, opus 4   SO
STIEHL, H.
Ungarisch, opus 79   SO
STOEGBAUER, ISIDOR
Sonate im alten Stil   ULL
STOJOWSKI, SIGMUND
Prologue, Scherzo et Variations   HE
STONE, GREGORY
Auld Lang Syne, as it would be
played in various nations   EMB
Burlesque Tzigane, Caricature of a
Famous Gipsy Theme on the
style of Great Composers
Dark Eyes, Paraphrase on the Fa-
mous Russian Gypsy Air   EMB
Great Rivers, International Rhap-
sody on Three Themes   EMB
Yablotchko, Dance of the Soviet
Sailors
STOYE, PAUL
Friendship Waltz   OD
STRAVINSKY, IGOR
Concerto per Due Pianoforti Soli   AMP
Sonata for Two Pianos   CPL
Scherzo à la Russe (transcription,
original for orchestra)   CPL
Dumbarton Oaks Concerto
(transcription)   AMP
STRELETZKI, ANTON
Grande Prélude   HAI
STRONG, MARK
Sir Roger de Coverley, Paraphrase   GS
STRONG, TEMPLETON
Drei sinfonische Idyllen, opus 29   JO
STURM, AUGUST
Elegy, opus 16   BOS
SUESSE, DANA
Concerto in E minor for Two Pi-
anos and Orchestra
Danza a media noche (Dance at
Midnight)   JF
SUGARMAN, LOUIS
March of the Puppets   EMB
Spanish Nights
Waltz Serenade
TAILLEFERRE, GERMAINE
Jeux de Plein Air (suite of two
pieces)   DFC
Concerto for two pianos, orches-
tra and chorus
Valse Lente

TAKACS, JENÖ von
Tarantella, opus 39   UE
TALMA, LOUISE
Four Handed Fun   CF
TANEIEV, SERGEI IVANOVITCH
Prelude and Fugue, opus 29   RUS
TANSMAN, ALEXANDER
Sonatine Transatlantique (transcribed from piano solo)
Carnival Suite   LEE
Suite for Two Pianos with Orchestra   AMP
TARENGHI, MARIO
Eight Variations on the Minuet theme opus 99 of Robert Schumann, opus 40   C
Nine Variations on Prelude XX by F. Chopin, opus 68   GR
Serenata (arr. by composer)   HB
Prelude and Fugue in G minor   GR
TEDOLDI, AGIDE
Habanera   GR
TELLEFSEN, THOMAS DYKE ACLAND
Sonata, opus 41   CO
THALBERG, SIGISMUND
Fantasy on "Norma," opus 12
THERN, KARL
Romance, opus 48   RE
Scherzo, opus 58   RE
Notturno, opus 66   RE
Theme and Variations in the Italian Manner, opus 67   RE
Andantino, opus 72   RE
Tarantella, opus 73   RE
THIÉRIOT, FERDINAND
Concerto for Two Pianos and Orchestra in F, opus 77   RB
Two Pieces, opus 36 (Intermezzo, Humoreske)   RU
Two Pieces, opus 40   GBR
Two Pieces, opus 82
THOMAS, GUSTAV ADOLF
Fuga eroica, opus 12   KNT
THOMPSON, ROY
Aubade   OUP
THOMSON, VIRGIL
Synthetic Waltzes   EV
TIPPETT, MICHAEL
Fantasia on a Theme of Händel   AMP
TOCCHI, GIANLUCA
Three Favolette   DS
TODD, ESTHER COX
Suite for two pianos

TORNIEPORTH, H.
Duo on the Waltz "Voices of Spring" by Joh. Strauss   SO
TRIGGS, HAROLD
Valse   GS
Spiritual (from Beaufort, Carolina Low Country) "Death ain't yuh got no shame?"   GS
Autumn Legend   JF
Tyrolienne (Waltz)   JF
TRIMBLE, JOAN
Sonatina   BO
The Bard of Lisgoole, Irish Air   BO
Buttermilk Point (Reel)   BO
Humours of Carrick, Hop Jig   BO
TRUXELL, EARL
Valse Chantée   V
Tango   V
TURINI, FERDINAND
Sonata in D major
TURNER, OLIVE
Cap and Bells   OUP
Two Cornish Sketches   OUP
TUTHILL, BURNET
Come Seven, Rhapsodie (arr. by composer from orchestra)   BTH
UNGER, HERMANN
Chamber Variations ("Kammervariationen") on an own Theme, opus 8   T
URSPRUCH, ANTON
Variations and Fugue on a Theme by Bach, opus 13   CRA
VALLE DE PAZ, EDGARDO
Scenes de Ballet, opus 39
VENEZIA, FRANCO DA
Fantasia for Two Pianos
VOGEL, ADOLF BERNHARD
Andante and Variations, opus 14   KNT
VOGT, JEAN
Prelude and Fugue, opus 18   BH
Prelude and Finale Fugato, opus 82   CH
VOLKMANN, ROBERT
Variations on a Theme by Händel, opus 26   SO
VOUILLEMIN, LOUIS
Four Classic Dances, opus 16   DFC
WACHTMEISTER, AXEL RAOUL
Prelude and Fugue   JC
WAGENSEIL, GEORG CHRISTOPH
Concerto for Two Claviers
Divertimento for Two Claviers, opus 5

WALDECK, CARL
Twelve Variations on the Minuet
from "Don Juan" by Mozart,
opus 22 FIN
WALKER, ERNEST
A West Africa Fantasy, opus 53 OUP
A Waltz Suite, opus 60 OUP
WALTER, FRIED
Concert Waltzes Z
WEHRLI, WERNER
Variations and Fugue on a Jolly
Song, opus 18 HU
WEINBERGER, JAROMIR
Polka and Fugue from the opera
"Shvanda" (transcription) AMP
WEISGALL, HUGO
Fugue and Romance MC
WEISMANN, JULIUS
Suite, opus 19
Nine Variations on a Theme in A
major, opus 64 STE
Partita, opus 107 STE
Sonatine "Ille terrarum," opus 122 STE
WELLEBA, LEOPOLD
Concert Waltz, opus 1 D
WHITTEMORE, ARTHUR and
LOWE, JACK
Paganini Caprice, No. 24 (with ac-
knowledgments to Franz Liszt)
WIDOR, CHARLES MARIE
"April Tales," opus 64, Suite Con-
certante for Two Pianos IIB
WIENIAWSKI, JOSEPH
Fantasy, opus 42 SO
WIENSINGER, EDUARD
Menuett and Scherzo, opus 60 GUT
WILCKENS, FRIEDRICH
Robes Pierre & Co., Kriminal-
Balletsketsch UE
WILLIAMS, BECKET
Impromptu and Double Fugue CUR
WILLIAMS, JEAN
Mitzie Polka SG
Sevilliana SG
WILLIAMS, RALPH VAUGHN
Introduction and Fugue CF
Concerto for Two Pianos and Or-
chestra
WILLIAMSON, ESTHER
Sonata for Two Pianos MC
WILLNER, ARTHUR
Variations on an own Theme,
opus 20 DRE

WILM, NIKOLAI von
Valse-Impromptu, opus 2 RE
Two Character Pieces, opus 60 RE
Preludium and Sarabande,
opus 62 L, HB
Variations, opus 64 L
Waltzes, opus 72 L
Easy Variations on "So viel Stern'
am Himmel stehn," opus 94 RB
WINKLER, ALEXANDER
ADOLFOVITCH
Variations and Fugue on a Theme
by Bach, opus 12 BE
WOLF, LEOP. CARL
Phantasiestueck, opus 24 BH
WOLLFAHRT, HEINR.
Introduction and Fugue, opus 5 ROT
WORTH, AMY
Purple Heather HFA
WOZENCRAFT, MARIAN LEITCH
Twin Pieces CS
WRIGHT, N. LOUISE
From the South (Plantation Dance) CFS
YAYSNOFF, JUNE AND IRIS
Symphonic Suite for Two Pianos
and Orchestra
Ode to China for Two Pianos and
Orchestra
YSAYE, THÉOPHILE
Variations in E minor, opus 10 SO
ZACK, VICTOR
Free Variations on an original
Theme, opus 2 RO
ZELLNER, JULIUS
Three Pieces, opus 3 MB
Duo, opus 12 MB
Duo, opus 16 D
Wedding March, opus 31 MB
ZILCHER, HANS
Night and Morning, for two pianos,
string orchestra and tympani
ZILCHER, HERMANN
Symphonie, opus 50 BH
(*Not* an arrangement of an or-
chestral work)
ZILLMANN, EDUARD
Duo on the Folk Song "A Schlosser
hot an G'sellen g'hot," opus 24 BRA
Four Quartettinos, opus 38 HTH
ZIZOLD, W.
Konzertstueck, opus 13, (Introduc-
tion and Scherzo) LI

CHAPTER XXV

RECORDED TWO-PIANO MUSIC

1. Extent and Confines

The following list includes recordings of music played on two pianos. In view of the still rather limited number of such recordings, an approximately summary survey of the available material has been attempted. Consequently, the index includes original compositions for two pianos, without and with ensemble, as well as all types of arrangements. In the case of the latter, the name of the arranger, wherever available, is given in parentheses after the title of the composition.

A few recordings from the popular field are added to this list, since some of them have been made by leading concert teams and therefore will afford an opportunity to study the style and ensemble effects of the particular duo-pianists.

The manufacturer of each recording is indicated by a symbol, and a list of recording companies corresponds with the key given for each item.

It is hoped that this compilation will help to reveal the fragmentary state of coverage in which the recorded literature for two pianos still is found. Professional duo-pianists as well as record manufacturers here meet a wide open field for their initiative and enterprise.

2. KEY OF RECORD MANUFACTURERS

A S	L'Anthologie Sonore	N	New Music Recordings
B A M	La Boîte à Musique	P	Parlophone
C	Columbia	P o	Polydor
C o	Concert Hall Society	R	Roycroft
C o n	Conlin Records	R e	Royale
D	Decca	S	Schirmer
D i	Dial	T	Technicord
F	Friends of Recorded Music	T i	Timely
G a	Gamut	V	Victor
G r	Gramophone (His Master's Voice)	V o	Vox
M	Musicraft		

3. LIST OF RECORDED TWO-PIANO MUSIC
ARENSKY, ANTON

Romance from First Suite for Two Pianos, opus 15	Bartlett and Robertson	c
Waltz from Suite No. 1 for Two Pianos, opus 15	Bartlett and Robertson	c
	Bauer and Gabrilowitsch	v
	Vronsky and Babin	c, v

ARLEN, HAROLD

Stormy Weather	Morley and Gearhart	c
That Old Black Magic (arr. Whittemore & Lowe)	Whittemore and Lowe	v

ARNDT, FELIX

Nola	Rawicz and Landauer	c

BABIN, VICTOR

Etude No. 1	Vronsky and Babin	v
Russian Village	Vronsky and Babin	c

BACH, JOHANN SEBASTIAN

Concerto No. 1 in C minor for two claviers and orchestra	Manuel and Williamson Harpsichord Ensemble	M
	Scheck-Wenzinger Chamber Orchestra	GR
Concerto No. 2 in C major for two claviers and orchestra	Bartlett and Robertson, String Orchestra, cond. J. Barbirolli	GR
	Ruggero Gerlin and Marcelle Charbonnier with String Orchestra, cond. by Curt Sachs	AS
	Manuel and Williamson Harpsichord Ensemble	M
	Artur and Karl Ulrich Schnabel with London Symphony Orchestra, cond. Boult	v
Concerto No. 3 in C minor for two claviers and orchestra	Manuel and Williamson Harpsichord Ensemble	M
Jesu, My Heart's Joy (from Cantata No. 147) (arr. Horne)	Bartlett and Robertson	c
Sheep May Safely Graze	Bartlett and Robertson	c
Sicilienne from Sonata No. 4 for Clavier and Flute (arr. Maier)	Nemenoff and Luboshutz	v
Sonata No. 4 in E minor (arr. Babin)	Vronsky and Babin	v
Sonata No. 5 in C major (arr. Babin)	Vronsky and Babin	v

BARROSO

Brazil (arr. Whittemore & Lowe)	Whittemore and Lowe	v

BARTLETT, ETHEL (arranger)

Elizabethan Suite	Bartlett and Robertson	c

Contains: Variations on John, Come Kiss Me Now and Earle of Salisbury's Pavan by William Byrd; His Conceit, A toye, Tower Hill Jigge, Tune for Two Virginals, His Dreame by Giles Farnaby; The Fall of the Leafe by Martin Peerson; The King's Hunting Jigge by Dr. John Bull

BARTÓK, BÉLA

Sonata for Two Pianos and Percussion	Béla Bartók and Ditta Pásztory	vo
	William Masselos and Maro Ajemian	DI

BEETHOVEN, LUDWIG van

Turkish March (from "Ruins of Athens") (arr. Thern)	Bartlett and Robertson	c

BERLIN, IRVING

Russian Lullaby	Morley and Gearhart	c

BIZET, GEORGES

Excerpts from "Carmen"	Jordan and Kent	D

BORODIN, ALEXANDER

Dances of the Polovetzki Maidens from "Prince Igor" (arr. Babin)	Vronsky and Babin	v

BOWLES, PAUL

Sonata for Two Pianos	Gold and Fizdale	co
Concerto for Two Pianos, Winds and Percussion	Gold and Fizdale	c

BRAHAM

Limehouse Blues	Morley and Gearhart	c

BRAHMS, JOHANNES

Liebeslieder Walzer, opus 52	RCA Victor Chorale with Luboshutz and Nemenoff	v
Variations on a Theme by Haydn, opus 56 b	Bartlett and Robertson	c
	Luboshutz and Nemenoff	v
	Whittemore and Lowe	v
Five Waltzes, opus 39 (Nos. 1, 2, 11, 14, 15)	Vronsky and Babin	c
Waltzes, opus 39 (Nos. 6, 15, 2, 1, 14, 10, 5, 6)	N. Boulanger and D. Lipatti	GR

BULL, DR. JOHN

The King's Hunting Jigge ("Elizabethan Suite")	Bartlett and Robertson	c

"By Jupiter"—

"By Jupiter" Medley, with rhythm acc. (1) Ev'rything I've Got (2) Careless Rhapsody (3) Nobody's Heart (4) Jupiter Forbid	Fingerle and Schutt	D

BYRD, WILLIAM

Earle of Salisbury's Pavan ("Elizabethan Suite")	Bartlett and Robertson	c
Variations on John, Come Kiss Me Now ("Elizabethan Suite")	Bartlett and Robertson	c

CARMICHAEL, HOAGY

Stardust	Morley and Gearhart	c

CHABRIER, EMMANUEL

Trois Valses Romantiques	Robert and Gaby Casadesus	c

CHAMBERS, DR. J. CLARENCE

All American, A Satirical Suite for Two Pianos	José and Amparo Iturbi	v

CHANDLER-WHITE-COHEN

Canadian Capers	Victor Arden and Phil Ohman	v

CHOPIN, FRÉDÉRIC

Minute Waltz	Jordan and Kent	D
Rondo in C major, opus 73	Bartlett and Robertson	C
	Luboshutz and Nemenoff	V
	Leonard Shure and Karl U. Schnabel	V

CONRAD, CON

The Continental (arr. Whittemore & Lowe)	Whittemore and Lowe	V

COPLAND, AARON

Danzon Cubano	Aaron Copland and Leo Smit	CO

COUPERIN, FRANÇOIS

Musette de Taverni (Bagpipe Tune)	Manuel and Williamson Harpsichord Ensemble	M

CREAMER-LAYTON

After You've Gone	Thomas Waller and Bennie Paine	V

CUI, CESAR

Orientale—from "Kaleidoscope, Opus 50" (arr. Luboshutz)	Luboshutz and Nemenoff	V

DEBUSSY, CLAUDE

En Blanc et Noir	Bartlett and Robertson	C
Fêtes (Festivals) (arr. Ravel)	Josef and Rosina Lhevinne	V
Fêtes	Fray and Braggiotti	D
Golliwogg's Cake-Walk	Fray and Braggiotti	D
La Cathédrale Engloutie	Fray and Braggiotti	D
L'Isle Joyeuse	Fray and Braggiotti	D
Reverie	Fray and Braggiotti	D

"Deep River"—

Deep River, American Negro Melody (arr. Alexander Kelberine)	Behrend and Kelberine	V

"Doubling on the Ivories"

Doubling on the Ivories (two piano tempo) Contains: light music by Porter, Wilder, Freed-Brown, Dubin-McHugh, Robin-Rainger and Johann Strauss	Whittemore and Lowe	V

DUBENSKY, ARCADY

Gossips (arr. Whittemore and Lowe)	Whittemore and Lowe	V

DUBIN, AL and McHUGH, JIMMY

South American Way (arr. Whittemore and Lowe)	Whittemore and Lowe	V

DVORAK, ANTONIN

Slavonic Dance No. 15	Bartlett and Robertson	GR

ELLINGTON, DUKE

Mood Indigo	Reginald Forsythe and Arthur Young	V
Solitude	Reginald Forsythe and Arthur Young	V

ENESCO, GEORGES

Roumanian Rhapsody, No. 1 (arr. Whittemore and Lowe) — Whittemore and Lowe — v

FALLA, MANUEL DE

Nana — Whittemore and Lowe — v
Ritual Fire Dance (from "El Amor Brujo") (arr. Luboshutz) — Luboshutz and Nemenoff — v

— Whittemore and Lowe — v
Spanish Dance No. 1 (from "La Vida Breve") (arr. Kovacs) — Bartlett and Robertson — c

FARNABY, GILES

A Toye ("Elizabethan Suite") — Bartlett and Robertson — c
His Conceit ("Elizabethan Suite") — Bartlett and Robertson — c
His Dreame ("Elizabethan Suite") — Bartlett and Robertson — c
Tower Hill Jigge ("Elizabethan Suite") — Bartlett and Robertson — c
Tune for Two Virginals ("Elizabethan Suite") — Bartlett and Robertson — c

FREED, ARTHUR and BROWN, NACIO HERB

Temptation (arr. Whittemore and Lowe) — Whittemore and Lowe — v

GEARHART, LIVINGSTON

Baby Boogie — Morley and Gearhart — c

GERSHWIN, GEORGE

I Got Rhythm — Jordan and Kent — D
— Morley and Gearhart — c
Rhapsody in Blue (arr. Iturbi) — José and Amparo Iturbi — v

GLINKA, MICHAIL IVANOVITCH

The Lark (arr. Luboshutz) — Luboshutz and Nemenoff — v

GLUCK, CHRISTOPH WILLIBALD von

Gavotte (arr. Doebber) — Bartlett and Robertson — c

GODOWSKY, LEOPOLD

Old Vienna — Sisters Jeanne Madeleine and Francis Terese — CON

GOULD, MORTON

Guaracha (Third Movement: Latin American Symphonette) — Whittemore and Lowe — v

GREEN, JOHNNY

Body and Soul — Morley and Gearhart — c

HANDEL, GEORG FRIEDRICH

Arrival of the Queen of Sheba — Bartlett and Robertson — c

HANDY,

St. Louis Blues — Reginald Forsythe and Arthur Young — v
— Thomas Waller and Bennie Paine — v

INFANTE, MANUEL

Andalusian Dances Nos. 1 & 2 (Ritmo and Gracia) — José and Amparo Iturbi — v
Danse Andalouse—Sentimiento — José and Amparo Iturbi — v

"Jazz Nocturne"—

Jazz Nocturne — Harry Fields and Marlene Fingerle D
Contains: Andalucia, Malaguena, Mardi
Gras, On the Trail, Soliloquy, Jazz
Nocturne, Deep Purple, Park Avenue
Fantasy

JESSEL, LEON

Parade of the Wooden Soldiers — Rawicz and Landauer — c

KERN, JEROME

All the Things You Are — Morley and Gearhart — c
The Song Is You (arr. Whittemore and — Whittemore and Lowe — v
Lowe)
They Didn't Believe Me (arr. Whittemore — Whittemore and Lowe — v
and Lowe)

KREISLER, FRITZ

Liebesfreud — Sisters Jeanne Madeleine and Francis
Terese — con
Tambourin Chinois, opus 3, (arr. Luboshutz) — Luboshutz and Nemenoff — v

LECUONA, ERNESTO

Malaguena, from Suite "Andalucia" (arr. — Bartlett and Robertson — c
Nash)
— Whittemore and Lowe — v

LEVITZKI, MISCHA

Valse Tzigane, opus 7 — Luboshutz and Nemenoff — v

LISZT, FRANZ

Liebestraum No. 3 (arr. Robertson) — Bartlett and Robertson — c
Liebestraum No. 3 (arr. Whittemore and — Whittemore and Lowe — v
Lowe)
Synthesis from Concerto in E flat — Whittemore and Lowe — v

MAC DOWELL, EDWARD

To a Wild Rose — Sisters Jeanne Madeleine and
Francis Terese — Con

MC DONALD, HARL

Concerto for Two Pianos and Orchestra — Behrend and Kelberine with
Philadelphia Orchestra, L.
Stokowski, cond. — v

MENDELSSOHN, FELIX

Allegro Brillant — Luboshutz and Nemenoff — v
Scherzo (from "Midsummer Night's — Bartlett and Robertson — c
Dream" Music) (arr. Philipp)
— Luboshutz and Nemenoff — v
Spring Song — Sisters Jeanne Madeleine and
Francis Terese — Con

MESSIAEN, OLIVIER

Visions de l'amen — Olivier Messiaen and Yvonne
Loriod — DI

MILHAUD, DARIUS

Scaramouche (Suite for two pianos) — Bartlett and Robertson — c
— Luboshutz and Nemenoff — v
— Vronsky and Babin — v
Carnival in New Orleans — Gold and Fizdale — c
Dreams — Gold and Fizdale — c

MOUSSORGSKY, MODEST

Boris Godounoff—Coronation Scene (arr. Luboshutz)	Luboshutz and Nemenoff	v
	Whittemore and Lowe	v

MOZART, WOLFGANG AMADEUS

Theme and Variations in G major K. 501 (one piano, four hands)	Appleton and Field	vo
Concerto for Two Pianos and Orchestra, in E-Flat, K. 365	José and Amparo Iturbi, with the Rochester Philharmonic	v
	A. and K. Schnabel with London Symphony Orchestra, cond. Boult	v
	Vronsky and Babin, with the Robin Hood Dell Orchestra of Philadelphia, Dimitri Mitropoulos, cond.	c
	Vronsky and Babin, with London Symphony, cond. Boult	v
Sonata in D, K.448	Castagnetta and Kaye	TI
	Nemenoff and Luboshutz	v
	Wiener and Doucet	c
The Marriage of Figaro—Overture (arr. Conus)	Luboshutz and Nemenoff	v

"NIGHT LIFE"—

Night Life on Two Pianos (set) Contains: popular items by Kern, Gearhart, Green, Gershwin, Braham, Prokofiev, Berlin, Carmichael, Arlen	Morley and Gearhart	c

PAGANINI, NICCOLO

Variations on Paganini Caprice, No. 24 (arr. Whittemore and Lowe)	Arthur Whittemore and Jack Lowe	v

PAGANINI-LISZT

La Campanella (arr. Taylor)	Bartlett and Robertson	c

PEERSON, MARTIN

The Fall of the Leafe ("Elizabethan Suite")	Bartlett and Robertson	c

PORTER, COLE

Begin the Beguine (arr. Whittemore and Lowe)	Whittemore and Lowe	v
In the Still of the Night (arr. Whittemore and Lowe)	Whittemore and Lowe	v
Night and Day (arr. Whittemore and Lowe)	Whittemore and Lowe	v

POULENC, FRANCIS

Concerto for Two Pianos and Orchestra in D Minor	Arthur Whittemore and Jack Lowe, with RCA Victor Symphony Orch. Dimitri Mitropoulos, cond.	v

PROKOFIEFF, SERGE

March (from "The Love for Three Oranges") (arr. Whittemore and Lowe)	Whittemore and Lowe	v
March, Opus 33	Morley and Gearhart	c

RACHMANINOFF, SERGEI

Floods of Spring, opus 14, No. 11 (arr. Babin)	Vronsky and Babin	v
How Fair This Spot, opus 21, No. 7 (arr. Babin)	Vronsky and Babin	v
Prelude in G Minor	Sisters Jeanne Madeleine and Francis Terese	Con
Suite No. 1, opus 5	Vronsky and Babin	v
Suite No. 2, opus 17	Vronsky and Babin	v
Synthesis from Concerto No. 2	Whittemore and Lowe	v
Vocalise, opus 34, No. 14 (arr. Babin)	Vronsky and Babin	v

RAVEL, MAURICE

Bolero	Fingerle and Schutt	D
	Fray and Braggiotti	v

REGER, MAX

Waltz (from "Ballet Suite") (arr. Whittemore and Lowe)	Whittemore and Lowe	v

RIEGGER, WALLINGFORD

New Dance	Luboshutz & Nemenoff	v

RIMSKY-KORSAKOV, NICHOLAS

Cradle Song from "Sadko"	Vronsky and Babin	c
Dance of the Tumblers from "Snegourot-chka"	Vronsky and Babin	c
Flight of the Bumble Bee	Vronsky and Babin	v

ROBIN-RANGER

If I Should Lose You (arr. Whittemore and Lowe)	Whittemore and Lowe	v

RODGERS, RICHARD

Falling in Love With You (arr. Whittemore and Lowe)	Whittemore and Lowe	v
Lover (arr. Whittemore and Lowe)	Whittemore and Lowe	v

ROSSINI, GIOACHINO

Barber of Seville—Largo al factotum (arr. Kovacs)	Luboshutz and Nemenoff	v

RUBINSTEIN, BERYL

Arabesque on Tunes from Lehar's "Merry Widow"	Rubinstein and Loesser	c
Suite for Two Pianos	Beryl Rubinstein-Arthur Loesser	v

"RUSSIAN MUSIC"—

Russian Music for Two Pianos (set) Contains: compositions by Arensky, Babin, Rimsky-Korsakov, Stravinsky	Vronsky and Babin	c

SAINT-SAENS, CAMILLE

Caprice Arabe, opus 96	José and Amparo Iturbi	v
Carnival des Animaux	Jeanne Behrend—Sylvan Levin with the Philadelphia Orchestra, under Leopold Stokowski	v
Danse Macabre	Luboshutz and Nemenoff	v
Scherzo for Two Pianos, op. 87	Rubinstein and Loesser	c
The Swan	Sisters Jeanne Madeleine and Francis Terese	Con
Variations on a Theme of Beethoven, opus 35	Bertram and Szreter	D
	Luboshutz and Nemenoff	v

SATIE, ERIC

Parade, Ballet	Georges Auric and Francis Poulenc	BAM
Deux Morceaux en forme de poire	Georges Auric and Francis Poulenc	BAM
Three Pieces in the Shape of a Pear	Robert and Gaby Casadesus	C

SCHUETT, EDUARD

Impromptu-Rococco, opus 58, No. 2	Bauer and Gabrilowitsch	V

SCHUMANN, ROBERT

Andante and Variations, opus 46	Bartlett and Robertson	C
	Luboshutz and Nemenoff	V
Etude in the Form of a Canon, opus 56, No. 4 (from Studies for Pedal Piano) (arr. Debussy)	Bartlett and Robertson	C
Synthesis from Concerto in A minor	Whittemore and Lowe	V
Träumerei	Sisters Jeanne Madeleine and Francis Terese	Con

SCOTT, JOPLIN

Maple Leaf Rag	Victor Arden and Phil Ohman	V

SHOSTAKOVICH, DMITRI

The Age of Gold—Ballet: Polka (arr. Luboshutz)	Pierre Luboshutz and Genia Nemenoff	V
	Whittemore and Lowe	V

SISTERS JEANNE MADELEINE AND FRANCIS TERESE

Legend	Sisters Jeanne Madeleine and Francis Terese	CON
Prelude	Sisters Jeanne Madeleine and Francis Terese	CON

"SONG OF THE VOLGA BOATMEN"—

Song of the Volga Boatmen (Russian Folk Song) (arr. A. Kelberine)	Behrend and Kelberine	V

"SONGS OF OUR TIMES"—

Songs of Our Times—1926	Fingerle and Schutt	D

Contains Medley of these Songs: I Know That You Know, Baby Face, Bye Bye Blackbird, The Blue Room, The Girl Is You and the Boy Is Me, The Girl Friend, Valencia, Where Do You Work-A, John?, Yankee Rose, Horses, In a Little Spanish Town, Mary Lou, Where'd You Get Those Eyes?, Gimme a Little Kiss Will "Ya" Huh, After I Say I'm Sorry, The Little White House, Tamiami Trail, When the Red, Red Robin Comes Bob, Bob, Bobbin' Along, The Birth of the Blues, Muddy Water, Black Bottom, The Desert Song, Lonesome and Sorry, One Alone, When Day Is Done, Charmaine, Someone to Watch Over Me.

Songs of Our Times—1929   Fingerle and Schutt   D

    Contains Medley of these Songs: Wedding
of the Painted Doll, Tiptoe Thru the
Tulips With Me, Singin' in the Rain,
Sunny Side Up, Jericho, Aren't We all?,
Happy Days Are Here Again, Why Was
I Born?, More Than You Know, With
a Song in My Heart, Can't We Be
Friends?, My Kinda Love, Moanin' Low,
Pagan Love Song, Love, Chant of the
Jungle, Siboney, When It's Springtime
in the Rockies, When the Organ Played
at Twilight, Beside an Open Fireplace,
Wedding Bells Are Breaking Up that
Old Gang of Mine, Ain't Misbehavin',
Little By Little, Weary River, I've Got
a Feeling I'm Falling, Romance, Should
I, Deep Night, Am I Blue?

Songs of Our Times—1936   Fingerle and Schutt   D

    Contains Medley of these Songs: With
Plenty of Money and You, Easy to Love,
I've Got You Under My Skin, The Way
You Look Tonight, A Melody from the
Sky, Pennies from Heaven, Moon Over
Miami, Lights Out, In the Chapel in
the Moonlight, Would You, When Did
You Leave Heaven, I'll Sing You a
Thousand Love Songs, Is It True What
They Say About Dixie?, South Sea Is-
land Magic, Goody Goody, It's Been
So Long, All My Life, Lost, Did I
Remember, It's a Sin to Tell a Lie,
Until the Real Thing Comes Along,
Goodnight My Love, There's a Small
Hotel, Stompin' at the Savoy.

STRAUSS, JOHANN

Waltz-Fantasy (arr. Whittemore and Lowe)   Whittemore and Lowe   V

STRAUSS, RICHARD

Rosenkavalier Waltz, opus 59 (arr. Babin)   Vronsky and Babin   V

STRAVINSKY, IGOR

Cinq pièces faciles   Gold and Fizdale   CO
Circus Polka   Vronsky and Babin   C
Concerto for Two Solo Pianos   Appleton and Field   VO
                                             Vronsky and Babin   C
Petrouchka Suite: Russian Dance   Luboshutz and Nemenoff   V
  (arr. Luboshutz)
Scherzo à la Russe   Vronsky and Babin   C
Sonata for Two Pianos   Gold and Fizdale   CO
Tango   Vronsky and Babin   C

TCHAIKOVSKY, PETER ILITCH

Waltz from "The Swan Lake" Ballet, opus 20 (arr. Babin)	Vronsky and Babin	c
Waltz from "Eugen Onegin," opus 24 (arr. Babin)	Vronsky and Babin	c
Waltz from "Serenade in C major for String Orchestra," opus 48, (arr. Babin)	Vronsky and Babin	c
Valse Sentimentale, opus 51, No. 6 (arr. Babin)	Vronsky and Babin	c
Waltz of the Flowers from "Nutcracker Suite," opus 71 a (arr. Babin)	Vronsky and Babin	c

"Tiger Rag"—

Tiger Rag	Reginald Forsythe and Arthur Young	v

"Traditional"—

Three Blind Mice (arr. Iturbi, José and Stoll, George) a. Waltz Version b. Boogie Version	José Iturbi and Amparo Iturbi	v

"Two Piano Recital, A"—

A Two-Piano Recital of Classical and Popular numbers: Contains: Sweet Sue, Just You, Honeysuckle Rose, I Got Rhythm, Turkey in the Straw, Minute Waltz, Excerpts from "Carmen," Three Blind Mice, (In the styles of Bach, Mozart, Chopin, Strauss, Rachmaninoff and Gershwin)	Bill Jordan and George Kent	d

"Two Pianos in Three-Quarter Time"—

Two Pianos in Three-Quarter Time: An Album of Viennese Waltzes	Appleton and Field	vo

WEINBERGER, JAROMIR

Schwanda: Polka and Fugue	Vronsky and Babin	v

WILDER, ALEC

Seldom the Sun (arr. Whittemore and Lowe)	Whittemore and Lowe	v
The Neurotic Goldfish (arr. Whittemore and Lowe)	Whittemore and Lowe	v

"You Were Never Lovelier"—

You Were Never Lovelier, Medley with rhythm accompaniment Contains: You Were Never Lovelier, Dearly Beloved, I'm Old Fashioned, Wedding in the Spring, "By Jupiter" Medley	Fingerle and Schutt	d

CHAPTER XXVI

ANNOTATED BIBLIOGRAPHY

1. *Statement of Extent and Confines*

This annotated bibliography is compiled from six general groups of reference material. The list includes the following sources of information:

1. Essays in books, encyclopedias and dictionaries. This category comprises authoritative contributions on the subject of duo-pianism which are of prime importance to the scholar;
2. Articles in magazines and other periodicals. This group contains the more casual and informal articles on two-piano activities, reports of interviews, recital criticisms, and press releases from or about duo-pianists;
3. Notes in concert programs and record albums. Included into the bibliography are a few significant items from this large field of reference;
4. Unpublished material such as theses, professional papers, radio scripts, and other documents pertaining to duo-pianism;
5. General reference literature. A selection of standard works which either directly or indirectly relate to the history and nature of duo-pianism. Also included are a few collections of
6. Printed music, such as the Fitzwilliam Virginal Book and the Bach-Gesellschaft edition of the complete works of J. S. Bach, because of their authenticity as sources of reference where rare or important works are concerned, and because of the information contained in prefaces and annotations of such collections.

The bibliography combines all aforementioned categories of reference material into one group and follows an alphabetical order. Annotations are provided where a definite connection between the reference source and the present work exists.

374

2. ANNOTATED BIBLIOGRAPHY

ADLER, GUIDO: *Handbuch der Musikgeschichte.* 2 vols. Berlin-Wilmersdorf: Verlag Heinrich Keller; 1930. Reference to the two-piano works of Max Reger; vol. II, p. 1017 (Paul A. Pisk).

AFFELDER, PAUL: *Concerto in D minor for two violins and orchestra (Bach).* Bridgeport: Columbia Records, Inc. Annotations to record album, with reference to Concerto No. 3 in C minor for 2 claviers.

AFFELDER, PAUL: *Concerto in E flat Major for Two Pianos and Orchestra K. 365 (Mozart).* Bridgeport: Columbia Records, Inc. Annotations to recording of this work.

AFFELDER, PAUL: *En blanc et noir (Debussy).* Bridgeport: Columbia Records, Inc. Annotations to record album.

ALTMANN, PROF. DR. WILHELM: *Verzeichnis von Werken fuer Klavier vier und sechshaendig sowie fuer zwei und mehr Klaviere.* Leipzig: Verlag von Friedrich Hofmeister; 1943. The index is arranged in groups of *A.* Original Works (1. study works; 2. Sonatas, Duos, Fantasies, Rhapsodies, Variations, Suites, suite-like works; 3. smaller character pieces, Rondos, Scherzi; 4. Dances and Marches; 5. with accompaniment of other instruments) *B.* Arrangements and Transcriptions of all types.

AMERICAN HISTORY AND ENCYCLOPEDIA OF MUSIC, THE. 2 vols. Toledo, O.: The Squire Cooley Co.; 1910. Vol. I, Musical Dictionary: W. L. Hubbard, Editor; Vol. II, Essentials of Music: Emil Liebling, Editor. Vol. II contains a section "Art of Music before 1750" by Arnold Dolmetsch, treating of clavichord, virginal, harpsichord, and spinet.

ANDERSON, EMILY: *Letters of Mozart and His Family.* Chronologically arranged, translated and edited with an introduction, notes, and indices by Emily Anderson. 3 vols. St. Martin's Street, London: Macmillan and Company Ltd.; 1938. References to Mozart's activities in the two-piano medium, as performer and composer.

APEL, WILLI: *Harvard Dictionary of Music.* Cambridge, Mass.: Harvard University Press; 1947. General reference work for scholarly research.

APPLETON, VERA and FIELD, MICHAEL: *Is There a Two-Piano Dilemma Today?* "Musical Courier;" August 1947, page 9. Deals with the literature of two-piano music and the problem of programming.

BACH BOOK, The Little. Edited by Theo. Hoelty Nickel. Valparaiso, Indiana: Valparaiso University Press; 1950. Contains essays by Kretzmann, Naumann, Nettl, Rosenwald, Fleischer, Buszin, and lists of compositions and recordings.

BACH-GESELLSCHAFT, editing society: *The Complete Works of Johann Sebastian Bach in 46 volumes.* Breitkopf & Haertel. Re-issued by Edwards, Ann Arbor. Reference source for Book I "The History," chapter II "Bach"; specific volumes of reference as indicated in the text of said chapter.

BACH READER, THE. A Life of Johann Sebastian Bach in Letters and Documents edited by Hans T. David and Arthur Mendel. New York: W. W. Norton & Co.; 1945.

BAGAR, ROBERT and BIANCOLLI, LOUIS: *The Concert Companion. A Comprehensive Guide to Symphonic Music.* New York: McGraw-Hill Book Company, Inc.; 1947. Some references on symphonic works by Brahms, Milhaud and others—originating from two-piano scores. Analysis of Poulenc's Concerto in D minor for Two Pianos and Orchestra. Comments on Bartók's Concerto for Two Pianos with orchestral accompaniment.

BAKER'S BIOGRAPHICAL DICTIONARY OF MUSICIANS. Fourth edition. Revised and enlarged. New York: G. Schirmer, Inc.; 1940.

BARTHOLOMEW, WILMER T.: *Acoustics of Music.* New York: Prentice-Hall, Inc.; 1946.

BAUER, HAROLD: *Harold Bauer, His Book.* New York: W. W. Norton & Company, Inc.; 1948. Autobiographical notes with only insignificant reference to Bauer's two-piano association with Ossip Gabrilowitsch.

BAUER, MARION and PEYSER, ETHEL E.: *Music Through the Ages.* New York: G. P. Putnam's Sons; 1946.

BAUER, MARION: *Twentieth Century Music.* How It Developed—How To Listen To It. New York; London: G. P. Putnam's Sons; 1933.

BEKKER, PAUL: *The Story of Music.* An Historical Sketch of the Changes in Musical Form. Translated by M. D. Herter Norton and Alice Kortschak. New York: W. W. Norton & Company; 1927.

BERKOWITZ, RALPH: *Original Music for Four Hands.* "The Etude," January 1944, pp. 27, 61. Remarks on the nature and the literature of music for one piano, four hands.

BERNSTEIN, MARTIN: *An Introduction to Music.* New York: Prentice-Hall, Inc., 1946.

BIE, OSCAR: *A History of Pianoforte and Pianoforte Players.* Translated and edited by Kellett and Naylor. London: J. M. Dent and Company; New York: E. P. Dutton and Company; 1894.

BITTER, CARL HERMANN: *Carl Philipp Emanuel Bach und Wilhelm Friedemann Bach und deren Brueder.* Berlin: W. Mueller; 1868.

BIVENS, VIRGINIA L.: *Problem of the Arrangement for Two Pianos of Iberia by I. Albeniz.* Unpublished. Thesis for the degree of Master of Music, Library of North Texas State Teachers College, Denton, Texas. Contains a discussion of arrangement and transcription.

BONAVENTURA, ARNALDO: *Bernardo Pasquini.* Monografia. Roma: Casa Editrice "Musica"; 1923. Contains a catalog of compositions. Lists under "Musica Strumentale" a Suite containing "14 Sonate a 2 cembali."

BRAHMS, JOHANNES: *Sämtliche Werke.* Leipzig: Breitkopf & Härtel. "Revisionsberichte" contain information on compositions for two pianos and works which at first were sketched in two-piano form.

BRODSKY, VERA: *The Art of Two-Piano Playing.* See Part VII of Albert Wier "The Piano"; pp. 338-374.

BRODSKY, VERA: *Two-Piano Playing.* See pages 1898-1905 of The MacMillan Encyclopedia of Music and Musicians.

BRYANT, JOHN EBENEZER: *Composers.* Part III of the "American College Course," published by the American College Society. Prof. Seymour Eaton, Director-in-chief; 1916. Essays on "The World's Great Musicians," Biographical notes, critical studies and reminiscences of Handel, Haydn, Mozart, Beethoven, Mendelssohn, Schubert, Schumann, Gounod, Verdi.

BUKOFZER, MANFRED F.: *Music in the Baroque Era.* From Monteverdi to Bach. New York: W. W. Norton & Company, Inc.; 1947. Standard reference for the Baroque period of music history.

BURK, JOHN N.: *Clara Schumann.* New York: Random House, Inc.; 1940. A few references on two-piano activities of Clara Schumann, especially with Brahms.

BUSONI, FERRUCCIO: *A New Esthetic of Music.* New York: G. Schirmer; 1911.

CALVOCORESI, M. D., and ABRAHAM, GERALD: *Masters of Russian Music.* New York: Tudor Publishing Company; 1944.

CANBY, EDWARD TATNALL: *Concerto for Two Pianos (Stravinsky).* New York: Vox Records. Annotations to record album; especially extensive and scholarly.

CHASE, GILBERT: *The Story of Music.* Broadcast Series of the NBC University of the Air. Handbook Vol. I; 1945. Handbook Vol. II; 1946. New York: Southern Music Publishing Company, Inc. Vol. I deals largely with the instrumental forms; Vol. II is devoted to the opera.

CHRYSANDER, FRIEDRICH: *G. F. Haendel.* Three Volumes. Leipzig: Breitkopf & Haertel; 1858-67.

COLLAER, PAUL: *Darius Milhaud.* Antwerp: N. V. De Nederlandsche Boekhandel; 1947. In French. No reference to two-piano works.

COPLAND, AARON: *What to Listen for in Music.* New York: Whittlesey House, McGraw-Hill Book Company, Inc.; 1939.

COUPERIN, FRANÇOIS: *Oeuvres Complètes de François Couperin.* Publié par Maurice Cauchie. Paris: Editions de l'Oiseau Lyre, chez Louise B. M. Dyer. Contains "Allemande à deux Clavecins" in the Sécond Livre de Pièces de Clavecin, Neuvième Ordre.

COWELL, HENRY: *American Composers on American Music.* Symposium edited by Henry Cowell. Stanford University, California: Stanford University Press; 1933. Contemporary American composers and their principal works. Mention of two-piano works by Brant and Roldan.

DAVIS, ENNIS: *More Than a Pitch-Pipe.* The Human, Professional, and Business Relations of the Music Educator to his School and Community. Boston: C. C. Birchard and Company; 1941.

DAVISON, ARCHIBALD T. and APEL, WILLI: *Historical Anthology of Music.* Oriental, Medieval, and Renaissance Music. Cambridge: Harvard University Press; 1946. Material on the English virginalists.

DENKMÄLER DEUTSCHER TONKUNST: Klavierwerke von Johann Pachelbel (1653-1706) nebst beigefuegten Stuecken von W. H. Pachelbel (1686-1764). Edited by Max Seiffert. Leipzig: Breitkopf & Härtel, 1901. Contains 3 pieces of W. H. Pachelbel under the title "Musikalisches Vergnuegen sowohl auf die Orgel als auch auf das Clavier."

DICTIONARY OF MODERN MUSIC AND MUSICIANS. Edited by J. M. Dent and Sons, Ltd., London and Toronto; New York: E. P. Dutton and Company; 1924.

DICTIONARY OF MUSICAL TERMS. Edited by Theodore Baker. New York: G. Schirmer, Inc.; 1923.

DOWNES, OLIN: *The Lure of Music.* New York: Harper & Brothers, Publishers; 1918.

EINSTEIN, ALFRED: *A Short History of Music.* New York: Alfred A. Knopf; 1947.

EINSTEIN, ALFRED: *Mozart.* His Character, His Work. Translated by Arthur Mendel and Nathan Broder. New York: Oxford University Press; 1945. Numerous references to the two-piano works and fragments.

EINSTEIN, ALFRED: *Music in the Romantic Era.* New York: W. W. Norton & Company, Inc.; 1947. Standard reference for the Romantic period of music history.

EITNER, ROBERT: *Biographisch-Bibliographisches Quellen-Lexikon der Musiker und Musikgelehrten.* New York: Musurgia. Year of preface, 1898. Important source of information.

ELSON, LOUIS CHARLES: *Elson's Music Dictionary.* Philadelphia: Oliver Ditson Company; 1933.

ELSON, LOUIS CHARLES: *The History of American Music.* New York: The Macmillan Company; 1915.

ENGEL, CARL: *Alla breve: from Bach to Debussy.* New York: G. Schirmer; 1933.

ENTRIKEN, REBECCA LOVE: *Problem of the Arrangement for Two Pianos of Sedlak by Jindr. Jindrich and Prelude opus 34 No. 5 by Dimitri Shostakovich.* Unpublished. Thesis for the degree of Master of Music, Library of North Texas State Teachers College, Denton, Texas.

ERB, J. LAWRENCE: *Music Appreciation for the Student.* New York: G. Schirmer, Inc.; 1926.

EVANS, EDWIN (SR.): *Handbook to the Pianoforte Works of Johannes Brahms.* London: William Reeves, Bookseller, Ltd.; 1912. Omits both opus 34b and opus 56b from discussion.

EVANS, EDWIN: *Stocktaking, 1930.* Music and Letters. London: 1931. A survey of early twentieth century music.

EWEN, DAVID: *Music Comes to America.* New York: Thomas Y. Crowell Company; 1942. A survey of musical development in the United States, including a chapter on "The Great Invasion" 1933-1942.

EWEN, DAVID: *Music for the Millions*. The Encyclopedia of Musical Masterpieces. New York: Arco Publishing Company; 1944. Includes some two-piano works.

FAULKNER, ANNE SHAW: *What We Hear in Music*. A course of study in music appreciation and history. Camden: RCA Manufacturing Co., Inc., Educational Department; 1936.

FELDMAN, HARRY ALLEN: *Music Appreciation*. Cleveland: The World Publishing Company; 1943.

FERGUSON, DONALD N.: *A History of Musical Thought*. New York: Appleton-Century-Crofts, Inc.; 1948.

FERGUSON, DONALD N.: *A Short History of Music*. New York: F. S. Crofts & Co.; 1945.

FITZWILLIAM VIRGINAL BOOK, THE. See Fuller-Maitland.

FOLDES, ANDOR: *Keys to the Keyboard*. A Book for Pianists. New York: E. P. Dutton & Company, Inc.; 1948.

FULLER-MAITLAND, J. A.: *Brahms*. London: Methuen and Company, Ltd.; 1911. A few references on Brahms' work in the two-piano field.

FULLER-MAITLAND, J. A. and BARCLAY SQUIRE, W.: *The Fitzwilliam Virginal Book*. Edited from the original manuscript, in 2 volumes. London and Leipzig: Breitkopf & Härtel; 1899. Contains nearly 300 pieces of virginal music, including "For two virginals" by Giles Farnaby (Vol. I, page 202).

GARROWAY, WILL: *Pianism*. New York: Carl Fischer, Inc.; 1939.

GATTY, NICHOLAS COMYN and TAYLOR, FRANKLIN: *Duet*, Grove's Dictionary of Music and Musicians, edited by H. C. Colles, II, 102-103. Page 103 contains a section on compositions for two pianos.

GEIRINGER, KARL: *Brahms, His Life and Work*. Translated by H. B. Weiner and Bernard Miall. Boston and New York: Houghton Mifflin Co.; 1936.

GILMAN, LAWRENCE: *Edward MacDowell*. A Study. New York: John Lane Company; 1909. Performance on two pianos with d'Albert before Liszt. (p. 17)

GOOD, CARTER V.; BARR, A. S.; SCATES, DOUGLAS E.: *The Methodology of Educational Research*. New York: D. Appleton-Century Company, Inc.; 1941. Methods of scientific research in the field of education.

GOSS, MADELEINE: *Bolero, the Life of Maurice Ravel*. New York: Henry Holt & Co.; 1940; Tudor Publishing Company, 1945.

GRAF, MAX: *Composer and Critic*. Two hundred Years of Musical Criticism. New York: W. W. Norton & Company, Inc.; 1946.

GRAMOPHONE SHOP ENCYCLOPEDIA OF RECORDED MUSIC, THE. New York: Simon and Schuster; 1942. Reference source of recorded music for two pianos.

GREAT CRITICS, The. An Anthology of Literary Criticism. Compiled and edited by James Harry Smith and Edd Winfield Parks. New York: W. W. Norton & Company; 1939. Essays on literary criticism from ancient to modern times.

GROVE'S DICTIONARY OF MUSIC AND MUSICIANS. Edited by H. C. Colles, Third edition, Five Volumes. New York: Macmillan Company; 1945. For general reference.

GROVE'S DICTIONARY OF MUSIC AND MUSICIANS. Supplementary Volume. Edited by H. C. Colles; New York: Macmillan Company; 1944.

GROVE'S DICTIONARY OF MUSIC AND MUSICIANS. American Supplement. Waldo Selden Pratt, Editor; Charles N. Boyd, Associate Editor. New York: Macmillan Company; 1945.

HALE, PHILIP: *Great Concert Music*. Philip Hale's Boston Symphony Programme Notes. Historical, Critical, and Descriptive Comment on Music and Composers. Edited by John N. Burk, with an Introduction by Lawrence Gilman. New York: Garden City Publishing Co., Inc.; 1939.

HALL, DAVID: *The Record Book*. New York: Citadel Press; 1946. A few commentaries on works for two pianos.

HAMILTON, CLARENCE G.: *Outlines of Music History*. Boston: Oliver Ditson Company; 1924.

HAMILTON, CLARENCE G.: *Piano Teaching, Its Principles and Problems*. Boston: Oliver Ditson Company; 1910.

HANSL, EVA B. and KAUFMANN, HELEN L.: *Minute Sketches of Great Composers*. New York: Grosset & Dunlap; 1932.

HARVARD Dictionary of Music. See Apel, Willi.

HAYDON, GLEN: *Introduction to Musicology*. A Survey of the Fields, Systematic and Historical, of Musical Knowledge and Research. New York: Prentice-Hall, Inc.; 1941.

HENSCHEL, GEORGE: *Personal Recollections of Johannes Brahms*. Boston: Richard G. Badger, The Gorham Press; 1907.

HOFFMAN, RICHARD: *Some Musical Recollections of Fifty Years*. New York: Charles Scribner's Sons; 1910. Relates of two-piano playing by Thalberg and Gottschalk as well as by Gottschalk and the author. (pp. 130-132)

HOWARD, JOHN TASKER: *Our American Music*. New York: Thomas Y. Crowell Company; 1946.

HOWARD, JOHN TASKER, with the assistance of Arthur Mendel: *Our Contemporary Composers, American Music in the Twentieth Century*. New York: Thomas Y. Crowell Company; 1941. Source of contemporary two-piano compositions by Berezowski, Howe, Bacon, and others.

HUGHES, RUPERT: *The Biographical Dictionary of Musicians*. Edited by Deems Taylor and Russell Kerr. Garden City, New York: Blue Ribbon Books, Inc.; 1940.

HUNEKER, JAMES GIBBONS: *Chopin, the Man and His Music*. New York: Charles Scribner's Sons; 1900.

HUNEKER, JAMES: *Franz Liszt*. New York: Charles Scribner's Sons; 1911. Comments on Concerto Pathétique, pp. 177-178. Symphonic Poems, p. 157.

HUTCHESON, ERNEST: *The Literature of the Piano*. A Guide for Amateur and Student. New York: Alfred A. Knopf; 1949. This work from the pen of one of the foremost duo-pianists mentions many two-piano compositions but omits a number of the more important items by Rachmaninoff, Debussy, and others.

IDELSOHN, A. Z.: *Jewish Music. In its Historical Development*. New York: Henry Holt and Company; 1929.

INTERNATIONAL CYCLOPEDIA OF MUSIC AND MUSICIANS, THE. Edited by Oscar Thompson. New York: Dodd, Mead and Company; 1938-1939. Contains a section on "Two Piano Playing" on pages 1936-1937.

INTERNATIONAL LIBRARY OF MUSIC, THE. The History of Music. Critical and Biographical Sketches of the Epoch Makers of Music. New York: The University Society; 1925.

IRVINE, DEMAR B.: *Methods of Research in Music*. Part I, Methods. Seattle, Washington. 1945. A methodology for scientific research.

JAHN, OTTO: *Life of Mozart*. Translated from the German by Pauline D. Townsend. Three Volumes. London: Novello, Ewer & Co.; 1882. Information on Koechel Nos. 242, 365, 426, 448, and 4 fragments.

JOHANSEN, DAVID MONRAD: *Edvard Grieg*. Translated from the Norwegian by Madge Robertson. New York: Tudor Publishing Company; 1945. Biographical information only.

JONAS, OSWALD: *Das Wesen des Musikalischen Kunstwerks*. Wien: Saturn-Verlag; 1934. Introduction to the teachings of Heinrich Schenker.

KALBECK, MAX: *Johannes Brahms;* Berlin: Deutsche Brahms-Gesellschaft m.b.H.; 1908. In 8 volumes. Traces the two-piano medium in the creative work of Brahms, in the original compositions for two pianos as well as in the sketches for symphonic works.

KATZ, ADELE T.: *Challenge to Musical Tradition*. A new Concept of Tonality. New York: Alfred A. Knopf; 1945. Expounds the Schenker concept.

KLATTE, WILHELM: *Franz Schubert*. Berlin: Marquard; 1907.

KÖCHEL, DR. LUDWIG RITTER von: *Chronological Thematic Catalogue of the Musical Compositions of W. A. Mozart*. Leipzig: Breitkopf & Härtel. *Chronologisch-thematisches Verzeichnis sämtlicher Tonwerke Wolfgang Amade Mozarts*. Nebst Angabe der verlorengegangenen, angefangenen, uebertragenen, zweifelhaften und unterschobenen Kompositionen. Mit einem Supplement "Berichtigungen und Zusätze" von Alfred Einstein. Ann Arbor, Michigan: Verlag von J. W. Edwards; 1947. Information on K. Nos. 242, 365, 426, 448, and four fragments of two-piano compositions; also on K. Nos. 501, 521, 608.

KOEHLER, WOLFGANG: *Gestalt Psychology*. New York: Horace Liveright; 1929. Referred to in Book II, "Nature, Applications and Problems," Chapter XIV.

KOLODIN, IRVING: *New Guide to Recorded Music*. Garden City, New York: Doubleday & Company; 1947. Reference source for two-piano recordings.

KREHBIEL, HENRY EDWARD: *The Pianoforte and its Music*. New York: Charles Scribner's Sons; 1911.

KREVIT, WILLIAM: *Music for your Child*. New York: Dodd, Mead & Company; 1946.

LABUNSKI, WIKTOR: *Adventures in Two-Piano Arranging*. A reprint, in excerpt, of a paper read at the Music Teachers National Association Convention in Chicago, January 1, 1949. "The Etude," March 1949, p. 150. Practical directions for experimentations on two pianos and for arranging for two pianos.

LANG, PAUL HENRY: *Music in Western Civilization*. New York: W. W. Norton & Company, Inc.; 1941. An extensive general survey.

LEICHTENTRITT, HUGO: *Music, History, and Ideas*. Cambridge: Harvard University Press; 1946. Aesthetically profound.

LENZ, W. von: *The Great Piano Virtuosos of Our Time*. Translated from the German by Madeleine R. Baker. New York: G. Schirmer; 1899. Memoirs.

LHEVINNE, JOSEF, and LHEVINNE, ROSINA: *Four Hands That Play as Two*. "The Etude," LI (December, 1933), pp. 809-810. Important essay on two-piano playing.

LHEVINNE, ROSINA: *The Spirit of Ensemble*. "Pan Pipes" of Sigma Alpha Iota, Vol. XLI No. 3 (February 1949) pp. 162-164. An essay on historical, aesthetical, and practical points of duo-pianism.

LOON, HENDRIK WILLEM van: *The Arts*. New York: Simon and Schuster; 1939. The integration of music into the general evolution of culture and the arts.

LUBOSHUTZ, PIERRE, and NEMENOFF, GENIA: *The Art of Piano Ensemble*. "The Etude," LIX (January, 1941) pp. 5, 58. Technic and aesthetics of duo-pianism.

LUBOSHUTZ, PIERRE: *The Two-Piano Recital*. New York: J. Fischer & Bro. A short essay on duo-pianism, contained on pages 14-15 of "A Little Book for Piano Teachers and Students."

LYLE, WATSON: *Saint-Saens, His Life and Art*. Preface by Leff Pouishnoff. London: Kegan Paul, Trench, Truebner & Co.; 1923.

MACMILLAN ENCYCLOPEDIA OF MUSIC AND MUSICIANS, THE. Compiled and edited by Albert E. Wier. New York: The Macmillan Company; 1938. Contains an essay "Two Piano Playing" on pp. 1898-1905. This reference is written by Vera Brodsky and contains essentially the same material which she has contributed in her essay in Wier's "The Piano."

MAIER, GUY: *Two Piano Ensemble*. "The Etude," February 1938, page 87.

MATHEWS, W. S. B.: *The Masters and Their Music*. Philadelphia: Theodore Presser; 1898.

McKINNEY, HOWARD D.: *Advocating Freer Use of Two Pianos*. Fischer News Edition, IX (October-December, 1933) pp. 1-10. A short sketch on two-piano history.

McKINNEY, HOWARD D., and ANDERSON, W. R.: *Music in History*. The Evolution of an Art. New York: American Book Company; 1940. Standard reference for music history.

MECK, BARBARA von, and DRINKER, CATHERINE: *Beloved Friend, The Story of Tschaikowsky and Nadejda von Meck*. New York: Random House; 1937.

MILLER, HUGH MILTON: *An Outline-History of Music*. New York: Barnes and Noble, Inc.; 1947.

MILLER, HUGH M.: *The Earliest Keyboard Duets*. "The Musical Quarterly," XL (October, 1943), pp. 438-457. Deals with Farnaby's piece for two virginals and with the two earliest duets for two performers at one keyboard.

MOLDENHAUER, HANS: *Duo-Pianism* (1945). Unpublished. Library, Spokane Conservatory. Term paper for a course in methodology of research, establishing several hypotheses for a dissertation and a job analysis of the project.

MOLDENHAUER, HANS: *Duo-Pianism* (1949) Ars Novissima Artis Novae. Slated for publication by the Philosophical Library, New York, as a section in "Encyclopedia of Musical Information" (Rosenwald-Nettl).

MOLDENHAUER, HANS: The Conservatory Hour. Library, Spokane Conservatory; 1943-1950. Program annotations serving as radio scripts for a weekly half-hour broadcast of two-piano music; material covers an extensive literature of original works and arrangements.

MOSCHELES, IGNAZ: *Recent Music and Musicians as Described in the Diaries and Correspondence of Ignaz Moscheles*. Edited by his wife and adapted from the original German by A. D. Coleridge. New York: Henry Holt and Company, 1879. References to two-piano performances of Moscheles with Cramer and Mendelssohn. His compositions in this medium.

MOSER, H. J.: *Musik Lexikon*. Berlin: Max Hesses Verlag; 1935.

MUSICAL MASTERPIECE SERIES: Suite No. 2 for Two Pianos, opus 17 (Sergei Rachmaninoff). Camden, RCA Victor Division, Radio Corporation of America. Annotations to record album; name of author not given.

NAUMANN, EMIL: *The History of Music*. Translated from the German by F. Praeger. Edited by Sir F. A. Gore-Ousely. Two Volumes. New York: Cassell & Co.; 1886.

NEF, KARL: *An Outline of the History of Music*. Translated by Carl F. Pfatteicher. New York: Morningside Heights, Columbia University Press; 1947.

NETTL, PAUL: *The Book of Musical Documents*. New York: Philosophical Library; 1948.

NETTL, PAUL: *The Story of Dance Music*. New York: Philosophical Library; 1947. Reference to the employment of two pianos in the rhythm section of Paul Whiteman's orchestra, pp. 335-336.

NEWLIN, DIKA: *Bruckner, Mahler, Schönberg*. Morningside Heights, New York: King's Crown Press; 1947.

NEWMAN, ERNEST: *Wagner*. As Man and Artist. New York: Tudor Publishing Company; 1946.

NIEMANN, WALTER: *Brahms*. Translated from the German by Catherine Alison Phillipps. New York: Alfred A. Knopf; 1929.

NIEMANN, WALTER: *Das Klavierbuch*. Geschichte der Klaviermusik und ihrer Meister bis zur Gegenwart. Leipzig: C. F. Kahnt; 1918.

O'CONNELL, CHARLES: *The Victor Book of the Symphony*. New York: Simon and Schuster; 1941.

OREM, PRESTON WARE: *About Pieces for Two Pianos*. "The Etude," LVI (September, 1938) pages 565-566. Fragmentary comments as to history and repertoire. Stresses the character of antiphonal effects produced on two pianos, and describes a technic of rearranging solo piano pieces for two pianos by means of contrapuntal devices.

OREM, PRESTON WARE: *All About Four Hand Music*. "The Etude," LVI, (February, 1938), pages 75-76, 128. Defining the registers of the piano for the exploitation of richer sonorities.

ORTEGA y GASSET, JOSÉ: *The Dehumanization of Art.* Translated by Pedro V. Fernandez. The Symposium, New York: April 1930. An essay on contemporary esthetics.

OXFORD COMPANION TO MUSIC. Edited by Percy A. Scholes. London; Toronto; New York: Oxford University Press; 1938. Short reference in section Pianoforte 21, pages 721-722.

OXFORD HISTORY OF MUSIC. W. H. Hadow, general editor. Seven volumes. Oxford: Clarendon Press; 1901-1905, 1934. Also see C. H. H. Parry "The Music of the Seventeenth Century."

PACHELBEL, WILHELM HIERONYMUS. See "Denkmäler Deutscher Tonkunst."

PAINE, JOHN K.: *The History of Music to the Death of Schubert.* Boston and London: Ginn and Company; 1907.

PAN PIPES of Sigma Alpha Iota. *Duo-Piano Issue.* Vol. XLI No. 3, February 1949. Menasha, Wisconsin: published by George Banta Publishing Company; 1949. This special issue, devoted to the two-piano ensemble, contains an essay by Rosina Lhevinne, biographical sketches of professional duo-piano teams, duonotes, fraternity piano duos, duo-piano recital repertoire, and duo-piano materials of teacher interest.

PARRY, C. HUBERT H.: *Johann Sebastian Bach.* New York: G. P. Putnam's Sons; 1910. Comments on the concertos for two claviers.

PARRY, C. HUBERT H.: *The Evolution of the Art of Music.* With additional chapters by H. C. Colles. New York: Pantheon; 1946.

PARRY, C. HUBERT H.: *The Music of the Seventeenth Century.* (The Oxford History of Music, Vol. III). Oxford: Clarendon Press; 1902.

PASQUINI, BERNARDO: *Selection of Pieces composed for the harpsichord by Bernardo Pasquini.* Edited by J. S. Shedlock. London & New York: Novello, Ewer & Company. Contains the Sonata for two cembali in D minor, edited by Shedlock. pp. 42-48. The preface by Shedlock refers to two-clavier works by Handel and Bach.

PATTERSON, ANNIE W.: *Schumann.* London: J. M. Dent & Sons, Ltd.; New York: E. P. Dutton and Co., Inc.; 1934. Reference to opus 46 on p. 44.

PIRRO, ANDRÉ: *L'Esthétique de Jean Sébastien Bach;* 1907.

PRATT, CARROLL C.: *The Meaning of Music.* A Study in Psychological Aesthetics. New York: McGraw-Hill Book Company, Inc.; 1931.

PRATT, WALDO SELDEN: *The History of Music.* A Handbook and Guide for Students. New York: G. Schirmer Inc.; 1935.

PRATT, WALDO SELDEN: *The New Encyclopedia of Music and Musicians.* New York: Carl Fischer, Inc.; 1924. Reference for numerous two-piano compositions; data on duo-pianists.

PROSNIZ, ADOLF: *Handbuch der Klavier-Literatur 1450-1830.* Historisch-Kritische Uebersicht. Leipzig-Wien: L. Doblinger; 1908. Well organized, valuable source. References to the early works for two pianos.

REIMANN, HEINRICH: *Robert Schumanns Leben und Werke.* Leipzig: G. F. Peters; 1887.

RIEMANN, HUGO: *Musiklexikon.* Edited and revised by Alfred Einstein. Berlin: Max Hesses Verlag; 1938.

ROLLAND, ROMAIN: *Beethoven the Creator.* Translated by Ernest Newman. New York: Harper & Brothers; 1929.

ROSENWALD, HANS: *Handbook of Music History.* Questions and Answers. With Foreword by Leonard Liebling. Chicago: Wilcox & Follett Co.; 1948. Concise yet comprehensive.

RUTHARDT, ADOLF: *J. C. Eschmanns Wegweiser durch die Klavier-Literatur.* 6th edition by Adolf Ruthardt. Gebrueder Hug & Co.; 1905. Chapter XII contains music for two pianofortes, four hands. Summary list up to the time of its publication. Critical remarks frequently interspersed. Interesting preface to this chapter.

SAFRANEK, MILOS: *Bohuslav Martinu, the Man and His Music.* New York: 1944. Mentions the concerto for two pianos and orchestra.

SAINT-SAENS, CAMILLE: *Musical Memories.* Translated by Edwin Gile Rich. Boston: Small, Maynard & Company; 1919. Contains a reference on the status of symphonic music and the role of two-piano arrangements by Czerny in Paris in the early 1850s (p. 193). Comments on the harpsichord, p. 173. There is an interesting chapter on "Art for Art's Sake," (p. 76 ff).

SALESKI, GDAL: *Famous Musicians of a Wandering Race.* New York: Bloch Publishing Company; 1927. Biographical sketches of outstanding figures of Jewish origin in the musical world including Bauer, Gabrilowitsch, Lhevinne, de Pachmann and others.

SAMAROFF STOKOWSKI, OLGA: *The Layman's Music Book.* New York: W. W. Norton & Company, Inc.; 1935.

SAUNDERS, RICHARD DRAKE: *Music and Dance in California and the West.* Richard Drake Saunders, Editor. Hollywood: Bureau of Musical Research, Inc.; 1948.

SCHAUFFLER, ROBERT HAVEN: *Beethoven, the Man Who Freed Music.* New York: Tudor Publishing Company; 1944.

SCHAUFFLER, ROBERT HAVEN: *Florestan, the Life and Work of Robert Schumann.* New York: Henry Holt & Company; 1945. Source material and analysis of Andante and Variations opus 46 by Robert Schumann.

SCHAUFFLER, ROBERT HAVEN: *The Unknown Brahms.* New York: Dodd, Mead & Co.; 1933. Crown Publishers, 1940. References to two-piano influences in opus 15, opus 34, opus 56.

SCHOEN, MAX (Editor): *The Enjoyment of the Arts.* New York: Philosophical Library; 1944. Contains chapters on "The Realm of Art" (Max Schoen), "Music" (Glen Haydon), "The Problem of Criticism" (George Boas), and others.

SCHOTT & CO. Catalogue of Pianoforte Duets, Trios and Quartets. Published by Schott & Co., London; 188— (no year given). Contains a section of music for two pianos, four hands. Included are Schott publications only.

SCHWEITZER, ALBERT: *Johann Sebastian Bach.* With preface by C. M. Widor. English translation by Ernest Newman. 2 vols. London: A. & C. Black, Ltd., reprinted in 1938. (German Edition: London, Breitkopf & Härtel; 1911) Comments on the works for two and more claviers, including the two fugues for two claviers from "Die Kunst der Fuge." See vol. I, pp. 278, 413-415, 427.

SCIONTI, SILVIO: *The Fascination of Two-Piano Playing.* The Etude, LVII (September, 1939), pp. 567, 602. Gives an abridged history, as well as a repertory of duo-pianism, in addition to some general opinions on the art of two-piano playing.

SLONIMSKY, NICOLAS: *Music Since 1900.* New York: W. W. Norton & Company, Inc.; 1938. Record of two-piano performances in the "Society for Private Musical Performances in Vienna," pp. 545-546.

SMITH, GEORGE HENRY LOVETT: *Edward Burlingame Hill.* "Modern Music," November-December; 1938. Reference to the composer's two-piano works.

SORENSON, HERBERT: *Psychology in Education.* New York: McGraw-Hill Book Company, Inc.; 1940.

SPAETH, SIGMUND: *Stories Behind the World's Great Music.* Garden City, New York: Garden City Publishing Company, Inc.; 1940.

SPAETH, SIGMUND: *The Art of Enjoying Music.* New York: Whittlesey House, McGraw-Hill Book Company, Inc.; 1933.

SPITTA, PHILIPP: *Johann Sebastian Bach.* His Work and Influence on the Music of Germany, 1685-1750. Translated from the German by Clara Bell and J. A. Fuller Maitland. 3 vols. London: Novello and Company, Ltd.; New York: Novello, Ewer and Co.; 1899. References to Bach's works for two, three, and four claviers; discussion of these compositions.

STRATTON, STEPHEN S.: *Mendelssohn.* London: J. M. Dent & Sons, Ltd.; New York: E. P. Dutton & Co.; 1910. Many references to Mendelssohn's two-piano activities with Moscheles, Clara Schumann and others. Appendix B lists two unpublished concertos for two pianofortes.

STRINGHAM, EDWIN J.: *Listening to Music Creatively.* New York: Prentice-Hall, Inc.; 1946.

SURETTE, THOMAS WHITNEY: *The Appreciation of Music.* New York: H. W. Gray Co.; 1907.

SWAN, ALFRED J.: *The Music Director's Guide to Musical Literature* (for Voices and Instruments). New York: Prentice-Hall, Inc.; 1941.

TERRY, CHARLES SANFORD: *Bach, a Biography.* London: Oxford University Press; 1928.

TERRY, CHARLES SANFORD: *The Music of Bach.* London: Oxford University Press; 1933.

THOMPSON, OSCAR: *Debussy, Man and Artist.* New York: Dodd, Mead & Company; 1937.

THORNDIKE, EDWARD L.: *The Principles of Teaching.* Based on Psychology. New York: A. G. Seiler; 1916.

TOVEY, DONALD FRANCIS: *Essays in Musical Analysis.* London: Oxford University Press; 1935-1939.

TREND, J. B. *Manuel de Falla and Spanish Music.* New York: Alfred A. Knopf; 1934. Reference to de Falla's debut in London when he played with Liebich on two pianos, (p. 65).

TURNER, W. J.: *Mozart, The Man and His Works.* New York: Alfred A. Knopf; 1938.

TUTHILL, BURNET C.: *Recordings of American Music.* An open letter. National Music Council Bulletin, Vol. X, No. 1, September, 1949, p. 3. A reference to the role of the performer of music is used in Chapter X "The Composers" of Book I "The History."

TWENTY THAT STRIKE AS ONE. "Newsweek," XXII (December 27, 1943), pp. 84-85. Notes on the recent popularity of duo-pianism and thumbnail sketches of several teams.

ULRICH, HOMER: *Chamber Music.* The Growth and Practice of an Intimate Art. New York: Columbia University Press; 1948. Does not include two-piano music. Reference to Sonata for two pianos by Brahms, opus 34, p. 324.

VARRO, MARGIT: *Contributions to Béla Bartók's Biography.* Abstract of a paper, Journal of the American Musicological Society, Vol. II No. 3, (Fall 1949), p. 200. Reference to Bartók's appreciation of Liszt.

VEINUS, A.: *The Art of Fugue (Bach).* Camden: RCA Victor Division, Radio Corporation of America. Annotations to record album.

VEINUS, A.: *Variations on a Theme by Haydn, opus 56 (Brahms).* Camden: RCA Victor Division, Radio Corporation of America. Annotations to record album.

WALLACE, LADY: *The Letters of Wolfgang Amadeus Mozart.* (1769-1791). Translated, from the Collection of Ludwig Nohl, by Lady Wallace. 2 vols. New York: Hurd and Houghton; 1866. Source of information on some of Mozart's two-piano activities.

WELLESZ, EGON: *Arnold Schoenberg.* London: J. M. Dent & Sons, 19...

WIER, ALBERT, E.: *The Piano.* Its History, Makers, Players and Music. London; New York; Toronto: Longmans, Green and Co.; 1941. Contains "The Art of Two-Piano Playing" by Vera Brodsky, (Part VII, 338-374), an essay dealing with I. The Essentials of the Art; II. A Survey of Original and Transcribed Music for Two Pianos; III. A List of Classical and Modern Works for Two Pianos.

INDEX